CONSUMING FANTASIES

This book is due for return on or before the last date shown below.

Consuming Fantasies:

LABOR, LEISURE, AND
THE LONDON SHOPGIRL, 1880–1920

Lise Shapiro Sanders

The Ohio State University Press
Columbus

Library of Congress Cataloging-in-Publication Data

Sanders, Lise, 1970–
    Consuming fantasies : labor, leisure, and the London shopgirl,
1880–1920 / Lise Shapiro Sanders.
        p. cm.
    Includes bibliographical references and index.
    ISBN 0-8142-1017-1 (alk. paper) — ISBN 0-8142-9093-0 (cd-rom)
    1.   English literature—19th century—History and criticism. 2.
Women sales personnel in literature. 3. English literature—20th century—History and criticism. 4.   Women sales personnel—England—
London—History. 5.   Working class women—England—London—
History. 6. Department stores—England—London—History. 7. Retail
trade—England—London—History. 8.   Women and literature—
England—London. 9. London (England)—In literature. 10. Sex role in
literature. I. Title.
    PR468.W6S26 2006
    820.9'3522—dc22

                                            2005029994

Cover design by Jeff Smith.
Type set in Adobe Garamond.
Printed by Thomson-Shore, Inc.

The paper used in this publication meets the minimum requirements
of the American National Standard for Information Sciences—
Permanence of Paper for Printed Library Materials. ANSI Z39.48–1992.

9 8 7 6 5 4 3 2 1

CONTENTS

LIST OF ILLUSTRATIONS

ACKNOWLEDGMENTS

This book began as a doctoral dissertation at the University of Chicago, and could not have taken shape without the support and encouragement of my codirectors, Elizabeth Helsinger and Elaine Hadley, and my readers, Lauren Berlant and Tom Gunning. Their scholarship served as both model and inspiration for my work.

The project was initially supported by a dissertation fellowship from the Andrew W. Mellon Foundation, and subsequently by a Newberry Library-British Academy Visiting Research Fellowship (for which I would like to thank especially James R. Grossman and Carol Rennie) and the Faculty Development Funds of Hampshire College. The generous financial support provided by these institutions enabled me to conduct research in England that I could not accomplish anywhere else—a true gift.

I am grateful for the expertise of many individuals at libraries and archives in the United States and the United Kingdom. I would like to thank especially the staffs of the Five College Libraries and the University of Chicago's Regenstein Library, especially the Interlibrary Loan and Special Collections departments; David Smith at the New York Public Library; Philip Stokes and Stewart Barcham at the British Library and Jill Albrooke at the Newspaper Library at Colindale; Kathleen Dickson and Luke McKernan at the British Film Institute/National Film and Television Archive; the staffs of the Women's Library (then the Fawcett Library) and the London Metropolitan Archives; and particularly the archivists at Harrods (Nadene Hansen and Sebastian Wormell), Selfridges (Fred Redding), and John Lewis (Judy Faraday), all of whom gave generously of their time to assist me in research. Nadene Hansen deserves a special thanks for introducing me to Norah Irwin Slade, a 1916 employee of Harrods, who offered me her gracious hospitality (and a delicious afternoon tea) during an interview in her home in 1998. The illustrations for the book were made possible through the efforts of Christine Campbell, Felicia Cukier, Sue Filmer, Nicholas Roberts, David Samuelson, and Sebastian Wormell.

My colleagues at Hampshire College have been a tremendous intellectual resource for the past six years, and have consistently impressed me with the caliber of their teaching and research. The manuscript greatly benefited as a result of conversations with Norm Holland, Brown Kennedy, Sura Levine, Sandra Matthews, Eva Rueschmann, Falguni Sheth, Susan Tracy, Jim Wald, and Jeff Wallen. I owe a particular debt of gratitude to Eric Schocket, whose work has inspired me to think about class in new ways, and to Mary Russo, whose scholarship and teaching first captivated me and who has been an invaluable mentor and friend for more than a decade.

I would also like to thank a number of people, both near and far-flung, for their interest and thoughtful comments on my work. The research suggestions of many scholars in Victorian literature, women's history, early cinema, and cultural studies were immensely helpful in the early stages. Particular thanks go to the respondents to my query to the VICTORIA listserv, including Miriam Burstein, Julie Early, Ellen Jordan, Eve Lynch, and Sally Mitchell, and to Judith Walkowitz, who introduced me to the work of Erika Rappaport. Erika's project in many ways made my own possible, and I am grateful for her detailed replies to my numerous queries. Thanks also to Kay Boardman, Margaret Beetham, Stacy Gillis, Fiona Hackney, Andrew Higson, Nicholas Hiley, Jon Klancher, Annette Kuhn, Laura Rotunno, Talia Schaffer, David Shumway, Ana Vadillo, and Elizabeth Wilson, all of whose research questions inspired and enriched my own. Meredith McGill, Andrew Parker, and Jutta Sperling each offered guidance during the early stages of the publication process, and the comments of several anonymous readers strengthened the project in its later stages. Pamela Walker read the penultimate version of the manuscript with care and attention.

The editorial staff at The Ohio State University Press have been a true pleasure to work with. Heather Lee Miller was a tireless advocate of the book, and Sandy Crooms, Malcolm Litchfield, and Eugene O'Connor have deftly shepherded the manuscript through publication.

My students at Hampshire have been a continual source of intellectual stimulation, and their perspectives on this material have often opened up new avenues of research. My thanks to Morgan Bernal, Devan Goldstein, and Patricia Miller, whose work dovetailed in surprising ways with my own, and to the members of my seminar "Odd Women: Gender, Class, and Victorian Culture," especially Meagan Foster, Miranda Ganzer, Megan Kennedy, Sara McCown, Henriette Recny, and Azadeh Shariatmadar, who constitute an inspiring new generation of Victorianists.

Many family members and friends have been an inexhaustible source of emotional sustenance. Among them are my extended family—the Foster, Shapiro, Sideman, Templeton, Rose, and Sanders clans—especially Judy and David Sanders, who have provided a home away from home wherever they might be; Mark, Kristina, and Natalia Sanders; and Lisa Foster, Marcus Lille, and Jon Shapiro, who never failed to remind me to have fun every now and again. Pat and Marisa Chappell and Adam Lowenstein were a source of camaraderie during the early years, as were

Rebecca Neimark, Lee Spector, Matt Soar, and Jen Turkstra later on. Audrey Brashich shared wonderful writerly insights. Viveca Greene, Chris Perry, and Jordan and Noe Perry-Greene provided the best distractions and companionship I could imagine. Allison Smith has been a wonderful reader, fellow enthusiast, and friend. Lastly, my thanks to Kate Rosen, whose friendship over the past twenty years has meant more than I can say.

My parents—Bennett M. Shapiro, Fredericka Foster Shapiro, Richard J. Sideman, and Jill T. Sideman—have each been a source of great wisdom and motivation. Themselves analytical thinkers, creative practitioners, and passionate readers, they have set the standard of excellence to which I aspire, and their investment in intellectual pursuits has long been my inspiration. I owe them an inexpressible debt.

Finally, Eric Sanders is the reason this book has come into being. He has lived with the manuscript from conception to conclusion—in stacks on the living-room floor and in seemingly endless conversations—long enough to know its pages by heart, and he has taken countless hours away from his own writing to spend on mine. For the many readings and rereadings, for his patience and unflagging commitment, for all these years of partnership, I thank him from the bottom of my heart.

A version of chapter 3 appeared as "The Failures of the Romance: Boredom, Class and Desire in George Gissing's *The Odd Women* and W. Somerset Maugham's *Of Human Bondage,*" *Modern Fiction Studies* 47, no. 1 (March 2001), and a portion of chapter 5 appeared as "'Indecent Incentives to Vice': Regulating Films and Audience Behavior from the 1890s to the 1910s," in *Young and Innocent? Cinema and Britain, 1896–1930,* ed. Andrew Higson (Exeter: University of Exeter Press, 2002).

Introduction

The Story of the Shopgirl

> When I came to the shop some years ago
>   I was terribly shy and simple;
> —With my skirt too high and my hat too low
>   And an unbecoming dimple.
> But soon I learnt with a customer's aid
> How men make up to a sweet little maid;
> And another lesson I've learnt since then
> How a dear little maid "makes up" for men!
> — *The Shop Girl* (1894)

In late Victorian England a new identity, the shopgirl, emerged in the midst of a heated debate about the nature of social, sexual, and moral practice for women employed in the public sphere.[1] This debate was made manifest in newspapers, trade union journals, and social histories of women's work, and represented a struggle between social reformers and trade union activists, department store managers, and members of Parliament, to shape the subjectivity of "the dear little maid" behind the counter. And yet this struggle represents only one scene in a complex narrative: to fully understand the cultural identity of the shopgirl, we must recognize her place within a turn-of-the-century culture of consumer fantasy. The shopgirl embodied the very moment at which fantasy entered the process of consumer exchange: her vocation required that she mediate the desires of consumers on the other side of the counter, be they women who longed to purchase the goods on display or men who might desire the shopgirl herself as another type of merchandise. Yet in a striking slippage between the processes of selling and consuming, shopgirls were themselves perceived by middle-class observers as consumers of goods and leisure products bound up in the fantasies produced by popular culture, particularly fantasies tied to the genre of the romance.

It is essential to note that "the shopgirl" is a construction, created by the society in which she emerged. Throughout this study I strive to separate the cultural type of "the shopgirl" from the female shop assistant, the actual social subject whom she represents in literary and cultural texts. This is

1

not to undermine the emphasis on the constructed nature of identity and subjectivity, but rather to facilitate an analysis of how cultural representation functions to both illuminate and obscure the experiences of actual, "everyday," or "ordinary" women. Those who purported to give voice to the shopgirl—Victorian and Edwardian social reformers, journalists, writers and publishers of popular fiction, music hall and theater managers, and department store owners, among others—replicated this slippage between subject and representation, resulting in a complex and often confusing set of discourses.

Recent historical research has begun to illuminate the working lives of shop employees in the late Victorian and Edwardian periods: census data and store records can assist us in identifying the demographics of shop workers, male and female, and can thereby begin to account for the varied life experiences of female shop assistants between the 1880s and the First World War. However, empirical research into the lives of shop assistants themselves is not the primary goal of this project. This is neither a social history of the late Victorian and Edwardian shop assistant, nor is it a straightforward analysis of representations of shop assistants in literature and popular culture. Rather, what I wish to elaborate here is the ways in which "the shopgirl," as a discursive entity, comes to embody a set of cultural assumptions about class, gender, and sexuality at the end of the Victorian period. Not only does the figure of the shopgirl trouble long-held ideologies of class and gender articulated through the language of domesticity, feminine propriety, and virtue; she also symbolizes the social and cultural transformations resulting from women's entry into a vast range of employments in the late nineteenth century. The "army" of young working women that came to "invade" professions formerly identified as the province of men (to paraphrase Mary Barfoot, George Gissing's feminist heroine in *The Odd Women*) included secretaries, clerks, and "typewriters," as well as bookbinders, watchmakers, and telephone and telegraph operators—to name only a few of the many kinds of employment viewed as appropriate for the modern "working girl."[2] Yet as the following study will elaborate, the shopgirl occupies a unique position in this range of new modes of identifying young women with work. As I will show, the constructed figure of the shopgirl symbolizes the intersection between conservative ideologies of gender and class and new models of female identity, behavior, and experience that suggest an ongoing resistance to or discomfort with these ideologies. As this introduction and the chapters that follow contend, the figure of the shopgirl demonstrates the instability of the notion of "separate spheres," divided by gender into public and private realms, and the effects of the transformations wrought by modernity on the lives of working women in London at the turn of the twentieth century.[3]

The archive for this study consists of an array of historical, literary, theatrical, and visual texts—writings in the trade and popular press, shop and store records, and the products of the mass entertainment industry including novelettes, serial magazines for girls and women, music hall songs and sketches, musical comedies, and early silent films—which I take as evidence of the cultural forces working to produce this new identity category during the 1890s and early 1900s. The narratives told by these texts raise a number of questions about the production of morality and the contested status of everyday life for working women in late Victorian and Edwardian shops and department stores.[4] Part of my investigation of this discourse stems from the contemporary cultural perception of the shopgirl as necessarily *between* classes, occupying a transitional position in a hierarchy based on appearance, demeanor, and relations with others in the social milieu of the shop. Shopgirls were often women of middle-class background who were compelled by financial hardship to take up "manual" labor, associating them with women of the working classes; yet their tasks involved a particular engagement of the body in the display culture of the shop or department store, a culture which demanded a certain gentility from its employees and provided a socially acceptable location for a type of public employment perceived as appropriate to their gender. In a similar vein, women whose backgrounds might be read as working-class (daughters of factory and agricultural laborers, for example) gained access to a sphere that tempted them with the possibility of upward mobility through employment in a shop, a social space of abundance and luxury imagined to imbue its inhabitants with the gentility characteristic of "proper" femininity.[5]

In numerous fictional texts, the shopgirl's transitional subject position is figured through the counter separating working women from their customers, which provided a barrier to class mobility at the same time that it suggested the possibility of self-transformation through a climb up the social ladder (often narrated as a romance plot culminating in marriage to a wealthy male suitor). The counter served to differentiate shopgirls from their customers, but through its placement in the front of the store it also differentiated shopgirls from factory workers and seamstresses, those who made the products for sale in the shop.[6] Moreover, in certain drapery establishments, the counter assistant might model the products for sale, thereby reflecting an image of the middle-class consumer while at the same time generating a fantasy image of herself as an upwardly mobile woman with access to the other side of the consumption/distribution process. The fact that the shopgirl was directly engaged in this circuit of exchange—that she handled both the goods and the money that went to purchase them, mediating the sale through her physical positioning behind the counter—

illuminates the contested definition of her placement within Britain's minutely delineated class structure and her centrality to studies of the late Victorian and Edwardian culture of consumption.

As socially constructed subjects of a culture based on commodity consumption and display, shopgirls synthesize cultural narratives of desire associated with the fantasy structures of the romance. Positioned as a consumer of mass cultural products and as a prospective romantic heroine, the shopgirl illuminates the operation of two modes of consumer fantasy: *absorption*, or immersion in a particular narrative trajectory, symbolized by the "complete story" marketed to readers of popular romance fiction, and the nonnarrative experience of *distraction*, symbolized by the "variety entertainments"—music hall sketches, revue acts, circus performances, and the like—that were increasingly characteristic of the period lasting from the mid-1880s to the First World War. I take these terms from contemporary accounts of popular leisure practice, but in framing my analysis in this way I have also been influenced by the writings of Walter Benjamin and Siegfried Kracauer, and especially by the latter's description of early-twentieth-century mass experience in several remarkable essays, particularly "The Little Shopgirls Go to the Movies" and "The Cult of Distraction," both written in the 1920s about Berlin's "picture palaces" but bearing a startling relevance to turn-of-the-century British culture.[7] The dialectic between absorption and distraction suggests that these two modes of fantasy have a reciprocal aspect, such that absorption in one narrative results in distraction from another. Yet distraction as an experience also works against the model of sustained absorption: distracted consumers shift their attention from one site to another, resisting the experience of sustained immersion and instead allowing themselves to be attracted to successive objects of desire. In essence, I view absorption and distraction as two sides of the same coin, each serving to define the other while expressing simultaneous yet discrete forms of consumer fantasy. The dialectical operation of absorption and distraction finds its clearest elaboration in the narrative structures of the romance, a genre dependent on the tension between the satisfaction of desire and the repeated and pleasurable deferral of that satisfaction.

Many of the texts which make up the archive of this project position the shopgirl within a sexual teleology of proper femininity in accordance with the conventions of the romance plot: fictional and historical narratives alike feature these women as heroines, imagining the shopgirl as the protagonist of a story about the social rise of a disadvantaged young woman through her marriage to a wealthy, often titled, man.[8] Indeed, what we might see as the paradigmatic "shopgirl story" goes something like this: a naïve but beautiful young woman, newly impoverished and forced to seek work, moves from the country to the city to find employment in a shop. There she suffers the hardships of too little pay, poor living conditions in a crowded dormitory, and the perception that she is sexually available to her male coworkers and customers. At this point her story can take one of two directions: the downward trajectory into "fallen womanhood" and prostitution, whether literal or metaphorical, or the upward trajectory into wealth, embodied by the moment at which the former shopgirl returns to the store as a consumer.[9] Not surprisingly, the shopgirl's upward mobility is frequently predicated on marriage as an escape from the drudgery of the shop, and the prospective husband therefore becomes the fairy-tale prince or "deliverer" who releases her from "shop-slavery" (both familiar phrases of the period). Consequently, a critical component of my analysis involves positing new ways to theorize the romance, a genre that constructs women as desiring subjects yet inevitably ends with a deferred promise of an alternative life story. I argue that the romance incorporates a complex exchange between fantasy and identification, one that holds out a promise whose utopian appeal is also its moment of despair: the fantasy of pleasurable experience provided by the romance lures its consumers with the simultaneous promise of absorption (in one story) and distraction (from another) but also withholds that promise, deferring its fulfillment and rendering satisfaction perpetually out of reach. For shopgirls, seen by many as the quintessential consumers of popular romances, the appeal of the romance plot lies in its offer of a continuity that would successfully bridge the gap between the scene of the fantasy and the "real" conditions of everyday life.[10]

Consuming Desires: The Romance of Fantasy

Katherine Mansfield's 1908 short story "The Tiredness of Rosabel" presents a fictional narrative of the shopgirl's vicarious pleasure in consumption that highlights the cultural significance of fantasy and the romance plot to the story of the shopgirl. Mansfield's heroine, Rosabel, spends her days working in a London hat shop and her evenings in a dull flat in the Richmond Road. The story takes place during the brief space of leisure time offered to young working women, narrating Rosabel's journey home on an omnibus and the solitary rituals she performs as she undresses for bed and contemplates the day's work. The story opens by characterizing Rosabel as a consumer who chooses aesthetic pleasure over practical considerations:

> At the corner of Oxford Circus Rosabel bought a bunch of violets, and that was practically the reason why she had so little tea—for a

scone and a boiled egg and a cup of cocoa at Lyons are not ample suf-
ficiency after a hard day's work in a millinery establishment. As she
swung onto the step of the Atlas 'bus, grabbed her skirt with one
hand and clung to the railing with the other, Rosabel thought she
would have sacrificed her soul for a good dinner—roast duck and
green peas, chestnut stuffing, pudding with brandy sauce—something hot and strong and filling.[11]

Mansfield's formulation of Rosabel's material deprivations suggests the
moral challenge inherent in the "sacrifice" shopgirls might be forced to
make: if not their souls, the argument went, then their bodies were certainly at risk. The contrast between pleasure and sacrifice continues as
Rosabel contemplates her surroundings: the jeweler's shops outside the
window appear "fairy palaces," but inside grim reality bears down on her:
"Her feet were horribly wet, and she knew the bottom of her skirt and pet-
ticoat would be covered with black, greasy mud. There was a sickening
smell of warm humanity" (3). Even the advertisements fail to move her:
"How many times had she read [them]—'Sapolio Saves Time, Saves
Labour'—'Heinz's Tomato Sauce'—and the inane, annoying dialogue
between doctor and judge concerning the superlative merits of
'Lamplough's Pyretic Saline'" (3). In this moment Rosabel is a critical,
cynical consumer, a stance which carries over in her attitude toward a girl
"very much her own age" next to her, who is reading a "cheap, paper-cov-
ered edition" of *Anna Lombard* (3). Mansfield uses this novel, written in
1898 by "Victoria Cross" (Vivian Cory), a New Woman novelist who
wrote popular romances targeted toward a mass reading public, to affiliate
the female reader of these fictions with the working classes.[12] This scene is
written as a voyeuristic spectacle in which Rosabel vicariously experiences
the act of reading and its effects:

> She glanced at the book which the girl read so earnestly, mouthing
> the words in a way that Rosabel detested, licking her first finger and
> thumb each time that she turned the page. She could not see very
> clearly; it was something about a hot, voluptuous night, a band play-
> ing, and a girl with lovely, white shoulders. [. . .] [The girl] was
> smiling as she read. (3–4)

Rosabel's revulsion toward the girl's habits of reading—habits that reveal
the sensory pleasures associated with popular fiction—separates her from
this young woman, replicating the class differentiation that becomes a
fundamental element in the construction of the shopgirl. When the bus
reaches her stop, Rosabel stumbles, apologizing politely, but the girl is too

absorbed in her reading to notice: "'I beg your pardon,' said Rosabel, but the girl did not even look up" (4). The girl on the 'bus symbolizes a type of absorption or immersion in fictional narrative which nonetheless occurs in public, and is thus both set against and influenced by the "agitated excitements"[13] associated with urban life in the late Victorian and Edwardian periods.

Rosabel, then, is not herself the primary reader of romance fiction, but nonetheless uses the romance plot to structure a fantasy which rewrites a shaming experience earlier in her day at the shop. Rosabel's interaction with a demanding female customer and Harry, the customer's companion, illustrates her humiliation in terms of both class and gender: the woman callously exposes the class difference between herself and Rosabel, while the man turns insolent and overly familiar, remarking on Rosabel's "damned pretty little figure" (6). After much searching, Rosabel finally locates a satisfactory hat—"rather large, soft, with a great curled feather, and a black velvet rose"—and the female customer insists that Rosabel try it on herself (5). When the woman sees the hat resting on Rosabel's head, the desire to consume the image leads her to exclaim, "Oh, Harry, isn't it adorable. . . . I must have that!" and, smiling at her reflection embodied in the shopgirl on the other side of the counter, comments, "It suits you, beautifully" (5). The woman's double-edged compliment inspires simultaneous feelings of rage and shame in Rosabel, who has become her own caricature, at once a commodity for the woman's consumption and a model for the display of the desired object, which gains its very desirability through the display:

> A sudden, ridiculous feeling of anger had seized Rosabel. She longed to throw the lovely, perishable thing in the girl's face, and bent over the hat, flushing. "It's exquisitely finished off inside, Madam," she said. (6)

In this scene, the carefully erected barriers of social position and wealth are threatened, as Rosabel is made to adorn herself in a luxury item for which she clearly is not the intended recipient. Moreover, this exchange depends on the involvement of Rosabel's body in the scene, as she is reduced to a mannequin—note the use of "it" and "that" in the woman's exclamation—and experiences the consequent loss of self and subjectivity.[14] This event, combined with Rosabel's emotional and visceral reaction, highlights the experience of class-bound shame which structures the shopgirl's everyday life, and precipitates the fantasy which rewrites the scene of class difference. In this scenario, fantasy functions both to contain and revise the painful self-exposure of such an event.

In the narrative of her fantasy, Rosabel imagines herself "changing places" with her female customer in order to remake herself both as a consumer and as the heroine of the romance plot. Her fantasy traces the teleological narrative of the romance—ending, as so often is the case, with marriage—but focuses on a scripted scene in which the elements of the setting are elaborated in detail.[15] The primary setting for the fantasy is a bedroom marked with the visual and tactile signifiers of upper-class life, in which Rosabel can enact in her imagination the process of being ministered to in the way she typically attends to customers:

> Then the great, white and pink bedroom with roses everywhere in dull silver vases. She would sit down before the mirror and the little French maid would fasten her hat and find her a thin, fine veil and another pair of white suède gloves—a button had come off the gloves she had worn that morning. She had scented her furs and gloves and handkerchief, taken a big muff and run downstairs. The butler opened the door, Harry was waiting, they drove away together. . . . (6)

In the space of fantasy, Rosabel returns again to describe the luxurious interior of her imaginary home, a description which heightens the contrast with the dull, grimy room in which she actually lives:

> The fire had been lighted in her boudoir, the curtains drawn, there were a great pile of letters waiting for her—invitations for the Opera, dinners, balls, a week-end on the river, a motor tour—she glanced through them listlessly as she went upstairs to dress. A fire in her bedroom, too, and her beautiful, shining dress spread on the bed— white tulle over silver, silver shoes, silver scarf, a little silver fan. Rosabel knew that she was the most famous woman at the ball that night; men paid her homage, a foreign Prince desired to be presented to this English wonder. Yes, it was a voluptuous night, a band playing, and *her* lovely white shoulders. . . . (7, emphasis in original)

Reflecting the environment in which she works—a space itself structured through fantasies of consumption—the setting of the fantasy here revolves around a dress which appears again at the conclusion to the narrative. The dress itself figures Rosabel as a desiring consumer, but also reflects the repetitions of her everyday life: she wears the same dress twice during this narrative, as one with limited means would, rather than supplementing it with new and more dazzling creations. The dress here seems to embody "the desire to desire"[16]: Rosabel longs both for the object itself, but also the pleasure produced by the act of longing.

By echoing the phrase from *Anna Lombard*—"a voluptuous night, a band playing, and *her* lovely white shoulders"—Mansfield demonstrates the role such novels were seen to have for young women of Rosabel's age and social class, promising release from the drudgery of mindless work through the romance narrative. The repetition of this phrase also affiliates Rosabel with the girl on the 'bus: having attempted to distinguish herself from the girl in the initial encounter, Rosabel is here drawn into a similar position as both covet the trappings of upper-class life in fictional or fantasy form. This moment in the fantasy relies on a relatively straightforward structure of identification in which the shopgirl occupies the place of the heroine in order to situate herself at the center of the fantasy. And yet, as Diana Fuss suggests in her reading of Freud's writings on identification and the unconscious, identification should be seen as a more complex process incorporating the metaphorics of "resemblance and replacement" in which the subject desires to be *like* or *as* another as well as facilitating multiple positions or points of entry.[17] Identification thus incorporates approximation and assimilation, but does so in a fragmented and fractured way, producing "identity" but also rendering it continually in flux.[18]

Mansfield's story uses the absorbing experience of fantasy to reimagine the shopgirl's experience, but also introduces the possibility of distraction as another type of consumer fantasy. Distraction, which (as I argue elsewhere in this project) is predicated on a greater permeability between the fantasy and the everyday, works in part on a formal level: Mansfield interrupts the fantasy narrative with ellipses and parenthetical descriptions of the "real" Rosabel, "the girl crouched on the floor in the dark" (7). Distraction is also a fundamental element on the level of the story's content, which in juxtaposing disparate leisure practices (reading, eating, shopping, opera-going—consuming in a variety of forms) constructs a fantasy that relies on distraction for its very possibility.

In describing the physical effects of Rosabel's labor as degrading and dehumanizing, Mansfield's story reflects the contemporary debate over the plight of the shopgirl. Mansfield provides her heroine with a compensatory mechanism, however, in the form of a "tragic optimism" (8) which operates through the dual fantasy of first becoming the heroine of a conventionally imagined romance plot and then (as an effect of the romance) acting as a consumer rather than as a seller of luxury goods. Rosabel uses her fantasy of upper-class pleasure to narrate a story which centers on the fulfillment of desire rather than on self-denial and suffering.[19] The practice of creating a fantasy structured through the desire to consume offers a way to survive the tedium and shame of everyday life, especially when (as so often in the case of the shopgirl) that experience is constituted in the painful disavowal of class difference.

The paradox embodied in the phrase "tragic optimism" suggests both the possibility and the limitations of Mansfield's characterization of the shopgirl. Rosabel's fantasy has the potential to operate as a mode of social critique, a practice which refracts and reappropriates the real, often mundane, experience of actual social subjects through its ability to produce both conventional romance narratives and alternative stories of life experience. Yet Mansfield's story has its limits: the story concludes with Rosabel's smile at the memory of her fantasy, a moment which echoes the smile of the girl on the 'bus and replaces her former feelings of anger and shame, marking Mansfield's retreat into a familiar version of fantasy as escapism. In the end, Mansfield shortchanges her protagonist by refusing to allow for fantasy as anything other than an escape from reality. One could imagine alternative trajectories for this story: one in which Rosabel would respond quite differently to her encounter with her customers, for example. Indeed, this was exactly the critical stance espoused by activists like Margaret Bondfield, a former shopgirl-turned-union organizer and MP who became the first female Cabinet Minister for the Labour Party in the 1920s, and whose life and work I discuss in greater detail in chapter 1. Bondfield's short stories for the shop assistants' union journal exposed the dangers of fantasy as a form of false consciousness, and rewrote the story of the shopgirl to emphasize the need for collective action and political change. But as my study of the popular fictions marketed to shopgirls shows, fantasy is more complicated than these formulations allow. The radical possibility of fantasy lies in its status as a creative practice: it opens up new possibilities for imaginative rewritings of everyday life, and therefore is essential as a first step in the process of social and political transformation.

Consumer Culture and the Gender of Modernity

Rita Felski begins her study of the relationship between women and the modern with the following questions: "What is the gender of modernity? How can anything as abstract as a historical period have a sex?"[20] In answering these questions through an analysis of competing cultural representations of the modern and the feminine at the turn of the twentieth century, Felski offers a new perspective on the "difference" made by reading modernity from a feminist perspective. Central to Felski's investigation is a nuanced analysis of "the aesthetic and erotic, as well as economic, dimensions of consumption" and the claim that "the emergence of a culture of consumption helped to shape new forms of subjectivity for women."[21] In focusing her discussion on ambiguous representations of the "voracious female consumer" in the works of Flaubert and Zola, particularly in the case of Zola's 1883 novel *Au bonheur des dames*, Felski positions the shopgirl as the "premodern" woman "completely free of the compulsion to consume," in stark contrast to her customers across the counter.[22] By contrast, as I argue here, contemporaneous British texts characterize the shopgirl as the paradigmatic consumer, a fact that has gone unremarked in the small body of existing scholarship on shop assistants in late Victorian and Edwardian England. Why then does the shopgirl come to signify the dangers of excessive consumption in Britain during this period? And what can a study of the shopgirl tell us about the relationship between consumer culture, gender, and modernity?

Although this study focuses on the late nineteenth and early twentieth centuries—a period many critics have identified as particularly and peculiarly "modern"—its foundations extend back to the eighteenth century.[23] Historians including Colin Jones, Jennifer Jones, Elizabeth Kowaleski-Wallace, Claire Walsh, and Erin Mackie have developed the argument originally presented by Neil McKendrick, John Brewer, and J. H. Plumb locating the birth of consumer culture in the late eighteenth century, tracing its antecedents to the early years of the eighteenth century, and identifying some strategies of commercial culture in the seventeenth century as well. These and other scholars of consumer culture have demonstrated how the processes and practices of consumption since the early eighteenth century have been predicated on the use of fantasy to create desires for commodity goods.[24] As Mackie observes, "An examination of the early-eighteenth-century commodity and the venues of its exchange and consumption show that such links between commerce and fantasy, pleasure and amusement were forged well before the nineteenth century."[25] Along similar lines, Kowaleski-Wallace's study of women and consumer culture characterizes the eighteenth century as "the age of the commodity," as this period marked "an important shift in the concept of the commodity and in new consumer activities designed to circulate commodities, chief among them the pastime known as shopping."[26] Walsh notes that browsing can be traced to the early eighteenth century, and views the eighteenth-century shopper as "a negotiator in a sophisticated cultural activity, an activity imbued with sociability, pleasure and the application of skill."[27] In contrast to arguments that shopping functions as a passive experience for its (primarily female) practitioners, Walsh contends that the verbal exchange involved in the selling process "was part of the pleasure of the shopping experience, particularly where it included compliments and flattery from the shop staff and, depending on the goods being sold, sexual innuendo and intimation . . . the counter was used as a form of display, but one that was not passive but active and interactive. The customer handled the goods, compared them, considered, selected and discussed them."[28] These studies reveal that modern retail strategies and consumer practices were in place well before the nineteenth century.

Critical analysis of consumer culture from the eighteenth century onward is complicated by issues of gender and sexuality. From an early stage women were identified as consumers in Britain and elsewhere: with the development of consumer culture women's supposedly insatiable appetites were directed toward commodities that were themselves linked to the body and were seen as a threatening, disruptive, and powerful influence. Kowaleski-Wallace comments, "With the birth of a consumer culture, women were assumed to be hungry for *things*—for dresses and furniture, for tea cups and carriages, for all commodities that indulged the body and enhanced physical life. . . . Though it had been necessary to the strong growth of the expanding British economy, female appetite for goods, by the end of the century, was also perceived as a sinister force threatening male control and endangering patriarchal order."[29] At the same time, however, a transformation occurs in which the female consumer, through her interaction with commodities under the spectatorial gaze of the (male) shop owner, becomes herself a commodity, foreshadowing the nineteenth-century association of women with goods and echoing the rhetoric of prostitution that characterizes numerous accounts of gendered consumption. Reading Victoria De Grazia and Ellen Furlough's collection *The Sex of Things: Gender and Consumption in Historical Perspective* and the cultural significance of two figures in the nineteenth century, the prostitute and the kleptomaniac, Mary Louise Roberts observes that "the nineteenth-century woman-as-commodity is the repressed, fantasy version of the eighteenth-century woman-as-consumer. . . . In the 'specularized' urban culture of arcades, boulevards and department stores, woman was inscribed as both consumer and commodity, purchaser and purchase, buyer and bought."[30] This tension between women's power as agents in the consumer environment and their subjection to the logic of commodification structures the discourse of consumption from the eighteenth century onward, and has prompted historians such as Roberts to call for a move beyond the Manichean dynamics that posit women as either "mighty consumers with advertisers at their beck and call or as pathetic victims of male expertise and control."[31] Among others, Erika Rappaport's study of the late-nineteenth-century women's commercial culture in Britain, *Shopping for Pleasure: Women in the Making of London's West End*, illustrates this kind of careful and complex historical scholarship, tracing the role of middle-class women as shoppers and urban actors in the metropolitan public culture of London. Rappaport's groundbreaking work has laid the foundation for this study of the women on the other side of the counter.

Several other critical studies of Victorian culture have paved the way for this project: these include Mary Poovey's *Uneven Developments: The Ideological Work of Gender in Mid-Victorian England;* Judith Walkowitz's *City of Dreadful Delight: Narratives of Sexual Danger in Late-Victorian London;* Deborah Epstein Nord's *Walking the Victorian Streets: Women, Representation, and the City;* and Sally Mitchell's *The New Girl: Girl's Culture in England, 1880–1915.* These and other scholars have explored the significance of class and gender to women's experience of urban life in the nineteenth and early twentieth centuries, and provide exemplary accounts of the cultural antecedents of the shopgirl.[32] Studies of nineteenth-century department store culture in the United States and Australia by Susan Porter Benson and Gail Reekie have also been influential in providing an international frame within which to view the shopgirl as a historical figure.[33] But literary and historical scholarship on shopgirls themselves remains elusive. With the exception of a few key studies placing shop assistants in the context of nineteenth-century class and gender ideologies, to date there has been no significant work focusing on the shopgirl as a pivotal figure in the late Victorian and Edwardian culture of consumption.[34]

This study contends that the shop is the central locus for the playing out of fantasy and desire in late-nineteenth-century consumer culture. The shopgirl therefore occupies an environment structured through fantasy, which, while generated through the processes of selling and consuming, intentionally lessens the distinction between the two. Consequently, as subsequent chapters argue, narratives of fantasy and consumption are bound up with the material conditions of the shop assistant's work experience and everyday life, at the same time that they mask the realities of that experience. The slippage between selling and consuming comes to constitute the story of the shopgirl, thereby obscuring the mechanics of the transactions taking place across the counter.

Labor, Leisure, and Experience

A primary feature of this study has been the effort to trace the construction of the shopgirl as both cultural type and historical figure, even as this figure is revealed to be less fact than fiction. This task has produced several methodological challenges regarding the question of "experience" and its status as evidence. Addressing this problematic, Joan Scott has argued for the constitutive relation between discourse and experience, suggesting that historians should attend to the situated nature of the knowledge produced in their study of particular subjects just as they should recognize the shifting and unstable production of identities.

> It is not individuals who have experience, but subjects who are constituted through experience. Experience in this definition then becomes not the origin of our explanation, not the authoritative (because seen or felt) evidence that grounds what is known, but rather that which we seek to explain, that about which knowledge is produced. To think about experience in this way is to historicize it as well as to historicize the identities it produces.[35]

Scott's imperative suggests the centrality of language and "the literary" to the historically and culturally situated project of analyzing the formation of social subjects, and likewise the importance of historical analysis within contemporary literary and cultural studies.

Another fundamental component of this study involves an analysis of the place of leisure within the study of lives structured around the daily rhythms of labor. An older tradition of historical analysis established labor, and the experience of work bound to the conditions of capitalist production, as a primary site for investigation. This tradition operated at the expense of histories of leisure, an omission that has been remedied through the writing and research of scholars like Peter Bailey, Hugh Cunningham, Gareth Stedman Jones, and others working from the example set by Raymond Williams and E. P. Thompson.[36] Within the two last decades, historians such as Chris Waters and Susan Pennybacker have enriched these foundational analyses of popular culture and mass leisure practices through a discussion of the politics of labor and leisure during the later nineteenth and early twentieth centuries.[37] In these studies, working-class history encompasses both work and play in an effort to analyze the intimate relation between these two components of everyday life.[38]

In what follows, I take this new model of historical scholarship and place it within the analytical context of cultural studies in an effort to study simultaneously the labor conditions experienced by the shopgirl and the leisure practices associated with her construction as a consuming subject.[39] Accordingly, chapters 1 and 2 analyze the struggle between competing forces which strove to transform the "sweated"[40] character of nineteenth-century shop labor into an enlightened and compassionate style of management. Using trade union journals and social histories of women's work and shop labor, the first chapter describes the attempt on the part of socialist activists to improve the working lives of shopgirls. These activists colluded with more conservative members of various middle-class philanthropic organizations in an effort to shape the leisure experience of shopgirls into one which would presumably benefit not only themselves but, more importantly, the cause of collective political mobilization. Chapter 2 examines a related narrative of shop labor in an analysis of the figuration of the female body within the social environment of the department store, an institution that transforms its female employees into mannequins, anonymous laboring bodies in the phantasmagoric display of consumer pleasure. To situate this narrative in its historical context, I trace a transformation in the rhetorical self-description of retail management from a familial model grounded in the tradition of benevolent paternalism, exemplified by Harrods and other British retailers, to a "scientific," Americanized model pioneered by Gordon Selfridge and based on Taylorist principles of centralized staff control. Harrods used the paternalistic model to elicit the fulfillment of filial duties from store employees whose individual well-being was subordinate to the collective enterprise of the store as substitute family; Selfridges, by contrast, used the rhetoric of individual advancement and upward mobility as part of their modern, "democratic" methods of leadership. The rhetoric of rational efficiency described in Selfridges' model, and the implicit use of Frederick Winslow Taylor's system of scientific management, cloaks a rather different version of department store labor, one in which the female body is made into an anonymous figure with little access to upward mobility except through fantasy. To articulate the imaginary possibilities provided by the fantasy of upward mobility, I examine two popular romance novels which narrate the other side of scientific management and the quest for efficiency, using the metaphor of the department store as machine: Charles and Anne Williamson's *Winnie Childs, the Shop Girl* (1914) and Arthur Applin's *Shop Girls* (1914). Reworking the concept of the "mass ornament," a term used by Kracauer to describe the visual spectacles of the turn of the century, I argue that these novels paradoxically reindividualize their shopgirl-heroines as sexual objects of display and desire rather than rendering them sexless or de-eroticized mannequins, thereby radically altering previous conceptions of the laboring body as either anonymous or masculine. The critique of anonymity offered by these novels operates through the promise of individuality and upward mobility, understood as an antidote to the alienating experience of industrial display labor for women in the department store.

In its discussion of gender, labor, and embodiment, the analysis in the second chapter paves the way for the discussion of pleasure which emerges in chapter 3. Here I address the critique of pleasure as such, describing the process by which physical and imaginative pleasure are rewritten as vulgar desire on the part of the shopgirl who aspires to class mobility.[41] In this chapter, I read the production of boredom and the desire for pleasure through stimulation as critical elements in the narrative of the shopgirl's romantic trajectory and subject formation. I compare the pedagogy of gentility emergent in etiquette manuals and marriage guides with two novels,

George Gissing's *The Odd Women* and W. Somerset Maugham's *Of Human Bondage,* both of which feature shopgirls who are both "extraordinary" and "abnormal," narrating the process by which the romance plots go astray. These novels, I suggest, rework the mid-Victorian ideology of proper femininity through their description of the failure of the shopgirl's marriage to live up to the romantic ideal, a failure which is largely dependent on the boredom inherent in the afterlife of the romance and the temptation to pursue new plots that will provide the "interest" necessary to render everyday life more aesthetically engaging. The failed romance plots expressed by Gissing and Maugham, and their concomitant critique of marriage as an economic system, provide a hint at the role of fantasy for readers of the romance (as the shopgirl-heroines of these fictions indeed are): they allude to the possibility of imaginative desire as an alternative mode of experience.

The desires expressed in these novels, metaphorically represented by the processes of reading for pleasure and pursuing leisure entertainments in public, provide the transition to chapters 4 and 5, which explore the industries that targeted shopgirls as consumers of socially sanctioned fantasy in the popular forms of the novelette and girls' magazine, the popular stage, and the silent cinema. In these chapters I confront the challenge of analyzing the reception of texts whose audience's reactions are almost entirely untraceable. One way to negotiate this task—although a problematic one in historicist terms—would be to gauge the reactions of more recent viewers to these texts, as Janet Staiger has suggested in her analysis of various reception strategies in film studies. Staiger's response is to propose a "historical materialist approach" which combines the analysis of contemporary social formations with an examination of "historically constructed 'imaginary selves,' the subject positions taken up by individual readers and spectators."[42] This study combines a similar attention to the historical and material conditions that produced the cultural type of the shopgirl as a reader-viewer-spectator with a commitment to theorizing the possible ways in which her experience might have been shaped by the texts she consumed.[43] In the final two chapters, I outline an alternative model of consumption in which fantasy and the everyday are characterized by a sense of exchange and permeability between texts and practices. The separation of this analysis into two chapters reflects my effort to differentiate between two types of leisure practice: the first a form of narrative or textual consumption, often imagined to be a private (insidious, dangerous) activity, and the second an interactive, public (illicit, immoral) experience. These two types of consumer practice are intimately connected nonetheless, as the modes of consumption structured by absorption and distraction converge in the arena of popular leisure.

The fourth chapter argues that novelettes and girls' and women's magazines, although dependent on the teleological narrative of the romance ("the old, old story of meeting, parting, and the church-door in the last chapter"[44]), provide an alternative model for imagining the practice of reading as a process of consuming fantasy. To a great extent, these genres encourage absorption on the part of the reader, involving her in a coherent fantasy which may be consumed as a discrete narrative; this is especially true in the case of the novelette, which in its form and content invites readers to lose themselves in scenes which create the fantasy of an alternative life. However, particularly in the case of the serialized writings in the genre of the magazine, they also offer the possibility of a deferred pleasure through the experience of distracted reading, a process facilitated by the disjunctive, "tit-bit"-style of the magazine's serialized form. The absorption-distraction model finds further confirmation in the use of fashion illustration in the novelettes and magazines targeted to shopgirls as a consuming audience: the fashions described in the stories were rendered in meticulous detail and often paired with patterns on the following pages, thereby reproducing a distracted pleasure in consumption, whether real or imagined.[45] This chapter contends that this alternative model of readerly experience permits a greater permeability between the romance narrative and the lives of its readers, at the same time allowing for a flexibility in the structural conditions of fantasy and consumer identification.

Chapter 5 describes a parallel mode of consumption—now made public and interactive rather than private and individualized—in the similarly distracted model of consumer practice exemplified by the variety format of music hall, popular theatre, and early cinema. Music hall songs and sketches and musical comedies featuring shopgirls helped to produce an atmosphere of interactive consumption that incorporated the model of distracted pleasure described in the previous chapter. Likewise, early fashion films incorporated techniques of nonnarrative display associated with the "cinema of attractions," echoing the strategies used by shops and department stores to entice potential consumers. The pleasures and dangers associated with these popular leisure practices resulted in a series of attempts to standardize the mass entertainment industry, paralleling the historically situated rise of classical film spectatorship and rendering the distracted mode of consumer pleasure less sustainable than it had previously been.[46] This chapter concludes the temporal trajectory of this study by acknowledging the historical transformation of leisure practice, signified most clearly by the changes to the structure and use of consumer fantasy constitutive of the second decade of the twentieth century and after.

Finally, a brief conclusion addresses the continued influence of the late Victorian and Edwardian shopgirl as a cultural figure throughout the twentieth century and up to the present day. Cases discussed in the final pages of the book—which include a 1907 murder trial as well as popular media from the turn of our own century—demonstrate the ongoing cultural fascination with the shopgirl and suggest what we may still have to learn from her story.

CHAPTER 1

Constructing the Shopgirl: The Politics of Everyday Life

As [the shop assistant] comes to self-consciousness and catches the spirit of the age, she too strains at the yoke of capital on labour. She knows the meaning of trade-unionism, the dignity of the common rule exchanged for subjection to autocratic degree. She claims a standard rate, a standard day, but first of all the right to spend her wages in her own way, to form her own life, to choose her own friends, to make her own home, the right, in fact, of the free man or woman to absolute and individual control, not over labour, but over leisure.[1]

In the latter half of the nineteenth century, many women of working- and lower-middle-class backgrounds found employment in the rapidly growing number of shops and department stores in London, as well as in other industrial cities and towns across England. As positions for shop assistants increased, so too did their number, until by 1907 it was estimated at one million or more. "No other class of workers," claimed two members of the National Amalgamated Union of Shop Assistants (NAUSA), was considered "at once so numerically strong and so economically poor."[2] The increasing numbers of women working in urban shops and department stores, institutions that were seen to lack the socially regulated environment of the domestic context or the sphere of apprenticed labor, contributed to an increased perception of shop assistants as impoverished subjects, not only on an economic level but also in terms of social practice. Beginning in the late 1880s, social historians and trade union activists began to decry a perceived transformation in the shop assistant's working conditions from an atmosphere of "light and pleasant" work to a dangerous and morally degrading environment. Historians of women's work narrated the experiences of shop workers from a middle-class philanthropic perspective in order to raise social awareness of the shop assistant's plight, while activists like Thomas Sutherst, Joseph Hallsworth and Rhys Davies,

William Paine, P. C. Hoffman, and Margaret Bondfield (all former shop assistants who denounced the "sweated" elements of their trade) periodically incorporated the testimony of store employees in their exposés of shop life, providing us with one of the few areas in which the experiences of actual shop assistants have been recorded.[3] In the argument that follows, I draw from these and other texts constituting an archive of women's labor conditions in the Victorian shop and department store in order to identify the particular characteristics associated with shop assistants as a social group and to develop the contention that the female shop assistant proved central to a controversy over labor, leisure, and gendered social mobility during this period.

During the period from the late 1880s to the First World War, the female shop assistant, or "shopgirl" as she came to be identified, became the figure for a contested and transitional subjectivity, a new social identity for turn-of-the-century working women. This change in terminology results in part from a historical shift in the modes of production and distribution of goods in the second half of the nineteenth century: with the effacement of artisanal labor and shop apprenticeship and the modernizing influence of the department store, the draper's assistant of the 1850s became the "shopboy" or "shopgirl" of the turn of the century. However, shop workers were still termed shop assistants in the majority of nonfictional accounts well into the twentieth century, so the change was not entirely a historical progression. Rather, this transformation masks a more complex narrative of gendered subject production narrated through the cultural mechanics of the romance plot. In essence, the shift in name reveals the "girling" of the shop assistant during the late Victorian era, in terms of age as well as gender. Thus, although female shop workers "belong[ed] to every age, to every diversity of taste, temperament and character," such differences were elided as these women came to be seen as "girls" in their teens and early twenties who embodied the transitional qualities of adolescence.[4] The dual components of femininity and youth contributed to the sense that the new category of the "shopgirl" consolidated a set of social practices associated with young working women living independent of chaperonage or supervision in urban areas.[5] Predominantly considered to be single wage-earners unencumbered with dependents, they had few expenses beyond their personal needs, and as unmarried women they had the liberty to spend their leisure time, however little there was, as they pleased.[6] Living away from the familial home (or at any rate spending a significant period of time—their lengthy workdays—beyond the confines of the domestic arena), female shop assistants occupied a relatively unsupervised sphere of social interaction, and therefore possessed a certain degree of freedom of action both at work and in their leisure practices. As a result, the figure of the shopgirl organized a number of late-Victorian middle-class anxieties over sexuality, morality, and class position, eclipsing the distinctions in age, social status, background, and experience which characterized actual shop workers. My discussion of the discursive forces producing the shopgirl as a transitionally classed and contested identity will describe the methods by which shop assistants were transformed into "shopgirls," delineating the process by which female shop workers came to be seen as endangered social subjects and analyzing the resulting efforts on the part of social reformers to mold these laborers into exemplary political actors.

In framing the shopgirl's identity as a contested production, I intend to account for the repeated displacement of the voices and histories of women who actually worked in turn-of-the-century shops and department stores. Part of my project has been to analyze the rhetoric of social reform which places middle-class men and women in the position of "speaking for" the young women who form the analytical subjects of trade union propagandist writing and social histories of women's shop labor.[7] This positioning of middle-class reformers as the narrators of the lives of female shop assistants whose own voices are occluded began with the formation of the Society for Promoting the Employment of Women in the 1850s and lasted (at least) through the first two decades of the twentieth century. Not all those who charged themselves with narrating the experience of the exploited shop assistant originated from or identified with the middle classes, however; many of the union texts were written by shop assistants who self-identified as working class, and therefore present a different set of concerns connected to working-class politics and labor reform. Even though many of the sources discussed in this chapter mask the class affiliation of their authors, I nonetheless draw distinctions where possible in order to avoid collapsing the various groups who worked toward different ends in their efforts to transform the everyday lives of Victorian and Edwardian shop workers.

Surviving accounts of the conditions of shop life for Victorian and Edwardian women fall into two categories: the first includes trade union journals and social histories of women's work, while the second combines memoirs, correspondence, and other autobiographical writings with fictionalized accounts of the vicissitudes of shop experience. However, these categories frequently overlap, since shop assistants wrote both fictional and nonfictional pieces in union journals as well as mainstream newspapers, frequently positioning themselves as experts on the experience of shop workers as a class. These writers combined exposés of the exploitative conditions of shop labor with stories casting the shopgirl as the heroine of a tragic romance plot, in which the ultimate scene of love or romantic union between an employee and her lover is repeatedly truncated through the mechanism of death or another type of deferral of the pleasures produced by the romance. The stories, such as those published by the *Shop Assistant* (NAUSA's monthly journal), frequently used the "real-life" experiences of actual shop assistants as "evidence" for their fictional narratives, and then in turn used these narratives as a way to mediate the emotional involvement of the readers who were themselves shop assistants invested in union politics and social reform. These stories allow us to perceive the rendering of actual experience as a fictionalized romance plot, in which the shopgirl occupies the role of the protagonist and must be protected, through legislative and ideological influence, from the narratives of degraded labor which were seen to characterize the conditions of everyday life in the shop.

As trade union activists fought for better living and working conditions for shop assistants as a class, they paid particular attention to the moral and physical risks attendant upon the shopgirl's experience. Describing the story of the shopgirl as one of sexual and moral endangerment by the conditions of shop labor, union activists colluded (strategically or unwittingly, depending on the particular case) with more conservative social reformers in an effort to expose prostitution as the trade to which impoverished female shop workers might be forced to turn. Furthermore, despite the popular cultural perception of the shopgirl as an upwardly mobile social subject who would relinquish the need to work through a fortuitous marriage (exemplified by the genres of popular romance like the novelette and the early feature film), much of the middle-class concern over legislation and the fight for more humane standards of living relied on the prevailing opinion that the female shop worker would never be "delivered" through marriage to a wealthy man.[8] Accordingly, while popular representations reproduced a fantasy of upward mobility through marriage, union activists attempted to create an alternative world for the rising female shop assistant founded on her newly imagined political involvement and her commitment to the collective union cause.

The epigraph with which I began this chapter depicts the female shop assistant as an enlightened laborer who recognizes her own exploitation by capitalist enterprise and who subsequently strives for the dignity inherent in the ideal of work as a rewarding rather than a degrading experience. The final sentence of the passage suggests the importance of freedom in the choice of leisure practices, and indeed the conclusion to the article reinforces this suggestion, stating that "freedom [. . .] comes not through Act of Parliament [but] through individual will." These excerpts reveal that collective political activism is a central element in prevailing concerns over the everyday lives of Victorian and Edwardian shop assistants: the last words of the article offer an exhortation to readers that "strength lies in trade unionism."[9] As is the case here, texts that uncover some aspect of the shop assistant's history also themselves construct that history as such, in this case guiding its course in the direction of a socialist critique of capitalism and industrialized labor in the sphere of consumption. The critique of labor is linked to the production of leisure for shop assistants, but intentionally shapes that leisure, ultimately for explicitly political ends.

Shop Labor and Feminine Sympathy, 1850–1880

Scholarship on consumer culture in England has represented the mid- to late-Victorian period as witness to the transformation of consumption from a duty to a pleasure, as shopping for goods changed from an everyday task to a leisure activity. For middle- and upper-class women, the department stores which developed from the smaller shops of the 1840s and 1850s symbolized a new world of abundance and display and a newly conceived public sphere.[10] As these female consumers became an identifiable market to be targeted by stores, employers began to seek out female employees who they imagined might more effectively serve the needs of the women on the other side of the counter. This assumption was predicated on a conception of feminine consumer desire that incorporated identification through fantasy, such that when a shop assistant employed behind the counter or in the showroom displayed merchandise for a customer, she embodied the projected fantasy image of possibility even while remaining differentiated from the consumer through her status as seller rather than buyer of goods. In the eyes of shop owners and advocates of women's employment in shops, this process depended on a gendered identification between the woman selling the goods and the woman buying them, and incorporated an ideology of sympathy between the shopgirl and her customer. In the words of one contemporary observer, Lady Jeune, women "understand so much more readily what other women want," offering expertise in their greater ability to "fathom the agony of despair as to the arrangement of colours, the alternative trimmings, the duration of a fashion, the depths of a woman's purse."[11] Although this observation masks the perception of class *difference* rather than parity between the shop assistant and her customer—a difference often assumed by wealthy consumers and ridiculed or denied by shop assistants—it allows us to read the ways in which fantasy and identification operate in the social environment of the shop.[12] The construction of women as "naturally" better suited to selling the goods which other women were more likely to desire resulted in the growing demand for female shop assistants in the late Victorian period, although the cheaper cost of their labor remained a significant factor in the increasing employment of women in this industry.[13] This section traces the history of social reform efforts to open up new areas of employment for women, arguing that selling goods in a shop became a socially sanctioned sphere for women who identified themselves as members of the impoverished middle classes or who aspired to rise into this class position (and perhaps eventually beyond, with the consequent release from shop labor). In the eyes of many middle-class reformers, the upward mobility of the shop assistant signified a promise for individual self-improvement; as the next section will show, trade union activists reframed this promise to extol the virtues of collective betterment in an effort to gain support for the union.

The construction of women as ideal shop assistants began in conjunction with the debate over "superfluous" women and the attempt to broaden employment opportunities for women who needed or chose to earn a living. After the findings of the 1851 census, journalists and social critics began to lament the unbalanced ratio of women to men in England: the much-cited figure of "above half a million" unmarried women had a tremendous impact on the public conception of women's lives and labor. In an 1859 article entitled "Female Industry," Harriet Martineau contended that "out of six millions of women above twenty years of age, in Great Britain, exclusive of Ireland, and of course of the Colonies, no less than half are industrial in their mode of life[;] more than a third, more than two millions, are independent in their industry, are self-supporting, like men."[14] Martineau's essay argued for the widest possible range of employments for women and for an increase in educational opportunities so that women would not be forced to earn their living by the needle or in the lamentable position of an impoverished governess, dependent on the will of a family in which she occupied a vaguely defined role. Several years later W. R. Greg, a liberal manufacturer who had written on the problem of prostitution in the 1840s, followed Martineau's treatise with an article on "redundant" women which proclaimed:

> There is an enormous and increasing number of single women in the
> nation, a number quite disproportionate and abnormal; a number
> which, positively and relatively, is indicative of an unwholesome
> social state, and is both productive and prognostic of much
> wretchedness and wrong.[15]

Greg's solution for dealing with this "residue" of women, who constitute "*the evil and anomaly to be cured*" (281), was to export five hundred thousand to the colonies and employ another half million in domestic service, thereby restoring the "natural" balance between men and women at home and abroad.[16] Greg then directs his philanthropic lens on the "odd women" of each class—the mill-girls, seamstresses, and needlewomen;

governesses and spinsters who eke out a scanty living; charity-givers, writers, and society women—in order to argue that as each segment is turned
to its appropriate function, those who remain in the home nation "will rise
in value, will be more sought, will be better rewarded" (307), and will
eventually find husbands and homes themselves.

Mid-nineteenth-century social reformers suggested different solutions
than emigration and marriage: they turned more often to the twin issues
of women's education and women's labor. By the late 1850s, middle-class
feminists like Barbara Leigh Smith Bodichon, Jessie Boucherett, Bessie
Rayner Parkes, Emily Faithfull, and others connected with the Society for
Promoting the Employment of Women, agitated for greater education and
advocacy on the part of the many thousands of single and widowed
women who could not rely on the security of wedded domestic life for
their social survival. Numerous articles in the *English Woman's Journal*
articulated the level of concern for that "immense female multitude" who
must gain the rights and abilities to fend for themselves in the public
sphere of labor, understood by many of these writers to be the province of
men.[17] Since these women could not be expeditiously exported to the "out-
lying provinces" or to Britain's colonial dominions, they argued, something
had to be done to address this concern in the home nation.[18] On behalf of
the society, Jessie Boucherett detailed their "plan for the prevention of this
distress, and of the many evils arising from it": they would open a school
in which women might be educated in trades "well suited" to them,
including printing, hairdressing, and the like.[19] Functioning as a "depot for
information of every kind relating to the employment of women," the
society understood itself as providing a viable and rewarding alternative to
menial labor, starvation, and eventual prostitution for the many educated
"odd women" who were faced with the prospect of financial independence,
whether voluntary or involuntary.

The members of the society advocated the replacement of men by
women in one trade in particular: that of the shop assistant. In an article
from the *English Woman's Journal* on the society, the committee analyzed
the disproportion in men's and women's labor opportunities, and demanded a redress of the imbalance:

> Let us then look round, and see whether men are never to be found
> occupying easy, remunerative places, that could be as well or better
> filled by women; places that originally belonged to them, and that
> they would have remained in possession of to this day, had not arti-
> ficial means been used to displace them. We refer to those depart-
> ments in the great shops, which are devoted to the sale of light arti-
> cles of female attire. Why should bearded men be employed to sell

ribbon, lace, gloves, neck-kerchiefs, and the dozen other trifles to be
found in a silk-mercer's or haberdasher's shop?[20]

Here, the authors strategically argue that women have been deprived of a
trade which was rightfully theirs, implicitly referring to a precapitalist history of the shop in which women assisted their families in selling the
goods within their gendered province. The "artificial means" by which
women were displaced from their original positions (presumably the
efforts by men to corner a lucrative trade) imply that shop work is more
"natural" and fitting for women, anticipating the argument for sympathetic identification articulated at the end of the century by Lady Jeune and
suggesting that the gendered reflection across the counter or on the showroom floor results in an increased desire to purchase those goods for sale.[21]
Therefore, argues the society, women should be returned to the "light and
pleasant" work of the shop, despite opposition from those who claim that
women are too little educated and insufficiently experienced in retail sales,
not to mention their physical handicaps (in being unable to lift bales of
sheeting and heavy velvet). The society's statement dismisses the latter
complaint with the claim that men might be employed for the "heavy
work," and moreover that "the active life of a shopgirl is less injurious to
health, than the sedentary one of a seamstress," and reveals its intention to
remedy the complaint about women's lack of business training through
the creation of a school to educate female shop assistants in their trade:

> It is the intention of the Society to establish a large School for girls
> and young women, where they may be specially trained to wait in
> shops, by being thoroughly well instructed in accounts, book-keep-
> ing, etc.; be taught to fold and tie up parcels, and perform many
> other little acts, which a retired shopwoman could teach them. The
> necessity of politeness towards customers, and a constant self-com-
> mand, will also be duly impressed upon them.[22]

This passage marks the shift in focus from the shopgirl's "natural" ability
to the need to educate women in the process of acquiring the appropriate
behavior and knowledge for shop employment. The emphasis on training
women in gentility and self-command suggests the society's assumption
that the women they sought to instruct might not inherently display the
proper characteristics of middle-class femininity, and would thus need to
be "thoroughly well instructed" in the behavior and appearance that
would define their new role as objects and mediators of the consumer
desires of their customers. The notion of education in the manners of the
shop, and the necessity of maintaining (as an 1897 tract published by the

Fabian Society put it) "a neat and prosperous appearance,"[23] proves to be central to the cultural construction of the female shop assistant as industrious worker and public servant.

Producing the Shopgirl as a Transitional Subject

Since most of the texts which comprise the archive for this chapter discuss the class of the shop assistant at length, it is necessary to begin with an analysis of contemporary perceptions of the shopgirl's place within the class structure of late Victorian and Edwardian society in order to clarify the ways in which class as a descriptive and associative term contributed to the shopgirl's subject formation. The authors of *Women's Work and Wages,* concerned with the "Social Problem" of women's working conditions in 1906 Birmingham, imagine the shopgirl as emerging from the "masses" of unskilled laborers to take up semiskilled employment:

> [. . .] sometimes a girl whose ambition has been aroused through the
> refining influence of her evening club or Sunday class raises herself to
> a higher social level by changing her situation, either leaving heavy or
> dirty work for lighter duties of the same kind, or giving up ordinary
> factory work for a place in a warehouse, a small shop, or, more rarely,
> in domestic service.[24]

This passage constructs the shopgirl as an ambitious, upwardly mobile young woman whose transition from factory to shop would accompany the "refining influence" of the better forms of leisure. Her ambition is couched in the language of desire for an identifiably better social place which would be characterized by the lighter and cleaner setting of the shop. However, the authors go on to argue that this class mobility occurs less often than might be expected: they assert that "most kinds of work are performed by distinct classes of girls [. . .] in most cases a girl's class is fixed before she starts work, and this is the determining influence in her choice of a trade."[25]

The perception of class fixity reappears in the 1915 article on shop assistants in the *Women's Industrial News,* in which the shop assistant belongs to "a wide social scale":

> In the good-class trade she is the daughter of a small tradesman, a
> clerk, a manager, a farmer, a skilled artisan, and has perhaps two years
> or more of secondary education before she begins her career about
> the age of sixteen. While [*sic*] in the cheap-class trade she comes from

a plain working-class home and starts work straight from the board
school. (323)

In this case, class distinctions inhere in each shop or store, for although the
counter assistant and the showroom saleswoman ostensibly belong to the
same class, "the fine bearing and assured manners of the latter are sometimes
said to denote a difference in breeding" (326). This article understands the
employer to be the best judge of the customers' desires for an "impressive"
showroom with "tall and elegant" saleswomen to match: employers assume,
"'No lady cares to be served in the showroom by a five-foot nothing'" (325).
The most talented saleswomen combine "personal advantages" with an array
of other qualities including "taste, tact, patience, savoir-faire, and gifts of
speech, powers of suggestion, persuasion [and] resource" in an effort to
engage consumer desire through a sympathetic identificatory strategy incorporating the fantasy reflection of the female consumer (325). But, as the
authors then note, "the difference in manner" between the counter assistant
and the showroom model or saleswoman is also one of opportunity, "for the
counter assistant has less scope to develop a rare order of talent" (326).
Counter assistants merely have access to "quick wits, a clear head, [and] an
honest heart," all assets which nonetheless do not permit them to advance
in salary: women employed behind the typical shop counter could rarely
earn more than £15 to £30 annually, while the head saleswomen in the
stores of London's West End might earn upward of £100 to £200 a year.

    These distinctions—based on the physical and social manifestations of
class—intensify in the competition for higher wages and available posts,
especially in the metropolitan drapery and millinery trades, which carry
the association of genteel, appropriate female labor and therefore remain
in high demand. In a pamphlet calling for increased union participation
on the part of shop assistants, the Fabian Society described the struggle for
employment between temporary and permanent shop workers:

> Those who are solely dependent upon their situation for a livelihood
> have to compete for employment with others who are attracted by
> the apparent gentility of such occupations, and either receive assis-
> tance from parents in fairly comfortable circumstances or supple-
> ment their earnings from other sources. Fellow employees who are
> exceptionally well dressed and well supplied with money make
> things much harder for poor and vain juniors who look upon such
> possessions with envy.[26]

This passage underscores the tensions among women working behind the
counter, and provides the historical basis for many of the shop fictions,

with titles like "That Pretty Shop Girl," "A Shop Girl's Revenge," and "The Soul of a Shop Girl,"[27] which describe an atmosphere of rivalry and divisiveness taken to be characteristic of shop life. The authors of this article imagine the culture of the shop to be affected by the superficiality of the fashion industry, viewing the interactions between employees as defined by the desire to signify wealth and security through dress and appearance; the description of junior sales assistants as "poor and vain" must be taken in this light, perpetuating a perception of shop assistants as self-interested workers concerned merely with individual social ascendance rather than collective improvement of the welfare of the class as a whole.

According to Fabian Socialists, shop assistants' lack of social consciousness and communal organization, combined with their self-identified gentility, allow the deplorable conditions of shop labor to go unchecked. This perceived or imagined gentility is elsewhere termed the "false pride" of the young assistant who believes that "any disclosure of her income to her fellows is 'unbecoming a lady,'" and therefore can never succeed at the attempt to obtain a standard wage from her employer.[28] The only solution, argue proponents of union organization, is for assistants to disregard their pretensions to middle-class status and form a politically motivated class of workers—in effect, to acknowledge their connection to the working classes:

> Social status, not economic law, is the ruin alike of shop assistants
> and clerks. Very many of them are prevented by their sham gentility
> from helping in the organization of their class. These "gentlemen"
> and "ladies" feel that it is quite beneath them to belong to a common
> Trade Union like navvies or bricklayers.[29]

The declarative tone of this article negates the possibility that shop assistants might not self-identify as working class, instead choosing to define them as such in order to state the necessity of increased participation in the effort to transform working conditions in the shop. The authors presume that any effort to signify middle-class status on the part of shop assistants would result in the exposure of their gentility as a "sham," a failed performative attempt to embody the qualities that would allow them to resist association with the working classes. In the narrative impetus for collective organization produced by unionist texts like the Fabian Society pamphlet, we receive a version of the shopgirl as a figure caught in the midst of discursive formations of class and gender identity which position her on the border between descriptive classes, subject to the unarticulated possibility of social transformation.[30]

In these discussions of shop life and labor, the class transitionality and identity formation of the shopgirl is complicated by the regional migration of workers and the seasonal fluctuation of the industry. Working from material evidence collected by the National Amalgamated Union of Shop Assistants in 1915, the *Women's Industrial News* noted the perception that "in London about 75 per cent. of the assistants in West End establishments are said to be country women" (323).[31] According to this account, after apprenticeships or junior positions in smaller country towns, young women would migrate into the larger industrial cities to take their places amidst the throngs of workers, lured by any number of personal and social amenities:

> The call to the country girl from the great city—the glamour and boasted salaries and opportunities, the preference of the West End employer for the country girl—her good looks and physique or perhaps her greater amenability, the convenience of the living-in system to a girl away from home, the dislike of the London girl to live in, the reluctance of the West End house to train apprentices, the excellent training in the provinces and suburbs, one and all go to swell the army of young women who, having finished their apprenticeship, pour into London each spring from Devon and Cornwall, and the South of England and Wales. (323–24)

These young country women, many of whom constitute the body of "ordinary women" workers, having relocated to the city, compete with two other types of migratory workers: the "blackleg," an assistant who gains temporary experience in the metropolis before settling down in the provinces, and the "casuals," a large reserve of temporary workers, either married women or daughters who return to the city for a few weeks every year or others who have fallen out of permanent positions and follow the season "from place to place, from trade to trade, from the sale-room to the tea-shop, from the tea-shop to the bar, from the bar to the theatre or exhibition, as shop assistants, waitresses, barmaids, programme-sellers, stallholders, attendants, etc." (327). The account of these women's travels in location and type of employment narrates a certain descent in the perceived status of the shopgirl: as is the case in this description, the draper's assistant (in counter and showroom) was often placed at the top of the social ladder and the tea-shop girl, waitress, and barmaid on lower rungs (even if their wages did not differ materially).[32] Union activists argued that the migrational character of shop life and the perpetuation of a casual labor force contributed to the difficulty in organizing assistants as well as the separation of each store into discrete and hierarchized factions.

The last, and arguably most important, aspect of the shopgirl's transitionality and its relationship to labor organization is her placement within a teleological narrative of eventual marriage and departure from the labor of the shop to the imagined leisure of the home. The cultural perception of the shop assistant as a proto-wife and domestic woman in the making, whose character is shaped through her daily interactions in the shop, in effect takes the form of a real-life romance plot in which the shopgirl is positioned as the protagonist of a love story whose ending promises release from the shop. Several aspects of the shopgirl's positioning within the dominant gender ideology are germane to my discussion, among them the perceived age and marital status of female shop assistants as well as the presumption that their desires would "naturally" be directed toward the ultimate normative objective of the heterosexual romance, namely love and marriage to a male suitor. Women whose lives did not fit this normative model therefore presented complications for the romance plot, suggesting one set of alternatives to the stereotype of the shopgirl as a young woman on her way to a lifetime of marital bliss.

The disjunction between the lives of turn-of-the-century female shop workers and the behavior and activity prescribed for women of an earlier period, who were more likely to remain within the structured environment of the home than to live alone or with other girls in lodgings, contributed to the perception in some of the more conservative social histories that these young, single women might act upon their intention to marry by flirting with their male customers across the counter. This largely middle-class perception depended on the presumption that female shop assistants imagined themselves as the heroines of a fantasized romance plot in which they would be "delivered" from the exhausting labor of the shop through marriage to a wealthy man, which in turn would provide them with the leisure that was such a precious commodity in their daily lives. M. Mostyn Bird, the author of a 1911 history of women's work, reveals this contemporary perception most vividly:

> The young girl starts work with no [. . .] sense of permanency, for of the two main roads that lay before her, marriage or spinsterhood, that of marriage is sure to be the one that she elects and expects to follow: therefore she will inevitably look upon any work she does between leaving school and going to the altar as something of a temporary and stop-gap nature.[33]

This assured tone of Bird's assessment in this passage, and in her subsequent claim that even women who love their work are unable to resist the "demands" of the "dominating male creature[s]" who will become their husbands, suggests her participation in the ideological reproduction of the romance plot in which the "Visionary Deliverer" engages the fantasies and desires of the laborer doomed to monotonous toil in the shop or factory. This formulation intimates that even though working women know that the "Deliverer" may come with "counterfeit coin in his purse," and that they may well have to return to the sphere of paid labor, the promise of the "possible husband" holds out a tantalizing possibility for women who long for another life than their own.[34] In Bird's representation of women's working lives, female shop laborers are reconceived as shopgirls who long for the solace and leisure of marriage as an alternative to the shop, a narrative that purports to documentary status but which strategically replicates the fictional/fantasy romance plot that characterizes the story of the shopgirl.

Working Conditions and Everyday Life

> And there is the girl behind the counter, too—I would as soon have her true history as the hundred and fiftieth life of Napoleon or seventieth study of Keats. . . .[35]

Although a full account of the "true history" of the girl behind the counter may always elude us, it is possible to use surviving documents from the trade and mainstream press in conjunction with modern histories of shop labor to piece together a preliminary history of everyday life for Victorian and Edwardian women employed in shops and department stores.[36] Several aspects of the working conditions of shop assistants between the mid-1880s and the First World War require attention here, among them the number of hours worked both daily and weekly, the financial returns of such employment (wages, commissions, fines, and other deductions, and the truck controversy), the living-in system, and the brief amount of time allowed shop assistants to pursue their leisure activities. This section addresses each of these subjects in turn, and then examines the reforms advocated by trade unions, guilds, and other organizations in each case. By using texts which provide partial accounts of the working lives of female shop assistants, I mean to elaborate the cultural concern over the perceived social and moral dangers such working women faced in their participation in the public sphere of labor in late-nineteenth- and early-twentieth-century London, and thus to draw out the various influences on the construction of the shopgirl as a new cultural type during this period.

    Any treatment of the relationship between work and leisure for women in Britain at the turn of the century must take into account the lengthy workday and the little time individuals were allowed for their own pursuits. In the case of the female shop assistant, working hours ranged from fifty per week to, in the worst cases, upward of one hundred; for most of this period, the only regulated hours of labor were for women under the age of eighteen, who were only allowed to work seventy-four hours a week or less. The majority of women would work from 8:30 in the morning until 8 or 9 at night four nights of the week, with a half-holiday one day beginning at 2, 3, or 4 PM (yet only in some cases until the Shop Hours Act of 1912) and Sundays off (except in smaller shops and less fashionable areas); however, on Fridays and Saturdays shops stayed open until 10 or, in some cases, 11 PM, and some assistants would not leave the shop until after midnight.[37] Meal times were largely unregulated until late in this period, and thus the workday would be extended even more, with few chances to rest over the course of the day. Assistants lamented the injustice of not being allowed even a folding seat to rest on briefly during the hours of standing: the authors of *The Working Life of Shop Assistants* noted that "the evil of confinement for long hours is aggravated by the rule in force in some establishments that the assistants must not lean against the walls or on the counter, even when they have no customers to serve" (67). And the work itself, although sometimes less taxing than factory labor, was by no means always as "light, clean, easy, and pleasant" as some advocates of women's shop employment imagined:

> The strain of constant attention on customers, the rush of business in a fashionable house, the impatience and exacting demands of the fashionable customer, the long hours of standing—seats being for the inspector rather than the assistant who, busy or not, is expected to appear so, the overheated or vitiated air in one house, the chill and draught behind the counter in another, the artificial ventilation and light in underground departments, the day is an exhausting one[. . .].[38]

The long hours of unrewarding, unregulated labor present a particular concern for this and other writers, who perceive other types of laborers (particularly in the industrial/productive trades) as the recipients of higher wages and better treatment; here as elsewhere, the distributive trade is framed as one of a list of "sweated" industries in order to express the necessity of organization for reform of working conditions.[39]

The public concern over long hours was related to the problem of income, such that assistants and reformers alike voiced their concomitant demands for "a standard day and a standard wage."[40] The debate over wages illuminates a larger concern about the relationship between men's and women's work and the relative value of women's labor. As women moved into the skilled and unskilled workforce in greater numbers, taking jobs that had previously been held by men, they invariably received a lower wage (often one-third to one-half of men's wages).[41] Again, to be sure, income varied greatly depending on the perceived social status of the position: throughout this period, shop assistants in higher-class establishments earned significantly more than those in less prestigious or smaller shops. In cheaper-class shops, women might earn as little as 10-/ to 15-/ a week, sometimes less than 2d. an hour.[42] Many employers avoided paying a fixed salary by promising premiums on the sale of damaged or unpopular merchandise and commissions on higher-priced goods; employees often preferred the former, however, since earnings were less certain under the commission system, and since they disliked the practice of "forc[ing] an undesirable purchase on an unwilling or unwitting customer."[43]

Unscrupulous employers might take advantage of shop assistants in several ways: through an elaborate system of fines for breaking shop rules, through payment in truck (goods) rather than wages, and through the living-in system. These methods of reducing the actual earned income of shop assistants were widely considered grievous offenses, since they were a largely unlegislated aspect of shop employment until the early years of this century. The system of fines as a means of regulating employee behavior, although declining in usage by the teens, was still in effect throughout the period between 1890 and 1914: assistants might receive deductions ranging from 1d. to 2s. 6d. for unpunctuality, carelessness, negligence, or a host of other infractions. To middle-class observers and proponents of reform through union activity and legislation like the members of the Women's Industrial Council, as well as to shop assistants themselves, the most unreasonable of these regulations included exhortations against personal adornment and decoration, in keeping with the narrative of the shopgirl as a vain consumer ("Rings and other showy adornments must not be worn in business"; "No flowers to be put in water glasses or bottles"), and invasions of privacy ("All employés are liable to be searched at any or every time of leaving the premises, the doorkeeper having full authority for that purpose").[44] These regulations allowed superiors to exercise undue control over junior-level assistants, and to the editors of the *Women's Industrial News,* "the fine in the hands of a bully [changed] from a means of discipline [into] an instrument of persecution" (330).

The truck system, too, was seen as merely a method by which shopkeepers and managers might regain some of their employees' income. Draper's assistants were often expected to purchase goods from the shop as a form of advertisement, and for young female shop assistants, this practice was seen by some middle-class writers as a temptation which led them further into debt and (potential) moral decline:

The girl loses in self-control and self-respect. She overspends herself in dress, and, tempted by the credit as well as the discount, runs up bills with her employer—an unscrupulous but not uncommon practice which secures the return of her wages to himself.[45]

This formulation depends upon women's "natural" desire to purchase ever more elaborate fashions and suggests the ways in which the shop assistant might be seen as placing herself at risk through her desire for goods. Other methods of payment in truck included often compulsory contributions to shop funds for recreational use of a shared library or piano and for medical assistance (the "House Doctor" despised by many shop workers), and purportedly voluntary subscriptions to the hospital, early closing, and Prince of Wales' funds.[46] In many (if not most) cases, shop assistants preferred to make their own choices about health care and leisure activity, yet were prevented from doing so by a system which frequently rewarded them with goods and products for which they had neither use nor desire.[47]

The most controversial aspect of payment in truck involved the living-in system, in which shop assistants were paid a portion of their wages in board and lodging. Most of the texts which narrate the plight of late-Victorian shop workers lament this system and its tendency to foster such qualities as "irresponsibility, improvidence, want of initiative, dependence, [and] reliance on others."[48] Although actual overcrowding and legal infractions such as "insanitary conditions, double beds, dirty linen, vermin, and rats" were relatively rare, shop employees still had material grounds for complaint. Such complaints generally focused on the lack of privacy and crowded living quarters engendered through the system, in which women slept "two, three, four and five to a room"; rooms themselves might be dingy and dark, with an "unhealthily close" atmosphere in the mornings due to the windows having been closed throughout the night.[49] Bathrooms were provided in up-to-date establishments, but often in a ratio of one to every twenty-five to one hundred assistants; shop assistants would usually be allowed a hot bath once a week. Meals, provided by the employer, were reportedly monotonous at best, but could be a great deal worse: rancid butter, stale bread, and ill-cooked and badly served food were common complaints, and meals of bread, butter, and weak tea often had to be supplemented in the form of "extras," paid for out of the employees' wages. The time allotted for meals was often insufficient as well, and since assistants might well be asked to return to the counter (in smaller shops) or might be delayed in reaching the dining hall (in larger stores), they were often forced to bolt their meals or go without. These hurried and insufficient meals were seen to have detrimental effects on their health:

A hot dish for breakfast, a glass of milk at 11 o'clock, a "relish" for tea, a hot supper, these so-called luxuries are in fact necessities to a growing girl or delicate woman, who is unable to eat the solid but unpalatable mid-day meal. [. . .] [T]he anemia, indigestion, and other forms of debility from which the older women suffer are often attributed to their inadequate diet in those years when they were most in need of good food, but least able to afford it.[50]

The lack of proper nourishment to sustain ten or twelve hours of standing labor, combined with the temptation to spend their meager weekly earnings on extras provided by their employers, meant that women shop workers were faced with a dilemma: they might invest all their money in the necessary food, or accept offers of meals from young men, even strangers—a habit seen to be demoralizing and to put them at risk for further moral and personal decline.

In the minds of reformers, the living-in system was objectionable on "nonmaterial grounds" as well, in its violations of the personal freedoms of "normal" daily life. The writer for the *Women's Industrial News* frames the problem thus:

> The segregation of young men and young women into herds, the forced barrier between the sexes, the lack of interests or responsibilities and discipline of normal living, the restrictions of the communal state without the willing bond of friendship, common cause, or spiritual purpose, the want of privacy, a society familiar but not intimate, the absolute dependence of one human being upon another, a whole existence confined to the atmosphere of the shop, the system is said to pervert mind and nature, destroying personality and freedom of spirit. (334)

This passage represents the living-in system as a perversion of the "natural" relations between men and women, separating them into gendered categories and restricting both their privacy and their collective sharing of "interests." Generating closeness rather than intimacy, producing the superficial familiarity of overcrowded living conditions without the bonds of friendship and communal effort, this system alienates its workers and renders them hardly more than animals ("herds") or automatons who have little access either to individuality and "freedom of spirit" or to the agency of collective political and social identification.

As this writer and other social critics (both union activists and middle-class historians) understand it, the living-in system's worst aspects lie in the absence of "a proper social or home life" and the simultaneous lack of self-possession and supervision by friends or chaperones.[51] These concerns about the lack of propriety and moral supervision engendered by the living-in system reveal a deeper cultural anxiety about the inability of shop assistants to make appropriate choices as to their sexual conduct and romantic partnerships. Union supporters like the Women's Industrial Council lamented the extremes of sexual practice experienced by shop workers: on the one hand, they were subject to the "enforced celibacy" of sex-segregated dorms, while on the other they could effectively exercise their sexual desires without the supervision of a more regulated domestic context. Marriage between shop assistants generally required the employer's permission, a favor rarely granted since it would result in living-out and a demand for wages to be paid in full, and therefore the potential loss of the position altogether. However, the sexes were understood to have differing perspectives on the prospect of marriage: as a Fabian pamphlet stated, "While the men are forced to shun marriage for fear of losing their work, the women hail it as a means of escape from their slavery, and would, as one girl expressed it, 'marry anybody to get out of the drapery trade.'"[52] Nonetheless, as the previous section suggested, contemporary social historians such as M. Mostyn Bird saw women's desire for marriage as a fantasy of deliverance that would remain unfulfilled, and the vast majority of articles on female shop assistants assert that most remained unmarried.[53]

From these complaints about the decay of moral and social propriety, it was only a short step in the eyes of middle-class reformers to the most degraded of moral practices: "the oldest profession in the world," prostitution either actual or metaphorical. The dinners from strangers, the evenings at the theatre or the music hall, the temptation to "hoodwink the housekeeper and spend the night with friends"—all these suggest the prevalent concern over the risk of moral and social ruin, for always implied was the possibility that the suitor might demand restitution in the form of sexual favors.[54] Moreover, women might be tempted to supplement their wages with earnings from prostitution, and shop assistants who lived in were occasionally given latchkeys in a tacit recognition/disavowal of the presence of this custom. Finally, when these young women were dismissed from their positions, which often happened without notice, they often lost their home and social resources as well.[55]

Although many writers and union activists denied the actual practice of female shop assistants prostituting themselves (even displacing that practice onto women of another vaguely defined class, those without the shop assistant's "character, intelligence, and education"), the anxiety over prostitution surfaces throughout these texts in another arena: the issue of these women's leisure practices. Since the living-in system did not provide supervision in the form of family, friends, or a responsible older woman, shop

workers were allowed a latitude in their leisure time that might not have
been afforded women living in a more regulated domestic context.
Moreover, the experience of shop work was seen to engender a desire for
goods which might prompt a "penniless and friendless girl," having lost
her position in the store, to turn to the only remaining alternative: as one
writer framed it, "one thing she has to sell, her poor little hungry body and
the starved soul that aches for vanities and laughter and pretty clothes and
all that she comprehensively terms 'fun.'"[56] The desire to amuse oneself
with such "vanities" and "fun" was seen by the *Women's Industrial News* as
"natural," but circumstantially threatening:

> A young girl needs, besides fresh air and exercise, a run, a change of
> scene. The night, the lights, the throngs of men and women, youth
> is called to adventure. Her chosen playground is thus the street—a
> place of hazard, if delight, for a pleasure-seeking, but inexperienced
> young lady away from her home and friends.[57]

The combination of hazard and delight in this passage conveys the dangerous thrill which many took to constitute the pleasures of urban leisure
for working-class women.[58] The implication here, considering the union-
affiliated source from which this observation is drawn, is that once a
young lady gained more "experience," she would follow one of two paths:
the temptations of pleasure might introduce her to an environment based
on sexual barter and economic exchange, or she might learn from experience the necessity of placing herself within a supervised domestic context,
and of regulating her own desires accordingly.

The potential for the young female shop assistant to simply become
one of the crowd, lowering herself to the hazardous level of "common"
amusement, signified for these authors the possibility of degradation
inherent in the culture of mass leisure.[59] For others, however, the desire to
participate in the amusements of the crowd revolve around the higher-
class tastes engendered by the shop as opposed to the factory:

> With a certain refinement of taste, with the desire for amusement
> and the lighter side of life natural to youth and high spirits, with the
> cultivation of personal charms and extravagance in dress encouraged
> in a thousand subtle ways, she is turned out at 7 P.M. into the gayest
> streets of the town, with all their attractions and temptations.[60]

The urban street as a site of temptation and attraction, in which the shopgirl becomes a spectacle through her dress and demeanor: this perception
complicates the definition of the urban crowd as a site of anonymity, and

underscores the metaphoric and ideological links between female flânerie and prostitution.[61] In the eyes of M. Mostyn Bird and others, the shopgirl who aspired to the leisurely consumer practices of the flâneuse might instead become "saleswoman and wares in one" through prostitution.[62] For middle-class social historians writing the history of the shopgirl at the turn of the century, the practice of leisure was a priori considered within the context of sexuality. Every venture the young female shop assistant might make into an unregulated, public social space of leisure explicitly provoked a set of anxieties over her sexual and moral state. The primary response, on the part of trade union and guild activists and other social critics, was to regulate that confluence of sexuality and leisure so that the shopgirl's desires and pleasures might be channeled into more appropriate, productive practices—not coincidentally, practices which would further the cause of labor activism and the collective welfare of shop assistants as a class.

Union agitation and legislative reform activity centered on the three areas I have analyzed as the conditions of labor for shop assistants in this period: hours, wages, and payment in truck through the living-in system. Two major unions—the National Amalgamated Union of Shop Assistants and the Amalgamated Union for Co-operative Employees (AUCE)—worked in connection with such organizations as the Women's Co-operative Guild, the Women's Industrial Council, and the Fabian Society to further the cause of shop reform through legislation.[63] Although shop workers were generally seen to resist organization as a political class, parliamentary papers from the period between 1890 and 1914 nonetheless reveal significant advances in the reform of the distributive trades. Of course, many of these advances centered on shop assistants as a whole, rather than female shop workers in particular. However, women's experience of the shop was often used as an example of the dire necessity of reform, highlighting the degrading labor conditions of this "sweated" industry whose atmosphere of luxury and abundance masked the sufferings of its female employees.[64]

Because of its visibility, the length of hours shop employees worked was a central concern targeted for reform by philanthropic and unionist groups alike. In the 1880s, working in connection with the NAUSA, Sir John Lubbock, advocate of the National Early Closing League and the Shop Hours Labour League, introduced into Parliament the Shop Hours Regulation Bill, later to become the Shop Hours Act in 1886. This legislation had a limited scope, however, merely limiting the number of hours per week to seventy-four, and that only for people under the age of eighteen. Several more acts passed between 1892 and 1895 did little to address the loopholes in the 1886 act, especially as they made no provision for inspection and enforcement of the new laws. From 1894 to 1904 Lubbock pressed Parliament to accept his Early Closing Bill (which called for legal

TAKING THE LAW IN ONE'S OWN HANDS.

Fair but Considerate Customer. "PRAY SIT DOWN. YOU LOOK SO TIRED. I'VE BEEN RIDING
ALL THE AFTERNOON IN A CARRIAGE, AND DON'T REQUIRE A CHAIR."

"Taking the Law in One's Own Hands." *Punch,* 24 July 1880. Reproduced by permission of Punch, Ltd.

enforcement of voluntary early closing), but gradually the NAUSA ceased to support this legislation and called instead for compulsory early closing and the regulation of Sunday trading. The NAUSA shifted its attention to Sir Charles Dilke, who worked from 1899 to 1913 to pass a number of bills which would mandate a weekly half-holiday beginning at 1 PM and evening closing hours of 7 PM on three days of the week, 9 PM on one day, and 10 PM on one day. The Shops Acts of 1912 and 1913, although still plagued by a lack of inspection and enforcement regulation, encompassed all previous legislation and mandated a maximum workweek of sixty-four hours for all employees, thereby reducing considerably the time shop assistants had to spend behind the counter. The legislative activity in

Parliament was largely influenced by trade union agitation and social reform, and as I have suggested, resulted in an increase in leisure time for shop assistants, which then was placed in the hands of various political and commercial interests.[65]

In the case of wages, the AUCE demanded a minimum wage of 24s. weekly for male workers twenty-one or over for all societies encompassed by their organization in 1896, but legislation for women was not successfully introduced until more than a decade later. Meanwhile, the NAUSA worked throughout the decades before the war to win higher pay for all employees. However, in both cases, women were consistently paid less than men who worked the same job, a situation which was not legally rectified until the passage of the Equal Pay Act in 1970. Both unions also fought to include the distributive trades under the Trade Boards Act of 1909 in an attempt to set minimum pay rates for all workers, a reform they did not achieve until after the First World War. In short, shop assistants, women in particular, did not attain "a standard wage for a standard day" until long after this period. Nonetheless, union agitation worked diligently to effect small-scale reforms through collective bargaining and social cooperation, a strategy which furthered the cause of higher pay and greater disposable income for shop workers.

The unions used legislative pressure as well as public sympathy to effect changes in the third aspect of shop experience: the truck system, the problem of fines, and the question of living-in. The Truck Act of 1896, and the NAUSA's attention to its enforcement, resulted in the voluntary abolition of fines by many employers, a significant victory reflected in the later articles on the conditions of shop experience.[66] However, shop assistants were not technically included as workers covered by the Truck Acts, and therefore shop reform advocates began to agitate for revision of those legal strictures. With reference to the living-in system, the NAUSA had previously advocated modification rather than abolition, but as the years passed, shop workers' representatives began to shift focus to the idea of paying shop assistants the supposed cost of their room and board (often ranging from £20 to £50 a year)—a change which would in effect double the salaries they received.[67] Those who pled the shop assistants' case claimed that the problem of shop assistants' moral and ethical development was hindered rather than aided by the living-in system; however, the Truck Committee was largely unconvinced, and did not recommend inclusion of shop assistants in the act's provisions. Eventually, however, the living-in system began to prove economically unfeasible for employers, and the system as a whole began to die out toward the end of this period.

The reforms effected in the arenas of hours, wages, and the truck system eventually contributed to a marginal increase in the quality of life for shop workers, which in turn meant that a circumscribed space of time was carved out of the working day for the pursuit of leisure. As the next chapter indicates, the modernizing influence of the department store industry also impacted the everyday lives of shop assistants, often operating in loco parentis to shape the working conditions and leisure practices of the men and women who worked behind the counter. This new leisure time fell under the constraint of various social forces whose objective was to manage that leisure according to their different ends. In the case of the mass entertainment industry, the publishers of popular reading matter and the owners and managers of theatres, music halls, and early cinema auditoriums targeted shop workers, particularly women, as potential consumers. By contrast, union organizers conceived of this new leisure potential as an untapped resource through which they might engage the political investment of formerly apathetic shop employees, and subsequently provided social and ideological structures by which workers might edify themselves, including evening classes, union meetings, conferences, and other similar events. My point here is not that all union representatives necessarily condemned the pursuit of leisure as such, for it is certainly the case that many found leisure a stimulating alternative to the everyday conditions of shop labor. Rather, I want to suggest that many proponents of collective organization within the distributive trades ideologically positioned themselves against the culture of mass entertainment in order to impress upon potential union members the necessity of a commitment to political action, subtly influencing the types of leisure practices that might be open to shop assistants within this environment. Hence, in comparing the divergent narratives of leisure practice that emerge within these texts, we can trace the tension between labor, leisure, and politics for the construction of the shopgirl as a new cultural identity at the turn of the century.

The Politics of Leisure:
The Life and Writings of Margaret Bondfield

As a conclusion to this chapter, I turn now to the case of one female shop assistant and labor activist: Margaret Bondfield, whose life and writings reproduce the tension between labor and leisure in the narrative of the Victorian and Edwardian shopgirl. Bondfield's experience, written in memoirs and autobiographies as well as recorded in the articles and short fiction she wrote in the late 1890s and early 1900s for the *Shop Assistant,* illuminates some of the challenges in reading the constructed history of the shopgirl as a transitional subject.[68] Since here I confront the necessity of relying on an autobiographical account for another kind of "evidence" of the shopgirl in history, I should note that the same sorts of biases and issues arise in this case. As Bondfield herself remained involved in labor politics to the end of her life, her memoir articulates an array of practices and life choices that differ from the popular accounts of the shopgirl which will form the subject of the following chapters. In examining Bondfield's memoir *A Life's Work,* I focus on the distinctions between the life of a shop assistant who became, in her words, a "convinced" unionist early on, and the fictional experiences of shopgirls who appear as the heroines of popular fiction, theatre, and film, experiences I discuss in detail in subsequent chapters. To begin with, we must read her memoir as itself a construction of a life, a production of subjectivity constellated through specific historical and social events.[69] It is also significant that this version of the life experience of a young female shop assistant has been carefully and methodically recorded, while the lives of the vast majority of young women employed in London shops have escaped the public record. In her own writings, Bondfield reproduced her life as the history of British Labour politics, implicitly suggesting that such a narrative of one woman's life deserves a place in the historical record—as indeed it does. It is striking, however, that such explicit and autobiographical narratives of the politics of everyday life occupy a primary place in the construction of the shopgirl as a cultural type. And of course, Bondfield's story cannot be taken as representative of anything more than one woman's experience. Margaret Bondfield's life story complicates the dominant conception of the shopgirl as a leisured consumer, in that it centers largely on expressly political concerns rather than an engagement with popular culture. My analysis of her autobiography suggests that, although it relates the experience of an individual who may represent a small body of politically conscious shop workers, it diverges from the popular narrative of the shopgirl which circulates throughout late Victorian and Edwardian culture. I interpret several examples of Bondfield's short fiction as a rewriting of the conventional romance plot which, for readers of the union journal in which the stories were published, underscore the necessity of politically motivated reform and a pragmatic perspective on social experience. Bondfield's stories resist the fantasies produced by popular romance fiction, instead figuring the shop romance as a tragic example of the sufferings of female employees whose lives are not enriched through affiliation with an organization that would labor on their behalf. Her writing therefore participates in the subtle effort to persuade shop employees of the importance of politics instead of pleasure, or rather the pursuit of individual pleasure and fulfillment through collective political activism.[70]

Margaret Bondfield was born in 1873 in Furnham, near Chard in Somerset, the tenth of eleven children of Ann Taylor and William

Bondfield; her father worked as a foreman in the Chard lace factory for over forty years. Writing of her youth, she claimed that nature, rather than books or other leisure activities, formed the primary influence on her childhood experience:

> I do not remember learning to read, but I do remember that it was held against me by my brothers that I would read anything I could get hold of from *The Boy's Own Paper* to Grandpa's Old Sermons. I believe that to be an unfounded accusation. While I admit that books always had a fascination for me, I protest that I was no book-worm, but a very ordinary out-door child.[71]

This claim differentiates the author's practices from the popular perception of shopgirls, in the lack of emphasis on reading as a formative experience. This resistance to popular leisure pastimes, and an insistence on the importance of nature and, later, work, characterize the text as a whole, and draw an important distinction in relation to the majority of shop assistants whose everyday lives were imagined rather differently during this period. Bondfield emphasizes the "ordinary" quality of her youth in order to suggest that she was influenced by others rather than emerging with her politics and social perspective intact. As we shall see, she writes her personal history as a narrative of grateful apprenticeship in Labour politics in order to underscore the potential for influence among activists invested in bettering the conditions of life for shop assistants as a class. Even in these early years, though, she sets herself off from those other "ordinary" girls who read to gain pleasure from their leisure time; instead, she turns to the more pragmatic aspects of everyday life, outdoor recreation and like activities, to describe her childhood leisure practice.

In terms of education and employment, however, we can see a degree of similarity between Margaret Bondfield's experience and that of the majority of young women who sought work as shop assistants in urban centers. In 1882, she began the requisite four years of elementary education and, after a brief stint as teacher in the Boy's School in Chard, entered the "readiest available wage-earning occupation": shop work.[72] At the age of fourteen, she became an apprentice to the proprietor of a Brighton shop in which "the relations between customer and assistant were of the most courteous and friendly, and the assistants, of whom [she] was the youngest, were treated like members of the family" (24). During her apprenticeship she learned "the details of an exclusive trade, most of which was by post to India," consisting primarily of fine ladies' trousseaux, layettes, and "liberty" frocks (24). None of her experiences in this "genteel" little shop prepared her for "the realities of shop life," as she took on a junior position in W. Hetherington's, a large drapery establishment in Brighton. Here, she was no longer treated as a family member, and instead had to struggle with the difficulties of the living-in system. Among these difficulties were the problem of getting a bath—the young women would race to the public baths after closing for a fifteen-minute interval before returning to the sleeping apartments—and the persistent attentions of strange men:

> On Race Week men—evidently making repeat visits—knocked at our ground-floor windows and tried to pull them down. The occupiers of the room facing the street were not that kind of girl, and after a slight struggle the window was shut and bolted. That experience did frighten me. . . . (25)

This passage, and others in Bondfield's autobiography, construct her as a relatively innocent young woman with little interest in the opposite sex or in the liberty provided by life in the shop. She looks back on her adolescence with the wisdom gained from adulthood and a more liberal attitude toward the education of young girls, commenting with irony, "All I knew of sex was the shaming gossip of schoolgirls. I felt hot all over if I saw a pregnant woman, because one was not supposed to know anything about a baby until or unless it appeared—*and* as a result of marriage" (26). Here, Bondfield conveys her awareness of the sexual risks posed to young female shop assistants and her perspective on sex as only one aspect of women's experience. This straightforward narrative of adolescent sexual knowledge (or the lack thereof) contrasts forcefully with the popular romance's emphasis on love and marriage and its repeated disavowal of sexual desire between men and women, again revealing the more pragmatic account of everyday life given by Bondfield's story, whose "facts" are rarely clouded by fantasy.

On moving to London, Bondfield gained employment in a shop after three months' exhaustive search, only to discover that the oppressive conditions she had experienced at Brighton were in fact universal to the industry.[73] In a 1928 pamphlet entitled *The Meaning of Trade,* Bondfield recalled:

> The condition of trade in its last state of degradagion became known to me through personal experience, when, from the place of my apprenticeship, I graduate through "Emporiums" and "Bazaars" to large stores in Brighton and London, where everything from pins to elephants could be obtained. Assistants became "numbers" and "hands." . . . At this period—the end of the nineteenth century—the

conditions under which we worked, even in the "West End" trade, were deplorable. Hours of labour ranging from 7:30 AM (for the juniors) to 8 PM, with only a half day off once a week by permission, were the normal hours; while "late shops" kept open till 10 or 11 o'clock on one or two nights of the week. . . . Small wages were made still more meagre by a system of truck known as "living in," by which the employer provided board and lodging as part payment for service. Overcrowded, insanitary conditions, poor and insufficient food were the main characteristics of this system, with an undertone of danger to the young boy and girl "up from the country." In some houses both natural and unnatural vices found a breeding ground.[74]

Such conditions were troubling both to Bondfield and to those philanthropic middle-class women who made her acquaintance; a Mrs. Martindale, who gave her "understanding and knowledge of life," also lent her books on "social questions," which, in the author's words, "prepared me to take my proper place in the Labour Movement." Bondfield's experience of mentorship by an older, socially conscious woman seems anomalous: the majority of young women working in shops were rarely exposed to such philanthropy, due in part to their hesitation (read by many as apathy, but often driven by the fear of losing their jobs) to reveal the actual conditions of their work experience. Bondfield remembers Martindale's "influence" with gratitude, although she insists that this influence was not politically motivated but rather concerned with simply "drawing out the best in others" and making them recognize their own independence and ability. Nonetheless, she comments, "I cannot bear to think of the difference it would have made to my life if that influence had not reached me when it did," inspiring speculation as to the possibilities she might have imagined for her life otherwise, and perhaps her aversion to leading the life of the politically apathetic, superficially concerned shopgirl of social stereotype.[75]

Bondfield's life, written retrospectively and through the lens of labor activism and union politics, constructs a coherent narrative of gradual ascendance through the ranks of unions and labor leagues to an eventual position in Parliament. Once in London, she first joined the Ideal Club, an organization dedicated to breaking down class barriers, where she took classes on Browning and Whitman and met George Bernard Shaw, Sidney and Beatrice Webb, and other socialist activists, and then joined the National Union of Shop Assistants, Warehousemen and Clerks. While there, she began to write monthly articles and short stories under the pseudonym "Grace Dare," some of which I discuss in more detail shortly. At this time (in 1896), Bondfield met Lilian Gilchrist Thompson, a member

MISS M. E. BONDFIELD (Grace Dare)

Margaret Bondfield ("Grace Dare"), *Shop Assistant*, c. 1897. Reproduced by permission of the British Library, S100.

of the Women's Industrial Council and an instigator of the surveys of shop life which later formed the basis for reports in the *Daily Chronicle.* Margaret Bondfield undertook the position of undercover investigator for these surveys, obtaining engagements in shops and judging conditions therein (32). From there she became assistant secretary to the shop assistants' union in 1898 at the age of twenty-five, and worked with the Women's Trade Union League and the National Federation of Women Workers to better conditions for women working in all trades.

After resigning from her post at the shop assistants' union in 1908, Bondfield worked as a member of the Independent Labour Party, with which she was associated for the remainder of her life.[76] In 1923 she won a parliamentary seat at Northampton, and in 1924 served as Parliamentary Secretary to the Minister of Labour, becoming herself the first woman Cabinet Minister in 1929. Like many other female shop assistants, she remained unmarried throughout her life, but her story rejects the marriage plot associated with shopgirls in the popular imagination. Instead, in her writings and in her practice, she advocated women's freedom to choose to marry or remain single, as in the following excerpt from an 1898 article:

> Many married women find their highest happiness in waiting on their husbands during the brief hours they have together. . . . All honour to her if she does her work well, she is helping to build up a nation. Other women have no aptitude for housework, their minds have been trained in other directions; they would sooner tackle a German grammar than a cookery-book recipe. These women also are helping to build up a nation. The injustice lies in the fact that the woman of the latter type is too frequently condemned to a domestic life through the economic pressure of our times.[77]

In part, we can read Margaret Bondfield's claims for women's independence (economic, social, sexual) and freedom of choice on an individual level as reflective of her own experience. Both her memoir and Mary Hamilton's biography suggest that Bondfield's intimate partnerships were with women rather than with men.[78] Overall, however, as the autobiographical narrative constructs her experience, she immersed herself in work rather than romance, devoting the bulk of her attention to social reform and the transformation of industrial labor.

The pieces Bondfield wrote for the *Shop Assistant* construct an alternate version of the romance plot, transforming the conventional story of the shopgirl's upward mobility through marriage into a cathartic tragedy of loss and suffering. The trauma of loss suffered by some of her heroines parallels the underlying theme of many of the stories, which often detail the suffering endured by shop workers and whose appeal lies in the emotional identification experienced by readers. These stories, unlike others analyzed in subsequent chapters, rarely use fantasy or the luxurious splendor of the department store to motivate readerly sympathy and identification; rather, they incorporate a visceral response through their emphasis on the painful quality of the shop assistant's everyday life. This response in turn, I argue, encourages readers to use the narrative as an emotional release but also to turn their efforts and energies to union participation and activist politics, a strategy that would ultimately result in a therapeutic treatment for the sufferings of life in the shop. For Bondfield, the ability for readers to work through their often negative experience of shop life through the text is, I suggest, a step on the path to eventual collective and communal betterment of the class of shop workers as a whole.

Under the pseudonym "Grace Dare," Margaret Bondfield published several types of writing in the *Shop Assistant* during the late 1890s, many of which combined the genres of documentary realism with fictionalized narratives of romantic love and familial devotion. Several of these were addressed specifically to women readers and printed on the journal's "Women's Page," and most featured the experiences of female shop employees: "Jean," for example, tells the story of a country girl's negotiation of the competition between saleswomen in the London shops, while "An Imaginary Interview" describes an exchange between two women regarding a utopian fantasy of shop life in a socialist future, in which short hours and high wages are complemented by individual incentive and the free pursuit of edifying leisure for men and women alike, who interact as equals in a classless society.[79] Bondfield's success in rendering the everyday experiences of shop assistants appealing as fictional accounts presumably depended on her ability to balance between readers' desires to see their own lives reflected in the pages of the journal and the necessity of marking a difference between the real and the imagined worlds. "An Imaginary Interview" uses the contrast between a utopian future and an insufficiently satisfying present to encourage the collective abolition of such outdated notions as the censoring influence of "Mrs. Grundy" and the hierarchical class system which depends on inequality between workers and employers: the closing exchange between "Grace" and "Polly" hints at the hope provided through such fantasies and the call to action they engender. Certain of Bondfield's stories thus work to provide inspiration for readers sympathetic to the union in the explicit connection they draw between fantasy and everyday life. Others, by contrast, write the story of the shopgirl as a tragic narrative of loss in which the promise of happiness inherent in the fantasy remains forever inaccessible and unfulfilled. These stories provide an emotional outlet for the sympathetic and identificatory sufferings of Bondfield's readers, resulting in a similar end: both the utopian fantasy and the tragic romance work to imbue the shopgirl-reader with a consciousness of her own experience and a drive toward political reform of the conditions under which shop assistants labor. In this respect Bondfield's writings reflect the "influence" she herself experienced, operating as narratives which would instigate politically motivated collective activity on the part of individual readers.

The textual mode of address of Bondfield's stories strives to engage the sentimental feelings of shopgirl-readers to produce an emotional catharsis that in turn suggests the possibility of using that emotion to political ends. An article on the women's page from 1898 entitled "The Case of Janet Deane" tells the "heartrending" story of one shop assistant's physical debilitation through the taxing circumstances of the shop, narrating her decline from a "strong healthy girl" to a weak and thin victim of malnutrition and unintentional neglect by an overworked housekeeper and a drunken doctor; an eventual hemorrhage results in her death at age twenty-two. Likewise, "The Manageress of the 'A' Department" (February 1897) describes the heroine's transformation from a bright young girl engaged to be married to a sorrowful but courageous victim of sadness and unfulfilled longing. Jenny's rise in the shop to the position of "manageress" is here seen as small compensation for the death of her fiancé, which occurred on his journey to Southampton, at which point he was to take her out of shop life and provide her with a future of love and domestic happiness. The narrator, who had worked with her during the early period and had known of the suffering she would endure on losing her lover, describes the physicality of her despair:

> Jenny was thin and grey, and carried clearly the mark of her great sorrow, in the pitiful droop of her mouth. There was something grand in the stern, set face. I knew as I looked that she had fought well, had gained the victory over her grief, she had taken up the burden of life with all her mind and strength, *but she had not forgotten!*[80]

The dramatic conclusion to this passage, combined with the "grand" figure that Jenny appears to have become as a result of her suffering, produces an invested emotional identification on the part of readers who themselves may bear the physical traces of their sufferings, even if those sufferings are otherwise induced. In fact, I would contend that it is the possibility of a parallel between actual and imaginary suffering that facilitates the readerly appeal of Bondfield's fiction. The happiness that Jenny anticipates as a result of her marriage and her departure from shop life, and the unconsummated desire she experiences as a result of the unhappy conclusion to her story, can be seen to reflect one version of the perceived desires of readers for their own marriage plot. The tragic ending to the narrative—Jenny dies on the thirty-first of January, the very day of her intended union with her lover—prompts a cathartic emotional reaction in sympathetic readers, allowing them to work through their own suffering in an attempt to survive the more mundane aspects of their everyday lives.

The catharsis of Bondfield's sentimental fiction has another side, however, which incorporates a critique of marriage I discuss in greater detail in chapter 3. In a short story entitled "And Gross Darkness Covered the Earth" (March 1897), Bondfield expressly counters the pressures on women to leave shop work upon marrying by narrating the collapse of a hopeful but unsuccessful marriage and its effects on the story's heroine. Bondfield uses passages describing the fog that envelops London, deepening the gloom of a small shop presided over by a tall, sorrowful figure, to draw a metaphoric critique of the injunction for a husband and wife to remain married despite their mutual unhappiness. The story recounts the marriage thirty years previously of Minnie Jennings to Arthur Scott, at which time Minnie gave up her lucrative position in a West End showroom in accordance with her new husband's wishes, and then moves forward to the present, eventually concluding with Minnie's death. Scott, having lost his business through speculation, taunts his wife with her success at supporting the family through the management of a tiny shop; she loathes him, but resists the temptation to break her marriage vow. This temptation is figured through her "intimate friendship" with John Redmond, who like her remains married to someone unsuited to him, in this case a woman who suffers from unspecified "excesses." Yet Minnie's honor requires that she encourage Redmond to "restor[e] his wife to her better self," and in so doing she sacrifices herself to the failure of her marriage.[81] Bondfield's short story rewrites the hardships experienced by female shop assistants as the sufferings of failed marriage, and much like the novels by George Gissing and W. Somerset Maugham I discuss in the third chapter of this study, argues against the "duties" required of women who submit to the demands of marriage. Stories like this one reconfigure the shopgirl's romance plot, serving as an object-lesson for readers who might themselves be contemplating a union with an unsuitable man. Implicitly, for Bondfield, the romance plot's inevitable conclusion in marriage entails the risk of exploitation and hardship paralleling women's sufferings in the shop. Her critique, which rewrites the shopgirl's romance as a tragic failure, encourages readers to vicariously experience the anger and pain of her heroine in order to avoid replicating that suffering in their own lives.

Reading the life and writings of Margaret Bondfield as one version of the story of the shopgirl presents certain challenges for a study of the relationship between labor and leisure at the turn of the century. This text, like the writings of female mill-workers, workshop employees, and domestic servants included in Margaret Llewelyn Davies' *Life as We Have Known It* (1931), reveals a political consciousness and social activism largely absent from popular narratives of the shopgirl. In conjunction with the activist thrust of Bondfield's writing, however, there emerges a marked critique of mass leisure practice. In part the emphasis on labor at the expense of leisure can be explained through the way Bondfield's memoir functions, in her own words, as a memoir of Labour Party politics:

> If, occasionally, it is difficult to separate my personal adventure from the history of the Labour Party, that is perfectly in harmony with the facts. I have been so identified with the Movement that it is not always possible to see where one ends and the other begins.[82]

On another level, however, the absence of mass entertainment in her life and writings suggests a different interpretation. In the analysis of Bondfield's stance toward popular leisure, it becomes evident that their exclusion from her narrative reveals an attempt to construct another version of leisure, one linked to the development of political consciousness through socialist and union activism. A story called "'Jim'—A Memory" (September 1896) describes the callousness with which "'Jim' (otherwise Jenny Moore)" treats her encounters with men, a "faithless and reckless" attitude derived from her exposure to the fact that men want sex rather than love. "Jim" offers the voice of a stereotypical shopgirl, coveting the sumptuous temptations of amusement provided by an evening with a male suitor:

> I love the glitter and gay flowers. I love the flattery of the men—real gentlemen (?) who take me out. I love pretty things, and they buy them for me. I love the suppers and the opera. . . . But [I've] learnt my lesson, and [since being "jilted"] I never *misunderstand* a gentleman. I get as much of their money as I can. I get my suppers, my opera boxes, my balls and my ball dresses, and I laugh at them. I shall never again be guilty of trusting them. But, Grace, it's dangerous, and I loathe myself. I know one day I shall go a step too far.[83]

In Bondfield's view, the risk of desire for leisure is equated with the risk of "going too far," of acknowledging the connection between one type of illicit pleasure and another for women of the shop assistant's transitional class. Accordingly, the possibility of pleasurable consumer leisure is negated in Bondfield's writings, which set themselves so clearly against the commodification of women at the hands of a culture based on desire, display, and the exchangeability of the female body. In this sense, the absence of consumer leisure in Bondfield's life and writing produces a resistance to the hazardous pleasures of consumption—a resistance which resembles the following passage on shop life, written by a female shop assistant and included in a contemporary study of women's work:

> There is one bad use in shop life and this is dress and following the fashions of the world such as regular theatre going and dancing and out somewhere every night of the week and if all the other girls in the shop follow these fashions you get a very trying life if you do not join them and it requires great firmness to keep from These pleasures which when taken too far are very wrong for we cannot do our duty to our Master the next day if every night we are seeking our own pleasures, but this can be turned into a good use for if you are a true

Christian girl you not only have daily work for your Master to do but you have a great field of labour for your heavenly Master by trying to come into close contact with the other girls and showing them the wrong of too much of there [*sic*] worldly pleasures and in this case you have good work cut out in your shop and by so doing making your shop life a very happy one.[84]

For the young author of this passage, the pleasures and temptations of urban leisure must be countered through Christian morality and proper social conduct. This writer's conflation of her daily work for the "Master" employer and the "labor" involved in imparting the wisdom of the "heavenly Master" to other girls suggests the various moralizing narratives associated with the consuming pleasures of the shopgirl. For Bondfield, these pleasures form no part of the consciousness and practice of political activism. As I have indicated, however, texts such as Margaret Bondfield's autobiography and short fiction tell only one version of the story of the shopgirl. I contend that it is both possible and necessary to read the popular narrative of the shopgirl's leisure practices, themselves a site of fascination for the late Victorian public imagination, as a text through which we can understand the relationship between fantasy, pleasure, and desire and the operation of these terms within the alternative life plots provided by the genre of the romance. The remainder of this study seeks to address this claim.

CHAPTER 2

Figuring the Female Body: Labor, Sex, and Desire in the Department Store

In her 1911 investigation of women's work in England, M. Mostyn Bird compared the efficient management of the industrial machine to the management of the "human machine," that laboring body which manufactured and distributed the "vast agglomeration of goods" produced for the consuming public in the late nineteenth century.[1] Bird's description of the experience of "toiling women" in factory, shop, and home emphasizes a concern for all branches of women's remunerative work, in an effort to produce a comparative analysis of women's labor and to argue for increased union activity and organization within the "sweated" trades. The metaphor of the machinelike body, however, suggests a consciousness of the industrialization of disparate types of labor. Of course, the historic associations between the machine and the worker's body stretch back to the industrial revolution: nineteenth-century critics of capitalism and industrial working conditions repeatedly described the effects of alienated labor practices on the autonomy and identity of the working classes.[2] In Bird's analysis, however, it is no longer the factory alone which constructs the worker's body as machine: any task involving the expenditure of energy can be understood as creating the parallel between these structures of mechanization. Furthermore, Bird contends, if the work and the worker are not made to operate in an efficient and harmonious manner, the labor process risks disintegration, as "the human being whose energy and capacity are not called out by the mechanical labour to which he subordinates his forces is stunted and dwarfed by its easy monotony" (1). To successfully combat the degrading aspects of mechanization in the rationalized culture of technological modernity, both industrial and human machines must undergo the appropriate adjustments to produce a culture of labor based on dignity and self-fulfillment rather than alienation and exploitation.[3]

Bird suggests that, in the minds of many upwardly mobile young women, shop labor fills an interval between the factory and the home, allowing them to leave behind the working-class atmosphere of the factory and providing the possibility of public employment instead of domestic service. The shop, moreover, furnishes an environment in which working women might have the opportunity, whether real or imagined, to meet and be courted by men above them in wealth and social station, thereby marking their path toward creating their own domestic sphere.[4] The display-oriented culture of the shop contributes in large part to this perception. Especially in the case of the late Victorian department store, women on both sides of the shop counter were imagined to participate in a panoramic vision of glamorous and luxurious consumption. For middle- and upper-class women, the department store was a source of pleasure, a tantalizing urban spectacle displaying luxury items behind plate-glass windows which, in a striking parallel to the cinema screen, reflected a fantasy image of the female consumer.[5] This reflection recalls the practice of saleswomen and models serving as mannequins for the goods on display, thereby resulting in a vexed situation where shop assistants themselves mirrored the female consumer, engaging strategies of sympathetic identification and desire to sell consumer products. In this setting, working women came to be figured as laborers within an economy of embodiment and self-display, fixtures in the phantasmagoria of the store and symbols of the increasing centrality of commodity goods and consumer desire to turn-of-the-century British culture. But shopgirls came to symbolize more than the universal desire to consume: as representative objects, their bodies were offered up to consumers both as sexualized recipients of male desire and as mediators for female consumers' fantasies and identificatory pleasures. In this sense, contemporary perceptions of the shopgirl's position complicate the description of the department store as a sphere of feminine pleasure, making the scene of consumer desire into one of sexual and social risk and placing the female worker's body in the midst of a swirl of competing discourses around the gendering of desire, embodiment, and identification.

This chapter addresses the institutional world of the department store and its impact on cultural perceptions of the shopgirl's role within the consumer-oriented society of the later nineteenth and early twentieth centuries. For shop assistants, the department store represented at best the improbability of gratifying their own desire to consume the goods they sold, and at worst the depths of labor exploitation through overwork, low wages, and crowded living conditions. The effects of modernization and new technologies of labor developing in America and later in England resulted in a transformation of working conditions within the department store, as Taylorist models of industrial efficiency expanded to fit the newest institutions which employed the laboring masses.[6] The familiar narratives of the worker's body as machine subsequently migrated from the industrial factory to the metropolitan department store, so that employees came to represent cogs in the machine of what I will term the "display culture" of the store, itself figured as an efficiently operated, fine-tuned system. In this sense, the earlier model of the industrial laborer's body-as-machine becomes reimagined within the rationalized industry of display and distribution.[7]

Such modernizing strategies produce a transformation in the gendered description of the body of the worker. In contrast to earlier depictions of the industrial laborer's body as masculine, in the dream world[8] of the department store the representative body is female, one of the many separate elements which combine to create and maintain the efficient machine of the store. Here, the female worker's body—on display as mannequin and luxury item, employed in the service of commodity circulation—serves to gender the sphere in which it operates, retaining rather than subsuming its identity in the modernized setting. This argument contests the perception that gender is evacuated by the technologies of modern life (articulated most vividly by Frankfurt School theorist Siegfried Kracauer in his writings on the "mass ornament," on which more shortly), suggesting that for women employed in the modern department store, sexuality and the erotics of display remained all too present, constitutive elements of their participation as laboring bodies within the feminized world of commodity distribution and consumption.

In a 1927 pair of articles on the visual spectacles of the late nineteenth and early twentieth centuries, Kracauer analyzed the *ratio*, or "murky reason" of modern life, as an integral part of the capitalist production process through the concept of the "mass ornament." In his formulation, the spectacular patterns formed by military-style cabaret troupes and stadium crowds are based on the abstraction of the body, revealing their distance from natural or organic forms and their immersion within a culture of rationalization. His argument is based on the contention that "only as parts of a mass, not as individuals who believe themselves to be formed from within, do people become fractions of a figure":

> These products of American distraction factories [revue acts like the Tiller Girls] are no longer individual girls, but indissoluble girl clusters whose movements are demonstrations of mathematics. . . . The ornaments are composed of thousands of bodies, sexless bodies in bathing suits.[9]

Kracauer's central claim is that the technologies of production employed by modern capitalism rely on an abstractness which leads the masses away from the "progressive potential" embodied by this new model for collective organ-ization.[10] However, his argument depends on the assertion that the bodies of the girls lose their gender identity in creating the mass ornament, no longer functioning as erotic objects: unlike the ballet, whose kaleidoscopic orna-ments retain "the plastic expression of erotic life," "the mass movements of the girls take place in a vacuum; they are a linear system that no longer has any erotic meaning but at best points to the locus of the erotic."[11] As this chapter suggests, the display culture of the department store, as figured through the ideology of the romance, maintains rather than discards the emphasis on the erotic identity of its figures: the shopgirls who form part of the visual spectacle of the store are continually reminded of their status as objects which mediate the sexual and consumer fantasies of their customers. These female employees, although part of a system which strives toward the linear standardization of rational, "scientific" management, nonetheless pro-duce a disjunction with that rationalization through their fictionalized place-ment as heroines of the romance of the department store.

This chapter begins with a brief history of the growth of the department store in England, describing the institutional transformation from the small shop to the large-scale luxury emporium. I then analyze the history and employment practices of two competing London stores: Harrods, which symbolized the height of luxuried consumer practice for the upper echelons of Victorian society, and Selfridges, which offered itself up to middle-class women as an affordable female pleasure. In 1909 an intense competition between these two stores, occasioned by Selfridges' opening and Harrods' "Diamond Jubilee" (thought by many to be a marketing ploy rather than a commemoration of an actual historical event), resulted in extensive discussion in the mainstream press of the "Americanization" of the London department store industry according to modern methods of labor management. The transition from the traditionally "British" model of retailing used by Harrods to the "science of shopkeeping" imported by Gordon Selfridge from Marshall Field's in Chicago parallels the modern-ization of the factory which reached its apex in the principles of disciplined labor power and efficient production developed by Frederick Winslow Taylor at the turn of the century. Much as Taylor described the scientific transformation of the labor process as a beneficial change for workers as well as management, Gordon Selfridge and his staff manager, Percy Best, used a rhetoric of self-improvement to encourage their employees to par-ticipate in a system which was intended to produce obedience and loyalty in the staff. By comparing Selfridge's "science of shopkeeping" to Taylor's system of scientific management, I intend to reveal the ideological strate-gies by which Selfridge and Best attempted to rewrite the mundane expe-rience of department store labor as individual and collective betterment.

   In order to examine the influence of contemporary perceptions regarding the transatlantic exchanges of department store culture, the final section of the chapter uses several popular novels as an entry point into an emergent critique of labor relations and working conditions within these new urban establishments, arguing that these novels provide evidence for the unmasking of Taylorism within the rhetoric of the department store. *Winnie Childs, the Shop Girl,* a 1914 novel by the Williamsons (Charles Norris and Alice Muriel, the latter of whom wrote for *Forget-Me-Not,* Harmsworth's popular magazine for young women), describes the experiences of a London shopgirl who finds employment in a New York store called "The Hands." This novel's emphasis on the dangers associated with industrial display labor presents a critique of the sexualized dismemberment of the shopgirl's body as she becomes one of a mass of numerical representatives. In a similar critique of the modernization of the department store, Arthur Applin's novel *Shop Girls,* published in 1914 as one of the Mills and Boon series of paperback romances, depicts the intrusion of Lobb's, a giant industrialized store operating on the new and mysterious model of labor efficiency, into a sleepy provincial town, subsequently shifting the focus of the narrative to the heroine's experiences of working life in London. The subterranean warehouses and cavernous dormitories linked to the central store in Applin's novel, as well as the Taylorist technologies of labor efficiency represented through the store, suggest the modernizing influence of new regulatory methods on the bodies of store employees and elaborate what I will term the threat of figuration, in which the shopgirl's body is rendered a figure for the desires of consumers. These two novels are examples of a new subgenre emerging in the popular romance fiction of the early 1900s, providing a subtle but suggestive critique of the exploitation of workers, and especially of women, in the department store as an institution.[12] By positioning the shopgirl as a romantic heroine, these fictions reproduce the cultural conflict between maintaining individual autonomy and becoming one of the masses. At the same time, they reindividualize the shopgirl through the narratives of the romance plot in a tactical resistance to the rationalized, dehumanizing effects of modern life. These department store romances suggest that the rhetorical emphasis on individual self-improvement espoused by proponents of the "science of shopkeeping" in fact merely produces the illusion of autonomy and upward mobility, prompting the conclusion that it is in the plot of the romance itself that we can locate the most extensive elaboration of the fantasy narrative of self-fulfillment and collective transformation.

A Brief History of the Department Store

The historical development of consumer society in England stretches back to before the eighteenth century, shaping cultural perceptions of the British as, in the now famous words of Napoleon, "a nation of shopkeepers" and, by extension, a nation of consumers.[13] The Great Exhibition of 1851, held at the Crystal Palace in London's Hyde Park and showcasing manufactured goods from around the globe, marked the beginning of a process which transformed the retail trade into a capitalist enterprise modeled on the spectacle of cultural abundance.[14] As Thomas Richards has suggested, the 1851 Exhibition combined the nascent forms of the world's fair, the department store, and the arcade (which later transformed into the shopping mall of the twentieth century) and in so doing raised the value of the object to a symbolic entity embodying the boundless possibilities of remaking the self through the process of consumption.[15] The growth of the department store in the decades after 1850 is intimately linked to this shift in cultural perception.

Social and economic historians have charted the transformation of the small grocer's, dry-goods', and draper's shops of the early nineteenth century into the palaces of modern consumption which symbolized cultural wealth and democratized access to purchasing power in a variety of national contexts.[16] It is only recently, however, with the shift in critical focus from work to leisure and the consequent study of social relations surrounding the consumer practices of all classes, that the British department store has begun to receive the kind of comparative analysis pioneered by American scholars like William Leach and Susan Porter Benson.[17] This is not to say that the histories of individual British stores and chains, including Whiteley's, Lewis's, Harrods, and Selfridges, went unrecorded; however, the available texts which do describe the institutional history of these stores are of varying utility, since they were often written as commemorative or souvenir editions and therefore do not take on the project of historical interpretation.[18]

A survey of these texts, taken alongside twentieth-century analyses of the history of British retailing, reveals a period of gradual expansion for most department stores in England from the 1850s on, followed by a period of heightened activity in the several decades preceding World War I. Many of the stores seem to have evolved from one of two models: the first (and most prevalent) was the draper's shop which expanded to include a wide array of goods beyond the usual supply of textiles, and the second was the grocer's shop which later became the food hall of the burgeoning department store. Examples of the first model include Bainbridges of Newcastle upon Tyne and Kendal, Milne, and Faulkner of Manchester, both of which rivaled each other for the title of the first British department store. These stores emerged in conjunction with the industrialization of urban locales in the north of England in the 1830s and 1840s, and incorporated local markets and bazaars into their rapidly expanding premises. From the original drapery stock they went on to sell novelties including gloves, stockings, ribbons, and the like, as well as household fabrics and their accessories. Despite this gradual expansion of merchandise for sale, the early department stores of the industrial north reflected and reproduced the ideology of caution and thrift in consumer practice which defined the middle-class household.[19] In a similar vein, the small grocer's shops which later became Sainsbury's and other chains maintained an atmosphere of necessity and utility in selling goods which appealed to the needs, rather than the desires, of the middle classes.[20]

By the second half of the nineteenth century, however, the formation of the department store as an institution in England began to be impacted by the development of the Parisian *grands magasins* (many of which were constructed according to the architectural and visual standards of exhibition buildings like that for the Grand Exposition of 1855) and the recreation of American dry-goods stores as splendid monuments to display aesthetics and consumption. The Bon Marché (1852) and the Louvre (1855), and later their rivals including Printemps (1865), Samaritaine (1870), and Galeries Lafayette (1895), incorporated quintessentially "modern" strategies for engaging the interest of the consumer. The 1855 Exposition had showcased merchandise with price tags attached (a technique already in use in some drapery houses in Paris and in the north of England), and had combined this reassuring denotation of cost and accessibility with the spectacular display of desirable commodities; likewise, the Paris stores attracted shoppers into dazzling architectural surroundings and tantalized them with an atmosphere of abundance, draping goods along the railings of the upper floors.[21] In subsequent decades American stores like Macy's, Wanamaker's, and Marshall Field's modified the Parisian model of the "walk-around shop" by utilizing the newest technologies of electric lighting and the show-window display techniques pioneered by L. Frank Baum and Arthur Fraser.[22]

These strategies for producing and perpetuating consumer desire were gradually incorporated into British retailing, eventually transforming the more straightforward presentation of available goods into an atmosphere of abundant supply and consumer satisfaction. Many of the new stores advertised themselves as institutions created for the sole purpose of catering to the consumer's every whim. Establishments like Whiteley's in Westbourne Grove used publicity, even notoriety, to sell goods—William Whiteley collapsed his own identity with that of the store, calling himself "The Universal

Provider"[23]—while Harrods' telegraphic address was listed as "Everything, London" in an effort to convey the range of possibilities the store provided. With the inspiration of the success of stores like Whiteley's and the model of the great emporiums in Paris, New York, and Chicago, other London businesses began to expand their premises: among these were Dickens and Jones, Marshall and Snelgrove, Swan and Edgar, and Debenham and Freebody.[24] This period, from the 1860s through the end of the century, marked the construction of massive and ornate architectural structures to house the new department stores, many of which followed the guidance of *Draper, Draper's Record,* and other trade journals in an attempt to recreate the successful selling environment of the French and American models.

Harrods and Selfridges, arguably two of the most developed examples of the influence of consumption on everyday life at the turn of the century, occupied similar positions within British department store culture to the French and American prototypes. As the next section shows, both stores reworked older models of the store as the site for necessary purchases by making shopping into a leisure practice. The former embodied the conception of consumption as a luxury practice for the upper echelons of Victorian society, while the latter offered itself up to middle-class women as an affordable leisure activity and one which incorporated the experience of browsing without the pressure to buy. As Erika Rappaport's research on the West End department store suggests, these new emporiums were devoted to the pursuit of "women's pleasure," rearticulating the identity of the consumer through their description of the well-to-do female shopper out for a day of browsing in the stores.[25] At the height of its success in Edwardian London, the department store symbolized the bloom of modernity through its dual focus on the practice of leisure through consumption and on new methods for producing efficient labor among store employees. Stores like Harrods and Selfridges now suggest the ongoing effort to produce a feminized culture of pleasure through display and the presentation of desirable goods to middle- and upper-class women, simultaneously developing alongside industry attempts to define and regulate the experience of women employed in the stores. The shopgirl was caught in the middle of these interconnected processes, embodying the contested relationship between labor, desire, and identification in her placement behind the counter.

Case Studies: Harrods and Selfridges

Although their emergence in the late-nineteenth-century consumer landscape differed by a period of sixty years, these two stores marked important turning points in the history of the London department store and in the conceptualization of modern labor practices. By the end of the period addressed in this study, both stores were concerned to represent themselves as models for the exemplary treatment of staff, providing employees with pension systems and investment clubs, social and athletic activities, and opportunities to better themselves through upwardly mobile activities. This section traces the change over time which resulted in the ideology of upward mobility presented by the stores, contrasting the different styles of retailing used in each case and describing the competition which eventually made the stores appear similar in their treatment of staff. Harrods, an institution which grew from a small shop into a great establishment dedicated to consumer luxury, modeled itself on a "British" system of benevolent paternalism toward store workers which nonetheless retained a strict and authoritarian managerial structure. Selfridges, by contrast, entered the London retail industry as a fully formed institution which emphasized its difference from the British stores by self-consciously instituting an "American" system for store efficiency and providing employees with business classes and opportunities for professional advancement. Neither store used the detested system of living-in, and fines were gradually abolished altogether by Selfridges. Moreover, staff magazines, memoirs, and histories of both stores describe them as testaments to the good feeling between managerial staff and employees. The rhetoric used by both stores to create an environment of pleasure and fulfillment through work rather than one of degradation and alienation suggests the investment of each store's managerial structure in reproducing their own institutional history as one of unhindered collective progress for employees and management alike.

In creating this environment of social advancement, Harrods and Selfridges expressly countered the stereotype of the department store as a site for sweated labor described in the previous chapter. Each store represented itself as a model for the transformation of labor relations in the hierarchy of capitalist enterprise: Harrods through the strategy of recreating its staff as a family of workers, Selfridges through the system of efficient management intended to benefit the employee as well as the store. Yet, as we shall see, the archival records of both stores reveal a certain degree of anxiety over the challenge of modernization within an increasingly competitive industry. Despite their rhetorical insistence on an ideology of fairness and opportunity for all, these institutions nonetheless participated in the systematization of labor during the late nineteenth and early twentieth centuries, and aided in the development of an increasingly rationalized culture of mass distribution and consumption in the years preceding the First World War.

I. Laboring Amid Luxury: Harrods, "Society's Favorite Store"

As Harrods expanded from a small storefront in Knightsbridge to the massive institution it became in the twentieth century, a parallel transformation occurred in the management's attitude toward employees of the store. This transformation was, in fact, an evolution in style: the store began in the tradition of the small London shop, owned and operated by one man who was assisted by his family members and a few hired employees; as the store's wealth and resources expanded, so did its staff, resulting in a managerial structure based on the extended family. Purchased by the younger Harrod from his more conservative father, the store was run according to a paternalistic structure in which the owner (and later, his general managers) exerted complete authority over the store employees. This relation was increasingly characterized as a benevolent system in which workers were seen as members of a substitute family and treated accordingly, even on occasion referred to as a cohort of siblings cooperating in the advancement of the familial unit's wealth and social position. In order to reproduce this benevolent paternalism, Harrods' management worked to create an ideology of the store employee as a committed worker whose ultimate end was the advancement of the store rather than his or her own individual mobility. Unlike Selfridges, whose management explicitly posited the betterment of the store as a whole as the result of the employee's upward mobility, Harrods left this possible connection to be formed by the worker, instead intimating that employees should welcome the chance to participate in the collective elevation of the familial enterprise. In consequence, Harrods recreated itself as a modern, family-owned establishment which countered any employee dissatisfaction through its rhetorical characterization of the pleasure and dignity staff members would find in the fulfillment of their filial duties toward the store.

In Harrods' version of its institutional history, 1849 marks the year in which the great store was founded; yet it took several decades before the store came to be recognized as a socially sanctioned destination, an environment in which one might satisfy one's consumer desires and mix with others of a similar standard of wealth and social standing. In the words of one writer for *Hearth and Home* in the 1890s, Harrods was "indeed a wonderful place," gratifying the physical and emotional longings of its customers: "The outer woman can be clothed and adorned there, whilst the inner woman can be vastly refreshed, and all her wants can be most tastefully and economically supplied, from a brocade dress to a tortoise-shell comb." The same article implicitly compared Harrods favorably with Whiteley's in its claim that it was "perfectly proper to meet a gentleman in [Harrods'] ground floor banking hall," since Whiteley's was by this point

well known for impropriety, its restaurant having been a "place of assigna-
tion" in a notorious divorce case.[26] In large part, then, the store's history
reveals the efforts of the managerial and publicity staff to create an environment for legitimate social interactions in the new world of mass consumption, and thereby to render the identity of the consumer secure and
distinct from that of those men and women working behind the counter.
For Harrods' management, the consuming public was to be repeatedly
and continually differentiated from store employees.

The early years of Harrods reveal the authoritarian familial structure of
the small shop which was to shape future relations between the store management and its employees. Henry Charles Harrod, a wholesale tea merchant, had first purchased a small grocer's shop from Philip Henry Burden
at 8 Middle Queen's Buildings, Knightsbridge; but it was his son, Charles
Digby Harrod, who foresaw the expansion of the neighborhood, and who
purchased the shop from his father in the early 1860s. By 1867 C. D.
Harrod had five shop assistants, a new storefront, and a plate-glass window, and by 1880 his staff numbered nearly one hundred. In the 1880s
store employees worked the long hours which were standard in the industry: 7:30 AM to 9 PM on weekdays, and to 11 PM on Saturdays. In reference to the exhausting and time-consuming nature of the work, one assistant remarked with veiled irony, "Hard going right up to closing time, 11
o'clock, put the shutters up, sweep up the shop, and the rest of the evening
to yourself."[27] Most records suggest that Charles Digby Harrod ruled his
staff by inspiring both fear and reverence in his employees, offering brief
words of praise or punishment through fines according to his will.[28]
Through the 1870s Harrod chose to employ male rather than female assistants in the shop, on account of their presumed increased efficiency and
loyalty to the firm; his resistance to hiring female employees was eventually overcome in 1885, with the appointment of Ida Annie Fowle as a clerk
in the counting house. Miss Fowle was to establish herself as a fixture in
the store, surrounding herself with other female employees who were
referred to as "Miss Fowle's chicks" and themselves were considered something of an institution.[29]

As the store and its merchandise expanded to fill the block-long
"island" site (owned entirely by Harrods Ltd., now a limited liability company, by 1911), so too did the store's staff: estimates suggest that between
four and five thousand were employed by the store in 1908, a large percentage of whom were women. The increase in employment meant that
the store required a general manager, and as a result Richard Burbidge,
formerly on staff at Whiteley's, was hired to supervise the store's employees in 1891. Many of the longtime employees had been anxious regarding
Burbidge's appointment, since Whiteley's had a reputation as a poor

Physical Culture Class, *Harrodian Gazette,* August 1914. Reproduced by permission of the Company Archive, Harrods Limited, London.

employer, and did not take references before hiring staff members; however, it seems that the new management assuaged these fears by immediately altering Harrods' methods for regulating staff behavior. The new store policies accorded with the Progressive politics of the London County Council and responded to the increasing agitation for better working conditions for shop assistants. Burbidge abolished fines for lateness, and reduced working hours in advance of the early closing legislation, arranging for the stores to close at 7 PM nightly and at 4 PM on Thursdays.[30] He held Sunday Bible classes for employees at his home, and established the Harrodian Club and the Harrodian Amateur Athletic Association, both located south of the Thames in Barnes on a property which Burbidge had donated to the firm in 1894 and which was expanded to include Mill Lodge and adjoining land in 1904. The club provided social outings and evening activities, while the athletic opportunities included physical culture classes and men's (and, during the war, women's) clubs for swimming, rowing, cricket, football, and hockey, as well as a ladies' rifle team.

Burbidge also established a Provident Society and a Benevolent Fund, and provided access to medical and dental care for store employees. In a similar vein, and in all likelihood in response to the entrance of Selfridges on the London retail scene in 1909, Richard Burbidge's son Woodman Burbidge, general manager of the store from 1911 to 1935, opened a Staff

Harrodian Ladies' Hockey Team, *Harrodian Gazette,* May 1915. Reproduced by permission of the Company Archive, Harrods Limited, London.

Office for the purposes of attending to employees' needs. In the two years before the war he started a staff newspaper, the *Harrodian Gazette,* and instituted evening classes through which employees might better themselves and gain the chance to move upward within the store's hierarchy. These classes were supported by another initiative involving "a scheme of yearly free scholarships, which provides for training in arithmetic, handwriting, commercial English, typewriting, French or Spanish, business efficiency and salesmanship, and special training on matters purely connected with the business of the house."[31] Much in the style of Gordon Selfridge, Woodman Burbidge gradually revised the brusque and paternalistic style of Harrods' previous management in order to remain in step with modern innovations in employee relations and changes in labor politics of the first decades of the twentieth century.[32]

Despite the management's efforts to describe Harrods as an institution attentive to modern methods for the treatment of employees, however, many of Harrods' archival documents nonetheless reveal the politically charged status of the staff hierarchy, and underscore the methods by which an ideology of "model" employee behavior was produced within the store. These documents include the posted rules and regulations for employee dress, manners, and comportment, as well as writings in the staff magazine which suggest a rather different story than the one told through

Harrodian Ladies' Rifle Team with Their Instructors, *Harrodian Gazette,* June 1915. Reproduced by the permissions of the Company Archive, Harrods Limited, London.

Harrods' official histories. In the first case, female shop assistants were requested to wear "neat plain black, made in good taste, and in keeping with the department they are employed in," accompanied by black stockings; jewelry was forbidden, as it would ruin the plain and unobtrusive image of the woman behind the counter. Indeed, a letter regarding this dress code appeared in the *Harrodian Gazette,* arguing in support of the uniform presentation of unadorned female figures: "May all of us who have not yet conformed to the rule remember that one or two can spoil the whole scheme, so let us try as much as we can to carry out this very reasonable regulation and then, when we do have a chance of wearing our pretties, we shall appreciate them much more."[33] In this formulation, female employees were expected not to detract from the visual splendor of the store merchandise, but rather to remain in the background, bolstering the image of the store as a theatrical display but themselves only effecting that display from behind the scenes. The only occasions on which female assistants were allowed to participate in the spectacle of display were when they served as mannequins in "fashion parades," modeling garments for the benefit of consumers. During the war, children of staff members were recruited as mannequins: in 1916, Norah Irwin, an employee in the juvenile costumes department and the daughter of a manager of the Removals department, modeled as a bridesmaid in an advertisement for the *Tatler.*[34] The employment of live models as participants in the spectacle of display continued for several decades, but the majority of employees were still expected to dress and behave in a subdued and deferential manner.

Richard Burbidge used an authoritarian managerial style in his attitude toward employees: although he rejected the common practice of fines and the living-in system, he maintained a strict attention to detail in his expectations of staff behavior, and made daily rounds of the entire store, inspecting the operation of each department and questioning assistants regarding their interactions with customers.[35] Among the general rules for shopwalkers and assistants on staff at Harrods were the usual injunctions against lateness and errors in calculating bills; Burbidge also retained the strict prohibition on loitering and gossiping among assistants. In addition, store regulations stated that "Assistants must do their utmost to please Customers, and under no circumstances allow a Customer to leave unserved without speaking to the Shopwalker or Buyer."[36] Under the directorship of Woodman Burbidge, store management maintained this strict attention to the needs of the customer: in a lecture on salesmanship, one manager exhorted staff to treat even the rudest customers with "quiet deference and courtesy," and to "consider the interest of the employer in every transaction": "Indifferent attention, careless remarks, unauthorized guarantees and promises, laziness in showing goods, impertinent questions and answers, delay in attending to customers, errors of department and various other common mistakes must be avoided."[37] In this sense the codes for staff behavior which characterized the management style of the Burbidge era suggest a gesture toward the past rather than an eye toward the more modern methods of labor management of the future. The patient and submissive shop assistant, deferring to the wishes of those above her in the store hierarchy, corresponded to the image of the exploited shop worker which formed the basis for the trade union agitation described in the preceding chapter, and reveals a marked difference from the concept of the worker as innovator introduced by Selfridge in his "American" model of store management.

Harrods' management gradually undertook the project of producing an image of its staff as dignified and self-improving employees rather than as mere anonymous workers, particularly during Woodman Burbidge's managerial tenure in the store. An exchange of letters in the *Harrodian Gazette* during its first few months of circulation describes two conflicting perceptions of women working behind the counter: the first was the enduring stereotype of the shopgirl as a generic, superficial figure concerned only with the petty intrigues of her workday and the pleasures she pursued during her leisure hours; the second, no less stereotypical image was the managerial ideal of the noble, loyal individual striving for humble perfection in all endeavors. The item which ignited the exchange was a series of fictionalized diary entries written by a "Miss Muddleton," a shopgirl whose attentions were focused more on courtship and leisure outside the store than on her employment and future career at Harrods. The archive does not hold an extant copy of the first number of the staff magazine (January 1913), but the second number of the magazine presents the second install-ment of the diary entries, which I reproduce in full below.

> *February 1st.* This opens a new month. Thank goodness I shall have a little time to make a few entries in my diary. It is disheartening to put in day after day "Very busy on account of sale" or "Working hard at stocktaking." Met a nice young gentleman, at least I did not exact-ly meet him, I ran into him in a passage and knocked him down. We had a long talk, and went to a picture palace, and saw "Love laughs at Locksmiths."

> *February 2nd.* Very interesting day, but am too tired to put in details.

> *February 3rd.* Back at work, and things very quiet. Gertie Thompson getting all the best lines. Complained to Mr. Casement, but he just said, "If you were getting good lines you wouldn't like her grum-bling." I think he has no backbone.

> *February 4th.* Pancake Tuesday. Things still quiet, but Casement does not have it all his own way. An old toff came in and went for him like a greased frying pan because he had been directed to six departments to find a silver mounted kangaroo skin cigar case. When I got home I had six pancakes for supper, and felt better for a little nourishment.

> *February 5th.* Ash Wednesday, and things still quiet. A nice lady came in in the afternoon, and bought about twenty pounds worth of my stuff, as she was going abroad. I should have felt very pleased if that spiteful Thompson girl had not complained to Mr. Casement about my enticing away her customers.

> *February 6th.* Met my friend who knocked me down, and we went to the pictures. We saw "The Lovesick Cowboy Off the Beaten Track" and some other things which gave me chills all down my spine.[38]

These entries represent "Miss Muddleton" as an employee who gets a small degree of satisfaction from her daily exchanges with customers and coworkers, but nonetheless one whose attentions are focused more on pleasurable entertainments like the courtship ritual and the fascinations of the picture palace than on the self-improving atmosphere of the shop. This representation of one shop assistant's perspective on her labor expresses the potential banality of everyday life in the department store through the light, semisatirical treatment of the fictional character's recording of her daily encounters. "Miss Muddleton" does not experience her life as banal, however; rather, the store presents a series of daily events rendering the most mundane experiences of working life a species of entertainment which finds its apogee in the stimulating "chills" and thrills of the cinema.

The diary provoked vehement responses claiming that "Miss Muddleton" must be the pseudonym of a male member of staff, and an extended discussion over whether her dissatisfaction with work and her general "silliness" and other character deficiencies should be taken seriously. One writer, "M. B.," argued in defense of the young lady, viewing her as the mouthpiece of the "soulless worker" and protesting the caricature of the female employee which emerges in the diary entries:

> There must be many workers in so vast a store who rebel at their environment, who think that life must hold something higher, better, nobler for them than just "the daily round, the common task," of everyday existence. They realise the emptiness of all which is deprived of soul and brought to the sordid money-level, and their ideal is in their work. [. . .] These workers, who are fighting toward the light, are giving the best of themselves to the stores. They are giving that which cannot be bought, the real spirit of endeavor, without which nothing could succeed. Could it be otherwise that such "days" as described in the diary grate on the mind as empty, meaningless words[?] [. . .] As for the decidedly quaint encounters with the member of the opposite sex, and the evenings at the cinema theatre, [they] are almost beneath contempt. [. . .] The visit to the cinema displays the culpable ignorance of the male object who edits the "Diary." I believe in the future the cinematograph may prove a great educational factor, but at present our evenings are far too precious to be wasted on any "Cow Boy's Adventures," on or off "The Beaten Track." How little the writer knows of the way the average worker spends her evenings.[39]

The rhetoric of this letter reveals its author's intent not solely to improve the conditions under which employees might labor, but also to hold up the store as an ideal environment for the pursuit of noble and fulfilling work. Instead of wasting valuable space on such "would-be humorous" pieces, M. B. suggests, one might instead use its place in the magazine as a literary corner to provide an uplifting influence for the "Miss Muddletons" of the stores. Implicit in this protest against the diary entries, of course, is a critique of mass cultural amusements like the "would-be humorous" magazines and the sensational films described in the last two chapters of this study. Here again, as in the case of the trade union activism analyzed in the previous chapter, we see a struggle over the characterization of the shopgirl as a cultural type, combined with an attempt to make actual shop assistants into exemplary social subjects. This exemplarity, according to M. B., would depend on the individual store employee's commitment to the "ideal" of work, and on her effort to render the store a collective enterprise based on something other than capitalist progress in its most "sordid" form.

The final letter regarding the diary offers a different perspective on this struggle to shape the Harrods employee into a worker who finds dignity and fulfillment in her everyday experience. It relegates the entire exchange to one of "silliness," not worth the "virtuous and high-flown verbiage" given it by M. B.; and yet it also suggests that this exchange might be participating in the process of shaping employees into diligent workers intent on the "higher" aspects of their working lives. The last letter, published in April 1913, takes issue with M. B.'s claim for women's equality or superiority to men, arguing that "silly women *do* exist, even (low be it spoken, or I shall incur the vials of M. B.'s wrath next) at Harrods":

> If, as I take it, the writer of the much-to-be-condemned "diary" is a member of the staff, is it not possible that he or she hopes, by holding such pitifully small-minded, weak-brained members of the community up to well-deserved scorn, to induce them to mend their ways? This is but a suggestion: but surely no one in their senses *could* take that absurd girl as being seriously intended to depict the average working woman! And surely M. B.'s suggestion that the author only knows very inferior members of the fairer sex does not speak in favour of her co-workers at the stores. [. . .] Believe me, yours faithfully, A Woman Who Works.[40]

This item offers a new reading of Miss Muddleton's diary by suggesting that such a farcical piece of writing could only have been intended as an object-lesson for those readers who might see their own relation to work and leisure reflected in the diary entries. Of course, we have no way to know whether the exchange of ideas surrounding the diary continued outside the pages of the magazine, in everyday interaction among the staff members; but, judging from the few responses printed here, by 1913 (and after the entrance of Selfridges on the London retailing scene), Harrods had become invested in the ideological reproduction of the store employee as a serious and committed worker rather than a flighty youngster concerned only with the absurd pleasures of the masses.

Harrods strove to create a custodial environment in its treatment of staff, particularly its female employees, whose involvement in the enterprise inspired protective instincts in colleagues and management alike. In the words of a 1917 article on "The Increased Scope for Woman as Wage-Earner," the future held a great deal of promise for the "working girl": "Gone are the prejudices and restrictions hitherto prevailing against female labour. She enters on the same footing as her brothers, and receives all the encouragement and sympathy that the most devoted parent could desire for her."[41] By contrast, the newest store on the London retail scene, founded by a wealthy entrepreneur named Gordon Selfridge who had trained at Marshall Field's in Chicago, used a strategy of "scientific" efficiency in management which strategically represented the staff as aspiring and upwardly mobile individuals rather than as members of a substitute family.[42] This new institution brought its own share of conflicts to the politics of department store labor, and as the next section suggests, provided a context through which popular writers could imagine and critique the industrialization of labor in the department store. With its introduction of Taylorist rhetorical methods for store management, Selfridges represented shop labor as a fulfilling and uplifting experience, a conception of labor that contrasted markedly with other contemporary descriptions of the modern department store. As the next section demonstrates, Gordon Selfridge created a store environment that was gendered feminine, but that retained a degree of anonymity in its treatment of workers as members of an efficient, modernized system. The message of agency conveyed by Selfridge's managerial structure, when read through the uplifting language of individual betterment, can be seen to be motivated by economic rather than social concerns, holding out the elusive promise of self-transformation. As the final section of the chapter will conclude, this constantly repeated and deferred promise finds its most direct expression in the fiction of the department store romance.

II. "The Science of Shopkeeping": Selfridges

From its inception, Selfridge's Oxford Street store was conceived as the ultimate institution for shopping as a modern leisure practice, and one which disregarded the strict class boundaries typically associated with other West End stores. Gordon Selfridge, the creative influence behind many of the advertisements for the store (including the long-running series of newspaper columns by "Callisthenes," describing the progress of the retail industry with particular attention to Selfridges' successes), represented the store as a social space which provided democratic access to all. One of the most striking advertisements for the store's opening proclaimed, "We wish it to be clearly understood that our invitation is to the whole British public and to visitors from overseas—that no cards of admission are required—that all are welcome—and that the pleasures of shopping as well as those of sight-seeing begin from the opening hour."[43] The emphasis on sight-seeing and browsing meant that even those who were not able to buy the store's merchandise could participate in the great spectacle of the store in its first days of existence as a public institution. News clippings from the opening days of the store claimed its accessibility for wealthy and poor alike; in the words of one writer, "Here, if a rich woman, you may spend £1,450 on a sable cloak, or if a poor one, you may buy a yard of ribbon with equal facility."[44]

In conceiving of Selfridges as a new institution which would revolutionize the London retail industry through the "American plan" of democratic access and managerial leadership, Gordon Selfridge reconfigured contemporary debates around the politics of labor and the relationship between gender and consumer desire. As Erika Rappaport has demonstrated, the innovations in architecture, marketing and advertising methods, and display strategies introduced by Selfridge prompted contemporary journalists, retailers, and shoppers to reconsider the nature of consumption as a leisure experience; Selfridge placed himself at the center of a culture of female pleasure defined by the department store as a social setting for new relations between consumers and goods.[45] Selfridge did not limit his quest for modernization to the treatment of customers and merchandise, however: he consciously fashioned himself as a model manager, emphasizing the efficiency and fairness with which his employees were treated and positioning himself as the means by which the scientific methods of management could be disseminated throughout England. In this sense Selfridge, and the store which bore his name, came to symbolize the introduction of new labor practices which were envisioned by contemporary observers as quintessentially modern and emblematic of the American model of success through enthusiasm, personal endeavor and integrity, and above all perseverance.

Selfridge's personal history reveals a distinct effort on his part as well as on the part of his later biographers to place him within the familiar American stereotype of the self-made man. The eldest son of a widowed schoolteacher, Gordon Selfridge came to Chicago in 1879 at the age of twenty-three with an elementary education and some clerical experience; he accepted a position as stock boy on the wholesale staff of Marshall Field & Co. at a salary of ten dollars a week, and gradually worked his way up the ranks of the firm, first as a traveling lace salesman and finally making his way into the retail side of the business. It was from this early period that some of his later innovations in retailing were said to have stemmed, including the idea for a reception area within the store (inspired by the catalog of a Boston retailer), a "greeter" to show female customers inside, a house telephone system, and an extensive use of new display strategies including electric lighting.[46] Selfridge became junior partner in 1890 (reflecting in his own upward trajectory the firm's saying, "Office-boy today, partner tomorrow") and expressed his attention to progress and efficiency through his communication with store employees. He circulated sheets of instructions and rules among the staff, and extolled the virtues of the "Marshall Field & Company Idea," which enjoined staff members to shape their conduct according to the following principles:

> To do the right thing, at the right time, in the right way; to do some things better than they were ever done before; to eliminate errors; to know both sides of the question; to be courteous; to be an example; to work for the love of work; to anticipate requirements; to develop resources; to recognize no impediments; to master circumstances; to act from reason rather than rule; to be satisfied with nothing short of perfection.[47]

Many of these injunctions recall Selfridge's religious upbringing, through which he was inspired to see work as a sanctified endeavor and to believe firmly that individual enterprise would reap its own rewards. Others, including the stated necessity of "eliminat[ing] errors" and "act[ing] from reason rather than rule," suggest the emphasis on rationality and efficiency that was slowly taking hold in American industry and that would shortly fall under the term "scientific management," pioneered by Frederick Winslow Taylor during this period.

Selfridge's efforts to incorporate efficiency into new managerial strategies for the retail industry were shaped by concerns similar to those which prompted Taylor to embark on his time studies and to elaborate methods by which industrial laborers might contribute to the greater efficiency of the production process. In 1898 Taylor began his time-based analyses of the various movements involved in manual labor, from there extrapolating a "scientific" method for replacing human error with system-based rationality. In the case of the yard laborers at the Bethlehem Steel Works in Pennsylvania, for example, where Taylor spent several years analyzing "the science of shoveling" (a term later used derisively by critics of scientific management), the time to complete a task of shoveling raw materials was dramatically reduced, held to a standard set by the "first-class" workman on the job, and then rewarded monetarily on a piecework system. As a result, the cost of handling both material and manpower was cut in half, and the resulting increase in efficiency, according to Taylor, ended in improved relations between workers and management.[48] As his theory developed into what he then termed scientific management, Taylor argued that this modern system entailed a "complete mental revolution" on the part of laborers and the managerial staff, in which "the new idea of coop-eration and peace [is] substituted for the old idea of discord and war," incorporating "the substitution of hearty brotherly cooperation for con-tention and strife; of both pulling hard in the same direction instead of pulling apart; of replacing suspicious watchfulness with mutual confi-dence; of becoming friends instead of enemies."[49] For those on the House Committee investigating Taylor's system of scientific management in 1912, the rhetoric of good feeling between masters and men used by Taylor to defend his system against critics contradicted the centralization of control and the increased specialization which made the worker into an interchangeable part of the efficient machine.[50] The increasing automatiza-tion of the worker in such systems of scientific management (epitomized in Ford's assembly-line techniques of specialized, mechanistic labor) con-tributed to the contemporary perception that these new technologies of controlling labor extended to an entire way of life shared by the employees of the industries utilizing these systems.[51]

Gordon Selfridge imported several aspects of scientific management into his new enterprise in London, effecting a transformation in retailing which can be read as paralleling the shift from an older model of industri-al relations in which each laborer worked at his or her own pace (Taylor's day-rate) to the new model of the modern factory based on piecework and efficiency in production. Selfridge's model used the language of efficiency pioneered by Taylor to mask more fundamental concerns about the suc-cessful distribution of goods and the economic profit to be gained by the store and its management. The largest and most publicized of the great West End department stores, Selfridges seemed to spring up overnight, startling contemporary observers in its rapid construction (in less than a year) and in the sheer scale with which it towered over the smaller shops surrounding it. Such a vast establishment required a large staff, and of the estimated ten thousand applications received in the six months before the store opened, approximately twelve hundred people were employed in the store in 1909. Many of the new employees had worked previously as shop assistants and clerks in other London stores, and were attracted by the promise of the superior conditions they expected to experience at Selfridges. Since, like Richard Burbidge of Harrods, Selfridge resisted the living-in system, store employees were less subject to explicit disciplinary efforts on the part of the store management; yet he nonetheless incorporated an ideology of implicit social control into his relationship with store employees. One of the hallmarks of the new store was its introduction of "central staff control," a practice by which only executives or general managers had the power to render final decisions on the hiring and firing of employees. The advantage to this system, many believed, was that staff members were able to escape the tyranny of buyers and department heads, often turning to Percy Best, the store's staff manager, or even to Selfridge himself with complaints. One female applicant, interviewed by Best in 1908, expressed dismay on learning the name of her future boss, who (as Best recalled) "had certain weaknesses which might be objected to by nice women." Best responded by reassuring the young woman that she was not expected to do anything that was not "part of [her] duty to the House," to the evident relief of this prospective shop assistant.[52] The use of a centralized system of management, combined with the diffusion of methods for greater efficiency from above, recalls many of the components of Taylor's managerial system and conveys the store's efforts to shape the working experience of employees. Gordon Selfridge resisted the perception that his employees were merely cogs in the vast machine of the store, instead describing the values which created the employee as a successful individual in an effort to maintain an emphasis on democratic leadership. It is this very resistance, however, that facilitates an analysis of the rhetorical production of Selfridge's "scientific" system. He combined the managerial principles he had developed in Chicago with others touting the virtues of progress and the ideals of industry in his testament to "The Spirit of the House," which rearticulated many of the standards of the Marshall Field & Company Idea:

> To look upon each minute as precious and to be exchanged only for its full equivalent in Progress . . . To develop, continually, every faculty which helps to build greater judgment, energy, determination, mirth and good cheer, for each is necessary to the strong happy individual . . . To look upon Work during the working hours of the day as a privilege—as a game—as a requisite of the full and complete life . . . To look upon Idleness with disrespect, as a waste of Time, the only commodity of which everyone has an equal amount . . . To feel that the waking hours after the day's work is over, are best used in study, in agreeable companionship, in recreation, in those acts which build happier, stronger character and better health . . . To strive for

higher Standards and Ideals . . . To look upon the bright side of things and be Optimists in the best meaning of the word . . . To act quickly and avoid procrastination . . . To think always Broad-mindedly and to scorn Narrow-mindedness, Meanness and jealousy . . . To be Just and to despise Injustice . . . To punish Dishonesty with the utmost effort . . . To appreciate fully Intelligence, Originality, Loyalty—recognising merit and merit only as the door to advancement . . . To acknowledge no obstacles as insurmountable which stand in the way of splendid Progress[.][53]

In this passage, personal development occurs for the greater good of the store, with the "strong happy individual" as the center of a cooperative ideology of shared progress. Labor, in this description, becomes an activity which workers should long to participate in, incorporating self-fulfillment through work as necessities for "the full and complete life." Lest store employees be tempted to treat their working hours as solely pleasurable, however, and in keeping with the principles of progress within this new "science of shopkeeping," Selfridge enjoins his staff to value the efficient use of Time, a valuable "commodity" distributed equally among all. In the next sentence, however, the focus shifts back to the creation of the well-rounded worker, surrounded by the positive influences of wholesome recreation and fitting companionship. As a whole, Selfridge's testament to the ideology behind manager-employee relations in the store describes a cooperative effort similar to the Taylorist ideal, with an added emphasis on the individual lives of staff members. The critical aspect of the Selfridge system is its insistence on producing this cooperative ideology through an emphasis on the health and well-being of the individual worker in conjunction with the successful development of the store.

Like Harrods, in an effort to reproduce its staff as coherent, self-fulfilled individuals, Selfridges provided numerous opportunities for shaping the lives of its employees outside of their working hours. Sporting and recreational activities were organized by the Arlington Social and Athletic Association on the grounds at Wembley on weekends, followed by social events which served as mixers for the men and women on staff: Adela Hill, an employee who worked at the store in 1909, recalled that "nearly every Saturday afternoon and Sunday was spent there. Sport in the afternoons, then tea—I was on the Committee. Then dancing with the boy of one's choice."[54] Shortly after the creation of the association, the Selfridge Operatic and Dramatic Society was formed, and went on to produce a play written by the society's director entitled *The Suffrage Girl*, which was later followed by Gilbert and Sullivan's *HMS Pinafore* and, in 1918, the popular musical comedy *The Shop Girl*. This musical, originally produced at the

Gaiety Theatre in 1894, had as its heroine the plucky Bessie Brent (played by Joan Ritz) and, in the role of Ada Smith, a Selfridges employee named Violet Mawhinny, who worked in Umbrellas and who enjoyed the chance to perform a glorified version of her everyday life on stage: she told the *Daily Express,* "I have had no previous experience on the stage. I love playing the part in the evening and look forward to it all day while I am at work here."[55] These social activities engendered a sense of community among the single members of the staff, many of whom lived in a neighboring hostel owned and supervised by the store.

Selfridge's most marked innovations in staff relations came in the form of classes which were intended to provide education in the business of retailing and to train new recruits for employment in the store. These innovations contributed to a culture of upward mobility which differed significantly from the curtailed narrative of progress provided by Harrods, whose management refrained from actively encouraging the majority of their employees to climb the social ladder of the store's hierarchy. Articles in the daily press described Selfridges' instruction classes in which store employees learned how to receive customers, answer questions, and direct people, with the strict injunction, "no importuning to buy"; others recounted the lectures given to assistants as a means of rising in the store's hierarchy of staff.[56] Managers routinely visited London schools in a search for "a continuous supply of the right material" for employment in Selfridges. Boys and girls who were thus selected, or recommended for employment by staff members, were enrolled in a two-year training program consisting of lectures on house policy, on administration and business ethics, and on the store's strategies for buying and selling merchandise. Staff training was not limited to the London retail trade: each year two traveling scholarships were awarded which allowed their recipients to study foreign retail enterprise in the company of a buyer, and in 1912 a mixed group of employees journeyed to Paris to visit the largest stores there and further their knowledge of business methods.[57] These efforts on the part of Selfridges' store management articulate the conviction that with the proper training, the stock boy might work his way up the ladder within the store to become a high-level managerial figure. The situation for female employees was markedly different, however: in 1912 the women of the store were given a bronze tablet bearing the following inscription: "This tablet is a tribute to women's work in the establishing of this business, and is set up as a permanent record of their splendid loyalty and the quality of the service they have rendered." The tribute was given because, according to Selfridge, while "there was practically no limit to the heights to which a man of ability might succeed in the house, women, although they might go far, could never attain a commanding

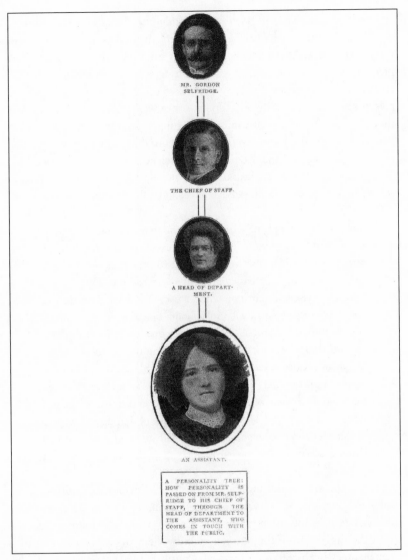

MR. GORDON SELFRIDGE.

THE CHIEF OF STAFF.

A HEAD OF DEPART-
MENT.

AN ASSISTANT.

A PERSONALITY TREE:
HOW PERSONALITY IS
PASSED ON FROM MR. SELF-
RIDGE TO HIS CHIEF OF
STAFF, THROUGH THE
HEAD OF DEPARTMENT TO
THE ASSISTANT, WHO
COMES IN TOUCH WITH
THE PUBLIC.

Selfridges' "Personality Tree," *London Magazine,* c. 1910s. The caption describes "how personality is passed on from Mr. Selfridge to his chief of staff, through the head of department to the assistant, who comes in touch with the public." Reproduced by permission of the History of Advertising Trust Archive, Norwich.

position."[58] The gendered nature of the store hierarchy is expressed visually in the "personality tree" used by Selfridges' management to demonstrate the transmission of proper business practice from the head of the store down through the ranks to the assistants behind the counter.[59]

Many of the managerial practices espoused by Selfridge were carried out, and perhaps conceived, by Percy Best, Selfridge's staff manager and the vehicle through which much of Selfridge's scientific method of store management was disseminated. In statements to the press from the store's inception, Best proclaimed the myriad advantages of Selfridge's system, which encouraged employees to "look upon their work, not as so much labour, which they were paid to do, and then to fly off as soon as they were released, but to feel that they were part of a band of comrades pushing forward a great enterprise."[60] Best emphasized the transition in industry from understanding business as a mechanical process to understanding it as a science. In a staff address entitled "Imagination in Business," Best described the ideal for employee conduct as emerging from imagination, perseverance, and enthusiasm:

> You will too, by applying science and philosophy into your daily work, soon be able to successfully diagnose customers who require your attention; you will be able to see at a glance that perhaps your first customer of the morning has come in in a very bad mood; you will at once adapt yourself to that mood, and, with tactful handling, the crochety lady or gentleman will probably not only leave a good impression on the takings of your department for that day, but will also leave in a much happier frame of mind. Your next customer comes in bright, happy, and evidently enjoying life; you will in this case rise to the occasion; you will respond to her brightness, will probably be able to interest her in your merchandise to a much greater extent than in the previous instance. [. . .] The whole game is one of starting and exciting imagination, and the higher our ideals and the more we strive after them, so surely shall we get ourselves far above the average.[61]

The emphasis on combining the "science of merchandising" with inspirational exhortations on the value of imagination, dignity, sincerity, and like qualities reveals the attempt on the part of Selfridges' management to resist the suggestion of the rational, deindividualizing aspects of scientific management in the retail industry. By contrast, a later series of articles by Best describing the evolution of business practices in Selfridges implies that Selfridge introduced a scientific model of retail management remarkably similar to the Taylorist model, but with little discussion of the negative effects this model might have on employees. In an article entitled "Building the Machine—and Organising the Men to Operate It," Best gave an account of this scientific system:

> Mr. Selfridge brought into this country a more highly organised management than up to that time we had felt was necessary in big

retail business. [. . .] The more detailed and scientific organisation introduced by Mr. Selfridge centred in the general management, the control of staff and merchandise. [. . .] The centralisation of staff control ensured a fair treatment of employees. Under the departmental management treatment of staff varied according to the character and temperament of the buyer, and on such departmental loyalty or otherwise depended. Under central staff control, however, there was a uniformity of loyalty to the business which, in Mr. Selfridge's opinion, made for greater efficiency.[62]

The rhetoric of efficiency and scientific organization used by Percy Best to describe the managerial structure of the store reflects, as I have argued, a centralized model of labor relations in which the store employees reported to a more highly skilled staff of superiors who guided the enterprise with a uniform hand. Selfridge incorporated this model in the making of his Oxford Street store in an effort to differentiate the new, democratized, American-style department store from the traditional, class-segregated shops of England's commercial history. Best's title for the section, "Building the Machine," reveals an important element of this scientific system, and one which did not go unnoticed by critics of the large-scale capitalist enterprises of which the new department stores like Selfridges were a symbol: for these critics, the metaphor of the machine, and particularly of mechanized labor within the great engine of the store, represented the disturbing potential of the unhindered forward progression of capitalism in the modernization of the retail industry. The most disturbing aspect of the industrialization of department store labor was the possibility of exploitation in the name of efficiency, such that store employees would become little more than numbers, interchangeable parts of a modernized system.

Needless to say, not all department store employees envisioned their labor as a source of pleasure. For many of the shop assistants whose working lives meant degradation rather than uplift, even the more enlightened stores could expose the negative side of shop labor. A surviving recollection of a Selfridges employee from 1909 suggests that her working life was physically taxing and degrading:

> I was that lowest form of animal life, a junior to wait on the seniors and hopefully learn salesmanship. This could be a dog's life, and very often was. [. . .] In the year 1911 we experienced the hottest summer anyone could remember—over 90 degrees in the shade, day after day. During this heat I wore a black serge long-sleeved, high necked

dress, black woollen stockings and sturdy black shoes, and the appropriate underwear. When the store closed at 6:30 PM, we had to go
into the Bathing Dress department to restore order out of chaos, as
these garments were in the main two-piece and we had to make the
garments match. This took some time, with nothing extra to eat or
drink and no money for overtime.[63]

This account contradicts the official history of stores like Harrods and
Selfridges, revealing the univocal rhetoric used to produce the staff and
management as one unit striving toward a common goal centered on the
profit of the enterprise. Unfortunately, these staff recollections, whether
they reinforce or contradict this institutional rhetoric, are few and far
between, and thus cannot be relied upon for a complete picture of the
range of perceptions held about shop assistants' experience of labor.
Another way to tackle the contradictory representations of working life in
the department store is to consider that institution's representation in popular fiction. The centrality of the great enterprise of the department store
in the popular romance novels of the early twentieth century, and its
relentless destruction of the small, outmoded nineteenth-century shop
through the mechanical turnover of capital and labor power, raises two
questions which are particularly germane to my analysis of the construction of the shopgirl as laboring subject: What happens to the interconnected systems of benevolent paternalism and scientific management of
stores like Harrods and Selfridges when these stores are imagined as sites
for the rational industrialization of labor? How did contemporary writers
mobilize the metaphor of the machine and its anonymous laboring bodies in order to critique the modernization of the retail industry?

Late-nineteenth- and early-twentieth-century novelists, particularly
writers of popular romance novels, repeatedly focused on the subject of
industrial display labor in the department store, using this subject to
express the sufferings and struggles of female department store employees
at the hands of exploitative managers and customers. Novels in this subgenre such as the Williamsons' *Winnie Childs, the Shop Girl* and Arthur
Applin's *Shop Girls* use the body of the woman worker as a vehicle for a
critique of the politics of labor and capitalist production in the Victorian
and Edwardian department store. Although she typically endangers her
virginal integrity through her labor within the store, in these fictions the
shopgirl-heroine's resistance to the ideology of systematic, rationalized
labor separates her from others who buckle under its influence. Rather
than becoming an anonymous part of the machine, the female department store employee is held up as an individual who represents the imagined promise of the humane and liberal treatment of workers, largely

through her capacity to transform the male store owner from machine to man. In keeping with the romance plots which typically drive these fictions, the promise of marriage in the final pages offers a consoling vision of the machine demechanized, in which the dehumanizing system is made human. As the following section shows, these novels offer a critique of the modernization of the retail industry at the same time that they celebrate its increasing power. Moreover, in describing the individual heroine's ability to triumph over the culture of desire which sexualizes and endangers her, they also gender the sphere of industrial display labor, rendering the female body the focus of the culture of spectacle embodied by the store. In this sense these novels dismantle the conventional assumption that industrial labor is by nature masculine: in the feminized world of the department store, labor as such becomes newly imagined as a feminine activity. Moreover, the individualizing narrative of the romance plot counters the anonymity of the scientifically managed store employee, providing a promise to satisfy the heroine's longing for self-fulfillment through an idealized marriage to the store owner, thereby remaking the store as a scene of pleasure rather than an alienating and degrading experience and reproducing the shopgirl as a desiring subject.

Critiques of Industrial Display Labor in the Department Store Romance

In Émile Zola's 1882 novel *Au bonheur des dames,* the eponymous *grand magasin* which tempts the "natural" desires of every woman is figured as a great machine working at maximum capacity:

> [T]he furnace-like glow which the house exhaled came above all from the sale, the crush at the counters. [. . .] There was the continual roaring of the machine at work, the marshalling of the customers, bewildered amidst the piles of goods, and finally pushed along to the pay-desk. And all that went on in an orderly manner, with mechanical regularity, quite a nation of women passing through the force and logic of this wonderful commercial machine.[64]

This factory-like emporium, a palace of luxury which markets its goods even to the poor through its much-lauded sales, bewilders and disorients its female clientele through an overwhelming abundance of merchandise, illogically positioned to encourage both browsing and impulse buying. Despite its ability to confound its consumers, however, the store operates with the "mechanical regularity" espoused by its managerial staff, the dour

Bourdoncle and his superior, the impetuous and flirtatious Octave Mouret, the man whose success depends on his innate understanding of women's desires and pleasures. In accordance with the feminine world of the "Ladies' Paradise," this store-as-machine is itself gendered female, an animated feminine body made up of luxurious fabrics and furnishings:

> [T]he stuffs became animated in this passionate atmosphere: the laces fluttered, drooped, and concealed the depths of the shop with a troubling air of mystery; even the lengths of cloth, thick and heavy, exhaled a tempting odour, while the cloaks threw out their folds over the dummies, which assumed a soul, and the great velvet mantle particularly, expanded, supple and warm, as if on real fleshly shoulders, with a heaving of the bosom and a trembling of the hips.[65]

For Zola, the mechanical culture of the department store, although it does succeed in crushing the small, family-owned shops which struggle in vain to compete with its superior selling power, is redeemed through the largely positive experience of its heroine, Denise Baudu, a country girl who works her way up to first hand in the store. Denise's story consists of her resistance to the temptations of the seducer Mouret and her hesitancy to marry him even when her honor would be unassailed; yet, at the end, both Mouret and his store submit to the taming influence of this honorable young woman. The Ladies' Paradise stands as a testament to the pleasures of the female consumer and the power of the female heroine over the man who believed himself able to conquer all women through their desire to consume.

Zola's depiction of the department store as a machine constituted by the bodies and desires of women differs from the version of the department store we receive in the popular romance fiction of the early twentieth century in that, rather than focusing on the consuming pleasures of this experience, the later writers emphasize the dangers women faced in the possibility of becoming anonymous members of a rationalized and dehumanizing culture. While Zola does portray his virginal heroine assailed by a lascivious inspector, he deemphasizes this danger by then narrating the story of Denise's increased independence and her rise to the top of the store's hierarchy. By contrast, writers such as the Williamsons and Arthur Applin figure industrial labor as a threat to the heroine's honor and integrity, representing her as a sexual subject imperiled by the male-dominated aspects of rational culture. *Winnie Childs, the Shop Girl* and *Shop Girls* both mount critiques of the Taylorist model of department store management through their descriptions of the anonymous worker reindividualized through her desire and her desirability as display object.

The female employees of these texts do fade into the background of the store, becoming part of the efficient machine and visual panorama that the store embodies, but their gender and sexual vulnerability at the hands of often unscrupulous male customers or employers necessitate the reassertion of their individuality and difference from the mere elements of the machine. In their presentation of the display culture of the department store as an inexorable force or system, these novels describe the exploitation of the female laboring body, but they also underscore the heroine's individuality and position as an "extraordinary" worker through a depiction of the sexual risks such women faced and their ability to triumph in the concluding chapters. In presenting this double-sided critique, these examples contradict the de-eroticizing technologies of modern labor, instead repositioning the mannequin-like figures of the mass ornament as individual gendered bodies. This type of labor critique occurs most markedly in the feminized, display-oriented culture of the department store, where working women's bodies become integral to the process of creating consumer fantasy and desire.

As is often the case with romance writers from this period, little is known about Charles Norris and Alice Muriel Williamson.[66] The two cowrote a number of popular romances during the decades leading up to World War I, and the latter also wrote serial fiction for popular romance magazines including *Forget-Me-Not*, a magazine I discuss in detail in chapter 4. These stories suggest her facility with the formula, style, and genre of the romance so often targeted to young female readers. *Winnie Childs* appeals to this population, particularly to the shopgirl-reader who forms the subject of the fourth chapter of this study, through its description of travel, romance, and risk in the urban environment of turn-of-the-century New York. The novel describes the trials of the eponymous heroine, a young woman from London traveling to America to earn a living, having received passage in exchange for modeling dresses for potential customers while on board the ship; once in New York, unable to find work as a journalist, she is engaged as an assistant at "The Hands," one of the newest institutions dedicated to the flights of consumer fancy. The remainder of the story relates her struggle to maintain her position and her integrity in the face of harassment by a wealthy male customer, and in the end resolves this conflict by allowing young Peter Rolls, the son of the store's owner, to rescue her from the clutches of an assailant and from the exploitative environment of the store, concluding in the manner fitting to the romance with a proposal of marriage. Several aspects of this seemingly conventional narrative are, in fact, quite striking: these include a critique of the treatment of employees in the store and a self-conscious irony regarding the subjectivity of the shopgirl-heroine. Despite its collusion with the ideology of the romance—through marrying the heroine to a wealthy man whose presence offers the promise of an alternative to her labor in the shop—this novel simultaneously criticizes the managerial structure of the store, substituting a newly individualizing and more humane environment for workers. As we will see, this critique of labor relations under the American system also emerges in a contemporaneous novel by Arthur Applin, although with a twist which renders the mechanical display of the department store as a dystopian nightmare figuring the frenzy of consumerism and suggesting the compromises involved in adhering to the structure of the romance narrative.

From its early chapters, the Williamsons' novel expresses an awareness of the coarse treatment of female employees of the fashion industry, offering a subtle critique of the exchangeability of women's bodies as models for clothes beyond their reach in terms of status and financial position. On board the ship, during one of her first conversations with Peter Rolls, Miss Child[67] explains that her engagement as a model was due to a speculation that she would fit the part: "'I got the engagement only by a few extra inches. Luckily it isn't the face that matters so much . . . I thought it was. But it's legs; their being long; Mme. Nadine engages on that and your figure being right for the dresses of the year. So many pretty girls come in short or odd lengths, you find, when they have to be measured by the yard, at bargain price.'"[68] Known among her fellow "dryads" on the ship for her wit and her determination to find humor in the most trying circumstances, Winnie here intentionally creates the metaphoric link between women's bodies and the fabrics which represent them; but she also establishes the interchangeability of these bodies, as long as one fits the established type in accord with the moment's fashions. Later, as she wanders past the windows of "The Hands," the store founded by Peter Rolls Sr., she envies the wax mannequins their ability to live the fantasy they provide to the eager consumers on the other side of the glass, as well as the luxury of leisure they embody. Winnie looks on as, in one window, maids prepare their mistresses for the glorious ball next door, while others portray a domestic scene, a classroom of children, winter sports in the Alps, and even a zoo populated by that emblem of early-twentieth-century commodity culture, "Teddy everythings" (80–81). These thrilling wax figures tempt Winnie to enter the store, even in the form of worker rather than consumer, in part because of the silence and serenity of their existence, which is then contrasted with her experience as a store employee. When hired as one of the "Hands" in the great factory-like machine, Winnie receives a number (#2884) rather than a name, by which she is identified within the store hierarchy. It is only her fellow shop assistants who call her by her name, thereby differentiating her from the many others laboring within the store. The other side of this differentiation, however, is Winnie's physical appeal and the fact that as "the tall English girl," she stands out from the crowd; and it is her sexual difference which makes her the target of an individual attention that becomes dangerous rather than redemptive.

Winifred's status as a "Hand" in Peter Rolls's machinelike establishment reinforces the synecdochic relationship between employee and store, as she and her fellow shop assistants are charged with the task of standing in for the store, representing the store to its public. Moreover, the use of the term "hand" underscores the importance of workers' bodies within the department store, metaphorically figuring employees ("manual" laborers) as parts of the store's body. The concept of workers as "hands" has a long association with the transformation of labor as an effect of the Industrial Revolution. Charles Dickens's novel *Hard Times* (1854), for example, describes the inhabitants of the industrial city of Coketown, "generically called 'the Hands,'" as "a race who would have found more favour with some people if Providence had seen fit to make them only hands."[69] The dismemberment of the body into its useful components returns in fictional narratives of shop labor in which the shopgirl is reduced to her hands, which process goods and money, or alternately to her legs, which mark her as a feminine, sexualized subject.

In the case of female employees, of course, their own hands were seen as indicators of their access to middle-class gentility (hence the emphasis in musicals like *The Shop Girl* on clean fingernails), but also signified their position as mediators of the exchange of goods across the store counter. In a crucial sequence of events in the Williamsons' novel, Winifred rescues a nurse whose clothing has caught on fire, in the process burning her own hands; shortly thereafter, back in the mantles department, her reddened hands (no longer the white, unscarred signifiers of her difference from the working classes) provoke her shame at being thought physically aberrant by a female customer:

> [T]he redness showed through, as if her hands were horribly chapped. She saw a lady who had asked her to try on a white lace evening coat staring at them.
>
> "What's the matter with your hands?" The question came sharply.
>
> "I scalded them a little this morning," Win explained.
>
> "Oh! I'm glad it isn't a *disease*."
>
> The girl blushed faintly, ashamed, glanced down at the offending pink fingers, and turning slowly round to display the cloak, suddenly looked up into the eyes of Peter Rolls. (301)

In this scene, the metaphoric significance of the "hands" acquires yet another layer: here, the shopgirl's hands stand in for her status as sexual

object, one of the many items on display to be consumed by male and
female customers (albeit with different ends).[70] In these several uses of the
"hands," the term used to identify workers in the store metonymically
comes to represent the body of the female employee, positioning her as a
signifier of industrial display labor in the department store.[71]

This eroticized figuration of the female body in *Winnie Childs* reveals
the authors' remarkable sensitivity to the central concern which structured
the lives of female employees of the Victorian department store: the fact
that their gender set them apart from the men beside whom they worked,
and the consequent sexualization of their roles within the store. Winnie
first experiences the mystery of an appeal to women's sexual influence as
she watches a fellow applicant persuade the superintendent to pay her
eight dollars rather than Winnie's six; she then learns of the romantic
intrigues between the saleswomen and the floorwalkers, and after a week
on the job is forced to negotiate an encounter with Meggison, her superi-
or, in which he lays a heavy hand over hers in a manner suggestive of the
ways by which women might rise within the store. Winnie, by contrast,
ascends the hierarchy through her integrity and flair for encouraging consumption in women desperate to purchase the latest craze. Nonetheless,
her integrity is consistently assailed by unscrupulous managers and fellow
employees—as in the young men who try to liven up their gray days by
pinching the shopgirls as they pass by—and by male customers like Jim
Logan, who after an unsuccessful attempt to detain her on the street, discovers her employment in the store and lures her to his empty house,
where he comes close to assaulting her before she narrowly escapes. In this
instance, and in her daily life at the store, the conflict between Winnie's
presumed anonymity and the evident spectacle she presents for the dangerous consumption of male employers and clients results in a crisis for
the heroine's sense of selfhood. Her embodiment of the eroticized figure
within the mass of workers, and her struggle to survive within the atmosphere of social and sexual risk that the store symbolizes, critically alters the
common perception that the laborers within the machine are simply
anonymous, desexualized parts of a larger whole. Instead, as this novel
suggests, because of her sex, the female worker highlights the centrality of
sexual display and the emphasis on the extraordinary individual heroine
within the display culture of that palace of consumption, the modern
department store.

At first glance, the remedy for the risks faced by shopgirls such as the
fictional Winnie Child lies, perhaps unsurprisingly, in marriage and the
possibility of another life, an alternative to the risk-producing culture of
shop life. The Williamsons' novel complicates this convention, however,
by linking the union between Winnie and the young Peter Rolls with a

narrative of compassionate treatment of the workers within the store. This benevolence is in part inspired by Peter's desire to undertake some philanthropic work, but is also, perhaps more importantly, shaped by Winifred's experience of life in the shop. Having learned of the weak fare offered by the staff restaurant, and the chairs provided behind counters tempting female employees to risk their positions by taking a moment to rest, Winnie concludes that "The Hands" follows the barest requirements of the law rather than acting in the true spirit of legal and social compassion. The women's rest room, for example, suggests the appearance of comfort and solace from the busy operations of the store:

> There were wall bookcases with glass doors, a few oak-framed engravings with a pale-green, "distempered" background, several chintz-covered sofas with cushions, and plenty of easy chairs. On small tables lay very back numbers of illustrated papers and magazines. The high windows had green curtains which softened their glare and (said Sadie) prevented dust from showing. The brown-painted floor had decorative intervals of rugs, like flowery oases. Altogether the room would have been an excellent "show place" if any influential millionairess began stirring up interest in "conditions of shop-girl life." (99)

This description reveals the authors' wry perspective on the effects of philanthropy on the actual "conditions of shop-girl life," suggesting that although such efforts may induce store owners to produce the appearance of kindly and caring managerial influence, they rarely fulfill their avowed commitment to the workers. Despite this room's superficial appeal, for example, it is rarely used for "rest"; rather, Winnie experiences it only once, as part of her training in using a check-book to record customers' purchases. Moreover, the staff and management are continually suspicious of spies from the Anti-Sweat League and other benevolent organizations, despite the store's apparently satisfactory fulfillment of the laws against exploiting workers. And, Winnie claims in a final confrontation with Peter which takes place over the counter, the "dignified barrier of oak" which separates the two, the management deserves to be anxious, for "The Hands" is the worst of its kind:

> We close at the right time, but the salespeople are kept late, often very late, looking over stock. Not every night for the same people, but several times a week. [. . .] We "lend" the management half the time we're allowed for meals on busy days—and never have it given back. The meals themselves, served in the restaurant—the dreadful restaurant—seem cheap, but they ought to be cheaper, for they're almost

uneatable. Those of us who can't go out get ptomain poisoning and appendicitis. . . . But nobody here cares how we live out of business hours, so long as we're "smart" and look nice. When we aren't smart—because we're ill, perhaps—and can't any longer look nice— because we're getting older or are too tired to care—why, then we have to go; poor, worn-out machines—fit for the junk shop, not for a department store. (309)

Convincing Peter of the many abuses committed by store management in the name of "business," Winnie then learns of the possibility of establishing a connection between Peter's convalescent home and those like Sadie Kirk, discharged because of her failing, consumptive body (one need hardly point out that, in this case, "consumption" for the employee means a very different thing than it does for the customer). The chance to bring philanthropic efforts to bear on the world of the shop dissolves the last remnant of her class-bound resistance to the love she has come to have for Peter Rolls.

Winnie's union with Peter, accomplished with aplomb on the last page of the novel, promises to transform the store's managerial structure: having experienced Winnie's passionate advocacy for "righting wrongs" done to the employees of the store—"Charity begins at home," she reminds him—Peter resolves to transform the business into an example of compassionate involvement rather than running the store with his father's managerial "hand" (305–13). This strategy suggests an anxiety about the effects of scientific and efficient management on the lives and experiences of workers, and claims to reintroduce the culture of benevolence which characterized the management policy of Harrods and other stores of its kind. Here, though, we find less a paternalistic style of governance than one based on the couple form, symbolized by the closing scene in which the elder Rolls approves of his son's marriage to Miss Child:

"You've got me, I tell you! And you can have Peter, too, if you want him. Do you?"

"I do," answered Win—and laughed again, the happiest, most surprised, and excited laugh in the world.

"Then we've got each other—forever!" cried Petro. "And, father, you and I will have each other, too, after this, as we never had before. You shall bless this day as I do, and as mother will."

"All right," said old Peter. "We'll see about that. Anyhow, shake hands."

Petro shook.

"And you, too, girl."

Winifred hesitated slightly, then held out her burned fingers.
Peter senior gave them deliberately to his son.
"There you are!" he exclaimed. "Now we're all three in the business."
"And this is the way we're going to run it in the future," said Petro.
"With love." (345)

This scene both recasts the traditional structure of marriage—by handing the son over to the prospective daughter-in-law rather than vice versa—and highlights the yoking of the romance to the industrial success of the store. The father's treatment of the marriage as a business partnership underscores the suggestion that the romantic couple signifies a new type of management, one based on the leadership of two people who know the store and their employees as intimately as they know one another, and who structure their managerial relations accordingly.

My analysis of *Winnie Childs, The Shop Girl* has addressed one formulation of the promise of the department store romance: in addition to providing the heroine with her destined partner, this novel also offers the assurance of a better life for all employees of a store run by a couple who embody the perfect union between laborers and management. As other chapters in this study of the shopgirl contend, however, this promise is in some sense always deferred, relegated, or postponed beyond the structure of the fictional narrative. After all, the marriage between the shopgirl and her employer inevitably concludes the romance rather than acting as a starting point for its story. This is in fact the case in Arthur Applin's novel *Shop Girls,* published in the same year: while *Winnie Childs* emphasizes an inexhaustible optimism in the title character's ability to "laugh at life," Applin's novel is characterized by a tone of anxiety over industrial competition and the deferral of the promise of personal and social transformation. Applin reformulates the deferred promise of the romance, leaving his readers with a much less fervent sense of the success of the department store romance as a genre which might extend the possibility of an alternative to the exploitation of industrial labor within the store. In this sense, *Shop Girls* conveys the other side of the utopian dream of the romance, articulating the failure of the romance novel to provide a narrative which satisfies its readers, and rendering their pleasure the center of an infinitely reproduced deferral, a longing for an alternative which becomes imaginable only in the context of fantasy.[72]

Like *Winnie Childs,* Applin's novel narrates the attraction shared between a shopgirl and her employer, but it does so in a dystopian environment of social and sexual risk which remains unresolved, or at least severely complicated, by the conclusion to the trajectory of the romance.

The plot follows the conventional structure of many fictions centering on women who are forced to take employment in a shop: the death of her father prompts the heroine, Martha Halliday, to seek employment first at Bungay's, a local department store in the quiet town of Birlington, and later at Lobb's, the newest competitor and the symbolic representative of the rapid expansion of capitalist enterprise into the smaller towns and cities of England. The contrast between Lobb's and the rural environs of Birlington is driven home in an early scene, in which Martha's pastorally induced reveries are disrupted when she ponders a billboard painted with the words "Lobb is Coming" in great black letters:

> Lobb had only been a name to its inhabitants, but now it threatened to become something more. The men and women living comfortable, self-satisfied lives had heard of Lobb as a monster, that the wilderness of steel, bricks, and mortar that London had in her agony of labour brought forth; a monster whose arms stretched over the countryside from city to city, threatening the prosperous tradesmen, snatching young men and maidens from home, robbing them of individuality, of freedom, and turning them into mere machines that made money.[73]

In this passage, Applin makes evident the explicit connection between the department store and its industrial laborers, but unlike Zola's Mouret, whose machine was a testament to efficiency and industrial progress, Lobb (and, by extension, the store that bears his name) is monstrous and terrifying, threatening to render its workers powerless cogs in the giant machine which distributes goods and creates consumers across the nation.

Martha's anxiety over Lobb's purported ability to turn "everything and everyone into a great piece of machinery; machinery which, once started, is never allowed to stop until it's worn out and cast into the scrap heap" contrasts markedly with her sister's imaginings, in which Lobb's power over his laboring bodies seems only "a fairy tale" (9–10). The former version of Lobb's comes to dominate the social landscape in Birlington, however, symbolizing the competitive spirit between the two stores: once the two begin vying for the attention of customers, sale goods and window displays tempt fickle buyers from one store to the other and back again. Even Martha, employed by Bungay to draw consumers away from Lobb's, finds herself inexplicably drawn toward Lobb's displays, which engage women's "natural" desire to adorn themselves with luxury goods:

> As Martha stared, jostled here and there by the increasing crowd, a feeling of awe of this wonderful Lobb was born in her breast, min-

gled with admiration. She looked and she longed. The blaze of colours blinded her, the wealth robbed from the world to glorify her sex, thrilled her body whilst it numbed her brain. She desired the rare flowers, the almost priceless feathers, the old lace, the ribbons arched like a rainbow from floor to ceiling, the delicate mousseline, the robes of sequins, the shoes of delicate tan, fawn, wine colour, purple, green, and lilac; the chiffons, the delaines, the soft linens, lawns, and Chinese silks, the bowers of imitation flowers that seemed to mock at nature's handiwork, and the veils, hand-painted. She desired these and the dangers they would bring. (84–85)

The descriptive repetition in this passage, with its sensual layering of fabrics and colors, contributes to the enthralling atmosphere of desire perpetuated by the store, reinforcing the novel's contention (à la Zola) that female consumers of all classes are unable to resist the temptation to buy the items which tantalize them.[74] Martha's position as head of the hosiery department during the desperate final phase of the battle between the stores allows her to counter Lobb's displays with her own captivating presentations of women's leg coverings, arranged in an abundance of colors to dazzle the eye. Unable to conquer the superior power of Lobb's (and the owner's ability to take on risk by underselling dramatically in order to gain an eventual profit), she is eventually forced to make the journey to London (another convention in the shop romance, here recast as her abduction from a peaceful home), or rather to Lobb's, which dominates the urban scene.

The bewilderment Martha had experienced in gazing into Lobb's Birlington windows pales by comparison with her first encounter with Lobb's great metropolitan store, a city in itself within the center of London. In the style of stores like Harrods, Lobb had built his store from a small Regent Street shop with a dozen assistants to a great emporium, referred to as "Everything, or merely Lobb's" (190). The first narrative description of the London branch occurs early in the novel, in which the store represents an admirable example of social progress, rivaling other urban structures in its architecture as well as in its industry:

Lobb filled three streets of the vast metropolis. There was no building in Europe to equal it in size or importance; architecturally it was beautiful, it formed a triangle, and on each side faced an open space filled with plane-trees; there were twenty-five departments. In the centre of each triangle was a great courtyard, and beneath the level of the ground a city of store-houses, stockrooms, ice chambers. A subterranean street led from the building to Clements' Street; the whole of which was owned by Lobb[;] here he housed and fed his assistants. Here were asphalt tennis courts, swimming baths, playgrounds, and a vast gymnasium. (91–92)

Lobb's innovations in retail management prove to be the central focus of both his supporters and his critics: while Martha's acquaintance Miss Despard admires the opportunities offered by the store (she comments, "[O]ne doesn't always get the sack if one marries"), others, including Martha herself, see Lobb's "model town" as a dangerous threat to traditional familial and social structures (54). In the words of the duplicitous but well-intentioned Mr. Brown, Lobb embodies the negative side of industrial progress, turning trees into ships, cattle into meat, steam into electricity, and men and women into slaves: "He'll pull down every house and cottage he can lay his hands on, and empty every home of father, mother, and children; he'll build a great hall for them, and instead of homes they'll find prisons—prisons so comfortable and luxurious that they'll be afraid to attempt to escape" (12). When Martha does in fact emerge from her disorienting journey into the cavernous store's subterranean regions, she experiences her misgivings in terms of the contrast between what she has been led to expect and what she sees before her:

> [S]he found herself in the midst of a hive. The human bees flitted to and fro buzzing softly in the manufactured sunshine. Crowds of them, Martha calculated them in hundreds, then in thousands, then she stopped calculating. She found herself in a lift, in another instant it had descended to the bowels of the earth; she was walking through a forest of bales and boxes and parcels; men and boys in their shirt sleeves were packing, others who were heaping goods into motor vans stood in two long rows down the centre of the subterranean room, against the walls where white eyes shone, a row of clerks were busy entering up their books. [. . .] Her brain, like a biographic film exposed too rapidly, refused to keep photographs of all she saw. The library, the gymnasium, the tennis court. Then across the square where, beneath the shadows of the artificial light, lovers stood whispering together, through the subterranean passage to the buildings where humanity was stabled. The barracks where Lobb's army slept. . . .
> (139–40, 142)

For Martha, Lobb's store signifies the deindividualization of workers into numbers; his display of the multitude of industrious workers who appear to gain pleasure from their employment provokes consternation on her part. The production of industrial efficiency in such a manner as to produce a new race of humans who thrive in an atmosphere that one would expect to crush them stuns her: as she gazes at the perfect body of a young woman emerging from the swimming pool, she cannot fathom that "these, at any rate, superficially happy, healthy girls, came from the showroom, the counter, slaves of Lobb" (141).

Martha's own status as Lobb's newest employee perpetuates the contradiction between the exploitative use of the female body in the service of industrial display labor and the supposed benefits provided by Lobb's managerial scheme. Engaged as a model in the outfitting department at a guinea a week, Martha experiences the loss of identity and individuality contingent on becoming part of the machine: "She ceased to exist. Martha Halliday was *just a number, a figure or model in flesh and blood,* on which other people's clothes would hang" (187, my emphasis). This quote reveals the complex position of the shopgirl as the heroine of the department store romance: she risks becoming an anonymous figure, a mere member of the crowd of beautiful women whose bodies are used as display objects, ideals of perfection to which customers may aspire. The women employed at Lobb's seem to confound the notion of the humble shopgirl: "The women seemed more beautiful and impossible—shop girls, assistants—Martha flouted the idea. They moved and dressed and looked like princesses of a fairy story, and their eyes were colder, and their mouths more scornful" (177). The inhuman beauty of these women is underscored by Martha's visit to the beauty department, where the renovation of the female body receives its most explicit treatment: in the words of Lobb, these rooms are dedicated to "the development of the body—if your breast is not developed, or your hands are too thin, or your ankles too coarse. Below us you say the making of hats and dresses, here you see the making of the women who wear them" (183). In this setting, women's bodies can be remade according to their desires, just as Lobb's model community can create "millions of champion men and women" to labor in his stores, rather than drawing from the "pigsties" of the urban metropolis, populated by foreigners and the "refuse" of the city. The risk for the shopgirl, then, is one of becoming a mere mannequin, one of many anonymous laboring bodies within the vast machine of the store; and yet these bodies are never wholly unmarked, for they maintain their status as sexual beings. Lobb's employees live in his model city in order to create a race of new workers for the store which will eventually populate the globe; he gives them the benefits they long for in order to maintain control over their breeding practices, thereby defining them solely as workers and breeders. Likewise, the mannequins who serve in the store, though shaped in the image of mechanical perfection, nonetheless retain their gendered identity, their bodies serving to tempt the consumer through the sexualized atmosphere of display. In this sense, then, the mannequin-like bodies of the women who work at Lobb's, rather than appearing as de-eroticized figures, "sexless bodies in bathing suits," instead symbolize the harnessing of female sexuality for the purposes of creating and perpetuating consumer desire.[75]

In the end, however, the romance narrative depicted in Applin's novel counters the figuration of the female body and the drive to render that body an "indissoluble girl cluster," a visual spectacle for the consumption of store customers.[76] Martha's final union with Lobb occurs because of his ultimate submission to a desire to experience the vulnerability of love; he trusts her ability to transform him into a fallible human rather than an exemplary and efficiency-driven machine, and in so doing (again in keeping with the conventions of the genre) takes her out of her position as subordinate within the store.[77] The implied results of their union include the ultimate re-creation of the shopgirl as a consumer, someone who, through her marriage to the store owner, can wear the store's merchandise as her own rather than only in the process of displaying goods for the consumption of others. This is also, however, a narrative which renders the potentially anonymous shopgirl an individual, effecting a particularization of the heroine as an extraordinary or exemplary figure. This individualizing narrative is based primarily on her desirability, but also incorporates her own production as a desiring subject. In this sense, the shopgirl becomes reconceived not as one of many exploited bodies or parts within the mechanical operations of the store, but rather as the heroine of the romance as a genre, and one whose life promises alternatives to the everyday experiences of actual shopgirls whose bodies were employed in the service of the store. And yet, as I suggested earlier, the promise of fulfillment offered by the romance—with marriage on the final page and the promise of complete, blissful, and eternal union ever after—remains only partially fulfilled. As I contend in chapter 4, it is the promise itself which sustains the reader and the heroine alike, and the perpetual deferral of the many disconcerting, unsatisfying, or otherwise mundane narratives which might follow on the conclusion to the romance may itself provide pleasure for the reader. The romance as a genre, then, attaches a certain vital importance to the maintenance of these two alternatives, the utopian promise and the pain contingent on the hardship and loss which characterize the everyday. It holds these two contradictory pieces in constant tension, and in that moment of possibility lies its readerly appeal.

CHAPTER 3

The Failures of the Romance: Boredom and the Production of Consuming Desires

I was sick of the starve and the stint and the grind of it all—sick to death of the whole grey life—and so I settled to have a royal time while the money lasted. All the things that I'd wanted—wanted horribly, and couldn't have—just because I was poor—pretty dresses, travel, amusement, politeness, consideration, and yes, I don't mind confessing it—admiration—they should be mine while the cash held out. I knew that I could buy them—every one—and I wasn't wrong.[1]

This passage, excerpted from Cicely Hamilton's 1908 feminist play, *Diana of Dobson's,* forms part of an impoverished shop assistant's confession to posing as a wealthy widow and spending an unexpected legacy of three hundred pounds to purchase the pleasures denied her in the context of her daily life. Formerly employed at Dobson's, a large drapery establishment characterized by "grind and squalor and tyranny and overwork," Diana decides to exchange her financial resources for a month of leisure, at the end of which she faces a return to the detested experience of the shop. In Hamilton's formulation, shop life is structured by the monotony of repetition, imagined by Diana as her inevitable future: "I shall crawl round to similar establishments, cringing to be taken on at the same starvation salary—and then settle down in the same stuffy dormitory, with the same mean little rules to obey—I shall serve the same stream of intelligent customers—and bolt my dinner off the same tough meat in the same gloomy dining room with the same mustard-colored paper on the walls."[2] The unremitting tedium of shop life, its dullness and drabness ("the whole grey life"), results in Diana's longing for an alternative atmosphere which would stimulate and invigorate rather than deaden her senses. Hamilton's depiction of the shop as a gray and drab existence structured through sameness and repetition transforms the scene of distribution and consumption from a glittering spectacle into a mundane environment drained of its attractions. Hamilton's critique of shop life spatializes and visualizes the banality of Diana's experience, producing an aesthetic version of the boredom produced by the culture of the shop or department store.[3] In this context, the stimulation provided by an escape from this stultifying experience is the only way to counter the monotony of the shopgirl's everyday life.

The contemporary conception of shop life as monotony resulted in part from the impoverished experience of time under the disciplinary conditions of shop labor.[4] Shop assistants, like factory hands, worked in an environment defined by repetition and routine, performing the same tasks on a daily basis and expected to reproduce an attitude of deference and readiness upon each encounter with a new customer. The department store's culture of industrial display labor, in which the employee becomes one of many elements in the display of goods for sale, rendered boredom a constitutive aspect of shop life, and resulted in a perceived desire on the part of the shopgirl for stimulation and excitement. The monotonous character of shop labor finds a corollary in the aesthetically depleted conditions of life outside the shop: shop workers often lived in a "plain and comfortless"[5] environment that contributed to the dullness of their everyday lives. I preface this chapter with Hamilton's characterization of shop life as dull and lacking in interest in an effort to describe the process by which the shopgirl became the focus of a set of cultural anxieties over the unsatisfied desires associated with late Victorian and Edwardian femininity. This process in turn worked to transform the shopgirl's identity in the popular imagination, rendering her a consuming agent whose desire for stimulation and excitement were imagined to shape her everyday practices.

Directed to an audience of middle-class readers and those who affiliated themselves with a cultural and intellectual elite, two British novels of the period, George Gissing's *The Odd Women* (1893) and W. Somerset Maugham's *Of Human Bondage* (1915), both portray shop labor as a degrading activity for women, particularly threatening to the performance of the gentility associated with "proper femininity."[6] In addition to its "sweated" aspects, shop labor is viewed as degrading in its production of boredom, an experience imagined as characteristic of the shopgirl's everyday life. As a result of the degradation of self produced by the shop, in the eyes of these writers, the shopgirl's desires themselves become debased: both authors depict desire, or the awareness of desire, as morally and physically degrading. When the shop fails to alleviate the boredom experienced by the shopgirl-heroines of these novels, they both seek stimulation, first in the form of marriage, and when their marriages fail, in the pursuit of extramarital, "illicit" pleasure envisioned in sexual terms.[7] In each novel, the shopgirl's reading practices are seen as symptomatic of her inappropriate longing for pleasure and stimulation, in turn rendering it impossible for her to assimilate herself to conventional norms for marital and domestic self-conduct. The shopgirl-heroine's perceived inability to mimic the signifying practices associated with gentility makes it impossible for her to occupy the place of the domestic feminine ideal. For these authors, gentility is positioned against its opposite, vulgarity, viewed in sexual and classed terms. It is precisely the distinction between the vulgar and the genteel, and the performance or occupation of these behaviorally located identities, that produces the causal narrative of boredom, desire, and stimulation operative in these novels. The following analysis tracks the ways in which desire, particularly working-class and sexual desire, makes the shopgirl into a vulgar parody of her upwardly mobile aspirations and produces marriage as an impossible solution to the problematic of the shopgirl's experience of boredom as a constitutive element of everyday life.

To put this argument another way, these novels narrate the pedagogy of identity for shopgirls who desire an upward trajectory out of the shop and into the secure position of the middle-class domestic woman. Integral to this pedagogical structure is a critique of the conventional conclusion to the romance, with its promised provision of marital and domestic fulfillment, as a fantasy unmasked. Instead, Gissing and Maugham depict the consequences fictional shopgirls might suffer through their apparent resistance or inability to satisfy the ideological demands of middle-class domesticity. As a result of their association with the "vulgar" sphere of public labor, the shopgirl-heroines of these novels fail to fully differentiate themselves from working-class desires and pleasures. Monica Madden and Mildred Rogers, both of whom leave shop labor for the promise of marriage and economic security, share an inability to reproduce the moral and social norms of proper femininity, a failure intimately tied to the threat of their affiliation with the working classes. Their failure to replicate a set of normative standards for identity and social practice produces a lack of domestic influence and industry, which in turn leads to boredom and the desire for stimulation, a desire sought and enacted through the consumption of fantasized romance plots. Monica and Mildred both turn to fantasy, here represented by the act of reading, to satisfy their desire for the pleasures provided by the romance narrative. Since, for Gissing and Maugham, such an act is inevitably linked with the degraded pleasures of the masses, both female characters subsequently endure the consequences of their association with sexual desire and with the class-inflected "vulgarity" of mass experience.

In constructing my analysis of these novels as a reading of the failures of the romance, I use the term "failure" in two ways. I have suggested that Monica and Mildred fail to reproduce an affiliation with middle-class desire and practice as a result of their association with the working classes. This failure occurs to varying degrees, becoming much more explicit in the case of Mildred, who is clearly written as working class throughout Maugham's novel. To some extent, however, we can and should also read this "failure" as an act of resistance in which the shopgirl-heroine successfully differentiates herself from the oppressive codes of middle-class domesticity, becoming a New Woman rather than an "odd" one.[8] But I also want to point to the ways in which the afterlife of the romance, here depicted as a series of failed marriage plots, fails to satisfy the desires of these novels' female protagonists. My analysis suggests that the conclusion provided by the conventional narrative of the romance remains unfulfilling for the shopgirl, presenting a markedly different ending from those that typically structure the romance plot as a fiction of consummated desire.

Boredom, Class, and the Production of Vulgar Desire

Gissing's female characters in *The Odd Women*, namely the Madden sisters and the proto-feminist figures of Rhoda Nunn and Mary Barfoot, continually strive to mark their own difference from the working classes, those perceived as more vulgar than themselves. While the majority of the "odd women" in this novel come from middle-class backgrounds, several characters reveal their vulgarism to be class-based (as in the twin cases of Miss Eade and Bella Royston) or character-driven (as in Mrs. Thomas, Everard Barfoot's sister-in-law, distinguished chiefly in her "base" disposition and attempts to make herself significant "in a certain sphere of vulgar wealth").[9] Gissing's version of vulgarity seems therefore, at first glance, to signify an identification with the commonplace, the ordinary, the banal.[10] For Gissing, to distinguish oneself from the vulgar masses one must make oneself into an extraordinary person. By "extraordinary" here I mean to point to a narrative of unconventional behavior and self-perception: in Gissing's novel such transgressive or nonnormative behavior occurs in the realm of sexual desire. In the case of his shopgirl-heroine, Monica Madden, Gissing creates a character who struggles against her middle-class upbringing and the moral injunctions which accompany it, instead seeking pleasure in a fantasy of romantic love. When she discovers the debasement of her own desire, however, she experiences that desire as shameful in its exposure of her inability to fully occupy the place of proper femininity. Monica's failure to successfully reproduce the ending of the romance within her own life causes her to pursue a fantasy romance plot which, in focusing on her transgressive sexual desires, offers the stimulation she seeks as an antidote to the monotonous conditions of bourgeois domesticity.[11]

A discussion of the middle-class ideology of proper femininity and its effect on the shopgirl's romance plot must take into account the expansive influence of Victorian moral standards for feminine propriety and the observance of social norms for conduct, whether public or private. Moral practice, as the English middle classes imagined it throughout much of the nineteenth century, encompassed a complex set of codes for regulating both the private self and the public sphere of social interaction.[12] As nineteenth-century conduct books and etiquette manuals reveal, middle-class women occupied an instrumental social position as upholders of propriety within the family and the home; in turn, their influence within the family was imagined to have wide-ranging effects outside the family circle, as the boys whom they educated went out into the public realm and the girls reproduced the ideals of motherhood and domesticity in miniature.[13] The insistence upon women's central role as arbiters of the morality of the family and the nation meant that, as Leonore Davidoff and Catherine Hall have argued, "canons of respectability" developed over the course of the nineteenth century. These injunctions for respectable individual and social behavior depended on an intricate set of practices (ranging from personal cleanliness, modesty, and domestic manners to language, speech, and social behavior) which, if properly maintained, would reproduce one's access to gentility and middle-class status.[14] In the case of *The Odd Women*, Monica Madden's failure to maintain such practices once she leaves behind the shop for the domestic sphere results both from a lapse in her education in normative femininity, such that she lacks the proper degree of moral instruction, and from her inability to censor her inappropriate emotions. Her failure to domesticate her desire in keeping with the ideology of proper femininity is figured through her lapse in concentration during a church service: she performs her religious observances "mechanically," with a "preoccupied look" that soon reveals the true focus of her attentions, the "adventure" of a budding romance with an older gentleman (33). The scenic remembrances of the "reverie" (36) which takes the place of the sermon operate in accordance with the structure of the romance plot, although in this case the object of Monica's desire will repeatedly fail to measure up to the fantasy.

For Gissing, Monica represents the financial and social aspirations of the upwardly mobile middle classes, but her history also suggests a critique of the inappropriate upbringing received by many young women, who lack both domestic skills and professional training. The untimely death of Dr.

Madden throws his daughters on their own resources, as their father had never made the transition from social respectability to financial security. Alice and Virginia, the two eldest sisters and the novel's most pathetic odd women, are forced to take employment in the homes of others, the former as a governess, the latter as companion to a gentlewoman. Three of their sisters die quintessential Victorian female deaths (one of consumption, another of suicide resulting from "brain trouble [and] melancholia," and the third "drowned by the overturning of a pleasure boat" [12]), while the youngest, Monica, resorts to employment in a shop, first as an apprentice to a draper in Weston, then at a large London firm. The drapery establishment—a business which generally sold bolts of cloth as well as ready-made garments and accessories—was the primary site for popular perceptions of the shopgirl's employment. This focus on clothing and fabrics seems to derive from the notion that shop employees, especially women, sold primarily luxury goods, or at least goods which could signify the class status of their wearers. There are many fewer stories of shopgirls employed in grocery shops or florists, for example, perhaps because these goods were less in the public eye as signifiers of wealth and luxury consumption. In keeping with the contemporary perception of the shopgirl as herself part of the display of merchandise, it is Monica's appealingly oxymoronic "dark and bright-eyed" (3) beauty (in contrast to her elder sisters' "unhealthy" [10] homeliness), rather than any gift for selling, that fits her for a position in the public eye: "To serve behind a counter would not have been Monica's choice if any more liberal employment had seemed within her reach. She had no aptitude whatever for giving instruction; indeed, had no aptitude for anything but being a pretty, cheerful, engaging girl. [. . .] In speech and bearing Monica greatly resembled her mother; that is to say, she had native elegance" (12).

From the outset, the novel positions Monica as a young woman who longs for "liberal" employment, here so unspecified as to suggest the vague alternatives (or lack thereof) offered to middle-class women with little practical training. Monica's difficulty in finding suitable employment stems from her unfinished education in middle-class femininity: in the hands of her guardians she is made "half a lady and half a shopgirl" (120). In one sense, Gissing's version of the shopgirl varies little from countless others: women who worked behind the counter were imagined to need no other talent or education than that of the ability to "engage" their customers. Monica's "native elegance," however, sets her apart from the other, "coarse" (51) and "vulgar" (54), women who work in the shop; the desire to maintain this "native" difference in class pervades Monica's experience throughout the novel. As others (most markedly her future husband, Edmund Widdowson) often remark, she is "no representative shopgirl"

(273), symbolically representing the extraordinary rather than the ordinary in character and manners. She brings to the role the "refinement" (75) of one born a "lady" (134), a term which in this novel signifies a certain gentility of character that separates Monica from the working-class girls with whom she lives. Gissing's depiction reflects the following perception, taken from a chapter entitled "In the Street," of an 1897 etiquette guide for young ladies of the middle and upper classes:

> [T]here is a quiet self-possession about the gentlewoman, whether young or old, that marks her out from women of a lower class, whose manner is florid. This is perhaps the best word to describe the lively gestures, the notice-attracting glance and the self-conscious air of the underbred, who continually appear to wish to impress their personality upon all they meet. [. . . While] a delicate sense of self-respect keeps [the well-bred woman] from contact with her neighbors in train or omnibus [. . .] the woman of the lower classes may spread her arms, lean up against her neighbour, or in other ways behave with a disagreeable familiarity[.][15]

In this passage, as in other depictions of women in public, class is defined by the bodily occupation of space. We might note that, while this guide to manners for the "really nice girl"[16] delineates the differences between middle- and lower-class women, it also serves the pedagogic purpose of effacing those differences even as it tries to maintain them. Remarkably, then, this etiquette guide subverts its own principles of inherent class difference through cultural pedagogy in feminine gentility, just as Gissing will subvert his own narrative of Monica's "native" elegance through the focus on the shameful quality of her desire. For Gissing, Monica comes to represent the aspiration to perform moral norms that are supposed to be inherent: in the early chapters her ability to signify her compliance with such norms forms an innate and essential aspect of her "nature," although she goes on to struggle with this compliance in later chapters.

The shop in which she is employed, like other establishments represented in social reform texts and popular fictions from this period, continually threatens Monica's "native" moral qualities, her honor (sexual chastity as well as integrity), honesty, and dignity. The chapter entitled "Monica's Majority," signifying her entry into femininity and adulthood, constructs the shop as the site of sexual and social license:

> In the drapery establishment where Monica Madden worked and lived it was not (as is sometimes the case) positively forbidden to the resident employees to remain at home on Sunday; but they were

strongly recommended to make the utmost possible use of that weekly vacation. Messrs. Scotcher and Co. acted like conscientious men in driving them forth immediately after breakfast, and enjoining upon them not to return until bedtime. By way of well-meaning constraint, it was directed that only the very scantiest meals (plain bread and cheese, in fact) should be supplied to those who did not take advantage of the holiday. (27)

Gissing's satiric depiction of these "large-minded men" and their "laudable regard for [the] health" (27) of their employees reveals his sympathy with the plight of young women driven away from their domestic habitations by the regulations of the living-in system. Moreover, Gissing suggests, the store's proprietors encourage the moral degradation of the young women through the latitude they allow their employees:

> Not only did they insist that the Sunday ought to be used for bodily recreation, but they had no objection whatever to their young friends taking a stroll after closing time each evening. Nay, so generous and confiding were they, that to each young person they allowed a latchkey. The air of Walworth Road is pure and invigorating about midnight; why should the reposeful ramble be hurried by consideration for weary domestics? (27)

The irony of this passage lies in its assumption of the reader's knowledge of Victorian codes for social and sexual propriety: young women of the higher classes were expected to be chaperoned on excursions into the city streets, and to "ramble" alone at midnight in the streets of London invariably implied one's similarity to those other "street-walkers" and "women of the night."[17] Indeed, Monica's association with several disreputable women in the context of the shop produces the metonymic link between her own desires for romantic fulfillment and the coded references to prostitution in the narrative of women walking the streets, unrestricted and unchaperoned.

Gissing's critique of the shop as a site of class degradation rather than ascendance centers on the social status of the shop assistant: in his description, few "ladies" work in the shop, and most employees are country women, the "dreadfully ignorant" daughters of small farmers (39), whom Monica habitually views as far below herself in moral and social position. These women are personified by the figure of Miss Eade, a "showily-dressed, rather coarse-featured girl" (51) who loiters in the streets, either pursuing Mr. Bullivant, a "mere counter-man" (54), or pestering Monica as to his whereabouts (51–52). Miss Eade is marked with the stereotypical attributes of the "ordinary" (read working-class) female employee: her voice "could not [be] more distinctive of a London shop-girl" (51). When, late in the novel, Monica encounters her in that other overdetermined public space of sexual and financial exchange, the railway station, the marked change in Miss Eade's appearance shocks the shopgirl-heroine into recognition: "Monica was confronted by a face which she at once recognized, though it had changed noticeably in the eighteen months since she last saw it. The person was Miss Eade, her old acquaintance at the shop. But the girl no longer dressed as in those days: cheap finery of the 'loudest' description arrayed her form, and it needed little scrutiny to perceive that her thin cheeks were artificially reddened" (341).

In this description, Gissing highlights the association of artificial face color and prostitution, encouraging readers to surmise along with Monica the turn Miss Eade's life has taken since leaving the shop.[18] Perhaps one of the most shocking, because destabilizing, elements of the shopgirl-turned-prostitute figure here is her ability to (almost) pass, to go (almost) *un*recognized; indeed, a complex series of codes for fashion and feminine beauty must be decoded to read her attire and appearance correctly. Of course, as nineteenth-century social theorists of prostitution suggested, the prostitute might also go unrecognized because of the change in her moral state, marked as physical deterioration: in the words of William Tait, "The effects of sin are not more plainly and fearfully displayed on any class of human beings than on fallen and decayed prostitutes. [. . .] The friends with whom they associated only a short time before, are now unable to recognize them."[19] In this context, the fallen shopgirl occupies a synecdochic relationship to the goods she sells, standing in for the display merchandise typically sold in shops marketing apparel and accessories. Monica's suspicion regarding her acquaintance's new trade is further strengthened by Miss Eade's explanation of the reasons she can be found loitering in the public spaces of the railway station: she claims to be awaiting the arrival of her brother by train, but (as the reader discovers), one man appears to be as good as another in this case: "Long after Monica's disappearance she strayed about the platform and the approaches to the station. Her brother was slow in arriving. Once or twice she held casual colloquy with men who also stood waiting—perchance for their sisters; and ultimately one of these was kind enough to offer her refreshment, which she graciously accepted" (343).

Miss Eade, this "public woman" whose showy dress and manner reveal the marks of her class difference, finds her counterpart in Amy Drake, the center of "shameful" (96) rumors about Everard Barfoot's history and the instigator of his disinheritance. Miss Drake, a working-class girl employed in a country shop and taken for an innocent, "spiritual young person,"

reveals herself to be "a reprobate of experience" and a "rascal" (107); as
Barfoot tells it, she "simply threw herself" (315) into his arms on a railway journey, occupying a solitary carriage with him and going to rooms
for the afternoon, then demanding that he marry her to forestall the "awk-
ward" consequences (108). His refusal to do so, and his identification of
her as a young woman of such "thoroughly bad character" ("she was a—
I'll spare you the word") marks him as a scoundrel and results in Mary's
disillusionment regarding his own morality; for the novel's metaphorics,
however, Barfoot's story thrusts responsibility for the sexual encounter
firmly on the shoulders of the working-class girl who, we are meant to
understand, knew what she was doing in her attempt to "get [him] into
her power" (316). In Gissing's depiction of women such as Miss Eade and
Amy Drake, working-class women with the sort of "animal nature" (67)
more virtuous (middle-class) women want to resist, the exercise of female
sexuality and desire, and its use for the purposes of power and financial
gain, becomes intimately linked to a debased class identity. The
metonymic link between the shopgirl and the prostitute suggests that
women who succumb to sexual instinct and physical desire reveal the
class-bound aspects of their nature at the expense of their ability to fully
inhabit the normative standards for proper feminine signification.

The atmosphere and living conditions of the shop result in health
problems as well as moral degradation in Gissing's conception, reflecting
an increasing public concern with the work experience of "sweated" shop
employees. Monica details the inequities she undergoes at the establishment, consisting mainly of exhausting work with little sustenance and
almost no rest. The assistants are allowed twenty minutes for each meal,
"'but at dinner and tea one is very likely to be called into the shop before
finishing. If you are long away you find the table cleared'" (38). In a discussion with Rhoda Nunn, her prospective employer and the book's feminist heroine, Monica describes the health problems of the staff, due in
part to being unable to sit down while behind the counter:

> "We suffer a great deal from that. Some of us get diseases. A girl has
> just gone to hospital with varicose veins, and two or three others
> have the same thing in a less troublesome form. Sometimes, on
> Saturday night, I lose all feeling in my feet; I have to stamp on the
> floor to be sure it's still under me."
>
> "Ah, that Saturday night!"
>
> "Yes, it's bad enough now; but at Christmas! There was a week or
> more of Saturday nights—going on to one o'clock in the morning.
> A girl by me was twice carried out fainting, one night after another."
> (38)

Without an early closing day, and with only a week's vacation in the year, the assistants experience multiple hardships but can do little to promote reform, and yet there are many waiting to take their place if they give notice or lose their positions. No woman is of any "particular importance[;] fifty, or for the matter of that, five score, young women equally capable could be found to fill [the] place" (71). Gissing's focus on the insufficient nature of the "benefits" provided for shop assistants, and the resulting dangers to their moral life, reflects the deprivation revealed in investigations and legislation against the shop system during the years preceding the publication of the novel.[20]

Throughout *The Odd Women,* Monica's choices are shaped by the decision to experience physical degradation on the one hand or moral degradation on the other: her "inherent" moral integrity repeatedly results in her choice of the former at the cost of her bodily strength. After leaving the shop, she attends the business school run by Mary Barfoot and Rhoda Nunn for only a short time before experiencing a physical breakdown, diagnosed as the consequence of "overstrain at her old employment," involving "nervous collapse, hysteria, general disorder of the system" (119). Unsurprisingly, the deplorable work conditions of the shop result in bodily suffering for those who "slave" behind the counter; in the case of female assistants, this suffering is framed as that most prevalent of late Victorian female maladies, hysteria[21]—here, however, described as chaos, a dis-ordering of the healthy worker's body-as-system. The implications of this collapse, as they appear in Gissing's critique of shop life, suggest not only that the quest for capital and power by store owners results in the decay of those exploited laborers who support the system, but also that middle-class workers (especially women, with their intimate connection to leisure and their struggle to identify appropriate "industry"), bored to the limits of resistance, will ultimately reject the degrading experience of their labor through a self-induced malady. Gissing imagines this resistance through illness to be the province of the middle-class shopgirl; the working poor could not be imagined to have the leisure, as it were, to bodily oppose their exploitation.[22]

Surprisingly, Gissing's novel provides little in-depth analysis of the actual labor involved in shop work; this absence is striking in light of his research into various other trades depicted in his fictional writings (the nascent field of advertising in *In the Year of Jubilee,* or journalism in *New Grub Street,* to name a few examples). Unlike H. G. Wells, who had himself worked as a draper's assistant and represented this experience in literary form in his 1905 novel *Kipps,* Gissing had little practical exposure to shop life and labor, and neglected to include more than a cursory glance at the tasks which occupied the workers' ten- to twelve-hour days. The contemporary accounts analyzed in the previous chapters, however, provide a preliminary sense of the kind of labor performed by shop assistants on a daily basis. In addition to showing merchandise to customers and on occasion modeling particular items, shop workers were expected to keep the counter tidy, to attend to the condition and supply of stock, and even to do light cleaning within the store; they could then proceed to work behind the cash register, or with the appropriate degree of skill (combined with good fortune) might eventually become forewomen or directors of showrooms.[23] Through their exposure to and experience with the vicissitudes of fashion and female adornment, shop assistants were imagined to gather invaluable knowledge for future enterprise; with the all-important access to capital, a clever young woman might set herself up in the dressmaking or millinery business.[24] In this novel, however, in order to construct the critique of conventional marriage that occupies the remainder of the plot, Gissing offers us few positive images of female shop experience. Instead, he focuses on the boredom produced by Monica's experience of working life, choosing to elaborate the causal relation between this experience and her subsequent actions.

Monica's labor fails to satisfy her desire for "change" (81) and adventure, instead stimulating her to seek pleasurable diversion in the public spaces of London. In the scenario of the shop, monotony and tedium combine in the experience of labor to produce a desire for leisure activity; the result is boredom, a longing for what one has not and a rejection of what one has, a desire that is not a desire. As Patricia Meyer Spacks has suggested in her analysis of the normalization of boredom in the Victorian era, the experience of boredom, which Martin Waugh describes as a "complex stalemate between fantasy, impulse, and threat," serves as a "negative impetus for action [and] an impulse for narrative."[25] In a similar fashion, boredom produces the desire to consume, whether fantasy plots or leisure entertainments, in both *The Odd Women* and *Of Human Bondage,* the novel to which I now turn. There are important differences in the class definitions of the shopgirls in each plot, however. Whereas in Gissing's text the story of the middle-class shopgirl forms just one of several threads which drive the plot, for Somerset Maugham the story of the working-class shopgirl becomes the more explicit center, the defining component from which Philip Carey structures his sense of self and his own access to middle-class status.

Maugham represents the working-class shopgirl's desire as overwhelming, producing a character who "naturally," because of the influence of her body over her actions, opts for moral rather than physical deterioration, although physical decay follows moral decay in this instance. With her false gentility and her shameless, vulgar sexuality (the latter resembling the "animal nature" which characterizes working-class women in Gissing's novel), Mildred Rogers serves as a means of figuring the deviant, impoverished, working-class self that Philip Carey wants to leave behind; it is only at the end of the novel, when Mildred is written out of the narrative, that the hero can fully inhabit the norms of middle-class selfhood and his distance from the version of identity and experience which she represents. In essence, it is Mildred's failure to mimetically represent middle-class social status, figured through her rejection of the conventional ending to the romance plot, that facilitates and reconfirms the class-based narrative of the novel.

Among the "odd women" who occupy Philip Carey's social and sexual world in Maugham's novel—including Miss Wilkinson, the aging governess; Fanny Price, the failed painter who commits suicide; Norah Nesbit, the popular novelist; and Sally Athelny, the country-born shopgirl with whom Philip will eventually find happiness—Mildred Rogers receives the most negative critical treatment. Contemporary critics found her "repugnant"[26] and "detestable";[27] more recently, scholars have labeled her "capriciously feminine,"[28] "despicable,"[29] "an odious creature [. . .] one of the most hateful, disagreeable female characters in fiction."[30] To be sure, Maugham produces her as such: with her pathetic attempts to mimic the mannered gentility of the middle and upper classes, Mildred would not be likely to appeal to all readers. In Maugham's construction, she coalesces a particular set of middle-class anxieties centering on the potential upward mobility of the working-class shopgirl, anxieties which engage and produce assumptions about the nature of working women's desire (vulgar) and pleasure (shameless). My reading of this novel takes Mildred as an example of the implicit dangers posed to shopgirls like Monica Madden, women from middle-class backgrounds who risk moral degradation through their association with working-class desire. In Mildred's case, that desire is explicitly figured as boredom: the state of being bored—or otherwise dissatisfied with the domestic ideology of proper femininity—produces Mildred's descent into prostitution, the literal figuration of what was only a metonymic connection in *The Odd Women*.

In choosing to employ Mildred as a tea-shop waitress, Maugham draws on an already existing social type to define her character and experience. As Barbara Drake's 1913 investigation for the Women's Industrial Council on the lives and working conditions of tea-shop employees suggests, "of the many varieties of the working girl there is none better known to the casual observer than the waitress of the friendly tea-shop, or none less known [. . .] to the critical student of social problems."[31] Drake's description of the class position of these working women, however, differs a great deal from Maugham's: while it becomes clear that the novelist views the tea-shop girl as firmly aligned with the working classes in her manner and character—through her employment and her residence in a lower-class suburb, her pretense to gentility and her underlying commonness in speech and behavior—the social investigator suggests that she might occupy any number of places in the social scale, from factory worker to shop assistant to daughter of a tradesman; some might even be ladies "by birth and breeding" (115). The characteristic all waitresses share, however, Drake claims, is a desire to marry: "She is, without exception, a marrying girl. To the work-girl of eighteen, who means to marry and to marry well, the tea-shop has something of the fascination of the ballroom for the leisured young lady of another class" (116). And, as Maugham's novel suggests, the possibility that the tea-shop girl will succumb to "the obvious temptations of her trade" (125) is a constant danger:

> [T]o a pretty and pleasure-loving girl the temptation is great to accept the presents from customers, over and above the regulation tip, which are never long in forthcoming. [. . .] Three or four girls, out of every staff of 12 or 14 [. . .] are said to be taken out or otherwise treated by customers. The drive in the taxi, the dinner at the restaurant, the excitement of the theatre, sweet flatteries and pretty things, after a long day in the tea-shop the delights of the evening out are almost irresistible. (125–26)

In both fictional and historical descriptions, the tea-shop girl occupies a role which, through her sexualized relationship to men and her negotiation of the economic necessities of work and marriage, requires that she market herself as much as the goods she serves. In this sense she occupies a role similar to that of the shop assistant, and unlike the position held by other working women (factory workers, domestic servants) whose lives are less mediated by public encounters with men of a higher class. Hence, too, the injunction that her appearance reflect "the right stamp of bright healthy young womanhood": the qualities she is expected to offer as employment assets include "youth, a good manner, a tall figure, a sweet smile, a bright complexion, sound teeth, [and] a good constitution" (115–16).

Drake's description of the tea-shop girl's physical disposition marks a point of distinction with Maugham's narrative, one which is crucial to the way the author imagines her relationship to the male protagonist of his novel. When Philip, then a medical student, first sees Mildred, he finds nothing especially attractive in her appearance: "She was tall and thin, with narrow hips and the chest of a boy. [. . .] She was very anaemic. Her thin lips were pale, and her skin was delicate, of a faint green colour, without a touch of red even in the cheeks. [. . .] She went about her duties with a bored look."[32] After she snubs his attempts at flirtation, Mildred becomes the increasingly intriguing object of his desire: "He could not get her out of his mind. He laughed angrily at his own foolishness: it was absurd to care what an anaemic little waitress said to him; but he was strangely humiliated" (275). This humiliation prompts Philip to seek her out, and after repeated visits to the shop, her appearance becomes perversely attractive, even "curiously fascinating" to him (277). The repetition of his attraction to her skin, which has a "chlorotic color" that Philip likens to pea soup suggests the unnatural quality of his attraction to her. This abnormal desire emerges from several kinds of simultaneous attraction and revulsion, based at first on physical grounds: "[I]t seemed impossible to him that he should be in love with Mildred Rogers. He did not think her pretty[. . .]. He loathed and despised himself for loving her" (283, 291). Philip's masochistic attraction has an element of class-based anxiety: he loves, and hates himself for loving, a woman whom he views as dreadfully "common" and from whom he wants to distance himself in class and sexual terms:

> Her phrases, so bald and few, constantly repeated, showed the emptiness of her mind; he recalled her vulgar little laugh at the jokes of the musical comedy; and he remembered the little finger carefully extended when she held her glass to her mouth; her manners, like her conversation, were odiously genteel. (283)

In contrast to Monica Madden, Mildred explicitly tries and fails to reproduce the signifying qualities of middle-class gentility. Indeed, Philip laughs scornfully at her attempts to distinguish herself from other working women, her inability to bear coarse language, her "passion for euphemisms"; he notes that "she scent[s] indecency everywhere," referring to trousers as "nether garments," and, thinking the action "indelicate," blows her nose "in a deprecating way" (291).

Mildred's attempts to mime the gentility of the upper classes are reminiscent both of the "false pride"[33] identified by M. Mostyn Bird as characteristic of the shopgirl's self-differentiation from factory workers or domestic servants, and of the pedagogical strategies used by writers of etiquette manuals and other guides for young women published during the nineteenth and early twentieth centuries. Mildred illustrates the presumed transparency of class identity as revealed through behavior and taste, an archaic formation dating from the early Victorian period. According to the author of an 1837 etiquette manual, vulgarity consists of "an inordinate desire to make people believe that you are of a higher rank or more refined

than you really are. [. . .] The waiting-maid bedecks herself in silks and
satins, that she may pass for a *lady*. The same feeling leads the half-bred
Miss to mince her words—to affect emotions which she never felt [. . .]
to be always in ecstasies is both unnatural and vulgar."[34] Likewise, an 1861
manual entitled *Etiquette for All* enjoins readers to at once avoid "majestic
and ridiculous airs" and a "loud and vulgar manner," and *Girls and Their
Ways*, an 1881 book "for and about Girls, by One Who Knows Them,"
provides numerous hints on cultivating modesty and details various "faults
to be avoided."[35] Mildred reproduces the negative effects of the failure to
heed these warnings, particularly through the lens of Philip's class bias: her
"odious" manners reveal the degraded signifying status of the term "genteel" in late Victorian culture.[36] Mildred's transparent failure to reproduce
true gentility reveals that gentility by nature involves performance, and
foregrounds the paradoxical project of etiquette manuals which promise to
recreate a supposedly inherent class affiliation in their readers. Moreover,
her inability to adequately meet normative standards for proper femininity is tied to the debasement of her desire, itself produced through her
experience of shop life and labor. For Philip, Mildred's failure to reproduce
gentility provokes the "odious" revelation of her "vulgar" nature, here
imagined as a signifier of her affiliation with the working classes.

The Failed Marriage Plot: Sex, Stimulation, and Shame

> By far the greater portion of the young ladies (for they are no longer
> *women*) of the present day, are distinguished by a morbid listlessness
> of mind and body, except when under the influence of stimulus, a
> constant pining for excitement, and an eagerness to escape from
> everything like practical and individual duty.[37]

This observation, written by Sarah Stickney Ellis in 1839, describes the
enduring nineteenth-century perception that young "ladies"—differentiated from "that estimable class of females who might be more specifically
denominated *women*"—embodied a tremendous susceptibility to the
vagaries of desire (6, 7). Ellis's solution to the feminine longing for excitement involves the production of domestic "influence" as a form of morally and socially sanctioned labor, here read as a "duty" that is reconceived
as pleasure in presiding over the private sphere of the home. Ellis focuses
her attention on "the cultivation of *habits*" in the practice of domestic life,
arguing that such an attention will counter the risk of moral lassitude (11,
emphasis in original). In the case of the shopgirl-heroines of the novels I
have been discussing, however, the unregulated social context of the shop

leads to the incomplete production of the habits associated with moral character, so much so that these young women are unable to resist their desire for stimulation. In this section, I read the effects of the shopgirl's failure and resistance to reproduce the norms of proper femininity as moments in the reshaping of her desire as shame, arguing that Gissing and Maugham imagine such desire as intimately linked to the sexed and classed identity of the shopgirl. For both Gissing and Maugham, the boredom produced by the shop results in the desire to seek stimulation elsewhere, whether through the acting out of a fantasized romance plot or through the urban amusements of the masses. The two novels treat that desire rather differently, however, according to the class affiliation of their shop-girl-heroines. In Gissing's novel, the banality of the shopgirl's working life effects a transition from the public sphere of the shop to the domestic sphere of marriage, since Monica's ramblings in the recreational spaces of the city lead to her encounter with her future husband, Edmund Widdowson. For Maugham, by contrast, Mildred's excessive desire for pleasure is reflected in the false marriage and other economic and sexual transactions by which her encounters with men are structured. In this sense, both authors offer a critique of marriage that nonetheless positions the shopgirl as the agent through which social identity and sexual desire are negotiated. These fictional narratives of the shopgirl stop short of imagining an alternative type of plot or mode of romantic identification which would counter the narrative of the shopgirl's shameful (or shameless) desire.

For Gissing, a critical aspect of Monica Madden's desire to wander about "with an adventurous mind" (42) is the reckless pleasure she experiences as a result of this respite from the circumscribed rhythms of the shop. Although her inherent (though endangered) proper femininity at first allows her to resist the temptations represented by one of her roommates in the shop dormitory—a woman with a "morally unenviable reputation" (54) who receives money with mysterious ease and who relates anecdotes so "scandalous" (54) other women are brought to earnest verbal protest—the fact that Monica obtains pleasure from solitary wanderings in the streets of the city threatens to compromise her access to middle-class propriety, assimilating her with her fellow shopgirls. This threat is made manifest in her encounter with a stranger in Battersea Park (42), a man of means who has all the appearances of a gentleman, but with whom she is unsure how to conduct herself, as they lack access to the conventional aspects of courtship such as a formal introduction and prescribed units of time for the playing out of their romance.[38] When she promises to meet him for a second time, she feels a mixture of shame, confusion, and recklessness: "[T]he knowledge of life she had gained in London assured her that in thus encouraging a perfect stranger she was doing a very hazardous thing" (42). The "hazards" involved in this encounter are tied to the transgression of the rituals of courtship, but also provide her with the pleasurable thrill of moral and social risk.

Monica's desire for an alternative to the exhaustion and tedium of shop life, brought on by the physical "disorder" she experiences as a result of her labor, produces her marriage to the gentlemanly stranger, Edmund Widdowson. This event, the typical conclusion to the romance plot, removes her from the "slavery" of shop labor and its alternative, the boredom of clerkship; however, for Gissing, this act merely places her within another form of institutional bondage. After their honeymoon, Monica begins to learn that her husband's cautious and methodical nature extends even more strongly to the sphere of her own conduct: he wishes her to remain at home, fulfilling his ideal for proper wifely and womanly conduct. In the early days of their marriage, Monica, approximating the middle-class domestic ideal, is content to follow Widdowson's prescribed routine for her education and employment, voiced as follows:

> Woman's sphere is the home, Monica. Unfortunately girls are often obliged to go out and earn their living, but this is unnatural, a necessity which advanced civilization will altogether abolish. You shall read John Ruskin; every word he says about women is good and precious. If a woman can neither have a home of her own, nor find occupation in any one else's she is deeply to be pitied; her life is bound to be unhappy. I sincerely believe that an educated woman had better become a domestic servant than try to imitate the life of a man. (173)[39]

Monica's resistance to Widdowson's demands is founded on the monotony she views as characteristic of marriage and domestic life: she wishes to exercise a moderate "freedom of movement" (174), liberty in her reading practices, friendship, and conversation, in all of which Widdowson attempts to exert his authority to restrict her choices. Most of all she longs for variety, the "change" that the society of people other than her husband would provide. A short while after their marriage, as a result of the increased stultification of her solitary life, she again falls ill; this "disorder," similar to the one she experienced while at the shop, subjects her to dramatic variations in emotion: "Her temper was strangely uncertain; some chance word in a conversation would irritate her beyond endurance, and after an outburst of petulant displeasure she became obstinately mute. At other times she behaved with such exquisite docility and sweetness that Widdowson was beside himself with rapture" (179). Gissing's description of Monica's shifting temperament in this passage suggests that her bodily disorder, metaphorically linked to the allegedly "disorder[ly]" domestic management which Widdowson attempts to discipline, is again a way of resisting the monotony of her everyday life.

Monica's moments of "docility and sweetness" represent the Ruskinian ideal against which she struggles, and her petulance and irritation mark her frustration with the conventional marital union. Indeed, the doctor who examines her upon the onset of this second malady asks questions regarding Monica's "mode of life": "Did she take enough exercise? Had she wholesome variety of occupation?" At such questions "Widdowson inwardly rage[s]" (179), for they reveal Monica's failure/resistance to approximate the virtuous "influence" of the proper middle-class woman, a behavioral mode repeatedly figured as work in nineteenth-century manuals on women's domestic labor.[40] In contrast to Sarah Stickney Ellis's position expressed fifty years earlier in her guide to conduct, *The Daughters of England,* it is the lack of *variety* of occupation that marks Monica's resistance to the monotony of the conventional marriage bond. Ellis contends that "It is this waiting to be interested, or amused, by anything that may chance to happen, which constitutes the great bane of a young woman's life, and while dreaming on in the most unprofitable state, without any definite object of pursuit, their minds become prey to a whole host of enemies, whose attacks might have been warded off by a little wholesome and determined occupation."[41] The critical difference between Ellis's description of interest as a substitute for desire and another version of interest as a sign of outwardly directed feeling (as Patricia Spacks argues is the case in earlier novels by Maria Edgeworth and Susan Ferrier)[42] is the self/other relation that structures the production of the shopgirl's desire. The problematic of desire created by Gissing's narrative lies in the inability of his heroine to direct her "interest" into the regulated marital/domestic sphere.

In arguing for increased liberty and freedom of choice in her marriage, Monica has recourse to comparisons with women's labor outside the home in order to highlight the necessity of healthy stimulation and variety to a successful relationship. Drawing on the confidence gained from her brief exposure to the women of Great Portland Street, Monica argues against inventing drudgery for the sake of duty:

> "I wish to do my duty," she said in a firm tone, "but I don't think it's right to make dull work for oneself, when one might be living. I don't think it *is* living to go on week after week like that. [. . .] Work is work, and when a woman is overburdened with it she must find it difficult to weary of home and husband and children all together. But of course I don't mean to say that my work is too hard. All I mean is, that

I don't see why anyone should *make* work, and why life shouldn't be as full of enjoyment as possible." (185)

In essence, Monica argues, once one has attained the ability to leave behind the boredom of working life, one should not impose on oneself the dullness of domestic work invented simply as an alternative to idleness. In demanding the freedom to "make more friends," to "hear people talk," and (with the greatest emphasis) to "read a different kind of book [. . .] that would really amuse [her] and give [her] something [to] think about with pleasure" (186), Monica claims the importance of producing "interest" rather than industry, pleasure rather than dutiful domestic labor. This effort marks her resistance to earlier Victorian norms for virtuous feminine influence and her desire to direct her "interest" to the fulfillment of her own pleasure rather than toward the happiness of others. Indeed, it is shortly after this scene that Widdowson, finding her reading "a novel with a yellow back" (187), suggests instead she take up *Guy Mannering*. The yellow-back novel reflects Monica's "degraded" literary tastes, signaling both popular paperback fiction and the writing associated with French literature and with the decadent culture of the 1890s, of which the short-lived periodical *The Yellow Book* was a self-proclaimed example. [43] It is Monica's resistance to Widdowson's commanding advice regarding her choice of reading matter that becomes a major point of contention between husband and wife.

Gissing implicitly compares the "slavery" (34) of shop life to the "bondage" (255) Monica experiences in her marriage, both sites which pathologize the shopgirl and render her unable to replicate the normative structures for feminine propriety. The marital union itself reflects the perversion of domestic ideology which ensues when the shopgirl attempts to approximate the ideal for womanly behavior:

> Every day the distance between them widened, and when he took her in his arms she had to struggle with a sense of shrinking, of disgust. The union was unnatural; she felt herself constrained by a hateful force when he called upon her for the show of wifely tenderness. [. . .] She thought with envy of the shop-girls in Walworth Road; wished herself back there. What unspeakable folly she had committed! (229–30)

Monica's interpretation of their relationship as "unnatural" results from her conviction that, despite cultural invocations to the contrary, woman should be a "free companion" to her husband, rather than his sexual and social "bondwoman" (230). Gissing's use of terms such as "slavery" and "bondage" to describe conventional Victorian marriage reveals his critique of the institution: the implicit link between the shop and the marital union is the metaphor of prostitution, in which women's bodies are exchanged for financial gain. In this sense Gissing's critique follows the trajectory taken up by dramatists like Cicely Hamilton and George Bernard Shaw, in which the strategy of associating marriage with prostitution becomes an effective method of arguing against women's economic and social exploitation.[44]

Without love or the sway of duty to induce her to continue their sexual relations, Monica turns away from the physical and moral degradation of her marriage and toward an idealized fantasy of romantic love. Monica's longing for stimulating intercourse as a contrast to the monotony of shop work or domestic life brands her with the stigma of adulterous desire, despite the fact that she never compromises the monogamous requirements of her marriage. Indeed, having entered into an affair with Bevis, a young wine merchant, under the influence of a fantasy circumscribed by the requirements of morally sanctioned romance, figured along the lines of the narrative of finding one's destined complement or soulmate, she experiences a "dreadful [. . .] disillusion" when this romance is revealed as an act of cowardice and vulgarity: "She had expected something so entirely different—swift, virile passion, eagerness even to anticipate her desire of flight, a strength, a courage to which she could abandon herself, body and soul. She broke down utterly [. . .]" (264). Bevis's failure to embody the romantic hero whose passion would ennoble rather than degrade her results in her discovery of the "shame" (260) and "ignominy" (281) which she views as characteristic of their affair.

Gissing's definition of female sexuality as shameful, all too close to the "animal nature" (67) of the "representative" (273) (working-class) shopgirl, provides a metonymic link with the public sites and subjects of this shaming desire. The spatial representation of Monica's shameful desire, first expressed in the street and in the neighborhood of the young man's flat, is the shop itself. When Bevis resolves to write her and tell her when to come to him, Monica confronts the necessity of finding some "obliging shopkeeper" (280) who might facilitate this exchange, not a difficult task. Although the commission is accepted by a "decent woman" (280) behind the counter, Monica emerges from the shop "with flushed cheeks," viewing this "ignomin[ious]" transaction as "another step in shameful descent" (281). The subterfuge of this encounter, combined with its very publicity, serves to make her "more hopelessly an outcast from the world of honourable women" (281). And it is shortly after this event that she returns home to find that Widdowson's detective has revealed her actions, although not their object: he denounces her behavior, attempting vainly to "sham[e] her guilt" (287) by comparing her (unfavorably, for lying) to "the prostitute in the street" (285). Widdowson's comparison is in fact an assimilation, in which Monica, the once extraordinarily moral, now all too "representative" shopgirl, metonymically becomes the ordinary woman who exchanges her body for "illicit" material gain and succumbs to expressive desire.

In *The Odd Women,* the narrative of vulgar desire and its class and sexual basis is obscured by the middle-class background of its shopgirl heroine. What might this narrative reveal if it centered on a working-class-identified shopgirl? Gissing hints at this possibility in Widdowson's encounter with a barmaid, that figure who represents the working-class-side of the service industry's class-demarcated border.[45] Just before discovering Monica's deception, Widdowson stops in a public house and meditates on the state of his marriage, comparing it with his own ideal:

> Whilst sipping at his glass of spirits, he oddly enough fell into talk with the barmaid, a young woman of some charms, and what appeared to be unaffected modesty. [. . .] Would he not have been a much happier man if he had married a girl distinctly his inferior in mind and station? Provided she were sweet, lovable, docile—such a wife would have spared him all the misery he had known with Monica. (272–73)

He continues, "My ideal of the wife perfectly suited to me is far liker [*sic*] that girl at the public house bar than Monica. Monica's independence of thought is a perpetual irritation to me" (273). In Widdowson, we find a man who, clearly unsympathetic in his treatment of his wife, nevertheless arouses readerly compassion in his self-representation as archaic in his desire for a simple "barmaid," a woman he views as his intellectual and social inferior. Gissing's pervasive concern with specifying and delimiting the appropriate type of marriage between two people here meets with a possibility unexplored in this novel.

The union between a middle-class clerk and a tea-shop girl—a woman not conventionally seen as occupying the same social class as the barmaid or the draper's assistant, but poised on the border between the two—receives a fuller depiction in Maugham's novel. Here, the shopgirl-turned-fallen woman represents the shift from shameful to shameless desire, from the world of "native" gentility to the world of falseness and vulgarity, thus revealing the anxieties produced over the threat she poses to entrenched systems of moral and sexual propriety. The fallen woman, as Judith Walkowitz has argued, functioned as a threat to Victorian networks of class and sexual propriety, representing "the permeable and transgressed border between classes and sexes" and serving as the "carrier of physical and moral pollution." In this discursive social formation, the prostitute became the repository of debased womanhood and social/sexual contamination, a polluted body which demanded regulation.[46] As in the case of Monica's longing for stimulation, symbolized by the romantic fantasies she constructs from fiction, the social and sexual risks associated with the desire for stimulation are embodied in Mildred's literalization of the shopgirl-prostitute narrative.

Having been disappointed in her romantic affair with Emil Miller, a quasi-bigamous relationship which parallels the familiar formula of women's victimization in the narratives of popular romance fiction, Mildred comes to view the world of sexual and economic exchange through hardened, pragmatic eyes. She treats her encounters with men as one of potential financial gain or loss, repeatedly evaluating her own exchangeability in the sexual marketplace. As she remarks to Philip after their first date, "Oh, if you don't take me out some other fellow will. I never need want for men who'll take me to the theatre" (281). When Philip proposes to her, Mildred responds in a manner taken from the novelettes which she reads voraciously: "I'm sure I'm very grateful to you, Philip. I'm very much flattered at your proposal. [. . . But] one has to think of oneself in these things, don't one? I shouldn't mind marrying, but I don't want to marry if I'm going to be no better off than what I am now. I don't see the use of it" (308–9). Mildred's focus on "use," her concern about the financial benefits of marrying Philip, here becomes a more coarse and callous version of the "lottery" detailed in so many nineteenth-century texts, fictional and critical.[47] In the hands of feminist writers of the same period like Cicely Hamilton and Charlotte Perkins Gilman, this strategy of pragmatic indifference appears the only option for women who have few employment opportunities and limited practical education.[48]

For Maugham, Mildred's resistance to marriage with Philip reflects her vulgar desire for wealth and her inability to let romantic ideals mask her sense of the practical elements of the sexual contract. Fascinated with her body and its functions, she views it as a productive object, whether of babies or of recompense for favors granted by men. When Philip assures her that she may depend on him for financial support until the birth of the child, she remarks, "You can't say I didn't offer anything in return for what you've done." This comment, with its implication of the only possession she has to offer, horrifies Philip; he cannot understand how she can treat her body so lightly, "as a commodity which she could deliver indifferently as an acknowledgment for services rendered" (358). To Mildred, however, all of her interactions with men are carefully calculated to give her the greatest benefit; whether her suitors provide her with food and entertainment or appease her "vulgar" appetites, she considers each one according to the extent to which he is able to satisfy her desire to consume and to appease the demands of her hypersexualized body.

Mildred's "vulgar" desire results in her moral and physical downfall, represented in the novel by her lapse into prostitution as the only career which will cater to her "natural" indolence and her trivial desire for idle pleasures. Like Gissing, Maugham spatializes Mildred's descent, metonymically associating her vulgar excesses with the public spaces of the city, the urban streets and amusement sites which become the province of the morally improper woman (likened to, if not actually practicing as, a prostitute). After her affair with his friend Griffiths, Mildred leaves Philip for the second time, and he does not reencounter her until, by chance, he sees her walking through Piccadilly Circus:

> She was crossing over from the corner of Shaftesbury Avenue and stopped at the shelter until a string of cabs passed by. She was watching her opportunity and had no eyes for anything else. She wore a large black straw hat with a mass of feathers on it and a black silk dress; at that time it was fashionable for women to wear trains; the road was clear, and Mildred crossed, her skirt trailing on the ground, and walked down Piccadilly. [. . .] She walked slowly along and turned down Air Street, and so got through to Regent Street. She walked up again towards the Circus. (455)

This passage, at first glance appearing to describe the actions and appearance of a woman innocently strolling through London's city streets, actually suggests the imminent collapse of Mildred's attempt to mimic the gentility associated with feminine propriety. The phrase "she was watching her opportunity" can be read as having another meaning than simply implying her wait for a safe passage across the crowded street: in light of Maugham's characterization of Mildred as a conniving, self-serving woman, out to satisfy her own interests before those of others, the sentence acquires new significance for the passage as a whole, marking this scene as one of commercial exchange. In addition, Mildred's apparently circular progress proves puzzling both for Philip and for readers, since "proper" (middle-class) Victorian women were understood to shirk the process of wandering, loitering, or rambling in the city. The next sentences, however, make Mildred's objective abundantly clear:

> She overtook a short man in a bowler hat, who was strolling very slowly in the same direction as herself; she gave him a sidelong glance as she passed. She walked a few steps more till she came to Swan and

Edgar's, then stopped and waited, facing the road. When the man
came up she smiled. The man stared at her for a moment, turned
away his head, and sauntered on. Then Philip understood. (455)

The scene of prostitution, here accomplished in front of a department
store (yet another hypersexualized site for the display of the female body),
marks women's experience of public spaces with the signs of visibility and
the rhetoric of immediate "recognition." Much like the scene from
Gissing's novel in which Monica recognizes the alternative to her experience in Miss Eade's manner, here Philip realizes all at once the depths to
which he imagines Mildred to have descended (and the corresponding distance he therefore holds from her experience). When, "overwhelmed with
horror" (455) at the evidence of her explicit self-prostitution, Philip confronts her, she at first attempts to conceal her actions, but then agrees to
take him to a room where they can talk—a dingy bedroom in a shabby
hotel which reflects the dishonor of her current occupation. There, Philip
continues his analysis of the visual signs of her descent, noting the clash
between the natural and the artificial in her appearance (reproducing the
visual rhetoric of fallen womanhood): "he saw now that Mildred's cheeks
were thick with rouge, her eyebrows were blackened; but she looked thin
and ill, and the red on her cheeks exaggerated the greenish pallor of her
skin" (456). This scene, lending a prosthetic, mannequin-like quality to
Mildred's body, marks her physical embodiment of the degrading narrative
associated with the working-class shopgirl.

Mildred's fall is reflected in her increasing desire to "acknowledge [the]
services rendered" through the use of her body, finally attempting to
seduce Philip outright:

[She] gave a soft, insinuating laugh. She sidled up to Philip and put
her arms round him. She made her voice low and wheedling.

"Don't be such an old silly. I believe you're nervous. You don't
know how nice I can be."

She put her face against his and rubbed his cheek with hers. To
Philip her smile was an abominable leer, and the suggestive glitter of
her eyes filled him with horror. He drew back instinctively. [. . .] But
she would not let him go. She sought his mouth with her lips. He took
her hands and tore them roughly apart and pushed her away. (494)

For Philip, who by now can only see her through the memory of her
lapse into prostitution, Mildred has become the most horrific kind of
woman he can imagine: coarse, self-interested, and degraded by her explicit and shameless sexual desire. Her transformation crucially occurs after his

own submission to physicality, and it is only when he is able to disavow his bodily desires that he can effect such a refusal. Maugham, however, refuses to imagine a disavowal or rejection of desire on Mildred's part; throughout the novel her "natural" character bubbles up from under her thin veneer of assumed middle-class gentility. Scenes which represent Mildred's anger at or rejection of Philip reveal her coarseness and lack of refinement, most evidently through moments when she lapses into the slang and "vulgar" speech associated with the un- or semieducated working classes.

Throughout the novel Mildred's vulgarity is filtered through Philip's perception, thereby disallowing an alternative reading of her behavior toward him. The striking exception is a short passage just preceding the above excerpt, a passage which provides readers with a first glimpse into Mildred's interior life. Here, as nowhere else in the novel, Maugham presents us with her version of recent events, including her humiliation at the fact that Philip has ceased to love her, and a description of her desire from her own perspective:

> She was the sort of woman who was unable to realize that a man might not have her own obsession with sex; her relations with men had been purely on those lines; and she could not understand that they even had other interests. [. . .] She suffered from pique, and sometimes in a curious fashion she desired Philip. [. . .] At last it became an obsession with her, and she made up her mind to force a change in their relations. He never even kissed her now, and she wanted him to: she remembered how ardently he had been used to press her lips. It gave her a curious feeling to think of it. She often looked at his mouth. (489–90, 491, 492)

Maugham's choice of the phrase "her [. . .] obsession with sex" reveals his construction of the working-class shopgirl from a middle-class point of view. For Maugham, Mildred's class is sexualized through the link between her false gentility and her appetite for amusement and pleasure, physical and otherwise; conversely, her sexuality is classed as base, excessive, and eminently "vulgar." Particularly in this passage, it becomes clear that Mildred Rogers is nothing more than a network of physical desires through which the monotonous events of her working-class life are filtered.

Here, too, Mildred's character contrasts starkly with the other shopgirl in the novel, Sally Athelny, the healthy, gentle country girl whom Philip will eventually plan to marry at the novel's end. Imbued with "natural" and unconscious sexuality in its positive form, Sally gives her body to Philip without resistance, commenting simply, "I always liked you" (617).

Although he claims he does not love her, he esteems her both physically and intellectually: "[H]e had a feeling for her which seemed to him ridiculous to entertain towards a shop-girl of nineteen: he respected her. And he admired her magnificent healthiness. She was a splendid animal, without defect; and physical perfection filled him always with admiring awe. She made him feel unworthy" (620–21).

Sally too is working-class, but represents the rural ideal of feminine innocence in contrast to Mildred's urban(e) degradation. While Mildred is marked through her physical imperfections, Sally embodies perfection of the social as well as the physical realm. In her ability to inspire admiration rather than perversity, Sally represents the possibility of class and sexual mobility for Philip, thereby allowing him to leave behind his class-bound history and effect the transformation of self which forms the center of his narrative.

Philip's attraction to Sally, described as a "soothing" feeling of companionship and respect (620), differs strongly from his relationship with Mildred, which by the end of the novel has decayed into a diseased state, symbolically represented by her afflicted body.[49] Mildred's seemingly inevitable relapse into her former occupation results in an unspecified (venereal) disease which Philip diagnoses gravely, "telling her of her own danger and the danger to which she expose[s] others" (558). Although his prescription has beneficial results, he suspects her of resorting again to prostitution to supplement her dwindling savings, and one day returns unobserved to confirm his suspicion:

> He fell back into the darkness and watched her walk towards him. She had on the hat with a quantity of feathers on it which he had seen in her room, and she wore a dress he recognized, too showy for the street and unsuitable for the time of year. He followed her slowly till she came into Tottenham Court Road, where she slackened her pace; at the corner of Oxford Street she stopped, looked round, and crossed over to a music hall. He went up to her and touched her on the arm. He saw that she had rouged her cheeks and painted her lips. (560)

This scene, occurring in front of a music hall, reveals the contemporary slippage over the practice of popular leisure, affiliating the shopgirl-prostitute with female members of the mass audience. Although she claims to be merely purchasing tickets for a show, Philip does not believe her, and when he confronts her with "It's criminal," she responds with "What do I care? Men haven't been so good to me that I need bother my head about them" (561). In this case, prostitution becomes more than just a way for Mildred

to make a living: bitter at her mistreatment at the hands of men, she considers this practice to be an implicit method of exacting revenge upon
those who support this trade in female bodies. Maugham does little to
explain why Mildred prefers selling herself to selling goods in a shop or
restaurant; rather, he characterizes her choice as arising out of her "natural
indolence" (491) and her desire to simply subsist on others' financial support rather than working for a wage. In this novel, the shopgirl-turned-
prostitute finds herself enslaved to the demands of her "nature" and the
culture of male desire through which she circulates. Of course, this
description of the prostitute's inherent moral lassitude, in which her labor
does not figure as such, predates Maugham by at least half a century.
William Acton, in *Prostitution Considered in Its Moral, Social, and Sanitary
Aspects, in London and Other Large Cities, with Proposals for the Mitigation
and Prevention of Its Attendant Evils,* describes the qualities which differentiate prostitutes from other women in his view: "Natural desire. Natural
sinfulness. The preferment of indolent ease to labour. Vicious inclinations
strengthened and ingrained by early neglect, or evil training, bad associates, and an indecent mode of life [. . .]. To this black list may be added
love of drink, love of dress, love of amusement[. . .]."[50]

Relegated to the sphere of vulgar passions, Mildred Rogers represents
another kind of failure: here, the romance plot fails to mask the economic conditions of marriage as the ultimate ending to the romance. Mildred
refuses to embody the pedagogic aspirations of the romance plot, instead
providing another kind of lesson in the consequences of a class-based lapse
in moral practice. Maugham's novel writes boredom as the effect of the
vulgar class position of its heroine, revealing her own "interest" to be self-
rather than other-directed. This inability to shape one's influence and
industry in the direction of the other, read as a failure to desire in an
appropriate manner, with the fitting object in view, confirms Mildred's
shameless resistance to moral and social norms for feminine behavior.

Coda: The Shopgirl as Romance Reader

The class-based narrative of the effects of romance reading suggested by
these two novels reveals the role such a leisure practice plays in the construction of the shopgirl's desire. Monica's fantasy of a romantic tryst with
Bevis, the young wine merchant, emerges from the romance fiction to
which she increasingly turns for solace and solitude:

> Sometimes the perusal of a love story embittered her lot to the last
> point of endurance. Before marriage, her love-ideal had been very

vague, elusive; it found scarcely more than negative expression, as a shrinking from the vulgar or gross desires of her companions in the shop. Now that she had a clearer understanding of her own nature, the type of man correspondent to her own natural sympathies also became clear. In every particular he was unlike her husband. She found a suggestion of him in books; and in actual life, already, perhaps more than a suggestion. (231)

Monica's susceptibility to "suggestion" and her "shameful" desire to act on the fantasy produced through reading the romance jeopardize her ability to act in accordance with moral norms for proper feminine behavior. Her moral if not literal fall occurs because she takes her reading too seriously, identifying too strongly with the heroine and inserting herself into a fantasy romance plot which absorbs her attention. The fact that she then reproduces this fantasy in her own life signals her inability to appropriately separate the real from the imaginary, and metonymically reframes that inability as bound to her insufficient practice of the habits of moral character.

Monica Madden and Mildred Rogers are simultaneously assimilated and differentiated through their leisure practices. Whereas Gissing's middle-class shopgirl, inherently unable to enjoy the pleasures offered to her fellow shop employees, opts for marriage and the fantasy of satisfaction through the idealized romance of absorbing fiction, Maugham's working-class shopgirl is more likely to satisfy the desires produced by her experience of everyday life and labor through "trivial" amusements. In Maugham's depiction, such products of the industry in mass entertainment—novelettes, music halls, and the like—cater to the shopgirl's craving for pleasure and "excitation," thereby working to vulgarize her all the more. Mildred's fondness for two-penny novelettes such as those written by Norah Nesbit under the pseudonym "Courtenay Paget" assimilates her to the status of the common service laborer. Mildred's comment, "I do like his books [. . .] they're so refined" (350) reminds Philip of Norah's self-description: "I have an immense popularity among kitchen-maids. They think me so genteel" (350). In representing the desires of the mass audience, Mildred reveals herself as "trivial" in several senses: she is one of the crowd, "to be found at every crossroads," associated with the banality of the vulgar everyday.[51] For Maugham as for Gissing, the inability to embody and thus perform one's acquiescence to such norms is figured through the inappropriate consumption of popular fiction. These authors understand the practice of popular reading to signify the moral and bodily risks faced by their heroines, risks constituted through the desire for a romantic plot that would not replicate the mundane conditions of ordinary life—that, in essence, would not be marked by the class-inflected failures of the romance.

CHAPTER 4

Imagining Alternatives to the Romance: Absorption and Distraction as Modes of Reading

All her spare time was given to novel-reading. [. . .] The girl's nature was corrupted with sentimentality, like that of all but every woman who is intelligent enough to read what is called the best fiction, but not intelligent enough to understand its vice. Love—love—love; a sickening sameness of vulgarity.[1]

Gissing's description of the effects of novel reading on Bella Royston, Miss Barfoot's strayed pupil and one of several "fallen" figures in *The Odd Women*, posits the romance novel as a cause of women's moral, intellectual, and emotional degradation. Having left the school in Great Portland Street to become the mistress of a married man, then abandoned and reduced to beggary, Miss Royston symbolizes the "vulgarity" of acting on illicit sexual desire; her actions, moreover, are imagined to be caused by her ability to identify with the female protagonist of the romance. Rhoda Nunn, Gissing's militant feminist figure, speculates that "women imagine themselves noble and glorious when they are most near the animals," and ventures to claim that "when she [Miss Royston] rushed off to perdition, ten to one she had in mind some idiot heroine of a book" (64). Rhoda's disgust at the sentimentalism and sensuality of these fictions reproduces a number of nineteenth-century discourses on reading practices and their effects on readers, newly conceived as a "public" since the 1840s and 1850s.[2] Critics and proponents of popular literature alike understood a causal relationship to exist between the intellectual, emotional, and moral occupation of reading and its physical effects. Many opponents of popular reading denounced the activity as unwholesome, harmful to the minds and bodies of those working- and lower-middle-class men and women who read sensational fiction and news stories, often the only cheap reading material to which they could easily gain access.[3] Supporters of reading as a leisure activity for the masses, by contrast, claimed that this practice, however sensational, kept them away from other, more tangible dangers and, through the force of contrast, taught them the value of "good" literature. Perhaps unsurprisingly, however, these factions concurred on the aims and objectives of expanding the popular readership: each group believed that the masses should be exposed to the "better" class of fiction, so that they might refocus their energies on moral and intellectual self-improvement. The rhetoric of building the self through wholesome reading emerges again and again in critical writings on leisure throughout the nineteenth century, and provides the prehistory for the late Victorian and Edwardian discourse on the reading habits of girls and young women analyzed in this chapter.

From the mid-1880s until the beginning of the First World War, a number of penny periodical publications, including novelettes and magazines targeted toward lower middle- and working-class consumers, flooded the market for cheap reading matter. Through tone and content, these periodicals created a virtual community of young female readers. This chapter contends that while the novelettes supplied these readers with a "ready-made" fantasy narrative of absorption which they might use to escape from the monotony of their working lives, the magazines produced a nonnarrative reading experience of distraction reflective of the "variety" entertainment that increasingly came to characterize popular leisure in the first decades of the twentieth century. My analysis consists of a brief account of the burgeoning market for popular reading matter and its focus on women as consumers of romance fiction; a discussion of contemporary middle-class accounts of the effects of reading on the female body; an examination of the workings of fantasy and identification in the romance plot; and an investigation of the correspondence (or lack thereof) between the world of fiction and the daily lives of the young female shop workers seen as the paradigmatic readers of popular romance fiction. The final section includes an analysis of several stories which featured shopgirls as heroines, stories which were thought to operate either as wish fulfillment narratives or object lessons for the women who read them. The chapter concludes by situating the model of distracted readership in the larger historical and cultural context of the popular leisure industry, comparing the more private experience of romance reading with the experience of public leisure practice in an increasingly consumer-oriented mass entertainment culture.

While a significant portion of my analysis examines a variety of historical accounts constructing the shopgirl as a consumer of popular romance fiction, the alternative model of reading I present here depends to some extent on imagining the potential relationship shopgirls might have had to the periodicals they consumed. Victorian and Edwardian shop assistants left few accounts of their experience of reading as a leisure practice, and even if such accounts did exist in significant numbers, they would provide only a limited perspective on the reading experience, and their presence would not mitigate the critical task of interpreting the institutional and discursive production of the shopgirl's consuming practices. It has therefore been necessary to undertake a careful analysis of existing documentation regarding contemporary perceptions of the shopgirl as a romance reader. Studying the mode of address of particular romance fictions—how the texts themselves construct a particular type of reader—has also proven useful as a strategy for illuminating the cultural context of women's reading in the late nineteenth and early twentieth centuries.

While contemporary accounts of women's reading describe a panorama of possible consumers of which shopgirls were only a portion, shopgirls are nonetheless a particularly useful population for an analysis of the workings of fantasy. The novelettes and magazines which form the subject of this chapter can be distinguished from earlier cheap publications in their reliance on the elements of a visually oriented display culture reflective of the spectacular environment of the luxury department store. The novelettes and magazines emphasize this atmosphere of fashion and display, encouraging their readers to consume the merchandise described and depicted in their pages. As a select portion of this readership trained in the mechanics of selling fantasy in a dress, shopgirls were directly addressed by these publications and therefore assist in the project of analyzing readerly experience during this period.

Moreover, the shopgirl's transitional class position places her at the center of a discourse of social mobility, providing a unique perspective on the significance of popular reading practices. Novelettes and magazines targeted to adolescent girls and women were consumed by working- and middle-class readers alike, implying a certain social mixing in the consumption of popular texts; the practice of middle- and upper-class women sharing their periodicals with servants provides one example of this exchange of reading material between women of different classes. Such publications were often marketed to a broad audience, but were still seen by some contemporaries as potential agents in the downward class mobility of their readers, so that middle-class readers might be at risk of occupying a similar position to their working-class counterparts. Because of the shopgirl's class transitionality, she comes to stand in for the paradigmatic or exemplary reader (often pejoratively conceived), mediating and legitimizing the class distinctions that were being simultaneously reproduced and leveled in the cheap periodical press.

In order to clarify my usage of generic terms, it is important to differentiate between several types of cheap periodicals discussed in this chapter. The phrase "cheap periodical" signifies any of the penny and halfpenny publications published during this period, including both the novelette and the magazine. Two other terms recur in turn-of-the-century accounts of popular reading, producing a generic slippage: these are the "serial" and the "weekly," both of which signify the practice of common practice of publishing "numbers" of a particular periodical. Contemporary commentators often grouped these together: both the novelette and the magazine are referred to as "serials," in that they were understood to follow one another in an identifiable sequence. They differ, however, in their treatment of fiction: while the novelette typically presented a "complete story every week," the magazine (often called a "paper" in light of its ephemeral quality) serialized its stories in installments which produced a deferral of the ultimate conclusion. Finally, since many of these periodicals incorporated the attractions of the romance plot, critics of women's reading tended to lump all such "degraded" products of popular culture together under the heading of "the romance," thereby facilitating the dismissal of a range of generic forms outright.

Partially as a result of this generic slippage, both the novelette and the magazine were clearly associated with and targeted to an audience of female consumers. The novelette, the epitome of nineteenth-century women's "trashy" reading, has a long history of association with feminine (or feminized) leisure practice. This type of popular fiction reproduces a formulaic romance plot, narrating the rise of a virtuous but lonely and often destitute young woman into the realm of the aristocracy through marriage and/or the discovery of noble birth. As such, the novelette was taken by contemporary critics to represent a mode of escape through fantasy. This argument suggests that the novelette produces readerly identification through absorption in the romance plot: the reader, subsumed in the sustained fictional narrative, loses touch with her everyday experience through the "wish-fulfillment" themes of wrongs avenged, desires fulfilled, and lovers reunited. We can locate a parallel to such absorption in the structure of the novelette: usually fourteen or sixteen pages of small print (approximately thirty thousand words), and published as "a complete story," the fictional material occupied nearly the entire text of the weekly serial, often accompanied by a column on fashion and society gossip and by advertisements for Beecham's Pills and other products claiming to refashion the female reader into the feminine ideal. The novelette facilitated a mode of readerly consumption dependent upon the disjunction from the mundane events of everyday life, a disjunction made possible by the production of a completed scene of reading: upon purchasing her new story for that week, the shopgirl-reader might spend an hour or two absorbed in the novelette and then return to her everyday life with these fictional fantasies intact in her mind.

By contrast, the new magazines targeted toward young unmarried working women, particularly the "girls" who worked in the shops and department stores of the new urban consumer culture, incorporated two or even three serialized stories in each week's number, accompanied by numerous "tit-bit"-style columns on dressmaking, employment, manners, and various leisure entertainments and the ubiquitous advertisements for a wide range of products. These magazines, with their emphasis on miscellanea and their fragmented structure, produced a new mode of reading characterized by contemporary critics as both feminine and working-class in nature. With their "cliff-hanger" aspect (in both the fiction and the miscellaneous columns), the magazines produced an experience of reading pleasure linked to the deferral of the conclusion, since each story took months to complete and new stories would be running in a staggered fashion in every issue. Much like shoppers who browse for the newest fashions with the intention of creating an entire outfit, readers of serialized fiction could consume their texts in a desultory manner, combining fashion advice, ads, and fiction to create their own fantasies. The subject matter of these magazines—narrating the adventures of mill-girls and madcaps, nuns and nurses, schoolgirls, female detectives, and circus performers— focused attention on alternatives to the romance plot of the novelettes while simultaneously attempting to negotiate their readers' desire for stories which would satisfy their adolescent longings for emotional and imaginative stimulation.

The two modes of readerly experience analyzed in this chapter derive from the formal structure of the periodicals themselves, but do not necessarily remain distinct in every instance. My analysis of the magazines posits an alternative model of distracted readership based on "variety," a cultural form which reflected the constitution of an increasingly commercialized urban culture based on leisure consumption. This alternative model suggests a greater permeability between the "real" or everyday world and the realm of fantasy, a permeability facilitated both by the form and content of these magazines. Nonetheless, we might also apply this model to the novelette, thereby opening up the possibility that shopgirl-readers might consume texts against the grain: in this reading the novelettes might leave a residue of imaginative energy that would allow for other imaginable plots and conclusions to the formulaic narratives presented therein. Indeed, the absorption and distraction models exist in dialectical tension with one another: the girls' and women's magazines reveal the other side of the fantasy-absorption of the novelettes, both forms producing the possibility of consuming in a fractured and distracted manner much like the process of shopping for luxury consumer goods. The shopgirl-readers who made up a portion of the target market for these periodicals might not be able to afford such luxury products in their everyday lives, but they could virtually attain them through the new mode of distracted consumption.

Gender, Class, and the Market:
Producing Popular Romance Fiction

As historians and literary critics have documented, the nineteenth century marked the growth of a mass reading public in England. Over the course of the century, literacy levels and access to cheap printed matter gradually increased, as did new institutions like the circulating library and the railway bookstall. Consequently, the working and lower middle classes, formerly hindered in their choice of reading as a leisure activity by issues of cost and education, became an immense new market for cheap fiction. Comprising the "Unknown Public" which so fascinated Wilkie Collins in 1858, the laboring millions consumed numerous types and genres of printed matter ranging from the "penny dreadful" and the novelette to the sensational newspaper and the miscellany. Collins, who conceived the Unknown Public to be "in its infancy" at midcentury, argued that this great audience must learn to read "in a literary sense," to "discriminate" in its choice of fiction;[4] but, as journalists made clear in the later decades of the century, the mass reading public had made a very definite choice. As a number of contemporary accounts suggest, the working and lower middle classes purchased, read, and circulated the products of the periodical press, shaping the types of fiction marketed to them and leaving behind a legacy of popular reading practices.[5]

The growth of the mass reading public produced an immense cultural anxiety on the part of middle-class commentators about the effects of cheap serials, particularly fiction, on working-class readers. Critics frequently voiced their misgivings over the potential of such popular fiction to destabilize the social structure of late Victorian culture, expressing the fear that the lower classes, from domestic servants to manual laborers, might find the seeds of insubordination and even revolt in the fictional narratives they read on a weekly basis. This narrative of class-based anxiety is especially germane to my discussion of the perceived reading practices of the shopgirl. Embodying the potential for social mobility on the part of young working women, shopgirls suggested to publishers a market of malleable readers whose fantasies and actions might be impacted by the new products targeted to a mass public readership.

The vast majority of fiction produced for mass public consumption was considered either sensational or sentimental, often blending these two affective modes in narratives of romance, crime, and adventure that explicitly contrasted with the drudgery of manual labor. Nineteenth-century observers claimed that the monotony of the laborer's working life impelled him to read solely for amusement and diversion: in 1844 Engels claimed that factory work was not work but tedium, "the most deadening, wearing process conceivable. The operative is condemned to let his physical and mental powers decay in this utter monotony[;] it is his mission to be bored every day and all day long from his eighth year."[6] In this description, the condition of modernity for the worker (by definition masculine, despite the fact that women also worked in factories during this period) depends on alienation from bodily experience as well as from any intellectual or emotional stimulation. Books, argued many, transported readers to livelier and more stimulating scenes, allowing them to forget the routinized and numbing conditions of their labor and escape into a foreign setting. Such was Sir John Herschel's argument in an 1833 address to library subscribers, in which he suggested that reading relieved the workingman's life of its "dulness and sameness" and provided intellectual companionship as well as a "diversified and interesting scene."[7] In fact, during this period reading itself became a habit, a routine in its own right: in 1935, Winifred Holtby commented that "travel by well-lit public vehicles has become a daily item in the routine of millions of workers, owing to the habit of building residential areas some distance from industrial sites and linking the two by trams and trains and buses"; moreover, she suggested, the "spell of changeful print" relieved the monotony of the repetitive commute between work and home.[8] Almost a half-century earlier, Agnes Reppelier noted how "imperative" the novelette was for third-class travelers, "outstrip[ping] other bodily requirements":

> The clerks and artisans, shopgirls, dressmakers, and milliners, who pour into London every morning by the early train have, each and every one, a choice specimen of penny fiction with which to beguile the short journey, and perhaps the few spare minutes of a busy day. The workingman who slouches up and down the platform, waiting for the moment of departure, is absorbed in some crumpled bit of pink-covered romance. The girl who lounges opposite to us in the carriage, and who would be a very pretty girl in any other conceivable hat, sucks mysterious sticky lozenges, and reads a story called "Marriage à la Mode, or Getting into Society" [. . .].[9]

For Reppelier, the pleasures experienced through reading become a substitute for physical needs like hunger, acting as a palliative which stands in for even as it masks the presence of bodily desire. As in the case of hunger, the desire for stimulation is reformulated as a recurring event, a habitual practice understood to reflect the repetitive qualities of working life. I will return shortly to the problem of "habit" in an analysis of the bodily effects of reading, but it is worth noting here the distinction between habits of leisure and the injunction to cultivate habits of domestic and moral influence dating back to the early Victorian period. In her series on the women of England, for example, Sarah Ellis described the necessity of reproducing "good" habits of industry rather than "bad" habits of idleness, and as Athena Vrettos has shown, the significance of habit was extensively discussed in Victorian philosophical and psychological writings.[10]

As Reppelier's comments also suggest, popular reading might not be gendered in the manner publishers imagined: most writers were apt to associate that "crumpled bit of pink-covered romance" with the fiction marketed toward young women, but as memoirs and other contemporary sources reveal, men and women often read material not necessarily targeted to them. Most familiar, perhaps, is the tomboyish girl who read her brother's penny papers—*Union Jack* or *Pluck,* for example, and others in the adventure genre—rather than stoop to the level of sentimental romance fiction.[11] By and large, however, girls and women were seen as the target market for romance fiction, and for many critics of the genre throughout the century, the romance novel (and later, the novelette and magazine) was the object of censure for its potential to endanger the moral state and physical condition of young female readers.

The romance novel had, of course, been suspect since its inception, in particular for its "continual feeding of the imagination [. . .] which, once deceived, becomes the deceiver," in the words of a writer for the *Christian Observer* in 1815.[12] This author's claim reflected the anxiety of many evangelical critics regarding popular literature's tendency to inflame the imagination and, as another writer put it late in the century, "fill [young readers'] heads with all kinds of unattainable ideas, and hopes that can never be realised":

> [I]nstead of embellishing life, as it is falsely represented to do, it heightens only imaginary and unattainable enjoyments, and transforms life itself into a dream, the realities of which are all made painful and disgusting, from our false expectations and erroneous notions of happiness.[13]

Many authors seemed to levy the most criticism at the falseness of romance fiction, especially in its ability to corrupt young readers and instill in them ideas of social relations and behavior unsuited to their stations. In 1845, a critic of the circulating library system lamented the "corruption" resulting from the sentimental fiction distributed by circulating libraries:

> To what an extent of corrupted views, impracticable notions, impossible wishes, and miserable regrets and disappointments in life; of seduction, of lazy and unsettled habits, of dishonesty, robbery, and even murder, the habit of reading the ever-pouring stream of high-flown and sentimental fiction from the circulating-library has been the origin—especially amongst females of the lower orders—it would be difficult to calculate; but it is awfully great.[14]

Similarly, George Humphery, writing in 1893, claimed that the result of reading "penny dreadfuls" was "the exalted opinions the young people entertain of themselves, even to the disuse of ordinary politeness," suggesting that in addition to their insubordinate activity, adolescent readers endangered the most fundamental codes of propriety and decency through the "habit" of reading popular fiction. These passages mark the location of a class-based anxiety which extends from the individuated realm of personal disappointment (when such "impracticable notions" are exposed as mere fiction) and internal corruption to the collective public sphere in which "young people" are imagined as a threat to social distinctions of rank and class.

Significantly, though, the romance novel and its subsidiary, the penny novelette, were seen to be at least as problematic as the circulating library novel and the penny dreadful, perhaps even more threatening because of their insidious nature. While (as some thought) boys' fiction explicitly drove young male readers to commit the petty crimes they read about in the cheap press, girls' fiction had a subtler but no less serious effect in the private sphere of the family:

> Because the influence of these love and murder concoctions among girls is not so apparent to the public eye as the influence of the burglar and bushranging fiction among boys, it must not be supposed that the influence is less real. It is, in fact, in many ways not only more real, but more painful. Boys may be driven to sea or to break into houses by the stories they read; their actions are at once recorded in the columns of the daily papers. With girls the injury is more invidious and subtle. It is almost exclusively domestic. We do not often see an account of a girl committing any very serious fault through her reading [. . . but it is likely that] the high-flown conceits and pretensions of the poorer girls of the period, their dislike of

manual work and love of freedom, spring largely from notions imbibed in the course of a perusal of their penny fiction. Their conduct towards their friends, their parents, their husbands, their employers, is coloured by what they then gather. They obtain distorted views of life, and the bad influence of these works is handed down to their children and scattered broadcast throughout the family.[15]

This passage creates a distinction between gendered forms of influence, in which boys are affected in their choice of actions while girls are affected internally and psychologically, paralleling their future sway over the private sphere of the family. This quotation describes an anxiety over the possibility that romance reading might problematize the operation of the domestic sphere, based both on the individual woman's influence over her own family and on the effects of that influence in the larger social and national context. Romance fiction for girls, then, inspired censure not simply for its ability to provide an "escape" from everyday life, but for its tendency to present "distorted," unreal, and unrealizable perspectives on social relations.[16] The distortion of the social fabric effected by romance reading suggested to more conservative critics the troubling possibility of insubordination on the part of working- and lower-middle-class subjects, and consequently the threat of a potential dismantling of the rigid class structure of Victorian England. Locating this threat within the home, and particularly within the sphere of feminine influence, critics of romance fiction avowed the necessity of subjecting reading practices to strict codes of supervision and social control in order to normalize the female body. By producing the sound and proper female subject, these writings imply, such regulatory methods would reproduce a prescribed set of sexual and class norms for social relations.

Embodiment, Education, and the Effects of Reading on Adolescent Girls

In 1899, Mary Wood-Allen, an American MD and the national superintendent of the Purity Department of the Women's Christian Temperance Union, published *What a Young Woman Ought to Know,* an advice manual targeting adolescent girls and their mothers and intended to inform both parties of the physical nature of girls' bodies and the "judicious care" necessary for managing those bodies.[17] The author describes a host of female maladies, among them painful menstruation, lassitude, nervousness, and hysteria, which she attributes to "disturbed nerves" and excessive mental and physical excitement. This troubling condition results, she asserts, from the "great evil of romance reading":

Girls are not apt to understand the evils of novel-reading, and may think it is only because mothers have outlived their days of romance that they object to their daughters enjoying such sentimental reading; but the wise mother understands the effects of sensational reading upon the physical organization, and wishes to protect her daughter from the evils thus produced. It is not only that novel-reading engenders false and unreal ideas of life, but the descriptions of love-scenes, of thrilling, romantic episodes, find an echo in the girl's physical system and tend to create an abnormal excitement of her organs of sex, which she recognizes only as a pleasurable mental emotion, with no comprehension of the physical origin or the evil effects. Romance-reading by young girls will, by this excitement of the bodily organs, tend to create their premature development, and the child becomes physically a woman months, or even years, before she should. (124)

In this passage, Wood-Allen collapses two different types of reading, the sentimental and the sensational, into a larger category which she variously labels "novel-reading" or "romance-reading," effecting the slippage between the novel and the romance so often evinced in late-eighteenth- and nineteenth-century assessments of the novel.[18] The tendency for the novel to "engender false and unreal ideas of life" in its readers was, as the previous section argued, a familiar site of anxiety for critics, prompting fears that such reading would bring about a "ruinous discontent" on the part of young women whose hopes, ideas, and sense of social position would be misdirected.[19] Wood-Allen's description of the relationship between these "morbid" mental and emotional states and the resulting physical evils takes the argument about reading's effects on the female body one step further, however, claiming that the sensations generated by romantic love-scenes result in the excitation of the sexual organs. This excitation in turn produces the "evil habit" of masturbation, or "self-abuse":

Girls often mature into women earlier than they should, because through romances, through jests of associates into beaus and lovers, and through indulgence in sentimental fancies their sexual systems are unduly stimulated and aroused. [. . .] The stimulation of the sex organs is accompanied with a pleasurable sensation, and this excitement may be created by mechanical means, or even by thought. Many girls who are victims of this most injurious habit are unaware of its dangers, although they instinctively feel that they do not want it known. Others who would not stoop to a mechanical exciting of themselves do so through thoughts, and do not know that they are just as truly guilty of self-abuse as the girl who uses the hand or other mechanical means. (151–52)

Here, female readers are imagined to be susceptible to the habit of impure thoughts as well as actions; the author later enjoins readers to direct their thoughts and actions into more "productive" activities. Wood-Allen's injunction against masturbation, or sexual stimulation of any kind outside the sanctioned sphere of marriage and procreation, recalls similar medical and moral pronouncements from earlier in the century.[20] However, she perceives the emotions produced by such stimulation as even more dangerous to the young girl than the physical actions, arguing that "feelings may be awakened by the imagination which are as wrong morally as, and more injurious physically than, actual deeds, and so may allow her mind to revel in fancies that would shock her as actualities" (154). These "imaginary scenes of love-making with real or unreal individuals," the "mental pictures which arouse the spasmodic feelings of sexual pleasure" (155), are all the more threatening to the adolescent girl's constitution because they are more insidious than actual activity, resulting in a less tangible form of sexual transgression. The stimulating activity of creating "mental pictures" and "imaginary scenes" produces a conception of fantasy as a direct threat to normative standards for proper feminine behavior.

Wood-Allen's argument—that reading, which produces fantasy and imaginary pleasures, leads to physical disorder and impurity in bodily practice—pathologizes the young girl's relationship to "normal" bodily functions.[21] Moreover, this formulation articulates the potential subversion of marriage and sex for procreation as threats to social institutions, the implication being that if young women attain their own pleasure without the help of men, the nation, even the species, will suffer the consequences. Her solution involves the relegation of sex to procreation, idealizing love as the goal of marital union and, somewhat paradoxically, using the promised conclusion of romance fiction to produce a desire for sanctioned emotional activity in the young female subject. She also advocates the early establishment of correct habits of dress, hygiene, and daily life, especially through the cultivation of the other senses. She encourages young women to turn away from fantasy and sensation to experience sensory pleasure in the natural world, enjoining mothers to keep their daughters "out of the realm of the artificial, the sentimental, the emotional" (158). These, of course, are exactly the terms used to describe the popular romance, with all its inflammatory potential. Despite its evident internal contradictions, *What a Young Woman Ought to Know* insists on the ability of the romance to produce premature development and its resultant disorders (in which

the sensations are more highly developed than the self-regulatory functions), disorders which in turn have the potential to undermine the social
and sexual codes Wood-Allen espouses.

One might counter Wood-Allen's argument by claiming that because of
the prevailing domestic ideology and the lack of access to education com-
parable to that which men received, middle-class women experienced idleness and boredom, driving them to seek out the stimulation of sensational fiction. Working-class women, for their part, suffered the habitual
monotony of manual and industrial display labor (as in the case of the late
Victorian and Edwardian department store), which in turn prompted
them to lose themselves in popular romances. In these scenarios, reading
is the attempted solution to, not the cause of, the physiological disorders
presumed to result from fantasy.

Less conservative writers, among them feminist and socialist thinkers
who supported reading as a form of individual betterment for the masses,
argued for reading as a solution to the monotony of the Victorian woman's
life in order to emphasize the necessity of widening educational and social
opportunities. Nonetheless, these writers were also disinclined to support
romance reading, urging parents and educators to substitute better literature
for this potentially subversive genre. In 1874, the feminist activist Dr.
Elizabeth Garrett Anderson underscored the inequity of male and female
education in England and America, responding to an article published in
the *Fortnightly Review* by Henry Maudsley entitled "Sex in Mind and
Education."[22] Maudsley had argued that because of the "extraordinary
expenditure of vital energy" required by the female "sexual system," women
should not be educated according to the standards available to men; this
type of assimilation of the female to the male mind would "unfit" women
for their appropriate sexual and social roles.[23] Garrett Anderson, by contrast,
contends that Maudsley misuses his data and exaggerates his claims; women,
she argues, have no desire to become men, nor do they experience adverse
effects if they disregard their "special" physiological functions. Working
women, she claims, are neither expected nor generally allowed to periodically avoid the strenuous manual labor by which they earn their living. In fact,
she suggests that work is by no means as serious a threat to the female organization as "dulness," a condition which young women attempt to ameliorate
through overstimulation of the emotional and sexual instincts:

> The stimulus found in novel-reading, in the theatre and ball-room,
> the excitement which attends a premature entry into society, the
> competition of vanity and frivolity, these involve far more real dan-
> gers to the health of young women than the competition for knowl-
> edge, or for scientific or literary honours, ever has done, or is ever

likely to do. And even if, in the absence of real culture, dissipation be
avoided, there is another danger still more difficult to escape, of
which the evil physical and moral results are scarcely less grave, and
this is dulness. [. . .] Thousands of young women, strong and
blooming at eighteen, become gradually languid and feeble under the
depressing influence of dulness, not only in the special functions of
womanhood, but in the entire cycle of the processes of nutrition and
innervation, till in a few years they are morbid and self-absorbed, or
even hysterical.[24]

Garrett Anderson attributes illness and nervous disorders to the "want of
adequate mental interest and occupation in the years immediately succeed-
ing school life" (590). Her solution does not lie in reading, however, but
in the emphasis on "solid intellectual work which demand[s] real thought
and excite[s] genuine interest," which she considers the "lasting refuge
from dulness" (591).

Garrett Anderson's use of the term "interest" to describe the necessary
and appropriate stimulation so often lacking in the lives of young women
recalls the words of John Ruskin, another proponent of female education
through "solid" intellectual matter. Arguing that girls should be encouraged to wander freely through "a good library of old and classical books"
and be given the same educational advantages as their brothers, Ruskin
nonetheless warns against the "fountain of folly" which characterizes circu-
lating-library fiction:

> [W]ith respect to that sore temptation of novel-reading, it is not the
> badness of a novel we should dread, but its overwrought interest. The
> weakest romance is not so stupefying as the lower forms of religious
> exciting literature, and the worst romance is not so corrupting as false
> history, false philosophy, or false political essays. But the best
> romance becomes dangerous, if, by its excitement, it renders the ordi-
> nary course of life uninteresting, and increases the morbid thirst for
> useless acquaintance with scenes in which we shall never be called
> upon to act.[25]

Ruskin's focus on the "interest" and "excitement" of romance fiction—its
sensational and affective aspect—posits the danger of reading in its ability
to create reader desire for the scenes and scenarios of fantasy. With regard
to romance fiction, opponents and supporters of the new educational
methods for women became unlikely allies, united in their condemnation
of the imaginary or fantastic aspect of these fictions and their absolute distance from the everyday.

During the Victorian period as in our own time, critics of popular romance fiction as a genre saw it as a method of "escape" through emotional indulgence and wish fulfillment. Few critics of the gendered consumption of popular texts have effectively investigated *how* the formal elements of the romance might have evoked (or provoked) such identificatory and fantasy processes; most have simply assumed that it did so in a relatively transparent manner.[26] In the next section, I analyze two different modes of consumer fantasy produced through absorption and distraction (the latter term evoking the prevalence of the "miscellany," in the style of George Newnes's *Tit-Bits* or Alfred Harmsworth's *Answers to Correspondents on Every Topic under the Sun,* both begun in the 1880s).[27] Paralleling the identificatory structures and processes of consumer fantasy, absorption and distraction work in tandem, shaping and regulating the reader's involvement in the romantic narrative and suggesting a range of possibilities for reading the shopgirl's consuming practices.

Absorption, Distraction, Fantasy: Romance Fiction for the Shopgirl

I. Imaginary Pleasures: Fantasy, Trauma, and Everyday Life

Fantasy occupies a critical position in the history of popular reading in part because of its negotiation of reader identification. As Cora Kaplan has suggested in her analysis of Colleen McCullough's best-selling 1977 novel *The Thorn Birds,* most critics of romance reading assume relatively straightforward strategies of reader identification: as the reader consumes the narrative of (to choose one of the most popular formulas) a budding romance between a poor but virtuous young woman and a handsome yet kindly aristocratic man, she transports herself into the heroine's world, creating a fantasy in which she takes the place of the heroine and vicariously experiences her emotions as well as the inevitable transformation in her fortunes. In her analysis, however, Kaplan contends that textual fantasy is much more complex than is generally assumed, combining original or primal fantasy with the more familiar reverie or daydream.[28] The transgressive textual fantasies produced on reading *The Thorn Birds,* she suggests, undermine the book's conservative politics, and demand a critical and careful engagement with the politics of their production.[29] So, too, I contend in the case of the romance fiction produced for the consumption of turn-of-the-century shopgirls: we cannot assume that the fantasies these texts intended to produce in their readers reflected the possible imaginary pleasures which might be experienced during the process of reading these romances. Rather, it is vital to attend to the multiple possibilities for identificatory and imaginary pleasure generated by the texts of romance fiction.

The relationship between original fantasy and the more conscious level of the daydream has been elaborated most fruitfully by Jean Laplanche and Jean-Bertrand Pontalis in their 1968 essay "Fantasy and the Origins of Sexuality," in which they articulate the fantasies of origins centering on three critical themes: the primal scene, the seduction fantasy, and the castration fantasy. In the original fantasy, the subject is "desubjectivized," able to occupy any of numerous positions within the scene: as the authors note, "the child is one character amongst many in the fantasy 'a child is being beaten,'" and the seduction fantasy 'a father seduces a daughter' is "a scenario with multiple entries, in which nothing shows whether the subject will be immediately located as *daughter;* it can as well be fixed as *father,* or even in the term *seduces.*"[30] In this sense of fantasy, then, the subject can transform his or her own placement within the fantasy, making the experience rather more liberatory (in terms of identificatory structures) than might be expected. Laplanche and Pontalis argue for a deeper understanding of the scenic quality of the fantasy, presenting it as a scenario in which the subject does not occupy a single position:

> [F]antasy is not the object of desire, but its setting. In fantasy the subject does not pursue the object or its sign; he appears caught up himself in the sequence of images. He forms no representation of the desired object, but is himself represented as participating in the scene although, in the earliest forms of fantasy, he cannot be assigned any fixed place in it. (27)

This type of original fantasy, desubjectivizing conventional processes of identification, differs from the daydream, a more secondary elaboration of desire. Following Freud, Laplanche and Pontalis argue that the daydream consists of "restoring a minimum of order and coherence to the raw material[, and] imposing on this heterogeneous assortment a façade, a scenario, which gives it relative coherence and continuity" (21). Laplanche and Pontalis underscore the connection between the daydream or reverie and the original fantasy, suggesting that the unity of the fantasy as an experiential process depends on the mingling of the structural and the imaginary in the subject's composition and reproduction of the fantasy. To account for the narrative quality of fantasy, Laplanche and Pontalis cite Freud's understanding of the "model" of fantasy as "the reverie, that form of novelette, both stereotyped and infinitely variable, which the subject composes and relates to himself in a waking state" (22). The reverie, here compared to a brief but absorbing fiction, incorporates and reshapes various forms of fantasy, at once sustaining the subject's experience of the "real" and marking it off as a category outside fantasy. To extend this reading, the novelette reproduces slight variations on a formulaic scene, thereby reflecting a number of possible transformations in the conventional narrative.

The novelette, an absorbing reverie in print form, produced a complex process of identification through fantasy that suggests a disjunction from everyday experience.[31] The plot and characters, formulaic for a number of reasons I detail below, encourage the reader to consume stories of aristocratic heroines in sensational or exotic circumstances, imperiled by villainous envy and greed, and saved from death and destruction through the efforts of a noble hero—all without the invasion of the mundane world into the scene of fantasy. The serialized romance fiction in girls' and women's magazines, on the other hand, featured heroines not unlike the readers themselves—virtuous but impoverished, hardworking and dedicated to proper Victorian values of honor and loyalty—in circumstances which transformed the experiences of "actual" shopgirls. These magazines, using a variety format of "tit-bits" including fashion, beauty, and health columns as well as the ever-popular "answers to correspondents" page, constructed a form of readerly fantasy which differed significantly from that of the novelette. This new form of fantasy, based on more explicit forms of identification with characters much like the ideal self of the shopgirl, involved a distracted experience of reading pleasure. The magazine's serial structure, with the culmination of any particular plot development always "to be continued," can be seen as productive of a greater permeability between the fantasy and everyday life than in the case of the novelette. This is not to deny the possibility that shopgirl-readers might in fact read "absorbing" fictions like the novelette in a "distracted" fashion; indeed, they might find themselves absorbed in quite different elements of the fiction than the conventional romance plot, identifying against the grain of what might be taken as a conventional identificatory process. The dialectical relation I formulate between absorption and distraction can serve to articulate some of the unexplored possibilities for romantic identification which emerge in a variety of fictions targeted to the shopgirl-reader.

II. "Gorgeousness of Effect": The "Absorbing Passion" of the Penny Novelette

Following Wilkie Collins's 1858 article, a number of journalists and social critics began attempting to ascertain the constitution of this "unknown public" of popular readers. In an 1883 article published in the *Nineteenth Century*, Thomas Wright contradicted the assumption that the unknown public was made up primarily of domestic servants; rather, he claimed, the majority of these readers came from classes which viewed themselves as "several 'cuts' above the domestic class":

> They belong to the "young lady" classes—the young ladies of the counters, of the more genteel female handicrafts generally, and of the dressmaking and millinery professions in particular. To these are added a numerous section of young ladies unattached—young ladies whose parents consider them, or who consider themselves, too genteel to go out to work. [. . .] As the young ladies carry their tastes into married life, the unknown public also includes numbers of wives of clerks, shopkeepers, and well-to-do artisans.[32]

Wright based his argument both on personal observation and experience as well as on internal evidence, detailing the ranks of young ladies and working men who habitually peruse the penny periodicals (novelettes and magazines), the former for the fiction and fashion supplements, the latter for the ubiquitous "answers to correspondents" pages.[33] Despite their exposure to "better" and more "permanent" literature (including Shakespeare, *Don Quixote,* and Farrar's *Life of Christ*), these members of the "lower, middle, or let-us-be-genteel-or-die" classes continue to choose this light and "easy" reading to while away their leisure hours. Unlike other critics such as Edward Salmon and James Payn, Wright contends that, according to the internal evidence of plot and character development, domestic servants cannot be the target or actual audience, since they hold no illusions regarding the aristocratic settings of the vast majority of these fictions: living in close contact with the upper classes, they are well aware of the difference between the fictional aristocratic hero and his counterpart in everyday life. Moreover, Wright argues, servants lack the time or inclination to read penny fiction on a daily basis, preferring other (but unspecified) forms of amusement.[34] For Wright, in short, the penny periodical addresses that middling class of readers who aspire to the genteel status of the leisured upper classes but have limited exposure to their way of life.

This version of the upwardly mobile, aspiring reader parallels the dominant conception of the shopgirl as a consumer of such cheap periodicals. Indeed, Wright's article is one of the first to discuss the reading habits of shop assistants, assisting in the periodization of this study. The first example I have found of a reader identifying herself as "a shopgirl" occurred just four months before the publication of Wright's essay, in Edwin Brett's long-running "Journal for Single and Married Everywhere," *Something to Read,* which published both serialized magazine-style fiction and novelettes over a thirty-year period from 1881 to 1910.

In Wright's formulation and elsewhere, the periodical romance and its subgenre, the novelette, merge into a generic form which, through luxurious and romantic settings, was imagined to provide readers with an escape, through absorption, from the monotony of everyday working life. Looking back to nineteenth-century fiction and drawing a correlation to the popular amusements of the 1930s, Winifred Holtby described this escapist model as a form of "emotional indulgence" shared by the shop assistant and the housewife:

> The popularity of Wild West, Foreign Legion and Gangster fiction among clerks employed in sedentary and monotonous occupations is obvious, just as "society" novels about guardsmen and peeresses, first popularized by Ouida, provide vicarious experience of luxury to housewives and shop assistants. The sumptuous settings of film scenarios and the marble pillars of Lyons' corner houses both flatter the same desire.[35]

In describing the desire of shop assistants for luxury and leisure, Holtby expresses the common perception that although shop workers might be surrounded by the dreamworld of the department store on an everyday basis, interacting with its wealthy consumers, they longed to immerse themselves in this world as its heroines rather than its minor characters, even if only vicariously through their reading practices. Moreover, in collapsing the shop assistant with the domestic woman, Holtby narrates the presumed romance/marriage plot that was thought to structure the lives and ambitions of the shopgirl. Like Holtby, Thomas Wright saw Ouida's novels as the epitome of the escapist fantasy for the "genteel young ladies" behind the counter, serving as the "acme of the penny serial style":

> In her they recognise the embodiment of their own high and inexpressible imaginings of aristocratic people and things. They believe in her Byronic characters, and their *Arabian Nights*-like wealth and power; in her Titanic and delightfully wicked guardsmen, in her erratic and ferocious but always gorgeous princes, her surpassingly lovely but more or less immoral grand dames, and her wonderful Bohemians of both sexes. In the same way they believe and delight in the manner in which their own Ouida lays it on with a trowel in the matter of properties, in the dream-like splendor of the abodes, and the no less resplendent dress and jewellery of her puppets[. . . .] The novelists of the penny prints toil after her in vain, but they do toil after her. They aim at the same gorgeousness of effect with her, though they lack her powers to produce it, to impress it vividly upon readers.[36]

Ouida, who adopted this literary pseudonym in place of her already "exotic" given name (Marie Louise Ramé), had been writing tremendously popular stories of romance and adventure in exoticized foreign locales since the 1860s, the most well known of which remains *Under Two Flags* (published in 1867).[37]

Other writers, however, found little of Ouida's "meretricious glitter" in the penny weeklies: they were likely to find such fiction unbearably dull rather than sensational or stimulating. The chief complaint, voiced most succinctly by Reppelier in her 1891 article on "English Railway Fiction," seems to be their formulaic quality:

> A gentle and unobtrusive dullness; a smooth fluency of style, suggestive of the author's having written several hundreds of such stories before, and turning them out with no more intellectual effort than an organ-grinder uses in turning the crank of his organ; an air of absolute unreality about the characters, not so much from overdrawing as from their deadly sameness; conversations of vapid sprightliness and an atmosphere of oppressive respectability—these are the characteristics of penny fiction.[38]

Reppelier speculates that rather than proceeding from an absence of dramatic incident, impropriety, or vice (as Payn and Wright claim), the "wonderful dullness" distinguishing penny fiction, particularly the romance fiction marketed to shop assistants, from other types of literature, results from the placidity and calm with which sensational plot twists are greeted by the central characters. She cites several instances which tend to confirm her argument, in light of the characters' matter-of-fact tone and modest acceptance of plot developments; and yet the vast majority of the penny weeklies in this study do not bear out Reppelier's claim, for the characters are much more likely to faint "dead away" or develop a dramatic and life-threatening illness than to simply accept the often quite surprising course of events. I suspect that these critics of penny fiction found it more conducive to their argument for a better class of literature to argue against those, like Salmon, who associated their sensational aspect with socialist tendencies, instead attempting to promote the cause of "discrimination" among readers through a shift in focus. If the penny novelettes were dull, they seem to suggest, readers might well grow appropriately dissatisfied with them and move on to texts by more "solid" writers, currently left to gather dust on the shelves of railway bookstalls.

By the 1890s, the debate over the penny novelette and other forms of cheap fiction had reached an impasse: some critics continued to warn the public about the dangerous effect of such fiction on feminine morality and conduct, while others argued that the novelettes, whatever their literary merit, had little or no negative effect on the morals of working- and lower-middle-class readers. This latter position resulted, it seems, from the widespread recognition that penny fiction had become a staple (or a habit) for the consumption of a large segment of the reading population, and could therefore only be discredited rather than eradicated entirely. Edward Salmon, who had condemned the penny novelette as "cheap and nasty," eventually concluded that the English penny papers were as a rule "more silly than vicious": "If they are not calculated to raise the moral tone of their readers above that which poverty and overcrowding may have engendered, they at least are not calculated to do any grave mischief. The worst that can be said of them is that they do help keep the moral tone of their readers low" (112, 114). Francis Hitchman went so far as to claim that "the popular literature of to-day is singularly pure in tone, and that any violation of decency would inevitably lead to such a falling off of circulation as would practically amount to the ruin of the paper guilty of it." Moreover, this author suggests, the attention to decorum, combined with the ignorance of novelette writers on all subjects connected to "society" life, produces some "anomalous" and striking results:

> It might, for example, be pointed out to [these authors] that peers of the realm do not as a rule look for their wives amongst the shop girls and milliner's apprentices of Regent Street and Bond Street; that baronets are not, as a rule, superhumanly wicked; that the chorus and "extra ladies" of the minor theatres are not necessarily superhumanly virtuous; that ladies of birth, family, and position, are not invariably much worse from the moral point of view than their own maids; and finally, that gentlepeople, of whatever age or condition they may be, have occasionally some notion of the value of self-restraint, and are sometimes actuated by motives a little higher than those of a sordid self-interest.[39]

Hitchman's flippant tone with respect to the factual inconsistency and lack of realism characteristic of the novelette suggests, as Kate Flint has noted, a broader tendency to condescension on the part of many critics of penny fiction.[40] If they could not blame the novelettes for their morals, it seems, they could certainly mock their inability to faithfully represent the wealthy and aristocratic environment which was the most frequent setting for the stories. Helen Bosanquet's opposing viewpoint, expressed in a 1901 article which analyzes a number of penny weeklies according to their formal characteristics, comes as a refreshing change from this critique: she cautions that "we must remember that [factual inconsistencies] would not be noticed by the readers for whom the stories are written; they are satisfied, and the author's purpose is served, if an atmosphere of luxury, of the unknown and mysterious world of wealth and leisure, is suggested, and for this purpose very slight and conventional indications are sufficient."[41] Moreover, she suggests, the middle classes are themselves guilty of complacency in regard to the conventional depiction of the working classes (and for that matter, the aristocracy) in the fiction they themselves consume.

Having set the stage for the historical debate over the "absorbing passion" of the novelette, I want now to shift to an analysis of the novelette itself through an examination of its form and content. The assumptions which emerge in contemporary accounts of popular reading were based on the novelette's formal characteristics and on the atmospheric description of sensationalized romance plots which produced the effect of contrast with the everyday life of the shopgirl. In terms of form, as I suggested earlier, the novelette worked like a condensed version of the novel, presenting a "complete story" in every issue and hence a sustained narrative for the shopgirl's consumption. Such stories were typically bookended by ads for patent medicines and articles of fashion intended to remake the body of the reader into an idealized form.[42] This form itself was reflected in the illustrations that accompanied the stories as well as in the descriptive content, a reflection which, as I discuss in more detail below, paralleled the positioning of the shopgirl as the image of fantasy for the consumption of customers in the shop or department store. Finally, two other items typically followed the presentation of the fiction, both of which contributed to the perception of the shopgirl as a reader aspiring to upward mobility: these were the gossip column and the "answers to correspondents" page, in which the reader received advice (both direct and indirect) on various strategies for refashioning her body and tastes into those of the aristocratic consumer.

The fictions included in the novelettes presented an astonishing array of characters to their reading audience, perhaps with the intention of providing a sensational and striking contrast with the actual and mundane encounters the shopgirl would have experienced on a daily basis. The majority of these fictions featured heroines whose day-to-day lives differed significantly from those of the working- and lower-middle-class women who read them on a weekly or monthly basis. Stories like "Gwendoline's Temptation" (*English Ladies' Novelettes*, 1891), "In My Lady's Keeping" (*Princess's Novelettes*, 1886), and "Esmée, or Under the Shadow of St. Paul's" (*Gipsy Novelettes*, 1900) recounted tales of beautiful young orphans adopted into aristocratic families or discovered to be long-lost heiresses, while others like "The Mysteries of Kenyon Court" and "Struggle and

Strife, A Woman's Life" (both printed in the first volume of the *Princess's Novelettes*, 1886) focused on mysterious betrothals and theft or murder, often featuring a school-age heroine who marries a duplicitous hero-turned-villain and later regrets her actions. The vast majority of these fictions describe an aristocratic world understood as foreign to readers from the lower and middle classes, and render it mysterious and sensational with tales of bigamy and deception. Occasionally, especially in the case of Edwin Brett's long-running *Princess's Novelettes*, authors provide a point of entry for the reader in the character of an impoverished art student or governess, either orphaned or struggling to support an ailing parent; likewise, stories featuring aristocratic or wealthy heroines typically humble them through appearance (as in "Ugly, an Heiress," *Princess's Novelettes*, 1887) or through the events of the story. More frequently, however, heroines come from what is represented to be an affluent middle-class background (as the daughter of an established country doctor, for example) or circulate in the upper echelons of wealthy and/or aristocratic society. The range of positions occupied by the heroines of these fictions suggests that the shopgirl-reader might use such texts to produce a variety of levels of contrast with her everyday life.

The content of the fictional romance narratives that formed the basic structure of the novelette paralleled the columns and advertisements in their reflection of a luxurious atmosphere of consumer pleasure not unlike that which the shopgirl was being taught or encouraged to desire. The world of wealth and leisure depicted in penny novelettes emerges primarily through the authors' use of setting to convey the sense of aristocratic luxury and leisure which was the perceived locus for the shopgirl's consuming desires. The most popular settings for the stories featured rural estates such as that described in "An Unknown Peril" (*Princess's Novelettes*, 1886) with "a richly-wooded park, splendidly laid-out grounds, [and] a castellated mansion"; authors would frequently leave the remainder of the scene to the reader's imagination, signaling the understated elegance of the country home through descriptions of the "fine old Elizabethan structure" in Devonshire ("Prince or Pauper?" *Gipsy Novelettes*, 1901) and "the old Manor House in Inglefield" ("She Did So Want to Be an Old Maid," *Gipsy Supplement*, 1901). Alternatively, stories would center on a country cottage, invariably described as "pretty" or "charming" to convey the modest yet comfortable circumstances of its inhabitants (see for example "A Wild Red Rose," *English Ladies' Novelettes*, 1891 and "The Mountain Maid," *Royal Novelette*, 1898). When set in London, stories revolved around stately mansions in Bloomsbury or in less central districts of the city, as in "Madeline's Lover" (*Dorothy Novelette*, 1889):

Her home was in one of those private mansions, whose dimensions are palatial, which are to be found round Hampstead and far Highgate. It was named "The Three Gables," and even its appearance denoted luxurious comfort, and seemed silently to inform the observant wayfarer that its inmates were undoubtedly possessed of every earthly blessing. The house stood on an elevation, and its pointed gables, round turrets, mullioned windows, and red bricks could be discerned here and there charmingly peeping through embowering trees, [giving] the place an aspect of sylvan beauty which any man might be pardoned for coveting.

The emphasis on setting works to absorb the reader in a pleasurable narrative, but might also be seen as contributing to a dislocation from the linear narrative of the romance plot, instead allowing the reader to lose herself in (and perhaps even identify with) the play of visual pleasure and the seemingly unending descriptive possibilities. The novelette's striking focus on setting and atmosphere often occurs at the expense of plot development, producing a relation to the text that might absorb the reader in an experience quite different from the experience of longing for a conclusion to the romance.

In other words, while the novelette was typically assumed to work on its readers through identification with the heroine, we may locate elements within the content of the romance fictions presented in novelette form that contradict this narrative of straightforward identification. "Madeline's Lover," for example, describes a number of subject positions with which the shopgirl-reader might identify, including the characters as well as the experience of desire that those characters represent. In describing the many suitors seeking the heroine's hand and fortune, this story creates a parallel between the luxurious estate and its sole heiress as objects of desire. The acknowledgment of the seemingly natural longing to possess such wealth and luxury legitimates the reader's desire to identify both with the heroine (as coveted object) and with the anti-hero, the Honourable Sigbert Cranbeigh, producing an imaginary relation to the narrative characterized by multiple identificatory positions. Subsequently, too, a change in Madeline's situation due to her father's careless speculation results in her employment first as a governess, then as a music hall vocalist, and finally as the wife of a handsome curate; these shifts in occupation (and identity, as Madeline works under the name Mary Horton) permit various possibilities for readerly identification. Indeed, the novelette typically provided a range of character types for each individual, reproducing such variations in identification on the part of the reading audience.

Frequently, authors would disregard the mechanism of plot entirely,

"Essie Armytage," *Dorothy Novelette,* April 1890. Reproduced by permission of the British Library, P.P. 6004.cam.

diverging into descriptions of the luxury goods with which the heroine might surround herself. Novelette writers typically included a lengthy account of the clothing and jewels worn by the heroine to a ball or other social event to underscore her wealth and position, whether actual or assumed, such as this passage describing the eponymous heroine of "Essie Armytage" (*Dorothy Novelette,* 1890):

> A fair, slender girl, with a delicate roseleaf-like complexion and glo-
> rious violet eyes. She was exquisitely dressed in rich trailing silk of
> the latest blue-green shade, profusely trimmed with the finest lace. A
> necklace of large pearls and armlets of dull gold set off the beautiful
> neck and arms to perfection, as she was led forward beneath the soft-
> ened light of silk-shaded rose-coloured lamps. (58)

In a similar vein, another author provides an elaborate account of the heroine's ball costume, made of "white silk, accordion pleated, and veiled with white net [with] a tracery of glittering steel paillettes [and] coral cabuchons," the bodice of which opens over "knots of rose-pink silk," and incorporating "an embroidered collar edged with a kilted frill." [43] As Helen Bosanquet commented in 1901, what this description lacks in design skill it makes up for in its ability to "stir the feminine longings of the girl-reader," although the imprecision with which Bosanquet imagines those longings reproduces the generic assumption of the shopgirl as the desiring consumer. If we take shopgirls as the intended audience of such fictions, however, we can understand how these descriptions may have also worked to reproduce mimetic identification in readers: these texts describe various ways in which the shopgirl might mimic the taste and appearance of the upper classes, reproducing the narrative of social mobility that emerges elsewhere in contemporary accounts of shop life. The amount of detail on fashion and appearance provided in these fictions—here, incorporating the approving whispers of the male spectators at this event and the wondering comments from the women, one of whom exclaims, "Must be one of Worth's dresses!"—comes perhaps as less of a surprise considering the emerging market of women readers working in the nascent fashion industry. This offhand mention of Worth, a contemporary couturier for the elite classes, underscores the novelette's emphasis on dress, fashion, and display, and firmly positions this type of romance fiction within a consumer culture based on the practice of shopping, itself a new leisure experience for women incorporating fantasy, desire, and identification. [44]

The focus on the fashions worn by novelette heroines receives even greater emphasis through the occasional practice of including a fashion "supplement" within the novelette, strikingly placed in the middle of the weekly publication and interrupting the flow of the fictional narrative. "Dorothy's Fashion Supplement" for April 1890, for example, includes columns on "Fashion's Fads," "The Treatment of the Hair," and "Practical Dressmaking by the Working Bee," each lavishly illustrated in the style of the period. The section on dressmaking contains a diagram for a "close-fitting ladies bodice" which women might reproduce and use as a pattern for their own garments; editorial comments suggest that a series of articles in this line would provide women with the practice to develop their dressmaking skills and, by implication if not explicitly, equip them to use those skills for the purposes of domestic economy or future employment. In addition, the fashion supplement included letters from readers on a range of subjects, the majority of which concern dress and appearance; the responses often involved lengthy descriptions of methods for alterations which would produce an elegant "new" outfit at very little cost. The fashion supplements,

"Dorothy's Fashion Supplement," *Dorothy Novelette*, April 1890. Reproduced by permission of the British Library, P.P.6004.cam.

along with the advertisements for dress improvers, electromagnetic corsets, and the like, explicitly reproduced the implicit strategies for rendering the reader's body fashionable according to the style set by the female protagonists of the weekly stories. In doing so, they contributed to the further democratization of fashion, revealing the ways in which "common" shop-girls might make themselves into elegant consumers through the purchase of a few crucial items.[45]

For turn-of-the-century consumers, the world of fashion presented an environment of endless attractions in the form of stylistic trends, producing a culture focused on serialized and distracted pleasures. The emphasis on ever-changing items of fashion in the pages of the novelette explicitly reflects a transformation in the late Victorian and Edwardian culture of consumption. During the 1880s and early 1890s, an era in which many women still made garments for themselves and their families at home, novelette readers were encouraged to create fashions in the style of those described in the stories themselves, thereby consuming fabrics and other dress materials rather than ready-made goods. The romance fiction of the early 1900s, by contrast, substituted notices of sales at the large London and regional department stores, encouraging women to consume particular fashion and beauty items. Although the novelettes did not use the fashion tie-up so prevalent in film culture in the decades following World War I, their emphasis on the minute details of the attire of their fictional heroines immersed women readers in the fashion industry and maintained the association of desire with identification through the processes of consumer fantasy.[46] Such strategies for producing and modulating the consuming desires of shopgirl-readers contribute to the production of what we might see as a nascent fan culture, in which the heroines step from the pages of the novelette and live the clothes, presenting a model image not unlike that embodied by the shopgirl in her reflection of the image of the female customer across the counter of the shop or department store.

Significantly, though, these narratives rarely if ever feature scenes of shop life, a common element of the girls' and women's magazines addressed in the next section. Those that do focus on a shop generally revolve around a heroine who chooses her profession on a whim, as does Peggy Lorraine, the fiction writer who decides to live the life of her heroine and disguises herself as "Mary Moore," proprietor-employee of a small stationery shop in a seaside town ("Peggy's Shop," *Princess's Novelettes* 1896). Other stories centering on the fashion and drapery trade describe two extremes in the characterization of their heroines: the overworked and exploited dressmaker's assistant ("A Queen of Sorrow," *Princess's Novelettes* 1886) and the fashionable *modiste,* a term generally used as a synonym for an elite dressmaker and stylist ("Madame Virginie," *Princess's Novelettes* 1895). In each case, however, the heroine differs from the majority of working women readers in her background as the daughter of a gentleman, and, of course, in the course of events which each story unfolds. Nola Marson, the protagonist of "A Queen of Sorrow," hastily wed and disinherited by her father, unwittingly commits bigamy and struggles to regain her home and position, while Flora Portland (alias Madame Virginie) borrows money from a wealthy uncle to start her own business and support her family, and after trading places with a friend to have a holiday in leisured social circles, eventually marries a member of the gentry. Much like the tales of long-lost heiresses and victims of crime and betrayal, the sensational plots traced in these two stories—bigamy and mistaken identity being two of the most popular formulas—provide the effect of a contrast with the everyday lives of the reading audience.

As Helen Bosanquet notes, in the case of girls' penny fiction there is but one theme, with characters drawn from the same stock of figures: "the old, old story of meeting, parting, and the church-door in the last chapter" (677), even when the characters have been married and separated in the course of the story. Typical endings achieve seemingly impossible heights of romantic union, as in the final sentences of "Two Dreams" (*Princess's Novelettes*, 1886): "The last doubt vanished by love's mystic touch, and their hearts beat in perfect unity and trust" (144). The formulaic conclusion, resolving all conflict and consummating the perfect love shared by the hero and heroine, intends to provide readers with the fantasy ideal of the union they were thought to long for in their own lives. The shopgirl-reader might be compelled to return alone to her dormitory room after an exhausting day's labor, the story goes, but she could lose herself and forget her lonesome surroundings in the fictional narrative of her weekly novelette. The problem with this exclusive and repetitive focus on the love story, of course, is that the romance takes precedence over any other possible stories that the reader might consume or imagine. Bosanquet's conclusion that "the constant suggestion that the whole point and interest of a woman's life is contained in the few months occupied by her love story must be narrowing and morbid," expresses this idea succinctly, but she concedes that the ideal presented in the stories—the "quiet domestic life" which seems their ultimate intent—is "not an unwholesome one" (680). Indeed, each story seems to offer an object lesson of sorts to its readers, providing a narrative of possible endings to their own love story. If the girl behind the counter were to marry the gentleman on the other side, she might achieve the wealth, title, and honor of the novelette heroine; on the other hand, she might also be entering into a disastrous union with a bigamist or murderer, unbeknownst to her. In one sense the frequency with which this narrative of the romantic deceiver appears in the novelettes could be seen to reflect the sheer difficulty of defining the companionate union in the shopgirl's life: as I have argued in previous chapters, the lack of chaperoned regulation of the shopgirl's interactions with men made the assessment of an "appropriate suitor" a challenging task. The stories featuring women victimized by villainous members of the impoverished aristocracy, however, usually provide a heroic partner for the troubled heroine by the end of the tale, again reassuring the reader that she will eventually achieve that romantic ideal. Primarily, the novelettes offer a catalogue of fictional possibilities which the reader can use as a guide against which to measure to make her matrimonial decisions. Mildred Rogers, the heroine of Somerset Maugham's *Of Human Bondage,* uses this comparative strategy to decline Philip's proposal; so, too, does Gissing's Rhoda Nunn as she imagines the causes of Bella Royston's fall. The danger, of course, lay in the failure of the reader to achieve the romantic and domestic bliss represented in the novelettes—hence the prominence of the "answers to correspondents" pages, in which editors carefully guided readers through the etiquette of courtship, marriage, and successful home life. In 1871, for example, *Wedding Bells,* one of Edwin Brett's early serials targeted to "single and married" (women) readers, ran a series of articles on the "etiquette of courtship and marriage." This series, addressing "the great object of our whole existence[,] the soul and essence of all happiness," reproduced the popular strategy of detailing the requisite behavior of "ladies" and "gentlemen" so that readers of lower rank and wealth might imitate the etiquette and manners of the aristocracy.

Penny novelettes therefore provided shopgirl-readers with a fantasy structure which allowed them to lose themselves in a world of luxury and sentimental feeling. The loss of self in the fictional world was paralleled by the structure of the novelettes, always provided to readers in the form of a complete narrative and frequently reprinted at intervals of a decade or more.[47] These fictions inevitably concluded with a romantic union and a promise of domestic happiness, usually complemented by wealth and often a restored title or inheritance. By contrast, many of the magazines produced for shopgirls and other young working women which ran serialized fiction alongside columns providing advice, commentary, and tidbits of factual information—particularly those published by Alfred Harmsworth, including *Forget-Me-Not, Girls' Friend, Girls' Reader,* and *Girls' Home*—produced a genre of fictional narrative which, although also occasionally domestic in its intent, provided a range of alternative lives through which readers were encouraged to play out their fantasy experience. These magazines differed significantly in structure and in subject matter, contributing to a distracted culture of consumption which produced the shopgirl both as a new kind of female reader and as a modern consuming subject. Moreover, because they incorporated realistic stories of shop life, the girls' and women's serial magazines I analyze in the next section were potentially even more inflammatory than turn-of-the-century critics might have imagined. In reflecting the exploitative labor conditions experienced by shop assistants themselves, these magazines made it possible for readers to imagine the promise of alternative conclusions to the plots narrated in their ordinary lives.

III. "A Habit of Loose Reading": Distracted Consumption

Many critics of popular reading in the late Victorian and Edwardian periods viewed the novelette, a prime example of the penny romance, as a double-edged sword in terms of its moral effects on female readers: while this genre lacked the literary quality to help lower-class readers out of their circumstances, it at least did them no identifiable harm. The troubling new popular genre, many middle-class writers believed, was the magazine. Modeled on earlier publications like *Bow Bells* and the *Family Herald,* a number of weekly magazines published in the 1890s and early 1900s addressed themselves to a reading audience made up of adolescent girls and young women placed at a critical stage in the linking spheres of domestic and working life.[48] These magazines incorporated the new "tit-bits" style of journalism, producing a mix of fiction, historical essays, anecdotes, jokes, comics, and advice columns in the style of the miscellany. Critics saw this fragmented style of reading as detrimental to young women's ability to focus on their reading matter, and articles from this period expressed an increasing concern about the dangers of "miscellaneous reading" and its possible effects on the quiet domestic life of the late Victorian and Edwardian home. Despite numerous attempts on the part of publishers and editors to imbue their magazines with moral and social propriety, this subcategory of the penny periodical remained troubling to middle-class observers, not so much by virtue of its content as its form. Instead of offering a "complete story" every week, these penny and half-penny papers provided a deferred reading pleasure through the process of serialization, delaying the conclusion of each week's story until the following issue. They produced a new form of leisure entertainment which offered variety and diversion, and a new type of reading pleasure based on what I describe as "distraction." I take this term from Siegfried Kracauer's description of early-twentieth-century mass experience, in which the senses are stimulated by a series of surface-level effects and impressions.[49] The distracted, desultory pleasures of serialized reading in the late nineteenth and early twentieth centuries implied a structural alteration in the nature of the process of consuming fantasy and its relationship to desire, identification, and everyday life.

Following the publication of George Newnes's *Tit-Bits* in 1880, a periodical filled with miscellanea which provided the model for Harmsworth's *Answers to Correspondents on Every Subject under the Sun* (1888) and

Pearson's Weekly (1890), journalists began to lament the "habit of loose reading" created by such popular literature. Edward Salmon, one of the first to do so, answered this complaint by asserting that "if the working classes did not read these papers they would read hardly anything save the novelette or the weekly newspaper; and, even though gained in a disjointed fashion, it is surely better for them to acquire pieces of historical information thuswise than never to acquire them at all."[50] This argument suggests that any education in history and factual knowledge is better than none, even when presented in such a fragmentary manner. To others, however, such reading habits produced an ephemeral, desultory experience which destroyed the reader's palate for more "solid" and "instructive" literature. James Haslam, author of a series of articles in the *Manchester City News* on the reading practices of the working classes in Manchester, expressed his alarm at the demand for periodicals filled with "'snips and snaps,'" and for those sensational papers describing the controversies of the divorce courts and "the spicy tit-bits of life in general"; observing the rush on rainy weekends for such popular reading matter, he commented, "These invariably go well among a class that read by fits and starts. Seeing that it is too wet to wander round and round the streets, they can only find comfort in the hasty perusal of ephemeral 'bits and bats.'"[51] George Humphery condemned the subsequent response on the part of such readers that "the study of a given subject is the height of monotony," decrying this reading practice as "degradation" rather than recreation, while "A Working Woman" commented in *Chambers' Journal* that "the information swallowed by this system of miscellaneous reading is enormous as far as the quantity goes, but it generally passes through the brain like water through a sieve."[52]

Most of these writers targeted the "tit-bits" genre of light or comic papers—among them *Great Thoughts, Rare Bits, Scraps,* and *Illustrated Chips*—which were read by working-class men and women alike. However, these magazines were thought to be so detrimental to the practice of reading "better" literature that critics increasingly began to effect a slippage between the "tit-bits" genre and the entire class of cheap publications. In the same year Haslam's series of articles were reprinted as *The Press and the People,* Florence Low wrote "The Reading of the Modern Girl," which develops the case against the desultory reading habit produced by the magazine industry and the free library system.[53] Having circulated a questionnaire to some two hundred teenage girls at secondary schools around England, Low found that girls read an average of three to five magazines monthly, rather than novels by more well-known authors like Dickens, Scott, and Austen. She found the magazines unobjectionable except for the miscellaneous style common to all, a style she viewed as likely to "destroy

all taste for serious and continuous reading" (280). She articulates the problem of the destruction of readerly "taste" through the familiar metaphor of
feeding, commenting that "the good literature is being pushed on one side
by the enormous mass of written stuff that is yearly issued by the press of
an inferior and second-rate quality, upon which our girls feed greedily,
with the very natural result that they cannot digest food of a superior
nature" (278). In this formulation, the process of feeding on light literature in cheap serialized form produces a population of young women who
"habitually" satisfy their desire for stimulation through the distracted
pleasure of reading "scraps and tags" of information. To Low, the mind of
the modern girl is an organism of limited capacity, and since girls "satiate"
their minds with "the second-rate, the insipid or the ultra-sentimental"
(282), they are consequently unable to read anything else. While she does
not censure the fiction published in novelettes and magazines per se, Low
does criticize the market for "rubbishy" novels, which themselves were
often republished from an original serialized run. The distributive branch
of the industry also causes her consternation, with the circulating and
public libraries producing particular anxiety through the mingling of different social classes in the reading rooms. In this sense we have returned
to the concept of reading practice as a threat to the social structure and the
organization of class hierarchy expressed by Edward Salmon some twenty
years before.

In an attempt to counteract the distracted pleasures and dangers of
reading, Low advocated strict parental supervision and informal censorship:

> Parents should sternly forbid the reading of more than one magazine
> a month, for the indiscriminate reading of magazines is perhaps
> more harmful than anything else; it creates a distaste for reading any-
> thing but "snippets" and the lightest of literature, and gives the read-
> er an air of superficial knowledge that is far worse than downright
> ignorance. The spaces in the mind may be filled; it is difficult to clear
> away rubbish. (286)

This strategy for managing the reading habits and practices of girls depends,
of course, on the existence of a regulatory structure like the family to control the consuming choices of adolescent women readers. However, women
employed in the new service and display industries, particularly those who
worked in urban shops and department stores, rarely experienced this type
of domestic or parental supervision. In the absence of such guidance,
women were free to make their own choices regarding their reading habits,
and thus to engage in and create new modes of consuming practices in

accordance with their more independent status. The success of a number of late Victorian and Edwardian penny and half-penny periodicals aimed at this body of readers attests to their consuming power and their very presence as members of the popular reading public. Magazines in this category include D. C. Thomson's *Girls' Weekly* (1912–1922) and the series of girls' magazines published by the Amalgamated Press (headed by Alfred Harmsworth) in the teens and twenties; for the purposes of this study I have chosen to focus on the Harmsworth publications spanning the 1890s and the first two decades of the twentieth century. These magazines—*Forget-Me-Not, Girls' Reader, Girls' Friend,* and *Girls' Home*—featured fiction and articles on the lives and experiences of "modern girl"–types like the "business girl," the "working girl," and the "shop girl." Although they did provide adolescent working women with a diverse range of heroines with whom to empathize, they too reinforced the domestic and romantic aspects of these women's lives, using conventional forms of reader identification to reproduce a fantasy of marriage with a wealthy suitor. The critical difference between these magazines and the novelettes analyzed in the previous section, however, can be located in their structural aspect: the serialized fiction presented in these magazines allowed for a deferred pleasure in reading which, in turn, facilitates an analysis of a heightened permeability between the fantasy and the everyday lives of the reading audience.

Alfred Harmsworth, born in 1865 into a professional London family, built his career and fortune on the cheap weekly paper distributed to the boys and girls of England. Although he eventually headed a number of long-running daily papers including the *Evening News,* the *Daily Mail,* the *Daily Mirror,* and the *Times,* many located the source of his power in the "millions of pennies and halfpennies plunked down on newsagents' counters every week" for the comic and story papers launched in the 1890s. Harmsworth himself recognized the growing body of young readers which would form the new market for popular magazines, commenting:

> The Board Schools [. . .] are turning out hundreds and thousands of boys and girls annually who are anxious to read. They do not care for the ordinary newspaper. They have no interest in society, but they will read anything which is simple and sufficiently interesting. The man who has produced this *Tit-Bits* has got hold of a bigger thing than he imagines. He is only at the beginning of a development which is going to change the whole face of journalism. I shall try to get in with him.[54]

And "get in with him" Harmsworth did, following each competitor's journal with one of his own, subsequently reaching out into new markets with periodicals targeted to gender-specific groups of readers. By the 1910s, the Harmsworth firm (renamed the Amalgamated Press in 1902) was producing a number of weekly magazines for girls, each of which combined serialized fiction with articles on the working lives of typists, nurses, teachers, domestic servants, and the seemingly limitless catalogue of "girl"-types (including, in addition to shopgirls, the telephone girl, the factory girl, the flower-girl, the Fourth-Form girl, and the stay-at-home girl, to name only a few).

In her book on girls' culture in England during this period, Sally Mitchell deftly analyzes the age-influenced separation of "girls" from "women" in a number of cultural texts including popular fiction for working- and lower-middle-class readers, arguing that Harmsworth (among others) identified and consolidated a new segment of the reading population. Members of his target readership could choose to occupy the position of a woman reading the romance, or that of a girl consuming stories of other girls' adventures in boarding or convent schools, as actresses on the stage or in the new picture palaces, or even as riders in the traveling circus.[55] However, Mitchell does not acknowledge what appears to be a significant contradiction in these magazines, the insistence on the simultaneity of girlhood and womanhood, represented in the same magazine and seen to coexist within the reader's own experience. While Mitchell views the culture of girlhood as a time of relative freedom from sexual and marital injunctions which was resexualized toward the end of the period she analyzes, my research suggests that the sexualizing narrative of romantic love and marital union exists throughout the period, barely concealed under the "madcap" antics of fictional girl-heroines. Certainly shopgirl culture had from its inception been imbued with a sexual teleology in which women were impelled toward the ultimate conclusion of the romance, the "church-door" of Bosanquet's description, even in magazines which might be read as offering new alternatives to the marital and domestic plots of female experience.

One alternative which did emerge, however, was a new mode for consuming the romantic fiction serialized in these magazines, based on the distracted pleasures associated with consumer fantasy. The fiction published in the pages of the Harmsworth girls' papers adhered to several tried-and-true narratives, creating a new formula for the popular magazine which differed from that of the novelettes but nonetheless incorporated some familiar elements. Numerous stories featured the shopgirls, mill and factory girls, typists, and housemaids who formed the majority of the magazines' readership; more often than not their adventures reflect the playful excitement which readers desired and found lacking in their own lives. The "trading places" plot, in which a lady and her maid change places, or a duchess disguises herself as a working girl, proved to be a favorite among working girls and women who longed to imagine themselves in someone else's shoes; the ensuing confusion added to the pleasure these readers experienced, as characters found themselves in hilarious and unlikely surroundings. A surprising number of stories centered on convent and boarding school life, a pleasurably unfamiliar milieu for girls employed in factories, shops, and offices in London.[56] Stories were serialized over several months, each weekly installment providing only two or three new pages and usually ending with a "cliffhanger" which would compel the reader to buy the next issue. Thus the immensely popular "Pollie Green" series of school stories, which first appeared in *Girls' Friend* in 1907 and was reprinted in *Girls' Reader* and *Girls' Home*, would often place its heroine in a vexing situation resulting from one of her adventures—wrongly accused of flirting with a boy at the neighboring school, for example—and only partially resolve the conflict, in the process creating another difficult set of circumstances from which the heroine would need to extricate herself (and which tempted the reader into her next purchase). This series, written by "Mabel St. John" (the pseudonym of Henry St. John Cooper, who wrote regularly as "Henry St. John" for the Harmsworth boys' papers), featured an attractive and sympathetic heroine and followed her education from Nunthorpe School, where she befriends Coosha, the daughter of a Zulu chieftain, to Mead House College, Cambridge, finally placing her in London society where she manages to reject the advances of a duke, yet still inherit his fortune and marry her impoverished but devoted admirer.[57] Mabel St. John's girls' fiction often described such a narrative, in which a working-class heroine manages to resist the snobbery and injustice inflicted on her by her upper-class peers at work or school, instead joining the circus or "going on the halls"; many of these heroines eventually marry their suitors, conveniently achieving financial security along the way (generally resulting in the decision to leave one's past adventures behind and settle down in a newly domestic environment). When one protagonist's narrative draws to its "natural" close, her friends become heroines themselves, as in "Coosha and Company, being the Adventures of Coosha, Pollie Green, Em Hammond, and a Caravan" (*Girls' Friend*, 1912) and "Daisy Peach, or, Pollie Green's Chum" (*Girls' Reader*, continued as *Our Girls*, 1915).

The stories of shop life serialized in the pages of the Harmsworth girls' magazines instilled shop culture with the adventure and excitement of the school, stage, and convent stories, while at the same time reproducing the reassuring narrative of the promised conclusion to the romantic union popularized by the penny novelette. *Forget-Me-Not* (*FMN*), one of the earliest of Harmsworth's magazines addressed to "ladies from fifteen to fifty," romanticized shop life in stories with titles like "The Adventures of a Shop

"Miss Raines!" cried Phœbe, "you had better come forward and confess the truth, and not bring dismissal on us all!"

"A Little White Slave," *Forget-Me-Not*, March 1904. Reproduced by permission of the British Library, g.1164(18).

Girl" (*FMN*, 1897), "That Pretty Shop Girl" (*FMN*, 1902), and "A Little White Slave" (*FMN*, 1904), and the later serials followed suit with "Kate Mercer: Shop Girl" (*Girls' Friend*, 1900), "Only a Shop Girl" by Mabel Strange (*Girls' Friend*, 1903), and "Slave of the Shop" (*Girls' Reader*, 1909). These stories frequently positioned their idealized heroines in circumstances familiar to those experienced by shopgirl readers, but created extraordinary events which made it possible for the heroine to escape the hardship of labor in the shop and eventually be restored to her legitimate position and/or inheritance.

In "A Little White Slave," for example, Isabel Raines, an employee of Messrs. Neilson & Gad's drapery establishment and a young lady of evident good birth and breeding, is wrongfully accused of theft and divested of her inheritance by Phoebe Lingdon, whose mother exchanged the two girls' surnames in infancy. Sir John Page, the handsome baronet who covets both Isabel and her fortune, kidnaps and eventually marries her, and only his death at the hands of the jealous Phoebe allows Isabel to be reunited with her virtuous lover Dick Denton.

A similar plot to steal a fortune from its rightful heirs forms the narrative of "Only a Shop Girl," in which Esther Dayle inherits three million pounds and the great drapery house of Harsent & Co., but forfeits the inheritance to her villainous second cousin Douglas Daunton because of a missing marriage certificate and, while the search continues for the document which will restore her name and fortune, instead fulfills the terms of her great-uncle's will by entering the shop herself as an assistant in the lace department. She, too, is accused of theft and subjected to cruel treatment by many of her fellow shopgirls, who are jealous of her beauty and the attentions she receives from the younger Daunton heir. The elder Daunton plots to marry his son Vincent to Esther, despite Vincent's previous secret marriage, simultaneously agreeing to ruin the prospects of Keith Carlton, an inventor of a revolutionary process for cotton-mill production and Esther's lover. When the certificate finally surfaces, Douglas Daunton is revealed to be the murderer of Esther's father, and Esther obtains her wealth and position as proprietor of Harsent's drapery firm, thereby righting the wrongs done to herself and her family.

This story in particular makes an effort to expose the indignities which shop employees suffered both in the showrooms and in the private quarters of London's drapery houses. The staff dining room at Harsent's contrasts markedly with Esther Dayle's sheltered past, with its "rough" tableware and heavy food served by overworked women; No. 15, the room she shares with twenty other women, is the dirtiest in the house, and several of the girls drink brandy on the sly. The close quarters and lack of privacy allow Elspeth Dork (or "Green Eyes," as the other girls have nicknamed her), the secret wife of Vincent Daunton, to persecute Esther through actions like ransacking her trunk and filling her washstand with an acidic solution. Through this focus on the underside of shop life, "Only a Shop Girl" reflects the emphasis in much of the Amalgamated Press shop fiction on revealing the hardships experienced by female drapery employees, who were often subjected to exploitation at the hands of managers and shopwalkers both in the shops of London and in the pages of magazine serials. The tyrannical shopwalker, a stock figure in much of this fiction as well as in musical comedies set in thinly disguised versions of London stores, represents the sexual harassment shopgirls could endure from unscrupulous superiors; Mr. Bulstrode (nicknamed "Bully") embodies the lecherous, patronizing attitude adopted by men who used fines and promotions to exert power over the employees they resented or admired.[58]

In almost all of these stories, the dignified lady employee speaks out against the injustices practiced by the greedy yet cowardly shopwalker, often concluding the story by firing the guilty man and instituting better working conditions throughout the establishment. This conclusion

"No, there isn't any mistake, miss. The lace has disappeared. Where is it?"
"Bully's" voice, guarded and almost polite at first, was suddenly raised loudly enough to reach the ears of every assistant behind the counter.

"Only a Shop Girl," *Girls' Friend,* October 1903. Reproduced by permission of the British Library, 1022.

resolves the shopgirl-reader's anxieties over her own experience of shop life, reassuring her of the rewards for enduring the trials of shop labor.

More importantly, however, the shopgirl stories presented in the Harmsworth/Amalgamated Press papers provide an alternative model for understanding the practice of consuming fantasy. The working- and lower-middle-class shopgirls who read *Girls' Friend* or *Forget-Me-Not* as they journeyed to work on the train or stole a few moments' reading at the close of the day might have been able to import the unfinished narrative of Esther Dayle or Isabel Raines into their everyday lives, renarrating their ordinary lives as fiction. Penny magazines such as those described above invite this alternative model, in that they posit an active reader who could use her imagination to shape the next installment of the story, thereby supplying an infinite series of possible resolutions to that particular tale. In turn, the fictional narrative such a reader produced through fantasy might then be read as influencing her everyday life in the shop, leading her to imagine herself as the model heroine, triumphing over adversity and winning the man she loves. This model, operative in a different form in the novelette's use of fantasy to diverge from the romance plot, provides an alternative to contemporary accounts of cheap fiction as escapist narratives of wish fulfillment, instead suggesting new ways of transforming the experience of the banal into something more stimulating and fulfilling.

However, it is important to remember that the promise provided by the fictions published in the Harmsworth magazines—that shopgirls, too, might find married bliss through an escape from the shop—remained distinct from the actual lives of many shop assistants themselves. In fiction, heroines married into wealth, title, and eternal happiness; in reality, female shop assistants often remained single or, if they married, exchanged one experience of mundane labor for another. Nonetheless, these magazines focused on marriage and its alternative, successful and fulfilling employment, in order to produce a different kind of life plot for the shop-girl. The Harmsworth papers combined editorial commentary on girls' chances of marrying well with articles written by London shop assistants with titles like "My Day's Work, by a Draper's Assistant" (*FMN*, March 26, 1904) and "Business Girl Chats No. 9: A Shop-Girl" (*Girls' Friend* no. 301, 1905). While each paper carried similar material, *Forget-Me-Not* seems to have targeted readers concerned with courtship and married life, while *Girls' Friend* and *Girls' Reader* tended to focus on representing the "actual" experiences of shop workers in order to convey some sense of working conditions to young women interested in shop employment. According to one article in *Forget-Me-Not*, for example, shopgirls might marry as well as girls of their class who stayed at home; moreover, they gained more experience in and exposure to public life, and subsequently would not be as susceptible to seduction by "worthless" men. The author claimed to know of several cases where shopgirls married into wealth and position, and in each instance "the young wife, when put into high authority, [. . .] never acted foolishly or put on airs because she had the good fortune to be very happy and successful in life."[59] This claim both reinforces the ideal of the shopgirl's upward social mobility and supplies a positive example by which readers who might be so fortunate could guide their behavior. Another article argued that "politeness is more important than beauty" in winning a wealthy man, citing shopgirls' positive qualities of punctuality, tidiness, and attention to others as the virtues shared by good wives.[60]

Indeed, the controversy over whether shopgirls were fit to marry and reproduce domesticity in their own lives reflected the tension between absorption and distraction as modes of experience. A series of articles on "Shopgirls as Wives" provides an interesting glimpse into the contemporary debate between middle-class commentators and shop assistants themselves over whether such work suited the shopgirl for domestic life. The first article, written by a female contributor, was later denounced by the editor as cruel and unjust in its assessment of shopgirls as slovenly wives, and provoked a flurry of letters from ex-shopgirls and their husbands as well as a response restating the appeal of punctuality and affection in the young wife. This article describes a situation in which the husband's illusions acquired during courtship quickly fade upon entrance into wedded life:

> During that blissful period, when love is young and love is all, his vision is ravished by the sight of a girl attired in the latest fashion, her coiffure equally à la mode; but once marriage has removed the necessity to serve behind the counter, the girl of fashion disappears and in her place is the slovenly woman, of the curling-pin order. The woman whose every garment is woefully demanding the ministrations of a needle and thread; the woman whose shoes are trodden over and unsightly; in short, the woman who doesn't care a pin how she looks![61]

Moreover, the author suggests, ex-shopgirls are too apt to become "gad-abouts," substituting the amusement of flirtation for care of her home. This narrative of swift descent clearly adopts the language of anxiety over socially appropriate behavior, suggesting the pressure exerted by middle-class domestic ideology on the management of the home and presenting an image of failed self-management, which is narrated through the stereotypical setting of working-class poverty (as in the examples of "shoes trodden over and unsightly," torn garments, and the like). This author locates the problem in the wife's boredom and frustration with the domestic routine, a narrative of failed reproduction of the norms of proper femininity reminiscent of Monica's disastrous marriage to Widdowson in Gissing's novel *The Odd Women*. Here, the ex-shopgirl, used to the "endless variation" presented by lovers and lovemaking, gets bored with the "'one life, one love' order of things" and longs for the stimulating, romanticized atmosphere of the shop.[62] This type of phrasing suggests that the shopgirl's failure might in fact be located in the distracting pleasures which shape her experience of labor and leisure, instead suggesting that she absorb her attentions in the more appropriate object of her husband and family. Conceding that the shopgirl may retain her womanly virtues if she marries for love rather than to escape her working life, the article nonetheless ends on a note of warning to those women who, no longer in their youth, may end up spinsters for lack of care and attention to the normative standards for character and conduct associated with marriage and domesticity.

The response from "another lady writer" returns to the ideal of the shopgirl-turned-devoted wife, couching the descriptions of the idealized union in the language of romance fiction:

> Just because she loves, she tries to be a good wife, and make her house a home, that the man she loves may find it the centre of his most cher-

ished ideals. Should the years as they pass bring bitter with the sweet, and tinge love's joy with pain, her's [sic] is not the voice to grumble because Fate has, with his inexorable hand, run things awry.[63]

In reply to the question asked of the "dear girl reader," "are you to-day brain-tired and weary with the toil of pleasing others, are you wondering whether into your life the advent of love will dawn with sweet-winged splendour?" the writer repeatedly reassures the reader that her own fairy prince will surely come "in Cupid's good time," at which point she will be able to enjoy the full measure of domestic and romantic bliss.[64] Husbands of ex-shopgirls expressed similar sentiments in their letters, writing of the "perfect happiness" they experienced upon marrying young women who were already so well versed in the art of pleasing others, for again the shop-girl's sympathetic ear and kind heart were imagined to prepare her well for the matrimonial marketplace.[65] The narrative of perfect happiness through absorption in others is here positioned against the disruptive desire for "variety" and stimulation embodied by the shopgirl who fails to reproduce the properly feminine in her own practice.

In addition to the editorial commentary on shopgirls' chances of mar-riage, the girls' papers often featured articles written by actual shop employees, detailing their earnings and prospects and describing the mun-dane activities which occupied their working hours. Most spent some time describing the living-in system and the fines levied on employees for late-ness or billing errors; others focused on the pressure to push "spiffs" (old or unsellable stock) on unknowing customers or the frustration of serving "querulous old ladies" when one has been standing for hours on end with throbbing head and aching feet.[66] The magazines reveal a contradictory perspective on shop labor: to some, it is "light and easy" work which any girl can do, while to others it involves drudgery and discrimination (by condescending shopwalkers as well as managers who only engage attractive female employees). The emphasis in articles by shop assistants themselves often falls on the task of representing the actual conditions of their every-day lives, a pragmatism which contrasts markedly with the romanticized narratives of the stories serialized in the same pages. I have not been entire-ly able to reconcile the tension between reading the romance and writing the real in these magazines, a contradiction made particularly evident through editorial claims to authenticity like that appended to the start of Mabel Strange's "Only a Shop Girl" (1903):

> This wonderful novel is the first published work of a talented young lady who is still engaged as a shop assistant in a large drapery estab-lishment. The delineations of character and surroundings are drawn

from the scenes amongst which the story has been written. The bitter struggles, trials, and temptations of the life of a lady shop assistant are portrayed with a vividness and truthfulness which will hold the reader spellbound from start to finish.[67]

This description gestures to the possibility of an alternative to the circumscribed narrative of shop work and marriage through the role of the author: the act of imagining the shopgirl as writer rather than wife or employee opens up an unexplored realm of possibility for the reader. Significantly, too, the editor's evident effort to market the story as a faithful representation of the shopgirl's working life effaces the distance between the romance narrative and the life of the reader so carefully constructed by the penny novelette. This slippage marks the permeability of the fantasy as a mode of rewriting everyday life, suggesting the necessity of creating and maintaining such a fantasy experience as a mode of sustenance for the shopgirl reader.

Ultimately, of course, the illusory narrative of upward mobility presented in these fictions might be faulted for its idealization of the romance plot as a method for transforming the banality of everyday life. Although these stories did pose a metaphoric threat to the entrenched Victorian class system, expressed through the mode of reader fantasy, this threat was far more likely to remain a promise, existing only in the realm of the imagination rather than exerting any significant influence over the working conditions of shopgirl-readers themselves. And yet it may have been the promise itself, its elusive qualities of deferral and suggestion, that rendered these narratives attractive to readers. The alternative identificatory structures provided by the romance fictions presented in these novelettes and magazines, which offered multiple modes for negotiating the relationship between fantasy and everyday life, suggest a range of consuming possibilities that do not emerge in contemporary middle-class accounts of the effects of such fiction. Although I want to acknowledge the difficulty of imagining how fantasy and its effects might be translated to the mundane world of the real, I nonetheless remain committed to producing an analysis of the utopian possibilities such acts of imagining represent.[68] This argument highlights the importance of reading such popular texts for the implicit and speculative fantasy narratives they produce, at the same time recognizing that these narratives necessarily cannot represent some version of the "true" consuming practices of actual shop assistants during this period.

In this chapter, I have examined the methods by which readerly fantasy and the absorptive model of escape through identification perpetuates the prevailing ideology of domesticity through the romance narrative. As my discussion of the novelette's focus on fashion and display revealed, however, the narrative of absorption in the romance plot might well diverge from its own teleology, instead producing a zone of free play which would permit new modes of desire and identification that might break the bounds of the conventional romance plot. As a corollary, my discussion of serialization in magazines targeted to the shopgirl has articulated how we might view turn-of-the-century distraction as pleasurable and productive, resulting in new modes by which women readers might use fantasy to transform their experience of everyday life. To construct a sense of the stakes behind these new modes of consuming fantasy, I have analyzed the middle-class response to the pleasures of reading, a reaction that reveals the cultural investment in the possible narratives, fictional or actual, which might ensue as a result of the shopgirl's reading practices.

In my discussion of the pleasures produced by popular reading, in which the distraction facilitated by an analysis of the serialized form of the magazine represents the other side of narrative absorption and identification, I intend to suggest the differences between the relatively private consumption of print and the more public experience of consumption in the context of the late Victorian and Edwardian culture of spectacle. In constructing this argument, I have drawn on scholarship on the concept of distraction as a constitutive element of modernity and social experience for consumers of turn-of-the-century mass culture. This project has been shaped by Tom Gunning's work on early film as a "cinema of attractions," in which spectators participate in an act of distracted viewing. Gunning uses Frankfurt School theorist Siegfried Kracauer's analysis of the "cult of distraction" which characterized Berlin's picture palaces in order to elaborate the substitution of discontinuity and fragmentation for the illusionistic absorption of classical film narrative.[69] With this in mind, the next chapter moves from the more private experience of readerly fantasy to the public sphere of mass fantasy embodied by popular entertainments. Chapter 5 analyzes the workings of distracted pleasure in the context of music hall, popular theatre, and early film, tracking the complex transformation of distraction into absorption and the increasing dominance of early film narrative in England. This concluding chapter analyzes the construction of the shopgirl as a member of the mass audience and theorizes the production of spectatorship through the enforced separation of the two modes of experience that were integral to dominant perceptions of the shopgirl's consuming desires and practices.

CHAPTER 5

Distracted Pleasures: Gender, Leisure, and Consuming in Public

In the popular imagination, as the target audience for penny romance fiction in the form of novelettes and serialized magazines, shopgirls read texts, images, and narratives in a manner which combined two modes of consumer fantasy: absorption and distraction. This model of narrative consumption depended on an individual's private engagement with the text, even if the act of reading occurred in the public spaces of modern urban life, the bustling city street or the crowded railway station.[1] The distractions provided by the atmosphere in which these penny romances were read contributed to the experience of distracted pleasure, in that the fantasy produced by the text might permeate or spill over into the contexts of the shopgirl's everyday life, and conversely that elements of the everyday might enter the scene of fantasy. As the previous chapter suggested, however, this permeable model of fantasy and reading pleasure often remained in the realm of the imaginary: shopgirls were no doubt less likely to act on the fantasies produced through reading than many critics of penny fiction presumed, and of course the actual rate of intermarriage between shop assistants and store owners or aristocrats was much lower than the romance plot would lead us to expect.[2] The vital conclusion we may draw from the analysis of popular romance fiction is the sense of possibility provided by the promise of an alternative ending to one's own life plot, even if this promise entails only wishful thinking.

If we consider the pursuit of distracted amusement in the mass public context of late-nineteenth-century spectacle culture, however, it becomes clear that a new set of romance plots began to emerge, reflecting a shift in the mode of consumer leisure during the end of the period covered by this study. As the following analysis illustrates, the model of consumer practice described in the previous chapter underwent a dramatic transformation during the first fifteen years of the twentieth century. During the decade from 1894 to 1904, a similar model of distracted consumption operated in tandem with the variety format of public entertainments. The music hall sketches, musical comedies, and early short films produced during this period reflect the fragmented, distracted experience of leisure consumption associated with the shopgirl. Gradually, however, the increased emphasis on absorption and immersion in the feature film narrative over the next decade, combined with the transformation of film's exhibition context through the creation of the purpose-built cinema, resulted in a shift in the mode through which such pleasures were experienced. In the earlier years of the period addressed in this study, shopgirls participated in an interactive consumer environment based on spectacle and defined through the rituals of romantic courtship and sexual desire, whether as part of the lively music hall crowd or as viewers of short films whose appeal lay in their strategic use of display. By the 1910s, however, shopgirl viewers were repositioned as spectators through a number of changes to the viewing experience, including the introduction of electric lighting in the interiors of darkened auditoriums and the informal and ideological censorship of music hall and film texts.

Most notable in this period, and most relevant for the study of working women's leisure, is the separation of absorption and distraction into discrete modes of consumer practice. The development of feature film narrative and the use of formulaic romance plots in early cinema meant that absorption came to dominate an industry which had formerly structured its use of fantasy through distraction. Viewers were urged to relinquish the distracted pleasures of the early public leisure experience, substituting for them the more highly individualized experience of absorption in a fantasy dependent on a sustained narrative. The structure of the feature film narrative meant that absorption was used to harness the formerly anarchic pleasures of the consuming audience, directing viewers to face the screen and, by the 1920s, addressing them as classical spectators. The relative success of this disciplinary narrativizing strategy meant that any vestiges of subversive activity within the auditorium (the couples entwined in the back rows of darkened theatres, for example) were intended for eventual eradication in an environment which emphasized control over the character and conduct of its formerly unruly audience.[3] The struggle to sustain this mode of interactive consumer experience in the face of pressures from censors and others anxious to maintain the moral standards of the masses underscores the significance of the debates over sexuality, morality, and agency that produced the shopgirl as a paradigmatic consumer of mass entertainments.

In this chapter, I address several such entertainment contexts, examining the texts and performances presented on stage and screen for audiences

of shopgirls and other leisure consumers. This analysis addresses the relationship between sexual knowledge and pleasure in an environment Peter
Bailey has identified as structured through the "knowingness" identified
with "parasexuality," a new form of "open yet licit" sexuality sanctioned by
a burgeoning mass consumer culture.[4] Alongside existing scholarship on
the relationship between fashion and glamour on the popular stage and
screen at the turn of the century, I situate the shopgirl's pursuit of distracted pleasure—the pleasure inherent in consumer and romantic fantasy.
After analyzing the place of shopgirls within the turn-of-the-century mass
audience, the chapter focuses on several exemplary textual genres that
epitomize the culture of fashion, glamour and sexuality associated with the
late Victorian and Edwardian shopgirl: the music hall sketch, the musical
comedy, and the early fashion film. In each case, a number of images and
ideologies associated with the figure of the shopgirl come into play: here
the shopgirl is at once a glamorous modern young woman, a potential
consumer of luxury fashions, and an object of sexual desire. All of these
characterizations merge in the context of the contemporary perception of
the department store, and by extension the city, as a site of sexual license,
embodying the pleasures and dangers posed to women by the urban environment.[5] As the chapter's conclusion suggests, a department store melodrama like *Damaged Goods,* a 1919 propaganda film starring a shop assistant as its fallen heroine, represents the other side of the romance plot,
demonstrating that the twin narratives associated with the figure of the
late Victorian and Edwardian shopgirl continue to flourish well into the
twentieth century.

Shopgirls and the Mass Audience

The turn-of-the-century spectacle culture of music hall, popular theatre,
and early film drew in part from the display culture of the shop and the
department store to constitute its audience: shop assistants, both male and
female, went in great numbers to theatres and music halls, and then to
purpose-built cinemas to view the latest technology of the moving picture.
They also patronized fairground entertainments and exhibitions and pursued outdoor recreational activities in the parks and public spaces of
London. In the popular perception and in the historical record, female
shop employees drew from a wide range of alternatives to find pleasure in
their leisure hours, despite the regimented working conditions under
which they labored. It is vital to examine the *perceived* leisure activities of
the shopgirl in order to account for the limitations of researching the consuming practices of a set of social subjects who left little trace of their actu-

al responses to the culture of public leisure practice. Although we can certainly identify female shop assistants as members of the late Victorian and Edwardian mass audience, it is next to impossible to locate surviving accounts which would convey the range of perspectives on that experience.[6] My strategy for meeting this challenge in this chapter has been to combine an investigation of surviving historical texts with fictional depictions of the leisure practices of the shopgirl. In addition, much can be gained from an analysis of the mode of address of certain music hall, theatrical, and cinematic texts, suggesting the ways in which these texts spoke to women employed in the fashion industry, itself an atmosphere which created and relied on consumer fantasy.[7] Without the benefit of accounts of individual reactions to and engagement with these texts, this analysis has its limitations; however, using a text-based strategy may assist us in understanding cultural assumptions regarding the atmosphere and characteristics of leisure for the London shopgirl during this period.

As members of the newest segment of the consuming public, shopgirls were perfectly positioned to participate in the making of the turn-of-the-century audience for mass entertainments.[8] Young, single women often living in shop dormitories and free from parental supervision, shopgirls frequently spent their leisure time in each others' company, or went to the theatre, the music hall, or the picture palace with a male suitor. In this context, popular leisure practice and the courtship ritual became intertwined as female shop assistants, unable to afford the luxurious experience of an evening on the town on their own, accepted the offers of men in order to provide themselves with stimulation and diversion. In such music hall environments as the Empire or the Alhambra, where the nightly promenades served as a meeting place for prostitutes and their clients, single working women were apt to be mistaken for prostitutes; of course, by accepting a man's invitation for an evening's entertainment, they risked placing themselves in a similar, if less explicitly articulated, situation.[9] Shopgirls were at particular risk of being evaluated in terms of their successful embodiment of respectability. The shopgirl's access to respectability, at work as well as during leisure hours, was mediated through dress and behavior: should an attempt to replicate the fashions worn by wealthy women fail (fashions found in the pages of penny papers like *Dorothy's Novelette* and *Forget-Me-Not*), her position as a woman aspiring to upward mobility and middle-class status, tied to her ability to represent "proper" femininity through visual and behavioral codes, was apt to be thrown into question. In the spectacle culture of mass entertainment, this association is literalized in a middle-class anxiety about "respectable" women brushing up against the bodies and morals of those women in the audience who were seen as "disreputable." The shopgirl's placement between the working and the middle classes, dreaming of a rise in the social hierarchy yet physically and perceptually tied to the labor environment of the shop, resulted in an increased sense of moral concern on the part of middle-class observers about the hazards of participating in the leisure entertainments of the masses.

In the late Victorian and Edwardian music hall—or variety palace, as it should more properly be called in keeping with its fragmentary format[10]— shopgirls as consumers were caught up in a narrative of social and sexual risk tied to their participation in the spectacle produced on stage as well as in the audience. The suggestive songs and sketches which were integral elements of the performance often featured the adventures of a country girl whose introduction to urban life involved sexual initiation, recreating the formula of the romance as a narration of the processes used by such young women to negotiate the rituals of courtship. These performances generally incorporated bawdy humor and comedic style to present an object lesson to young women who might themselves encounter a similar situation. Shopgirls were the implied referents of this narrative of a young woman's initiation into the pleasures and dangers of urban life, as they served most frequently as examples of the mobility and migration of working women from rural counties to the metropolis in the late nineteenth century.[11] Although the music hall sketches and songs did not always feature shopgirls as heroines—unlike that other popular turn-of-the-century stage genre, the musical comedy—the similarity in certain elements of these performances can be taken to suggest the identificatory exchange that many contemporary writers perceived to be occurring between shop assistants in the audience and the texts they consumed.[12]

We can identify a similar anxiety over the relationship between the text and the behavior of audience members in the case of early film exhibition, a public context which reflected and reproduced the distracted pleasures in consumption described in chapter 4. The earliest films were exhibited as part of the variety show of the late Victorian music hall, and as elements of the "cinema of attractions" they contributed to the distracted quality of turn-of-the-century spectacle culture.[13] This type of variety spectacle was eventually supplemented by the purpose-built theatres of the 1910s, a transition which involved efforts to subdue the distracted (and distracting) pleasures occurring within the cinema auditorium. As members of the early film audience—itself a cultural form undergoing a gradual transformation in class status and respectability during the later years of this period—female shop assistants participated in the transformation of the public consumer pleasures of the early film theatre, from a distracted, interactive environment to an atmosphere dependent on the absorbing pleasures of the feature film narrative and the establishment of classical models of film spectatorship.

"Palaces of Distraction":
Music Hall, Musical Comedy, and Variety Entertainment

As Dave Russell has argued, the turn-of-the-century music hall was an institution in transition, denounced by critics as a soulless commodification of an authentic tradition belonging to "the people," but hailed by supporters as a vital new form incorporating the latest popular entertainments.[14] The variety theatres of the 1880s and 1890s became "palaces" of amusement in the early 1900s, with architectural splendor contributing to an atmosphere of luxury and abundance paralleling that of the late Victorian and Edwardian department store. Likewise, the musical comedy—a form derived from burlesque, comic opera, and farce, but involving longer, generally romantic, narratives—evolved in the 1890s and early 1900s into an immensely popular genre, particularly for its use of spectacle and display to engage its audience.[15] The production of the music hall as a spectacle in itself had been underway since the 1880s: halls such as the Empire and the Alhambra, two of the most vilified examples of the need for censorship in the eyes of social purity campaigners, had incorporated "flamboyant" and splendid architecture, gilded interiors, and glittering lights since their inception.[16] In an 1890 article, F. Anstey described the Empire's lavish appearance as follows:

> Its exterior is more handsome and imposing than that of most London theatres, even of the highest rank. Huge cressets in classical tripods flare between the columns of the facade, the windows and foyer glow with stained glass, the entrance hall, lighted by soft electric lamps, is richly and tastefully decorated. You pass through wide, airy corridors and down stairs, to find yourself in a magnificent theatre, and the stall to which you are shown is wide and luxuriously fitted.[17]

The performances, like the decor, "satisf[ied] the most insatiate appetite for splendour," filling the stage with "bewildering combinations of form and colour" which culminated in a dazzling conclusion: "the ballet girls are ranked and massed into brilliant parterres and glittering pyramids, the première danseuse glides on in time to appropriate the credit of the arrangement, and the curtain falls on a blaze of concentrated magnificence."[18] Anstey's description of the hall's environment and entertainments anticipates the combination of surface splendor and mechanization described by Siegfried Kracauer in his 1927 essays on distraction and the mass ornament. Like that other institution dedicated to the culture of display, the department store, these "palaces of distraction" (to use another of

Kracauer's evocative phrases), appeal to and reproduce the desire for wealth and luxury in their patrons, disregarding the social background and class status of those patrons and shifting focus from the world of the everyday to the culture of fantasy and distraction.[19]

The performances taking place on the variety stage contributed to the production of distraction in the viewing audience. Alongside the comic songs from the earlier years of music hall, late Victorian and Edwardian variety theatres featured an array of novelty acts, including magicians, jugglers, strongmen, performing animals, and the new technology of the bioscope and the cinematograph. They also incorporated ballet acts and sketches like "A La Carte" (performed at the Palace Theatre of Varieties in 1913 and starring Gaby Deslys, the French dancer who would later become the mistress of Gordon Selfridge), many of which retained the sexual suggestiveness of the Victorian halls. Sensitive to the influence of social purity campaigners, however, managers were careful to characterize these performances as respectable, often emphasizing their artistic merit in an attempt to differentiate the products of high(er) culture from those associated with the pleasures of the masses.[20] The sheer multitude of performative elements on the variety stage meant that viewers were less likely to see an evening's entertainment in terms of absorption in a sustained narrative or plot, instead participating in a distracted consumer environment based on the pleasures of a range of visual and aural stimuli. For participants in the experience of variety entertainments, the possibility of creating consumer fantasy was literalized both by the nature of the spectacle and by the incorporation of visual splendor in the scene of display.

In contemporary literary representations of popular theatrical entertainments, the distracted pleasures of the spectacle are often complicated by the class and gender of the audience. In W. Somerset Maugham's 1915 novel *Of Human Bondage*, for example, Mildred Rogers, the tea-shop girl-heroine, persuades various suitors to provide her with the amusement she most enjoys: an evening out at a theatre or music hall.[21] Mildred's "vulgar" nature (read as working-class throughout the novel, as I argue in chapter 3) contaminates even the entertainments she attends: a night at the theatre with Philip Carey, the protagonist, is actually an evening of musical comedy, an experience considered somewhat less respectable for its popularity with the masses. Mildred attends several music hall performances as well, including the Tivoli with Philip's rival Miller, and the Canterbury with Philip himself, both performances which excite her interest and frankly expressed pleasure. In Maugham's view, the experience of a night out at the theatre or music hall suits Mildred perfectly in its vulgar, lower-class atmosphere; Mildred's character and the character of mass entertainment are intertwined, each defining and influencing the other.

In the first instance, Philip asks Mildred to attend a performance of the American musical *The Belle of New York,* with dinner at the Adelphi Restaurant beforehand.[22] His offer of "a couple of stalls" is expressly designed to attract her on an economic level, for "when girls went to the play it was either in the pit, or, if some man took them, seldom to more expensive seats than the upper circle" (278).[23] Philip's success in persuading Mildred to accompany him does not mitigate his distaste for mass entertainment, however:

> Philip was a very cultured young man, and he looked upon musical comedy with scorn. He thought the jokes vulgar and the melodies obvious; it seemed to him they did these things much better in France; but Mildred enjoyed herself thoroughly; she laughed till her sides ached, looking at Philip now and then when something tickled her to exchange a glance of pleasure; and she applauded rapturously.
>
> "The is the seventh time I've been," she said, after the first act, "and I don't mind if I come seven times more." (280–81)

Mildred's delight in the musical comedy metonymically comes to stand in for her class status, and foreshadows her fall: on this evening she compares herself favorably to other women in the stalls who wear paint and false hair, but as the novel progresses she adopts these very signifiers of dubious morality as she herself becomes a prostitute.

In a later scene, after Philip has agreed to allow Mildred and her baby to live with him in exchange for housework, the pair takes an evening tram through South London, passing "gaily lit" shops and crowds of shoppers in the streets (467). When they pass the Canterbury, Mildred exclaims, "Oh Philip, do let's go there. I haven't been to a music hall for months," and in response to Philip's hesitation over the price of seats in the stalls, replies, "Oh, I don't mind. I shall be quite happy in the gallery" (467). They obtain sixpence seats and Mildred "enjoy[s] herself thoroughly," with what Philip sees as a "simple-minded" pleasure (468). The subtext to this description is the fact that the Canterbury, a Lambeth hall catering to a local audience (including shopkeepers and their assistants, mechanics and laborers), would have facilitated the sort of mixing among classes so anathema to Philip, who has his own reasons for feeling socially insecure. As historian Dagmar Kift notes, audiences for suburban music halls such as the Canterbury tended to be relatively homogenous, consisting largely of working- and lower-middle-class patrons; others in this vein included the Metropolitan in Edgeware Road, the Middlesex in Holborn, the Winchester in Southwark, and Wilton's in the East End. The West End halls, by contrast, drew a more socially mixed male clientele consisting of aristocrats, bohemians, and students, often accompanied by female acquaintances who were perceived as more or less "creditable."[24] The struggle for upward mobility and financial security symbolized by Philip's efforts to gain a position as a country doctor depends on an enforced separation from the culture of the music halls, which for Maugham is tinged with base vulgarity in its appeal to the working-class desires of transitionally classed women like Mildred. As noted above, the music hall as class signifier is integral to Mildred's eventual descent into prostitution: her inability to separate herself from such "simple-minded" entertainments suggests her entrenchment in an identity which is both hypersexualized and emphatically working class.

Tensions around class and sexuality were prevalent in debates over the morality of the halls, particularly with regard to the presumed causality in the relationship between the songs and sketches performed on stage and the activities pursued by women in the audience. As scholarship by Lucy Bland, Tracy Davis, Judith Walkowitz, and others has shown, the turn of the century was characterized by an increased effort on the part of social purity campaigners to establish legal and social control over the "vice" and corruption they identified with London's streets and social institutions, one of the most prominent of which was the campaign against the music hall.[25] Both the material performed and the behavior of the audience were subject to multiple interpretations by inspectors, purity activists, and others who filed complaints about music hall activity with the London County Council (LCC).[26] The lyrics to music hall songs, as well as the "sketches" and the patter spoken by vocalists and comedians, were notorious for their potentially suggestive and "vulgar" nature, but such moral risks depended, as both industry members and reformers demonstrated, on the manner in which the songs and sketches were presented.[27] Songs like "The Bewitched Curate," in which the title character gazes at the legs of a young woman, were the subject of numerous complaints for their suggestive language. An apocryphal story recounts evidence given before the LCC Theatres and Music Halls Committee by Marie Lloyd, one of the stars of turn-of-the-century music hall culture, in response to charges of indecency: she sang the offending song "straight," without any accompanying gestures, and then followed it with "Come into the Garden, Maud," a "respectable drawing-room song" to which she added "every possible lewd gesture, wink, and innuendo" which would render it obscene in the eyes of the committee. Her conclusion, "It's all in the mind," shifted the burden of obscenity ruling from the performer to the individual viewer or listener.[28] Even Laura Ormiston Chant, a proponent of music hall regulation who styled herself "One of the Puritans," conceded that the interpretation of the lyric "meet me in the moonlight alone" would depend on "how it was sung and who sung it."[29]

Other popular music hall songs, like the American import "And Her Golden Hair Was Hanging Down Her Back," in which a country girl loses her innocence during a visit to London, explicitly relied on sexual innuendo to stimulate the imagination of the audience. The song describes the heroine's transformation from a shy maiden to a knowing woman with "a naughty little twinkle in her eye," a process set in motion when she strays into a "Palace" in "a Circus or a Square" (a coded reference to the West End halls) where she appears in a "tableau":

> She posed beside a marble bath upon some marble stairs,
> Just like a water nymph or an advertisement for Pears,
> And if you ask me to describe the costume that she wears,
> Well, her golden hair is hanging down her back.[30]

This verse positions the song's heroine in the midst of a culture shaped by various discourses targeting the consuming pleasures of the masses, namely popular illustration and advertising (recalling the Pears' soap ad featuring a naked child) and the spectacle culture of the music hall. Each verse of the song is punctuated with the title line, narrating the process through which this young woman gains knowledge and sophistication, first through her control over the precious commodity of her "golden hair" ("once a vivid auburn") and then through her seduction of a young man.[31] With the suggestiveness of the repeated final line, this song uses humor and innuendo to simultaneously disparage and reinforce the conception that a naive young woman's sexual awakening might result from exposure to the risqué urban environment of mass entertainment.[32]

"And Her Golden Hair" underscores the contemporary perception of the shop or department store as the ultimate destination for young women from the country seeking employment and excitement in the metropolis, particularly through its adaptation for the 1894–6 Gaiety production of H. J. W. Dam and Ivan Caryll's musical comedy *The Shop Girl.* Written by Felix McClennon and originally sung by Alice Leamar, "And Her Golden Hair" was adopted by Sir Seymour Hicks, the show's romantic lead and the husband of Ellaline Terriss, one of the stars who played Bessie Brent, the plucky shopgirl-heroine of the long-running show.[33] This show, set in the "Royal Stores" (inspired, according to Dam's account, by Whiteley's and the Army and Navy Stores), capitalized on the association of the department store with romantic advancement and intrigue.[34] Its romance plot, in which a foundling shopgirl inherits a fortune, unfolds with a nod to the spectacular displays thought to be so appealing to the mass audience in its self-conscious use of a burlesque show at the store's charity bazaar, performed by girls from the "Frivolity

Theatre" (a reference to the Gaiety). The songwriters revealed their awareness of the reaction of social purity campaigners to the possibility of suggestive display within the show, however, and incorporated several direct references to Laura Ormiston Chant's crusade against indecency on the stage and in the audience at the Empire music hall during the previous month, including the following verse:

> And the skirts traditionally worn by ladies of the ballet,
> We have banished altogether as intolerably scant:
> On the promenade improper we have sternly put a stopper
> And the only tune permitted is the Ormistonian Chant. . . . [35]

The shift in subject matter within this verse from ballet dancers' skirts to the promenade, as well as in Chant's efforts to reform the activities taking place both on and off the stage, reveals the contemporary perception that the indecency taking place on stage might well affect the manners and morals of women in the audience, especially those of the young, seemingly vulnerable shop assistants whose character and conduct itself formed a spectacle for middle-class observers in the crowd.[36]

A number of other musical comedies featured shopgirl-heroines during this period, among them *The Girl from Kay's* (Apollo 1902), *The Girl Behind the Counter* (Wyndham's 1906), and *Our Miss Gibbs* (Gaiety 1909). In each of these cases, as Erika Rappaport has argued, the spectacular elements of consumer culture merge with the romance plot as the shopgirl-heroine navigates the pitfalls of courtship against the background of the millinery shop or fashionable department store. Like the novelettes and magazine fictions described in chapter 4, in these narratives the ultimate goal for the shopgirl-heroine is marriage, but the fantasy of consumption is never far behind; the narrative functions to hold viewers' attention while simultaneously facilitating the distracted pleasures of consumer fantasy through the display of glamorous fashions and the women who model them. Several numbers underscored the connection between romance and consumption through their emphasis on the desirability of the shopgirl herself, who becomes the primary object of desire for the audience. In *The Girl from Kay's*, a chorus set in the resort town of Flacton-on-Sea makes this connection explicit:

> We are young ladies
>   From Kay's—from Kay's
> Trimming our trade is
>   Most days—most days,
> Wreathing with laces

And flowers—and flowers
Frames for such faces
   As ours—as ours!
When work is done with
   And ends—and ends,
We have some fun with
   Our friends—our friends,
Flacton parade is
   Ablaze—ablaze,
With the young ladies
   From Kay's—from Kay's!
To Twickenham Ferry
   Where folly and frolic are
We go and are merry
   On top of a trolley car.
The play is our passion
   We love to see actresses,
With hats that we fashion,
   On top of their black tresses!
To work when she works and to play when she plays
There's nothing like a woman—a woman from Kay's!
   Our ways amaze
We are nice little ladies from Kay's![37]

In this song, the milliner becomes a consumer of "fun," whether in the
streets or at a play, but she herself is also available for consumption according to the expectations of the romance narrative. Likewise, the assistants in
Our Miss Gibbs (set in "Garrod's Stores," a thinly veiled version of
Harrods)[38] sing the virtues of the weekend while simultaneously under-
scoring their sexual availability:

   Saturday afternoon!
The welcome bell gives warning,
Business is done and we'll have fun,
Right up to Monday morning!
So you will find us soon,
In quite a new edition,
Out for the day, seeing a play,
Or for the Exhibition

   . . . .

   Saturday afternoon

> To all the winds we scatter,
> Now the week ends we go with friends,
> Where, it does not much matter!
>   Frolic and flirt and spoon
>   Without an intermission—
> Ride on the cars, pay at the bars,
>   At the Exhibition![39]

The popularity of the musical comedy certainly drew from its use of spectacle and display to attract viewers—hence the sumptuous sets and design
features of the musical comedy theatre, and the use of Gaiety dancers to
incorporate aspects of burlesque and music hall performance—but may
well have depended on the consuming desires of its female audience members, among whom were shop assistants and other employees of the serv-
ice-oriented urban culture of turn-of-the-century London.[40] Most significant is the way in which musical comedy participated in and perpetuated
a mass entertainment culture centered on sexual "knowingness" that combined consumption and display of the female body with the consumption
and display of goods—all under the guise of a narrative of romantic desire
and satisfaction.

The "Little Shopgirls" at the Movies

> *February 1st.* This opens a new month. Thank goodness I shall have
> a little time to make a few entries in my diary. It is disheartening to
> put in day after day "Very busy on account of sale" or "Working hard
> at stocktaking." Met a nice young gentleman, at least I did not exact-
> ly meet him, I ran into him in a passage and knocked him down. We
> had a long talk, and went to a picture palace, and saw "Love Laughs
> at Locksmiths."

> *February 6th.* Met my friend who knocked me down, and we went
> to the pictures. We saw "The Lovesick Cowboy Off the Beaten
> Track" and some other things which gave me chills all down my
> spine.[41]

These two fictionalized diary entries, written by a Harrods employee
impersonating a typical shopgirl derisively named "Miss Muddleton,"
position the female department store employee as a consumer of the feature films of the early 1910s, pictures which she attends with a "gentleman

friend" and which thrill her with the romance and adventure of narrative plots completely unlike her own. Judging from the titles of the films (themselves satiric depictions of the sensational Westerns and romances becoming increasingly popular with viewers during this period), these were longer, more absorbing tales using the romance/adventure plot to differentiate the on-screen narrative from the everyday lives of shop assistants themselves. There were, for example, very few films featuring shopgirls (or if they existed, these films were not reviewed either in *Bioscope* or in the nascent products of women's fan culture, *Pictures* and *Picturegoer*[42]), an absence which might suggest that such narratives of daily existence in the shop—no matter how sensationalized—appealed less to consumers than did other, more "exotic" romance plots. The presumption of a direct relation between a lack of films on a certain subject and a rejection of that subject by the audience cannot be quite so easily made, however, since the ways in which early film industry representatives— writers, directors, and producers as well as theatre owners and managers—strove to shape the consuming desires of their audiences were in fact much more complex. In any event, the absorption produced by viewing these sensational feature-length romances resulted from an earlier culture of distraction characteristic of the "cinema of attractions," in which the viewing audience found itself fascinated with successive and stimulating views. The yoking of absorption to the romance plot of early feature films resulted in an increasingly individualized relation to the production and consumption of fantasy, and signaled a turn away from the radical possibilities of distraction.

This section focuses on the history of early film exhibition in Britain, describing its relationship to the variety form of entertainment and accounting for the distracted pleasures which resulted from such a stimulating variety of on-screen images. To middle-class commentators, I argue, the pleasures of the consuming audience, many of them seen to be intimate private acts, were inflammatory precisely because they were taking place in public. I examine several examples from a particularly intriguing genre of early film "views" which positions the shopgirls in the audience as distracted viewers: the early fashion film.[43] The focus then shifts to the impact of narrative absorption on the behavior of the audience, first via a discussion of various measures to control the potentially "illicit" activities taking place in the dark auditorium, and then to a remarkable essay on the shopgirl's viewing experience as imagined by Siegfried Kracauer. While Kracauer is writing on early film spectatorship in 1920s Berlin, we can trace similarities in the constitution of the absorbed female film spectator in the British context, in order to understand the ways in which distraction becomes less available as a mode for acting out one's fantasies in public and to track the subsequent reindividualization of fantasy through the absorbing experience of the romance narrative. In a concluding section to the chapter, I turn to the 1919 film *Damaged Goods,* in which a shopgirl figures prominently at the center of a narrative about the moral, sexual, and social health of the nation, exploring its significance in the context of modern urban leisure.

The cinema as a new mode of public leisure entertainment arrived in London on 20 February 1896, when the Lumière Cinématographe received its first public screening by Félicien Trewey at the Royal Polytechnic Institution. Shortly thereafter Trewey exhibited the Lumière machine at the Marlborough Hall on Regent Street and then for an eighteen-month period at the Empire, drawing crowds of elite viewers anxious to experience the newest technological wonder. At the same time, the Alhambra management engaged Robert Paul to exhibit his Theatrograph alongside their current music hall acts. As the industry advanced, films began to be included in the variety format as one of the music hall "turns," usually occupying a twenty- to thirty-minute period toward the end of the evening's program; like performers, operators might give more than one turn per night, maximizing their exposure and profits from a number of different halls. Of course, early film exhibition was not limited to the West End halls: as public exhibitions became more frequent in city centers and suburban areas, they became available to working- and lower-middle-class viewers through the cheaper halls and in the transitional exhibition contexts of the "penny gaff" or shop-show, the peepshow street cinematograph, and the traveling or fairground exhibition.[44] Early exhibition contexts struck some viewers as bizarre novelties, while to others they represented the dubious legitimacy of the medium.[45]

By the end of the first decade of film exhibition, however, purpose-built cinema theatres began to take the place of these transitional exhibition contexts, and by 1916 the public displayed their commitment to this form of entertainment by spending more on it than on all other public forms of leisure combined.[46] Women were a vital part of the cinema-going audience from its early years—according to some estimates, by 1916 they made up over 50 percent of the audience—and because of their presumed access to higher moral standards for behavior, they were incorporated into the ideology of respectability that was becoming increasingly dominant within the industry.[47] Consequently, with the increased amount of public attention paid to cinema as a leisure entertainment came a concern over the behavior of the audience, particularly its female members, and extended discussion over how that behavior might be affected by the cinematic image. The transformation of the audience into a controllable entity paralleled industry and individual efforts to improve the moral condition of the narratives taking place on as well as off the screen.

In some accounts of early film exhibition, the audience appears as a fractured mass, a crowd of viewers rather than an audience of spectators focusing on the film narrative. Nicholas Hiley has argued that this crowd formed and encouraged a communal environment: he cites one projectionist's recollection of "a tremendous air of friendliness and sense of social gathering, with patrons chatting in the queue and during the intervals," and describes the multiple interruptions for reel changes and comings and goings, all of which made the audience present to itself as a community of viewers.[48] These audience members (especially the younger and more "exuberant" patrons) developed strategies for influencing the presentation of images on screen: if they disapproved of the program they might slash the backs of seats with pocket knives, or disrupt the showing by shouting at the screen.[49] In this sense, though, the audience seems to me to be less communal than characterized by internal divisions: patrons who wished to watch in silence found themselves ridiculed by more vocal members of the crowd, and might even be driven from the theatre by kicks at their seats after they complained about the disruption.[50] The lack of audience consensus over how films ought to be viewed resulted in large part from their primary exhibition context, the music hall and variety theatre auditorium which had itself been subject to the subduing influences of standardization since the late 1880s.[51]

The first fifteen years of cinema in England, then, found audiences resisting assimilation into a new model of spectatorship which relied on the individual and silent enjoyment of the performance on screen rather than the communal performance created by the auditorium environment of the variety theatres and music halls which were the predecessors to the cinema. Instead, the earliest cinema audiences consumed films according to a distracted model which incorporated the interactive pleasures one might experience as part of the process of public leisure practice.

I turn now to the fashion film, an early film genre that uses the rhetoric of consumption and display developed in the department store and provides an ideal example of the distracted model of consumption. This genre raises several questions that are germane to this study: What conclusions can we draw regarding consumer fantasy when the fantasy process is produced by the spectacular display of alluring fashions on screen? What are the limitations of the cultural construction of the shopgirl as a desiring subject, consuming fashions not unlike the goods she sells on a daily basis, but consuming them through fantasy rather than in practice?

A number of early films held by the British Film Institute display various fashions in drapery and millinery, often couched as part of an emergent French couture industry and therefore marked as elite and exotic products unlike the everyday fashions worn by women of the shopgirl's

transitional class. Two of these films, both entitled *Paris Fashion,* display
the latest luxury items as modeled by women who attempt to act naturally in front of the camera, engaging in various "realistic" activities like
pouring tea while modeling gowns produced by the houses of Ernest
Radnitz and Francine Arnauld.[52] Films such as these used a common strategy of placing their female models on rotating discs, so that they would
revolve in front of a stationary camera. This strategy of display resulted in
the female model becoming an item for consumption as much as the
goods themselves, so much so that the attraction of viewing lies in the fascination with a constructed spectacle slowly rotating before the eyes of the
viewer. The gowns and hats themselves were often elaborate creations
made of silks, feathers, and lace, made more appealing on film through
toning and tinting processes. These early fashion films, along with others
like *Early Fashions on Brighton Pier* (1898), position the shopgirl-viewer as
a consumer of a spectacle constituted through the exchange of looks: the
models of Paris fashions, like the women strolling past the camera on
Brighton Pier, gaze into the eye of the camera and hence out of the screen
at the audience. These early fashion films, nonnarrative and reliant on the
attractions of display, reveal the deferred pleasures that might result from
the creation of a fantasy which combined the scenic elements of display
with the sequencing of events resulting from the fantasized possession of
luxury items. Such films replicated the culture of display created by the
department store, participating in the construction of the shopgirl as a virtual consumer who gained distracted pleasure through the successive
images of the elaborate creations shown on screen.[53]

The sustained narratives of the feature-length romance and adventure
films of the 1910s came to be imagined by some critics as the ultimate
fulfillment of the consuming desires of the masses, who were seen to long
for the escape into alternate life plots that such sensational film narratives
might facilitate. This was certainly the case with the fictional Harrods
shopgirl "Miss Muddleton," who found herself stimulated by the
thrilling romances taking place on screen. We can also see this assumption at work in Siegfried Kracauer's 1927 series of articles on female spectatorship entitled "Die kleinen Ladenmädchen gehen ins Kino" (translated as "The Little Shopgirls Go to the Movies").[54] Each of the eight short
articles satirically depicts the shopgirl (here conflated with the "Little
Miss Typist," seen by Kracauer as another example of this class of semi-
professional female workers[55]) as a certain type of classical spectator, one
who immerses herself in the film through empathetic identification and
absorption. When the films end with "a triumph and an engagement,"
Kracauer argues, the female spectators desire the same ending to their
own romantic plot; when wealthy lovers disguise themselves as poor men

and women in films like *Her Night of Romance* (Sidney A. Franklin, 1924) and *Le Prince Charmant* (Victor Toujansky, 1925), the "little shopgirls" might later perceive a passing stranger as "one of the famous millionaires from the illustrated magazines" (302). In Kracauer's formulation, the "little shopgirls" in the mass audience typify the absorbed spectator-consumer of fantasies produced by the mass entertainment industry of the feature film. This model of consumption permits only a very slight degree of interaction between the shopgirl and her lover inside the cinema auditorium: inspired by the narrative of marriage between a "young and pretty girl" and a wealthy and propertied gentleman, "the poor little shopgirls" in the darkened theatres "grope for their date's hand and think of the coming Sunday" (297), imagining themselves as the heroines of this absorbing romance plot. What such romantic film plots do provide the shopgirl-spectator, however, is the ability to pursue her own fantasy plot in the solitude provided by an audience of spectators absorbed in the narratives taking place on rather than off the cinema screen. The model of absorbed consumption taking place in public results in the paradoxical privatization of mass entertainments, such that the fantasy becomes a highly individualized experience. That experience reflects the transition to the classical model of film spectatorship in which consumers enacted an increasingly silent and solitary relationship to the film text. Although the film experience retained some elements of the distracted model of consumer fantasy so characteristic of the earliest years of cinema, these elements were gradually subdued within a culture based on the consumption of absorbing and coherent narratives.

It has been argued that the transition from the participatory experience of the music hall to the silent spectatorship of the cinema was an effect of managerial and government efforts to maximize profits and standardize the early film industry.[56] It is certainly true that the cinema constituted a vast new market to be exploited by filmmakers and distributors, theatre owners and management alike; but this argument, grounded in economic analysis, does not account for the cultural concern over the presence of sexuality in the audience as well as on the cinema screen. Part of early cinema's effort to cater to the increasing demand for respectable amusements that would nonetheless entertain the masses was an emphasis on the need for a more formalized censorship to regulate the material presented on screen, thereby controlling the behavior of the audience. The records of rulings and decisions made by the London County Council and the British Board of Film Censors suggest that the industry concern for profits was intimately linked to a national effort to improve the moral and social environment of the cinema through the simultaneous control of the acts taking place on as well as off the screen.

For the first decade of cinema in Britain there were few direct legislative controls by local or national government which addressed the question of the cinema's effects on public morals and social relations. This is
not to say that contemporary critics did not express their anxiety over
the cinema's influence on mass audiences: on the contrary, they blamed
the cinema for its escapist function and its tendency to foster juvenile
delinquency and crime, and saw cinema theatres as sites which, like the
music hall, licensed prostitution and facilitated the spread of contagious
diseases.[57] Several articles in the mainstream press suggest that local mag-
istrates as well as clergy and temperance campaigners believed that "cinematograph shows were responsible for the downfall of many young
people," contributing to the prevalence of theft and violence among
young men and, occasionally, their female accomplices.[58] As a result, the
Home Office came under increasing pressure from the metropolitan
police to control film content in order to resist the alleged glorification
of crime and immorality on the cinema screen. The only way to control
this potentially dangerous new medium, many believed, was to institute
a formal structure for film censorship and disciplinary measures for controlling the unruly or transgressive behavior of audience members.
Hence the formation of the British Board of Film Censors (BBFC) in
1913, a regulatory board proposed by representatives from the film
industry (including the well-known filmmaker Cecil Hepworth) and
headed by G. A. Redford, formerly a stage censor on the Lord
Chamberlain's staff. Films were judged according to a general principle
involving the elimination of "anything repulsive and objectionable to
the good taste and better feelings of English audiences," a principle
which embodies the efforts to control the morality of the masses
described in the previous sections of this chapter. A 1914 report speci-
fied twenty-two grounds on which films were either cut or banned,
including vulgar or immoral behavior, excessive violence, and the dispar-
agement of public figures or sacred subjects.[59] During 1913 and 1914,
thirty-four films were rejected; twenty-two of these were in the first year
of the board's activity.[60]

A *Times* report on the "moral dangers of cinematograph exhibitions"
from 1913 reflects the continued assumption of an intimate relation
between the "objectionable" film and acts of "indecency" within the cinema theatre throughout the first fifteen years of film exhibition in Britain.
A special committee ruling on licensing in Liverpool addressed both subjects in close proximity, stating that "from time to time complaints have
been made of indecency having taken place in cinematograph halls, and it
is obvious that such offences may be facilitated by the darkness in which
some of the halls are kept while the pictures are being shown."[61] By 1917,

when the National Council on Public Morals undertook an investigation of the cinema, social reformers were arguing simultaneously for more supervision of the audience and a greater reliance on educational subjects rather than romances or adventure films. Following their investigation, the National Council of Public Morals published a report which recommended the establishment of suitable conditions for viewing and expressed support for state rather than industry-controlled censorship. Their findings contributed to a standardization of the cinematic experience through control of lighting, projection standards, and increased audience supervision by patrolling attendants as well as through the continued influence over the types of films available to the audience. As a result, the council's recommendations contributed to the ongoing effort to discipline the public leisure experience.[62]

The effects of this effort to standardize the practice of leisure had substantial implications for the subsequent regulation of the viewing pleasures of shop assistants and other members of the mass audience in the decades following the early years of cinema. It is the relationship between viewing pleasures—the fantasies occurring in the mind of the individual—and the enactment of those pleasures in practice that has formed the crux of this chapter. The shopgirl-viewer was positioned at the center of the debate over the dangers of distracted consumption, which in turn centered on the presumed exchange between actual events and those constructed through fantasy. This analysis is predicated on the distinction between two related types of consumption, the individual experience of reading and the interactive experience of consuming in public: distracted reading, with its facilitation of an interruption of the fantasy by the vestiges of the everyday, parallels the music hall and early film context. Absorption, by contrast, centers on sustained narrative, and therefore in the film context results in a privatization of the fantasy experience, so that spectators are increasingly swayed by the influence of narrative logic. We may see the distracted fantasy produced by turn-of-the-century leisure entertainments as a radical possibility for alternative modes of imagining the everyday whose anarchic or utopian possibilities lose their viability in the narrativizing mode of absorbed consumption. Ultimately, of course, both modes of consuming fantasy are revealed to be wishful thinking rather than a transformation of the actual conditions of everyday life; the promise intimated by the experience of fantasy (for another gown, another love, another life) remains a promise whose fulfillment is perpetually deferred. Yet it is the pleasures produced by these twin processes of fantasy, and the enthralling variety of repetition both formulaic and variable, which work to construct and sustain the shopgirl's construction as a consuming subject in both private and public contexts.

Sex and the Urban Landscape: *Damaged Goods*

In 1919, a propaganda film warning viewers of the dangers of venereal disease entitled *Damaged Goods* was produced and screened in Britain. The film was based on Eugene Brieux's 1902 play *Les Avaries,* which had had a successful run in the West End and on Broadway and had already been made into a film in the United States with the original Broadway cast, and told the story of a wealthy family whose purity and integrity is imperiled through the spread of syphilis. In the British film version, George Dupont, an aspiring lawyer, has become engaged to Henrietta Louches; before they marry, however, George discovers that he has contracted syphilis, and instead of waiting the two or three years recommended by a legitimate physician, he opts for an unreliable six-month cure, thereby spreading the disease to his newborn child. Only after George agrees to undergo the proper treatment can his family be cleansed of the disease. Intercut with George's story is the story of Edith Wray, the woman from whom he contracted the disease, who had begun her career as a shop assistant and, having been raped by her employer and fired when discovered to be pregnant, has been forced to resort to prostitution to support herself and her child. This, of course, is the familiar story of the shopgirl's fall, here reconceived as an exemplary case of the dangers posed by sexual activity outside the bounds of marriage.

Of particular interest for this argument is the shopgirl's transformation from innocent shop worker to fallen woman, figured against the urban landscape and evoking associations with the violation of proper femininity. When Edith, described in an intertitle as "an orphan fresh from the country," first arrives in the metropolis, she notices a sign outside a shop advertising "Assistants Wanted"; she hesitates, but a man steers her inside. Having obtained the position after being physically sized up by the proprietor, M. Rouvenel, and his wife, Edith undergoes an uncomfortable conversation with a gentleman customer, who speaks to her too familiarly and looks her up and down as she holds an elaborately sequined gown, conflating Edith with the clothes she displays as each becomes goods available for consumption.

Sent upstairs, ostensibly to locate an item for a customer, Edith is cornered and assaulted by Rouvenel, who tells her, "If you shriek, out you go!" before the image closes with an iris on her vain struggle to escape. Henriette and George's mother, visiting the shop in quest of Henriette's trousseau, become "eye witnesses of Edith's disgrace" as Mme Rouvenel reprimands, "We don't want your class in our establishment. Get out you baggage! Only respectable girls are wanted here." Despite the fact of her sexual exploitation by her employer, Edith's fall is ultimately collapsed

Still from *Damaged Goods,* 1919. Reproduced by permission of the Samuelson Family Archives.

with her descent in class—she is no longer "respectable" as a result of sexual activity—and her violation of appropriate gender codes. Intertitles expressing the irony of public morality and the sexual double standard reinforce the visual representation of Edith's story: as Edith searches futilely for another job, an intertitle proclaims, "The great moral public neither forgives nor forgets," and as a sequence of shots depicts the convent in which Edith places her baby intercut with scenes of M. Rouvenel flirting with another assistant, another intertitle reads, "The woman alone pays." Finally, Edith reappears at the end of the film: she is seen smoking outside the office of the reputable physician who has taken George's case; after she tells her story, the doctor remarks, "This poor girl is typical. The whole problem is summed up in her." Here, the fallen shopgirl becomes once again "typical," representative of a host of concerns to do with the consequences of sexual license and endangered morality; as her character is transformed from innocent country girl to sexually knowing prostitute and conveyor of disease, she comes to stand in for the dangers posed to the bourgeois family even as she is herself a victim.

Crucially, two sequences visually represent the contaminating influence of extramarital sexual activity, lodged in the body of the shopgirl, through the iconography of the city. The first sequence explicitly places the narrative in London: the shot of an urban landscape at night that follows the

intertitle which reads "The sins of the fathers," glimpsed quickly in passing, reveals itself to be a shot of the statue of Eros in the center of
Piccadilly Circus. This district of London combined associations of metropolitan nightlife and leisure entertainment, particularly with the presence of the Trocadero Restaurant and Theatre, with the perception of the
location as one of both pleasure and danger.[63] The city, here figured
through the shot of Piccadilly Circus, comes to stand in for sexual activity for pleasure (in George's case) and economic survival (in Edith's), and
by the rhetoric of metonymic substitution, the shopgirl comes to be representative of the dangers associated with the modern city. In the second
sequence, the protagonists' disregard of the dangers of sexual activity are
represented as the result of ignorance, which the physician later labels "our
greatest enemy." A title reads "The ignorance of youth," and is followed
by two titled images: the first, "By day," portrays the shop, and the second, "By night," depicts a dancing hall. Again, the logic of metonymy
facilitates the connection between urban locations and sexual
pleasure/danger, here assimilating the shop to the dancing hall as similar
sites of sexual license. If we take "the ignorance of youth" to refer to Edith
as well as George—leaving aside the responsibility of M. Rouvenel for his
actions—the titles suggest that in Edith's case, innocence and ignorance
are one and the same: the shopgirl loses her innocence as a result of her
inability to recognize the dangers posed by the metropolis, and sexual
knowledge robs her of innocence, respectability, and proper femininity.
For George, "the ignorance of youth" is embodied in his careless approach
to premarital sexual activity: the dancing hall stands in for the sexual
license allowed to young men whose lapses from the practice of "industry
and clean living" are generally overlooked. The collapse of urban locations
and sexual acts—shop and dancing hall, sexual exploitation and sexual
pleasure—underscores the ways in which the shop, and especially the
shopgirl, comes to signify that urban pleasure and danger are, in these narratives, one and the same.[64]

  As Annette Kuhn has argued, the exhibition context of the 1919 version of *Damaged Goods* is relevant to the film's mode of address, which
constructs its spectators as "moral subjects."[65] Kuhn places *Damaged Goods*
in the context of a number of other contemporary films that were
designed to educate the public about the dangers of venereal disease,
including a 1918 American film entitled *The End of the Road,* which contrasts the stories of two women, childhood friends, one of whom becomes
an army nurse and educates others as to how boys and girls may avoid
"unwise conduct, dangerous to health and morals," the other of whom
finds work as a shop assistant in a New York department store, becomes
sexually involved with a man outside of marriage, and contracts syphilis as

a result.[66] Many of these films appear to have been made or screened primarily for educational and propagandistic purposes, often in consultation with vigilance and purity associations such as the National Council for Combating Venereal Disease (NCCVD), although as Kuhn notes, both *Damaged Goods* and *The End of the Road* were shown in commercial exhibition contexts as well as in specially arranged private screenings. *Damaged Goods* and other films of its genre figured centrally in ongoing debates over censorship occurring within the British Board of Film Censors and the Home Office: although the founder of the NCCVD had argued that a British version of *Damaged Goods* would "reach an audience that the play could not touch and . . . good might result," the Home Office saw the film as inappropriate for everyday film audiences, since "the Cinema differs greatly from the Theatre: the audience is less intelligent and educated and includes far more children and young people."[67] This argument regarding the vulnerability of audiences to film narrative echoes that expressed by the National Council for Public Morals discussed above, and, as Kuhn theorizes, raises the possibility of "resistant" or otherwise unstable readings of such films.[68] Hence a propaganda film like *Damaged Goods* or *The End of the Road* might on the one hand serve as a lesson in proper sexual knowledge and practice, but it might also be read against the grain, in unexpected and unintended ways.

Damaged Goods, then, provides a fitting conclusion to the argument described in this study in its positioning of the shopgirl at the center of a narrative of anxiety, danger, and consequence for young working women's moral subjectivity, sexual behavior, and class position. Likewise the film poses crucial questions about the consumption, meaning, and mode of address of popular texts, and figures importantly in the continuing debate over women's leisure in the urban context. With a visual language based on metonymic associations between images of the city and moral danger, and an articulation of its characters as representatives of various "types" or positions, this film offers a range of possibilities for critical interpretation of one version of the shopgirl's story.

Conclusion

In 1926, an editorial appeared in the *Times* under the headline, "The Word 'Shop Girl' No Longer Fits." Penned by "Callisthenes," the fictional persona used for Selfridges' print advertising campaigns, this piece quoted the following remarks, made by the head of the store: "I should like to do all I can to kill the expression. . . . The epithet 'shop girl' has become one almost of disrespect."[1] The article went on to observe:

> Every one who is familiar with ordinary usages knows what is implied by the phrase: "She is only a shop girl." It indicates a narrow, timid life; it hints at an inadequate education, at a lack of culture and ambition, at something second-rate in manners and appearance, and perhaps suggests the absence of a robust, physical life.[2]

This pronunciation, calling for the death of the term "shop girl" and all its associations of narrowness, inadequacy, and lack, suggests one ending to the shopgirl's story, in that it demands a new conception of identity based on the "modern facts" about the young women employed in shops and stores such as Selfridges.[3] Yet the narrative of the shopgirl, like the serial format in which it often appeared in fiction, resists the imperative to conclude, continuing to hold contemporary relevance for our own cultural moment.

This study has been necessarily limited in temporal scope and national cultural context for a number of reasons, the most significant of which is the historical emergence and consolidation of the shopgirl as a cultural type between the 1880s and the First World War. However, the figure of the shopgirl by no means vanishes in the 1920s; by contrast, she remains a cultural icon, a paradigm for a certain mode of consumer fantasy and the repository of societal anxieties over sexuality and moral propriety, particularly as regards young women. In these concluding comments, I hope to suggest the ways in which the shopgirl has continued to function as a symbol for the constellation of various markers of class, gender, and sexuality, from the turn of the last century to the turn of our own. To do so, I discuss a case in which the shopgirl becomes the center of a controversy over the practice of sexuality in the public sphere: the 1907 murder trial involving one of the great Victorian department store founders, William Whiteley. I then touch on several examples of the shopgirl's emblematic status at the turn of our own century, articulating the significance of this figure to issues of labor, leisure, and consumer fantasy in the present.

The Sensational Death of the "Universal Provider"

In January of 1907, William Whiteley, founder of the department store popularly known as the "Universal Provider," was shot and killed by Horace George Rayner, a young man claiming to be Whiteley's unacknowledged son.[4] Horace's mother, Emily Turner, was unmarried at the time of his birth, and the man she identified as his father, George Rayner, later denied paternity. Although his claim to be related to Whiteley was later disproved in court, Horace did have a connection to Whiteley through his mother's sister Louisa Turner, a onetime store employee and Whiteley's former mistress. She had, in Victorian parlance, been living "under the protection" of her employer from 1883 to 1888, when she and Whiteley quarreled and separated, three years after the birth of their son, Cecil, who is only mentioned in the news coverage of the case but did not appear in person (or in William Whiteley's will). Having learned of his cousin's existence, and believing he too could be a son of the famous merchant, Horace Rayner met with Whiteley and asked him for money, but was rebuffed. The murder, which took place immediately following the interview, occurred on the crowded store floor, and a panic ensued among the midday shoppers. Rayner subsequently turned the gun on himself and sustained several life-threatening wounds. Despite a defense based on a claim of insanity—which many sympathetic petitioners for his pardon saw as a natural result of brooding over the "cruel injustice of his ignominious birth"—Rayner was convicted and condemned to death; however, he was eventually granted a reprieve and his sentence was commuted to penal servitude for life.[5]

This case, with its parallels to other famous celebrity murder cases of the period (particularly the Stanford White affair in New York), is of interest for a number of reasons. First, it both reflects and reconfigures the paradigmatic story of the shopgirl. In the pages of late Victorian and Edwardian popular fiction, on stage and screen, the narrative of the impoverished shop assistant who is "rescued" by a wealthy suitor had time and again served to elaborate the possibilities involved in the fantasy of social mobility for young women who worked behind the counter. Louisa

Turner's relationship with Whiteley, who had separated from his wife, suggests the material rewards a young woman might gain from her involvement with her employer and benefactor. Although such a relationship was subject to social censure—for, of course, any woman who was sexually active outside of marriage was subject to public condemnation, despite the social status of her lover and the relative openness of their relationship—the conditions of women's shop employment certainly might prove tempting in providing an opportunity to "escape" from the shop. And, judging from the lengthy duration of their relationship and the fact that Whiteley did acknowledge paternity of Louisa's son, Cecil, we cannot assume that the affair between Turner and Whiteley was solely motivated by economic considerations. Reading between the lines of news coverage and court documentation, the affair between a shop assistant and her employer takes the fictional romance plot described in chapters 2 and 4 and complicates it with questions of the relationship between sexuality and economics that are of particular relevance for young working women in the public sphere.

This narrative differs from that of the shopgirl's rise out of the shop and her return as a customer in at least one crucial way, however: here, the shop assistant does not gain the social respectability of marriage to her employer. In this sense the Turner-Whiteley liaison destabilizes the opposition between the two narratives (ascent into marriage or descent into prostitution) that structure the shopgirl's story. In this case, an "illegitimate" liaison between shop assistant and store owner becomes a legitimate one, at least in the eyes of the young man who takes the starring role, relegating the shopgirl's plot to the background. The news coverage of the trial emphasizes the presumption on Horace Rayner's part that charging William Whiteley with paternity would lead to pecuniary assistance and potentially to greater social security than he had previously been able to obtain. The sympathy expressed by thousands of people who had followed the trial in the daily press for the bitter life Rayner had led, not to mention the heroic efforts of surgeons to save him, resulted in a petition for clemency signed by "persons of every rank of society."[6] Such an outpouring of support on the part of the British reading public suggests the ways in which Rayner's financial difficulties were rewritten as emblematic of a desire for social recognition—an end to the "bitterness" and "cruel injustice" of his illegitimate birth and the perceived ignominy of his life, structured as it was in comparing his own poverty to the wealth and luxury embodied in the figure of William Whiteley. This case, a seemingly perfect example of Freud's "family romance," in which the individual reimagines the conditions of his birth and parentage to provide himself with an alternative life story, illustrates the sway of narrative in giving voice to fantasies of social mobility.[7]

The news coverage of the case also underscores the significance of turn-of-the-century debates over sensationalism in the media, particularly in light of the rise of the "new journalism" and various related strategies for engaging the sympathies of the mass reading public. The London papers drew an explicit connection between the Rayner-Whiteley case and the Thaw inquiry in New York, taking place at the same time. The Thaw case was one of the most sensational murder trials of its day: in June of 1906, Pittsburgh millionaire Harry K. Thaw had shot and killed the prominent New York architect Stanford White, who had had an affair with Thaw's wife, the model and dancer Evelyn Nesbit, when she was sixteen.[8] The *Times* observed: "The subject matter of the two inquires has not a few points of strong resemblance. In both there is a question as to the relations of men of wealth and position with certain women. In both there was an opportunity for the Yellow Press of the two countries to publish or insinuate scandalous tales about the antecedents of the dead men." However, the article went on to note, "The contrast between the procedure in the two trials could not be greater. The long nightmare of the Thaw trial still goes on, and the end is still indefinitely distant. . . . We may be thankful that so far we have had small experience of trials which are almost as mischievous to society as the crimes which are investigated."[9] The phrasing of the similarities between the trials—particularly the reference to "certain women" and the criticism of sensational journalism—both suggests and reinforces the significance of using scandal to sell papers; indeed, the very reticence of the *Times* to publish further details of the "scandalous tales" circulated about William Whiteley and Stanford White seems paradoxically to play on the prurient interests and imaginative speculations of readers. The news coverage of the Whiteley case, even that of a "respectable" paper like the *Times,* therefore participated in and helped to perpetuate the culture of sensation that characterized the turn of the century.

Finally, it is significant that this case, with its yoking of sex, sensation, and scandal, turned on the sexual practices of the shopgirl at its center: Louisa Turner, mistress to the "Universal Provider" and aunt to a murderer, speaks only briefly in this narrative, and then only with regard to questions of sexual and moral behavior. The actual events which contributed to Louisa Turner's progress out of the department store and into the historical record will likely remain in shadow. Perhaps unsurprisingly, in this case as in others described throughout this study, the experience of the woman behind the figure of the shopgirl remains elusive; her story, replete with the gaps and fissures of the archive, will always exist to some extent in the realm of fiction.

The Shopgirl in the Twentieth Century

It is well documented that during World War I, as men were called into military service, women took their places in a range of new types of employment, including munitions and factory labor traditionally identified as men's work, not least because these jobs often paid significantly more than positions typically open to women. However, young women continued to find work in shops and department stores in ever-increasing numbers, and when many women returned to "women's work" after the war, the shop retained a prominent role in the employment of women and in the perceptions of young working women's lives.[10]

Accordingly, the types of characterizations described throughout this study—particularly the stereotype of the shopgirl as the paradigmatic consumer and the cultural identification of the shopgirl as subject to a culture of sexual and moral risk—endure throughout the twentieth century.

For example, in a review of a proposed serial radio drama by Irma Phillips, a pioneer in the development of radio serials directed to female consumers, one critic commented scathingly:

> This program . . . is another of the amateurish type of programs that have attained such popularity with a certain class of listeners . . . *it panders to the crude emotions of the shopgirl type of listener,* and it trades upon the maudlin sympathies of the neurotic who sits entranced before the radio, clutching a copy of "True Confessions" and (possibly) guzzling gin and ginger ale. Despite the many things that are wrong in a show of this type, it will undoubtedly be successful. . . . But to people who have an I.Q. of something higher than 15 years, it will be another of the dreadful things that the radio brings.[11]

Once again, the shopgirl comes to stand in for the overly susceptible consumer of popular texts, a correspondence dating back to the 1880s but here applied to the latest technology, presaging the stereotype of the sentimental female consumer of film and television (particularly melodrama and soap opera) in subsequent decades. By association, the shopgirl is conflated with the "neurotic" for whom reading and listening to the romance have the same entrancing urgency and who (possibly) numbs herself through the use of alcohol to the difference between her own life and the fictional narrative.

Similarly, the positioning of the shopgirl at the center of a heterosexual romance plot endures throughout the silent period and well into the era of classical cinema. Two American films are particularly compelling exam-

Ladies' Sitting Room, *Harrodian Gazette,* July 1920. Reproduced by permission of the Company Archive, Harrods Limited, London.

ples of this characterization. The silent film *It* (1927), inspired by Elinor Glyn's term for sex appeal and based on a 1926 novella serialized in *Cosmopolitan,* featured Clara Bow as a woman employed in a New York department store whose marriage enables her to pursue the pleasures of leisured consumption.[12] A very different story appears in the 1939 film *The Women* (adapted by Anita Loos from Clare Boothe Luce's play of the same name), in which Joan Crawford starred as the scheming husband-hunter who chooses her man from among the male clientele at the perfume counter where she works. In both cases, the fictional shopgirl becomes the vehicle for the performance of sexual desire and desirability by a female star, although in the former case the shopgirl is the heroine and the object of the viewer's desire, whereas in the latter the shopgirl turns villainess and destroyer of female associative bonds, echoing the rivalry and competition fictionalized in the penny papers of the turn of the century.

So ingrained is this narrative that even at the turn of our own century, the shopgirl remains a significant cultural symbol, updated and reconfigured under the conditions of late modernity. In the late 1990s, several articles from fashion magazines such as *Harper's Bazaar* and *Women's Wear Daily* represented the shopgirl as privy to a certain kind of elite knowledge regarding the world of haute couture, the locus of sartorial sophistication and superiority despite—or perhaps because of—her position behind the counter.[13] At other moments, the shopgirl's position as signifier of the everyday is highlighted: in the 1998 remake of *The Shop around the Corner* (1940), *You've Got Mail,* in which an e-mail romance figures prominently to shape the plot's central conflict between two store owners, Meg Ryan's character, Kathleen Kelly, goes by the e-mail moniker "shopgirl." Most vividly, in Steve Martin's 2000 novel (and 2005 film), *Shopgirl,* the plot revolves around a similar narrative of sexual experience: a young woman drifts into a liaison with an older, wealthier man who transforms from customer into lover. Yet this novel departs from the familiar shopgirl story in its conclusion, placing the heroine in a companionate relationship based more on shared affinities than consumer desire.

Finally, in the 2001–2002 season of the long-running television program *Friends,* the on-again, off-again relationship between Rachel (Jennifer Aniston) and Ross (David Schwimmer) incorporates the rivalry plot in the pregnant Rachel's angry response to Ross's flirtation with a saleswoman in a shop selling baby clothes: retelling the story later, she exclaims, " . . . and he's out picking up some *shopgirl* at Sluts-R-Us?" The emphasis on the word "shopgirl," standing in for the sexually forward, inappropriate woman (here inappropriate because she falls outside the bounds of the longed-for reunion between these two central characters), suggests the resonance of these associations into the contemporary moment.

It should, perhaps, come as no surprise that the shopgirl's role as signifier of cultural and sexual anxieties endures into the present: the feminization of the retail labor force continues to raise concerns regarding the exploitation of workers in a service economy and the production of a working- and lower-middle-class population of women employees subject to the machinations of corporate capital, as Barbara Ehrenreich's work on Wal-Mart, among other scholarship on labor, class, and gender, has demonstrated.[14] Likewise, the challenge of balancing the demands of work with the freedom to define oneself in relation to or apart from sexuality continues to resonate as female employees struggle against sexual harassment in the workplace on the one hand and insufficient accommodation for child care, parental leave, and the like on the other. Hence an understanding of the ways in which the sexual and social practices of actual women are fictionalized into easily comprehensible and containable narratives may assist us in grappling with the challenges women face today in their everyday working lives.

Notes

Introduction

1. My understanding of the shopgirl as a new identity category draws on concepts of performativity and discourse founded in the work of Michel Foucault, especially *The History of Sexuality, Volume 1: An Introduction,* trans. Robert Hurley (New York: Vintage, 1990) and elaborated with reference to gender by Judith Butler, first in her landmark study *Gender Trouble: Feminism and the Subversion of Identity* (New York: Routledge, 1990) and subsequently in *Bodies That Matter: On the Discursive Limits of "Sex"* (New York: Routledge, 1993), and Joan Scott, in *Gender and the Politics of History* (New York: Columbia University Press, 1988). In her influential essay "The Evidence of Experience," Scott notes: "Treating the emergence of a new identity as a discursive event is not to introduce a new form of linguistic determinism, nor to deprive subjects of agency. It is to refuse a separation between 'experience' and language and to insist instead on the productive quality of discourse." Joan W. Scott, "The Evidence of Experience," in *Questions of Evidence: Proof, Practice, and Persuasion across the Disciplines,* ed. James Chandler, Arnold J. Davidson, and Harry Harootunian, 382–83 (Chicago: University of Chicago Press, 1994).

2. On changes to women's employment in the late Victorian period, see Lee Holcombe, *Victorian Ladies at Work: Middle-Class Working Women in England and Wales* (Newton Abbot: David & Charles, 1973); Martha Vicinus, *Independent Women: Work and Community for Single Women, 1850–1920* (Chicago: University of Chicago Press, 1985); Angela V. John, ed., *Unequal Opportunities: Women's Employment in England 1800–1918* (Oxford: Basil Blackwell, 1986); Elizabeth Roberts, "Women's Work 1840–1940," in *British Trade Union and Labour History: A Compendium,* ed. Leslie A. Clarkson, 209–80 (Atlantic Highlands, NJ: Humanities Press International, 1990); Ellen Jordan, *The Women's Movement and Women's Employment in Nineteenth Century Britain* (London: Routledge, 1999); and Sally Mitchell, *The New Girl: Girls' Culture in England, 1880–1915* (New York: Columbia University Press, 1995). On female clerks, see Meta Zimmeck, "Jobs for the Girls: The Expansion of Clerical Work for Women, 1850–1914," in John, *Unequal Opportunities,* 153–77; and Christopher Keep, "The Cultural Work of the Type-Writer Girl," *Victorian Studies* 40:3 (Spring 1997): 401–26.

3. For more on the ideology of "separate spheres" and its influence on nineteenth-century gender and class relations, see Leonore Davidoff and Catherine Hall's influential book *Family Fortunes: Men and Women of the English Middle Class, 1780–1850* (Chicago: University of Chicago Press, 1987), as well as the authors' two essay collections: Catherine Hall, *White, Male and Middle-Class: Explorations in Feminism and History* (New York: Routledge, 1992), and Leonore Davidoff, *Worlds Between: Historical Perspectives on Gender and Class* (New York: Routledge, 1995). The artificiality of the public-private split was clearly acknowledged in the Victorian

era as today, and subsequent scholarship has challenged the dominance of the paradigm: see especially Amanda Vickery's critique drawn from her research on the letters and diaries of provincial women of privilege in the eighteenth century, first published in article form as "Golden Age to Separate Spheres: A Review of the Categories and Chronology of English Women's History," *Historical Journal* 36:2 (1993): 383–414, and elaborated in *The Gentleman's Daughter: Women's Lives in Georgian England* (New Haven: Yale University Press, 1998). For responses to the challenge articulated by Vickery and others, see Anna Clark, "Reviews in History," David Cannadine, ed., Institute of Historical Research, University of London: http://www.history.ac.uk/reviews/paper/anna.html (September 1998), accessed 18 November 2004; and Leonore Davidoff, "Gender and the 'Great Divide': Public and Private in British Gender History," *Journal of Women's History* 15:1 (Spring 2003): 11–27.

    4. In referring to the shopgirl's "everyday life," I intend to suggest the quality of lived social experience, and the tactical practices for managing that experience, outlined by Michel de Certeau in *The Practice of Everyday Life*, trans. Steven Rendall (Berkeley: University of California Press, 1984). For a useful discussion of the historical production of everyday life as a theoretical concept in the work of Roland Barthes, Henri Lefebvre, and others, see Kristin Ross, *Fast Cars, Clean Bodies: Decolonization and the Reordering of French Culture* (Cambridge, MA: MIT Press, 1996), 5–6. It is, in fact, no coincidence that an analysis of everyday life should center on women: as Ross suggests, "women, of course, as the primary victims and arbiters of social reproduction, as the subjects of everydayness and as those most subjected to it, as the class of people most responsible for consumption, and those responsible for the complex movement whereby the social existence of human beings is produced and reproduced, *are* the everyday: its managers, its embodiment" (77).

    5. This discussion recalls the mythic ideal of Victorian domestic ideology in which woman's role as wife and mother was to create and maintain the bourgeois home as a sanctuary from the "worldly" public sphere. A critical aspect of my argument is the contention that shopgirls, members of the broader generic category of "working women," obscured the artificial distinction between public and private life produced earlier in the century. My use of the term "proper femininity" has been shaped by Lyn Pykett's work on women's literary genres: see her *The "Improper" Feminine: The Women's Sensation Novel and the New Woman Writing* (London: Routledge, 1992). See also Mary Poovey's analysis of mid-Victorian constructions of class and gender, *Uneven Developments: The Ideological Work of Gender in Mid-Victorian England* (Chicago: University of Chicago Press, 1988).

    6. The mid-Victorian figure of the seamstress is herself the central figure for an earlier debate over gender, labor, and class in the nineteenth century. For critical discussions of the plight of the Victorian seamstress (or "distressed needleworker," as she was known at the time), see Beth Harris, *Famine and Fashion: Needlewomen in the Nineteenth Century* (Aldershot, Hants, England: Ashgate, 2005), and Joel H. Kaplan and Sheila Stowell, *Theatre and Fashion: Oscar Wilde to the Suffragettes* (Cambridge: Cambridge University, 1994), 84–89; for a fictional representation of a seamstress's "fall," see Elizabeth Gaskell's 1853 novel *Ruth*.

    7. In drawing this connection between absorption and distraction, my argument resonates with Jonathan Crary's analysis of the relationship between atten-

tion and distraction in modern life. Responding to the work of Kracauer, Benjamin and Georg Simmel via an analysis of "the rise of attentive norms and practices" in the nineteenth century, Crary argues that "attention and distraction were not two essentially different states but existed on a single continuum." Jonathan Crary, *Suspensions of Perception: Attention, Spectacle, and Modern Culture* (Cambridge, MA: MIT Press, 1999), 1, 47. Absorption, like attention, suggests a contemplative or concentrated state of perception, but this state is of necessity a temporary one. For another useful investigation of the perceptual logic of absorption, see Michael Fried, *Absorption and Theatricality: Painting and Beholder in the Age of Diderot* (Chicago: University of Chicago Press, 1980).

8. Throughout this study, I use the terms "narrative," "story," and "plot" intentionally, to signal the ways in which the story of the shopgirl is indeed a fictional account. Not only is it not my goal to recapture the "real" lives of Victorian and Edwardian female shop assistants, such a project would suggest an overly simplified approach to historiography. Rather, I use words that highlight the constructed nature of the story of the shopgirl in order to draw out the compelling nature of particular kinds of plots as modes of organizing the fragmentary and enigmatic nature of experience into a "story" that makes sense, that, most crucially, has an ending. For, as we shall see, the shopgirl's story is bounded by its own narrative logics and expectations.

9. The association of the shopgirl with the prostitute has a long history. Historian Judith Coffin locates the perceived link between the clothing trades and prostitution in the eighteenth century: "Eighteenth-century engravings of women workers in the clothing trades were often a pretext for pornographic or erotic fantasies and merged depictions of the commerce in fabrics and clothing with evocations of prostitution. Eighteenth- and early-nineteenth-century engravings of the lingerie trade, for instance, showed women flirting with their male clients and provided voyeuristic peeks at groups of women together behind closed doors." Judith G. Coffin, *The Politics of Women's Work: The Paris Garment Trades 1750–1915* (Princeton, NJ: Princeton University Press, 1996), 89. Mid-eighteenth-century trade manuals such as Campbell's *The London Tradesman* (1747) made the connection between millinery and prostitution explicit: "The vast Resort of young Beaus and Rakes to Milliners' Shops exposes young creatures to many Temptations, and insensibly debauches their Morals before they are capable of Vice. . . . Nine out of ten young Creatures that are obligated to serve in these Shops are ruined and undone: Take a Survey of all common Women of the Town, who take their Walks between *Charing-Cross* and *Fleet-Ditch*, and, I am persuaded, more than half of them have been bred Milliners, have been debauched in their Houses, and are obliged to throw themselves upon the Town for want of Bread, after they have left them. Whether then it is owing to the Milliners, or to the Nature of the Business, or to whatever cause is owing, the Facts are so clear, and the Misfortunes attending this Apprenticeship so manifest . . . it ought to be the last shift a young Creature is driven to." R. Campbell, *The London Tradesman* (1747), 208–9, cited in Elizabeth Kowaleski-Wallace, *Consuming Subjects: Women, Shopping, and Business in the Eighteenth Century* (New York: Columbia University Press, 1997), 120. Kowaleski-Wallace reads this passage as a sexualized representation of the dangers of business for women, noting that for Campbell, "The problem with the milliner's shop is that it is an imperfect house. The suggestion here is that, once a woman opens her *house*

to the public, she makes herself sexually available. In a real house a lady would not sell. In a real house a woman is protected against the debauchery of rakes (or so the logic seems to go). True domesticity, in contrast to the world of business, is depicted as enclosed, insular, protected from the salaciousness of the business world. The proper lady finds her protection from sexually predatory men inside a real house, and she eschews all other kinds of houses" (121). The association between the garment trades and prostitution also operated through the spatial characterization and use of London's West End: as Lynne Walker notes, in the 1850s and 1860s, the "double mapping" of Regent Street made the West End "by day one of the most elegant shopping streets in the world and at night the haunt of prostitutes," a metonymic connection drawn by the journalist Henry Mayhew and associating prostitution with "a 'large number' of working-class women employed in the shops and trades of the West End (milliners, dressmakers, pastry cooks, shop assistants, servants, and so on)." Lynne Walker, "Vistas of Pleasure: Women Consumers of Urban Space in the West End of London 1850–1900," in *Women in the Victorian Art World,* ed. Clarissa Campbell Orr, 75 (Manchester: Manchester University Press, 1995).

10.   This discussion has been informed by an extensive body of scholarship on the production and consumption of the romance. Most influential has been Janice Radway's *Reading the Romance: Women, Patriarchy, and Popular Literature* (Chapel Hill: University of North Carolina Press, 1991 [1984]). See also Kay Mussell, *Fantasy and Reconciliation: Contemporary Formulas of Women's Romance Fiction* (Westport, CT: Greenwood Press, 1984); Jean Radford, ed., *The Progress of Romance: The Politics of Popular Fiction* (London and New York: Routledge & Kegan Paul, 1986); Carol Thurston, *The Romance Revolution: Erotic Novels for Women and the Quest for a New Sexual Identity* (Urbana: University of Illinois Press, 1987); Jayne Ann Krentz, ed., *Dangerous Men & Adventurous Women: Romance Writers on the Appeal of the Romance* (Philadelphia: University of Pennsylvania Press, 1992); and Lynne Pearce and Jackie Stacey, eds., *Romance Revisited* (New York: New York University Press, 1995). For a useful analysis of the romance's role in the history of publishing, see Joseph McAleer's *Passion's Fortune: The Story of Mills and Boon* (Oxford and New York: Oxford University Press, 1999). My analysis of the promise provided by the fantasies inscribed within the narrative of the romance plot draws upon Lauren Berlant's work on femininity and desire: see especially "The Compulsion to Repeat Femininity," in *The City and the Politics of Propinquity,* ed. Joan Copjec and Michael Sorkin (London: Verso, 1999), and "The Female Woman: Fanny Fern and the Form of Sentiment," *American Literary History* 3:3 (Fall 1991): 429–54.

11.   Katherine Mansfield, *Stories* (New York: Vintage Classics, 1991), 3. Further references will be cited parenthetically.

12.   Victoria Cross, one of many popular female writers of the 1890s and early 1900s, has been virtually forgotten in twentieth-century literary history and criticism. To date only two articles on Cross's life and writings have been published: see Shoshanah Milgrim Knapp, "Real Passion and the Reverence for Life: Sexuality and Antivivisection in the Fiction of Victoria Cross," in *Rediscovering Forgotten Radicals: British Women Writers, 1889–1939,* ed. Angela Ingram and Daphne Patai, 156–71 (Chapel Hill: University of North Carolina Press, 1993); and "Revolutionary Androgyny in the Fiction of 'Victoria Cross,'" in *Seeing*

Double: Revisioning Edwardian and Modernist Literature, ed. Carola M. Kaplan and Anne B. Simpson, 3–19 (New York: St. Martin's Press, 1996). Cross is also mentioned briefly in several accounts of Decadent and New Woman fiction, including Ann L. Ardis, *New Women, New Novels: Feminism and Early Modernism* (New Brunswick, NJ: Rutgers University Press, 1990). Cross's short story "Theodora," first published in *The Yellow Book* in 1895, is reprinted in Elaine Showalter's *Daughters of Decadence* (New Brunswick, NJ: Rutgers University Press, 1993), 6–37.

13. The phrase belongs to Tony Davies, whose analysis of the twin genres of the railway novel and the romance has been influential to my understanding of popular reading at the turn of the century. See his "Transports of Pleasure: Fiction and Its Audiences in the Later Nineteenth Century," in *Formations of Pleasure,* ed. Formations Editorial Collective, 46–58 (London: Routledge & Kegan Paul, 1983).

14. By contrast, in numerous popular fictions and films of the period, such as August Blom's silent film *Daughters of the Department Store* (1917), the trajectory from woman to mannequin is the heroine's path to marriage and upper-class life. For a fuller discussion of the shopgirl as mannequin, see chapter 2.

15. See, on the scenic quality of the fantasy, Jean Laplanche and Jean-Bertrand Pontalis's claim that "fantasy is not the object of desire, but its setting." Jean Laplanche and Jean-Bertrand Pontalis, "Fantasy and the Origins of Sexuality," rpt. with a retrospect in *Formations of Fantasy,* ed. Victor Burgin, James Donald, and Cora Kaplan, 26 (London: Routledge, 1986). For further discussion of the scripted and sequenced model of fantasy, see J. Laplanche and J.-B. Pontalis, *The Language of Psychoanalysis,* trans. Donald Nicholson-Smith (New York: W. W. Norton & Co., 1973), 314–19.

16. I take this phrase from Mary Ann Doane's *The Desire to Desire: The Woman's Film of the 1940s* (Bloomington and Indianapolis; Indiana University Press, 1987); see especially chapter 1.

17. Diana Fuss, *Identification Papers* (New York: Routledge, 1995); see also Eve Kosofsky Sedgwick, *Epistemology of the Closet* (Berkeley: University of California Press, 1990), 61.

18. On the relationship between identification and identity, see Fuss, *Identification Papers,* 51. My account of fantasy has been shaped by Jean Laplanche and Jean-Bertrand Pontalis's 1968 essay "Fantasy and the Origins of Sexuality" (cited above), in which the authors rework Freud's diverse and often contradictory perspectives on fantasy and the unconscious in order to argue, in part, for the variability of identification within fantasy. Freud suggested this variability in "A Child Is Being Beaten" (1919), presenting the possibility of multiple gendered positions to be occupied by the fantasizing subject. Sigmund Freud, "'A Child Is Being Beaten': A Contribution to the Origin of Sexual Perversions" (1919), rpt. in *Sexuality and the Psychology of Love,* ed. Philip Rieff, 97–122 (New York: Collier Books, 1963). Laplanche and Pontalis clarify this point in reference to the fantasy of seduction: if the sentence "a father seduces a daughter" can be read as a linguistic statement of the content of the seduction fantasy, they argue, this statement provides multiple points of entry for the location of the subject: "nothing shows whether the subject will be immediately located as *daughter;* it can as well be fixed as *father,* or even in the term *seduces*" (22–23). I raise the question of the multiple

sites for identification within fantasy in order to resist the tendency to understand fantasy as merely providing an imaginary coherence for the shopgirl's identity. Instead, as I argue in chapter 4, the variability of identification provided by the experience of fantasy suggests that the shopgirl might occupy places within the fantasy that differ from that of the heroine; she might identify across gender and class, or she might as well identify with other elements (actions, objects, desires) within the narrative. This contention has been influenced by Cora Kaplan's work: see especially "*The Thorn Birds:* Fiction, Fantasy, Femininity," in *Formations of Fantasy,* ed. Victor Burgin, James Donald, and Cora Kaplan, 142–66 (London: Routledge, 1986).

As Laplanche and Pontalis's essay illustrates, fantasy may also incorporate a narrative component. To some extent the fantasies produced by the texts of late Victorian and Edwardian consumer culture—penny novelettes and magazines or early films, for example—operate according to the model of the reverie, which Laplanche and Pontalis characterize as "that form of novelette, both stereotyped and infinitely variable, which the subject composes and relates to himself in a waking state" (22). Similarly, Freud's depiction of the daydream often follows the terminology of the fictional scene or episode, in the case of women following a romantic plot or trajectory, since for Freud "[women's] ambition as a rule is absorbed by erotic trends." Sigmund Freud, "Creative Writers and Day-Dreaming" (1907), rpt. in *The Freud Reader,* ed. Peter Gay, 436–43 (New York: W. W. Norton & Co., 1989). Although the fantasy associated with the shopgirl may have related aspects of narrative progression, the tension between absorption and distraction suggests a less predictable relationship to identification than these descriptions of the reverie and daydream suggest.

19. Here I would distinguish between terms whose meanings are often collapsed: need, demand, desire, longing. In my description of the relation between fantasy and consumer/consuming desires, I read need and demand as primarily directed toward particular objects, whereas desire and longing suggest a more mobile or transitory set of associations. The shopgirl's desire for alternate life plots can be conceived through this more fluid model, in which the fabrics, settings, and romantic scenes that structure the fantasy operate on the level of surface effects rather than according to a psychoanalytic account of plenitude and its constitutive opposite, lack. This reading has been influenced by Elizabeth Grosz's work on desire: see her "Refiguring Lesbian Desire," in *The Lesbian Postmodern,* ed. Laura Doan, 67–84 (New York: Columbia University Press, 1994).

20. Rita Felski, *The Gender of Modernity* (Cambridge, MA: Harvard University Press, 1995), 1.

21. Ibid., 89–90, 62.

22. Ibid., 72.

23. The debate over the periodization of "modernity" intersects in important ways with the chronology of this study. Despite the evident continuities between the Victorian and Edwardian periods, the majority of literary criticism focuses on one of these periods at the expense of the other, or extends discussions of the Victorian period to encompass the years leading up to the First World War without addressing the cultural differences of the Edwardian era. However, several exceptions are worth mentioning: Ann Ardis's *New Women, New Novels: Feminism and Early Modernism* (New Brunswick, NJ: Rutgers University Press, 1990), and

Rita Felski's *The Gender of Modernity* (Cambridge, MA: Harvard University Press, 1995), discussed above. Felski's argument regarding the ambiguous and complex relationship between gender, urban experience, and consumption is echoed in Mica Nava's work: see especially "Modernity's Disavowal: Women, the City, and the Department Store," in *Modern Times: Reflections on a Century of Modernity,* ed. Mica Nava and Alan O'Shea, 38–76 (London: Routledge, 1996). As the following discussion should make clear, however, many of the defining characteristics of modernity can be traced to the eighteenth century, in particular the impact of industrialization and urbanization on gender relations and the relationship between public and private life. My effort here, then, is to analyze the ways in which the figure of the shopgirl in particular, and by extension working women in general, made use of the unique aspects of late-nineteenth-century urban culture in ways that reveal the relationship between gender, consumer fantasy, and modern experience, but that also show us how these elements were grounded in a much longer and more complex history. For more extensive analysis of modernity and its conceptual relevance for the study of British, European, and American culture during this period, the seminal work of Charles Baudelaire and Walter Benjamin presents a useful starting point: see especially Baudelaire's *The Painter of Modern Life, and Other Essays,* trans. and ed. Jonathan Mayne (London: Phaidon, 1964); Benjamin's *Illuminations,* ed. Hannah Arendt and trans. Harry Zohn (New York: Schocken Books, 1968); and *Reflections,* ed. Peter Demetz (New York: Schocken Books, 1986). Other useful sources are Georg Simmel's 1903 essay "The Metropolis and Mental Life," in *Individuality and Social Forms,* ed. Donald Levine (Chicago: University of Chicago Press, 1971), and the writings of Siegfried Kracauer, discussed at greater length in chapter 5. Secondary critical sources include Susan Buck-Morss's extensive work on Benjamin's Arcades Project, explored in *The Dialectics of Seeing: Walter Benjamin and the Arcades Project* (Cambridge, MA: MIT Press, 1989); David Frisby, *Fragments of Modernity: Theories of Modernity in the Work of Simmel, Kracauer, and Benjamin* (Cambridge, MA: MIT Press, 1986); Anthony Giddens, *The Consequences of Modernity* (Stanford, CA: Stanford University Press, 1990); and Marshall Berman, *All That Is Solid Melts into Air: The Experience of Modernity* (first published 1982; rev. ed. Harmondsworth, Middlesex: Penguin, 1988). For feminist critiques of the androcentrism of many writings on modernity, see Nava, "Modernity's Disavowal"; Felski, *Gender of Modernity;* Andreas Huyssen, "Mass Culture as Woman: Modernism's Other," in *After the Great Divide: Modernism, Mass Culture, Postmodernism* (Bloomington: Indiana University Press, 1986); Elizabeth Wilson, *The Sphinx in the City: Urban Life, the Control of Disorder, and Women* (Berkeley: University of California Press, 1991); Deborah L. Parsons, *Streetwalking the Metropolis: Women, the City, and Modernity* (Oxford: Oxford University Press, 2000); and the debate over the possibility of the *flâneuse* addressed in chapter 1, n. 59.

24. For two reviews of historical scholarship that pay particular attention to issues of class and gender, see Matthew Hilton, "Class, Consumption and the Public Sphere," *Journal of Contemporary History* 35:4 (2000): 655–66, and Mary Louise Roberts, "Gender, Consumption, and Commodity Culture," *American Historical Review* 103:3 (June 1998): 817–44.

25. Erin Mackie, *Market à la Mode: Fashion, Commodity and Gender in* The

Tatler *and* The Spectator (Baltimore: Johns Hopkins University Press, 1997), 53. See also Neil McKendrick, John Brewer, and J. H. Plumb, *The Birth of a Consumer Society: The Commercialization of Eighteenth-Century England* (Bloomington: Indiana University Press, 1982); Hoh-Cheung Mui and Lorna Mui, *Shops and Shopkeeping in Eighteenth-Century England* (Kingston: McGill-Queen's University Press and Routledge, 1989); John Brewer and Roy Porter, eds., *Consumption and the World of Goods* (London: Routledge, 1993); Colin Jones, "The Great Chain of Buying: Medical Advertisement, the Bourgeois Public Sphere, and the Origins of the French Revolution," *American Historical Review* 101 (February 1996): 13–40; Jennifer Jones, "Coquettes and Grisettes: Women Buying and Selling in Ancien Régime Paris," in *The Sex of Things: Gender and Consumption in Historical Perspective*, ed. Victoria de Grazia and Ellen Furlough, 25–53 (Berkeley: University of California Press, 1996); Elizabeth Kowaleski-Wallace, *Consuming Subjects: Women, Shopping, and Business in the Eighteenth Century* (New York: Columbia University Press, 1997); and Claire Walsh, "Shop Design and the Display of Goods in Eighteenth-Century London," *Journal of Design History* 8:3 (1995): 157–76, and "The Newness of the Department Store: A View from the Eighteenth Century," in *Cathedrals of Consumption: The European Department Store, 1850–1939*, ed. Geoffrey Crossick and Serge Jaumain, 46–71 (Aldershot: Ashgate, 1999).

26. Kowaleski-Wallace, *Consuming Subjects,* 74.

27. Walsh, "Shop Designs," 174, 157.

28. Ibid., 171–72. Walsh quotes a 1727 letter to the *Plain Dealer* from a mercer lamenting ladies who "tumble over my goods, and deafen me with a round of questions. . . . They swim into my shop by shoals, not with the least intention to buy, but only to hear my silks rustle, and fill up their own leisure by putting me into full employment" (cited 172). The sexualization of the consumer environment here and in other texts from the eighteenth century to the present is striking: the male mercer's silks rustle and his goods are tumbled by these forward, forceful female consumers that may remind readers of later examples in texts such as Emile Zola's *Au bonheur des dames* (1883).

29. Kowaleski-Wallace, *Consuming Subjects,* 5. See also De Grazia and Furlough, *The Sex of Things.*

30. Roberts, "Gender, Consumption, and Commodity Culture," 827, 818.

31. Ibid., 841.

32. A number of excellent critical studies in literary criticism and history have been published over the past two decades that explore the relationship between class and gender in the Victorian period, particularly with reference to women's working lives and the relationship between domesticity and the public sphere. In addition to those cited in notes 2 and 3, important early sources include Catherine Gallagher, *The Industrial Reformation of English Fiction: Social Discourse and Narrative Form, 1832–1867* (Chicago: University of Chicago Press, 1985), and Nancy Armstrong, *Desire and Domestic Fiction: A Political History of the Novel* (New York: Oxford University Press, 1987). Subsequent scholarship has refined and added to these pioneering studies: for examples, see Monica Cohen, *Professional Domesticity in the Victorian Novel: Women, Work, and Home* (Cambridge: Cambridge University Press, 1998); Dina M. Copelman, *London's Women Teachers: Gender, Class, and Feminism, 1870–1930* (New York: Routledge,

1996); Ellen Ross, *Love and Toil: Motherhood in Outcast London, 1870–1918* (Oxford: Oxford University Press, 1993); Deirdre D'Albertis, *Dissembling Fictions: Elizabeth Gaskell and the Victorian Social Text* (New York: St. Martin's, 1997); and Susan Zlotnick, *Women, Writing and the Industrial Revolution* (Baltimore: Johns Hopkins University Press, 2001).

33. Susan Porter Benson, *Counter Cultures: Saleswomen, Managers, and Customers in American Department Stores, 1890–1940* (Urbana: University of Illinois Press, 1988), and Gail Reekie, *Temptations: Sex, Selling, and the Department Store* (St. Leonards, Australia: Allen and Unwin, 1993). For articles on French stores, see Theresa McBride, "A Woman's World: Department Stores and the Evolution of Women's Employment, 1870–1920," *French Historical Studies* 10:4 (Fall 1978): 664–83, and Jones, "*Coquettes* and *Grisettes.*" For an excellent source on consumer culture in France at the turn of the century, see Lisa Tiersten, *Marianne in the Market: Envisioning Consumer Society in Fin-de-Siècle France* (Berkeley: University of California Press, 2001).

34. The earliest (and still most comprehensive) historical study of female shop assistants in England is Lee Holcombe's chapter from *Victorian Ladies at Work: Middle-Class Working Women in England and Wales* (Newton Abbot: David & Charles, 1973). Judith Walkowitz has begun to explore the significance of shop life to urban experience for women in the late Victorian period: see especially her "Going Public: Shopping, Street Harassment, and Streetwalking in Late Victorian London," *Representations* 62 (Spring 1998): 1–30. There is also a wide range of work on small shopkeepers and cooperatives in Britain that provides a useful context for this study. Christopher Hosgood has published several key articles including "The 'Pigmies Of Commerce' and the Working-Class Community: Small Shopkeepers in England, 1870–1914," *Journal of Social History* 22:3 (1989): 439–60; "'A Brave and Daring Folk': Shopkeepers and Trade Associational Life in Victorian and Edwardian England," *Journal of Social History* 26 (1992): 285–308; and "'Mercantile Monasteries': Shops, Shop Assistants, and Shop Life in Late-Victorian and Edwardian Britain," *Journal of British Studies* 38:3 (1999): 322–52. Other sources on British and European shops and cooperatives include Geoffrey Crossick, "Shopkeepers and the State in Britain, 1870–1914," in *Shopkeepers and Master Artisans in Nineteenth-Century Europe*, ed. Crossick and Heinz-Gerhard Haupt, 239–69 (London: Methuen, 1984); Ellen Furlough, *Consumer Cooperation in France: The Politics of Consumption, 1834–1930* (Ithaca, NY: Cornell University Press, 1991); and Peter Gurney, *Co-Operative Culture and the Politics of Consumption in England, 1870–1939* (Manchester: Manchester University Press, 1996). These studies have enriched the extensive literature on the emergence and development of the department store in the nineteenth century, which I discuss at greater length in chapter 1.

35. Scott, "Evidence of Experience," 370.

36. The foundational studies are Raymond Williams, *Culture and Society 1780–1950* (London: Chatto and Windus, 1958; Harmondsworth: Penguin, 1963) and *The Long Revolution* (London: Penguin, 1961); and E. P. Thompson, *The Making of the English Working Class* (New York: Vintage, 1963). For the field of leisure history, see Peter Bailey, *Leisure and Class in Victorian England: Rational Recreation and the Contest for Control, 1830–1885* (London: Routledge & Kegan Paul, 1978); Hugh Cunningham, *Leisure in the Industrial Revolution c. 1780–c. 1880* (New York: St. Martin's Press, 1980); and Gareth Stedman Jones, *Languages*

of Class: Studies in English Working-Class History 1832–1982 (Cambridge: Cambridge University Press, 1983).

37. Chris Waters, *British Socialists and the Politics of Popular Culture, 1884–1914* (Manchester: Manchester University Press, 1990); Susan D. Pennybacker, *A Vision for London 1889–1914: Labour, Everyday Life and the LCC Experiment* (London: Routledge, 1995). For an exemplary account of the relationship between gender and leisure during this period, see Catriona M. Parratt, *"More than Mere Amusement": Working-Class Women's Leisure in England, 1750–1914* (Boston: Northeastern University Press, 2001).

38. For models of this type of work in US history, see Nan Enstad, *Ladies of Labor, Girls of Adventure: Working Women, Popular Culture, and Labor Politics at the Turn of the Twentieth Century* (New York: Columbia University Press, 1999); Kathy Peiss, *Cheap Amusements: Working Women and Leisure in Turn-of-the-Century New York* (Philadelphia: Temple University Press, 1986); and Roy Rosenzweig, *Eight Hours for What We Will: Workers and Leisure in an Industrial City, 1870–1920* (Cambridge: Cambridge University Press, 1983).

39. Cultural studies has been notoriously difficult to define, but for a preliminary historiography of the growth of this interdisciplinary field of scholarship, and its connection to the Centre for Contemporary Cultural Studies at Birmingham, see Lawrence Grossberg, Cary Nelson, and Paula Treichler, eds., *Cultural Studies* (New York: Routledge, 1992), 1–16. Also useful are David Morley and Kuan-Hsing Chen, *Stuart Hall: Critical Dialogues in Cultural Studies* (New York: Routledge, 1996), and Angela McRobbie, "New Times in Cultural Studies," *New Formations* 13 (1991): 1–17.

40. The term "sweated" was used to describe exploitive working conditions in a variety of trades. As Judith Coffin notes in her study of the Paris clothing trades, sweating originally referred to "the particular exploitation involved in systems of contracting and subcontracting," and although not synonymous with homework, by the end of the nineteenth century in France, "most homework was contracted or 'sweated,' so commentators used the term interchangeably." Judith G. Coffin, *The Politics of Women's Work: The Paris Garment Trades 1750–1915* (Princeton, NJ: Princeton University Press, 1996), 173. However, in the British context "sweating" comes gradually to signify a lack of regulation and the prevalence of exploitation in shops and factories within and outside the textile industry. Contemporary analyses of sweating include Barbara Drake, *Women and Trade Unions* (1920; London: Virago, 1984), and Clementina Black, *Sweated Industry and the Minimum Wage* (London: Duckworth, 1907). For a modern analysis, see James A. Schmiechen, *Sweated Industries and Sweated Labor: The London Clothing Trades, 1860–1914* (Urbana: University of Illinois Press, 1984).

41. On the degradation of pleasure and its commodification as "leisure," see Fredric Jameson, "Pleasure: A Political Issue," in *Formations of Pleasure*, 1–14.

42. Janet Staiger, *Interpreting Films: Studies in the Historical Reception of American Cinema* (Princeton, NJ: Princeton University Press, 1992), 81.

43. Linda Williams makes a similar argument in her introduction to *Viewing Positions: Ways of Seeing Film* (New Brunswick, NJ: Rutgers University Press, 1995), 4.

44. Helen Bosanquet, "Cheap Literature," *Contemporary Review* 79 (May 1901): 677.

45. With its focus on the relationship between the fiction and fashion for the shopgirl-consumer, this chapter echoes Nan Enstad's research into the consuming practices of working-class women in the turn-of-the-century United States. In *Ladies of Labor*, Enstad argues that working women "formed subjectivities as ladies by using the fiction and fashion commodities available to them," using their consumer practices for expressly political purposes as well as for imaginative pleasure (4).

46. In drawing a parallel between the shift in consumer fantasy from distraction to absorption and the transformation of the fragmented visual display of the cinema of attractions into the sustained narrative of the feature film, I want to emphasize the simultaneous shift in viewer-text relations and the production of cinematic spectatorship. My aim has been to explore early British cinema's mode of address to its distracted female consumers, a project influenced by the scholarship of Tom Gunning and Miriam Hansen. See Tom Gunning, "The Cinema of Attractions: Early Film, Its Spectator, and the Avant-Garde," *Wide Angle* 8:3/4 (Fall 1986), rpt. in *Early Cinema: Space-Frame-Narrative*, ed. Thomas Elsaesser, 56–62 (London: BFI, 1990); "An Aesthetic of Astonishment: Early Film and The (In)Credulous Spectator," in Williams, *Viewing Positions*, 114–33; and Miriam Hansen, *Babel and Babylon: Spectatorship in American Silent Film* (Cambridge, MA: Harvard University Press, 1991).

Chapter One

1. "The Shop Assistant," *Women's Industrial News*, n.s.,19, no. 69 (April 1915): 336. Further references to this article will be cited parenthetically.

2. Joseph Hallsworth and Rhys J. Davies, *The Working Life of Shop Assistants: A Study of Conditions of Labour in the Distributive Trades* (Manchester: National Labour Press, 1910), 7. For an analysis of changes in the retailing trade during the nineteenth century, see James B. Jeffery, *Retail Trading in Britain, 1850–1950: A Study of Trends in Retailing with Special Reference to the Development of Co-operative, Multiple Shop and Department Store Methods of Trading* (Cambridge: Cambridge University Press, 1954), and Michael J. Winstanley, *The Shopkeeper's World 1830–1914* (Manchester: Manchester University Press, 1983).

3. Edward Cadbury, M. Cécile Matheson, and George Shann, M.A., *Women's Work and Wages: A Phase of Life in an Industrial City* (London: T. Fisher Unwin: 1906); M. Mostyn Bird, *Woman at Work: A Study of the Different Ways of Earning a Living Open to Women* (London: Chapman & Hall Ltd., 1911); Thomas Sutherst, *Death and Disease behind the Counter* (London: Kegan Paul and Co., 1884); Hallsworth and Davies, *Working Life;* William Paine, *Shop Slavery and Emancipation: A Revolutionary Appeal to the Educated Young Men of the Middle Class* (London: P. S. King and Son, 1912); and P. C. Hoffman, *They Also Serve: The Story of the Shopworker* (London: Porcupine Press, 1947). For Margaret Bondfield's writings, see the final section of this chapter.

4. "The Shop Assistant," *Women's Industrial News* (April 1915), 333. Christopher Hosgood has made a similar argument regarding the enforced adolescence of the male shop assistant in "'Mercantile Monasteries: Shops, Shop Assistants, and Shop Life in Late-Victorian and Edwardian Britain," *Journal of British Studies* 38:3 (1999): 322–52.

5. For a related analysis of young working women's experience of the urban environment, see Judith Walkowitz, "Going Public: Shopping, Street Harassment, and Streetwalking in Late Victorian London," *Representations* 62 (Spring 1998): 1–30.

6. Bird, *Woman at Work;* Cadbury et al., *Women's Work;* O. M. E. Rowe, "London Shop-Girls," *Outlook* 53 (29 February 1896); and The Fabian Society, "Shop Life and Its Reform" (London: The Fabian Society, December 1897).

7. Gayatri Chakravorty Spivak's articulation of the impossibility of speech for the subaltern female subject of British India has influenced my discussion of the various groups who occupy the position of "speaking for" women whose histories would go otherwise unrecorded. See Gayatri Spivak, "Can the Subaltern Speak?" in *Marxism and the Interpretation of Culture,* ed. Cary Nelson and Lawrence Grossberg, 271–313 (Urbana: University of Illinois Press, 1988).

8. On the contemporary perception of marriage as a "deliverance" from the shop, see Bird, *Woman at Work,* especially the introduction.

9. "The Shop Assistant," 343.

10. However, research by Claire Walsh and other eighteenth-century scholars has suggested that this transformation in fact began much earlier. Walsh's work suggests that the architecture, lighting, and furnishings of eighteenth-century shops encouraged customers to view shopping as "a leisurely pursuit and an exciting experience" and the shop as an atmosphere of elegance and luxury. Claire Walsh, "Shop Design and the Display of Goods in Eighteenth-Century London," *Journal of Design History* 8:3 (1995): 168. On the construction of shopping as a pleasurable leisure experience for bourgeois women at the turn of the century, see Erika Rappaport, *Shopping for Pleasure: Women in the Making of London's West End* (Princeton, NJ: Princeton University Press, 2000).

11. M. Jeune (Lady Jeune), "The Ethics of Shopping," *Fortnightly Review,* n.s., 57 (January 1895): 126.

12. Susan Porter Benson has analyzed the contested terrain of the counter and its mediation of class conflict in the United States during this period, but little work of this kind has been done on the British context. See Susan Porter Benson, *Counter Cultures: Saleswomen, Managers, and Customers in American Department Stores, 1890–1940* (Urbana: University of Illinois Press, 1986). For a further discussion of interactions between women in the department stores of London's West End, see *Shopping for Pleasure.* Christopher Hosgood's work on small shopkeepers has begun to redress this imbalance: see especially "The 'Pigmies of Commerce' and the Working-Class Community: Small Shopkeepers in England, 1870–1914," *Journal of Social History* 22:3 (1989): 439–60, and "'Mercantile Monasteries': Shops, Shop Assistants, and Shop Life in Late-Victorian and Edwardian Britain," *Journal of British Studies* 38:3 (1999): 322–52.

13. Other factors contributing to the feminization of shop work may have included the "deskilling" of women's shop labor as a result of the transformation of the retail industry; the increasing tendency of small shopkeepers to give their daughters, ideal shop assistants under the former system, a "young lady's education," necessitating a labor force drawn from outside the family; and the perception of female shop workers as a temporary and renewable labor force, since women were generally expected to leave the shop upon marriage. For the "deskilling" of shop labor, see Lee Holcombe's landmark early study, *Victorian*

Ladies at Work (Newton Abbot: David & Charles, 1973); and for an excellent summary of Holcombe, and the speculation regarding the education of shopkeepers' daughters, see Ellen Jordan, *The Women's Movement and Women's Employment in Nineteenth-Century Britain* (London and New York: Routledge, 1999), 68–71. Jordan likens the perception of female shop assistants as "unpromotable" to studies of the feminization of the clerical labor force, referencing Samuel Cohn, *The Process of Occupational Sex-Typing: The Feminization of Clerical Labor in Great Britain* (Philadelphia: Temple University Press, 1985), and Rosemary Crompton and Gareth Jones, *White Collar Proletariat: Deskilling and Gender in the Clerical Labour Process* (London: Macmillan, 1984).

14. Harriet Martineau, "Female Industry," *Edinburgh Review* 222 (April 1859): 335, 330–31.

15. W. R. Greg, "Why Are Women Redundant?" *National Review* 14 (April 1862): 434–60; rpt. in *Literary and Social Judgments* (1869), 276. For an excellent discussion of Greg's article and the connections between his solution for female redundancy and his solution to the problem of contamination and disease as linked to prostitution and morality, see Mary Poovey, *Uneven Developments: The Ideological Work of Gender in Mid-Victorian England* (Chicago: University of Chicago Press, 1988), 1–6.

16. Poovey notes that Greg's reliance on a diffuse conception of Nature's "golden rule"—that marriage operates through the human instincts as "the despotic law of life" (279)—constructs the problem of superfluous or "odd" women as one which contradicts the established order, both social and natural. For Greg, there are very few "natural celibates," and those who choose this path effectively write themselves out of the controversy: they are the anomalies par excellence, "abnormal and not perfect natures" (280). Rhoda Nunn, George Gissing's fictional version of the nineteenth-century militant feminist, views herself as a model for such women in her choice to remain single and celibate; in this she is not unlike Greg's "epicene women," those women "whose brains are so analogous to those of men, that they run nearly in the same channels, are capable nearly of the same toil, and reach nearly to the same heights; women not merely of genius [. . .] but of hard, sustained, effective *power;* women who live in and by their intelligence alone, and who are objects of admiration, but never of tenderness, to the other sex" (Greg, 280). Needless to say, the repetition of the word "nearly" in this passage signals Greg's attempt to contain the threat that such intellectual "odd" women provide; moreover, these women of power and intelligence are consigned to the margins of abnormality and imperfection, thereby in his eyes influencing only the few of their own sex who sympathize with them.

17. See the series of articles and letters on this subject in the *English Woman's Journal* between 1858 and 1863 (vols. 1–11); especially useful here are "The Disputed Question," *EWJ* 1 (1 August 1858); "How to Utilize the Powers of Women," *EWJ* 3 (1 March 1859); "Association for Promoting the Employment of Women," *EWJ* 4 (1 September 1859); "On the Obstacles to the Employment of Women," *EWJ* 4 (1 February 1860); and "The Balance of Public Opinion in Regard to Woman's Work," *EWJ* 9 (1 July 1862). For more on the *English Woman's Journal* and the women of the Langham Place Circle (so named after the building which housed the journal's editorial offices and the headquarters of the Society), see Candida Avin Lacey, Ed., *Barbara Leigh Smith Bodichon and the Langham Place*

Group (London and New York: Routledge & Kegan Paul, 1986). See also Sheila R. Herstein, *A Mid-Victorian Feminist: Barbara Leigh Smith Bodichon* (New Haven and London: Yale University Press, 1985); Pam Hirsch, *Barbara Leigh Smith Bodichon, 1827–1891: Feminist, Artist and Rebel* (London: Chatto & Windus, 1998); and Barbara Caine, *Victorian Feminists* (Oxford: Oxford University Press, 1992).

18. This phrase comes from "How to Utilize the Powers of Women" (ibid.); however, see also Greg, "Why Are Women Redundant?" In this article, Greg drew on his earlier articulation of the threat posed by prostitutes to both the economic and moral order of midcentury England in an essay entitled "Prostitution," published in the *Westminster Review* 53 (July 1850). On the relationship between Greg's two texts, see Mary Poovey, *Uneven Developments;* for an analysis of the "woman question" in this period, see Elizabeth K. Helsinger, Robin Lauterbach Sheets, and William Veeder, eds., *The Woman Question: Society and Literature in Britain and America, 1837–1883,* 3 vols. (New York: Garland Publishing, 1983).

19. "Association for Promoting the Employment of Women," *English Woman's Journal* 4 (1 September 1859): 59.

20. Ibid., 57.

21. M. Jeune, "The Ethics of Shopping."

22. "Association for Promoting the Employment of Women," 58–59.

23. The Fabian Society, "Shop Life and Its Reform" (London: Fabian Society, December 1897), 5.

24. Cadbury et al., *Women's Work,* 48.

25. Ibid.

26. The Fabian Society, "Shop Life and Its Reform" (1897), 7.

27. Terrick Mayne, "That Pretty Shop Girl," *Inglenook Novels,* no. 41 (London: Aldine Publishing Co., 1906); H. St. John Cooper, "A Shop-Girl's Revenge," *Woman's World 3d. Complete Library,* no. 27 (London: Fleetway House, Farringdon Street, 1914); Charles Pearce, "The Soul of a Shop Girl," *Mascot Novels,* no. 25 (London: Aldine Publishing Co., 1915). See also the examples discussed in chapters 2 and 4 of this study.

28. "The Shop Assistant," 327. For another discussion of the "false pride" of the country lass and the elementary schoolgirl who choose the shop over the factory or domestic service because of the higher social status, cleanliness, and lack of preparation necessary for employment, see Bird, *Woman at Work,* 65.

29. The Fabian Society, "Shop Life and Its Reform," 12; for the claim that shop assistants should not receive special treatment that would distinguish them from the rest of the working classes, see page 15.

30. In distinguishing between the descriptive and the transformative in my discussion of the shopgirl's class-inflected subject formation, I am drawing from Spivak's analysis of the dual forms of representation and re-presentation (*vertreten* and *darstellen,* or the difference between proxy and portrait) in Marx's *The Eighteenth Brumaire of Louis Bonaparte.* See Spivak "Can the Subaltern Speak?," 276–77. The relevance of Spivak's analysis for my discussion of the shopgirl's transitional and potentially transformative class-identity is the possibility that this transformation might occur differentially, through the work of communal political organization and collective interest described by Marx or, in a different register, on an individual level through the *fantasy* of self-transformation.

31. See also Bird, *Woman at Work,* 76.

32. See, for example, M. Mostyn Bird, *Woman at Work*; Cadbury et al., *Women's Work and Wages;* and Holcombe, *Victorian Ladies at Work*, 103–40.

33. Bird, *Woman at Work*, 2–3.

34. Ibid., 3, 9.

35. Virginia Woolf, *A Room of One's Own* (San Diego: Harcourt Brace Jovanovich, 1929), 90.

36. Again, I must acknowledge my debt to Lee Holcombe's chapter on women and the distributive trades in her *Victorian Ladies at Work*. Holcombe's work lays the foundation for many of the concerns I address in this chapter. However, she too easily aligns the shopgirl with the middle classes without taking into account the contentious and contested formation of her transitional class position and its transformative potential, and as a result flattens out the discursive forces producing the shopgirl as a social subject.

37. Will Anderson, *The Counter Exposed*, cited in Wilfred B. Whitaker, *Victorian and Edwardian Shopworkers: The Struggle to Obtain Better Conditions and a Half-Holiday* (Newton Abbot: David & Charles, 1973); Hallsworth and Davies, *Working Life;* "The Shop Assistant."

38. "The Shop Assistant," 329. The preceding quote on the "pleasant" quality of shop labor comes from Bird, *Woman at Work,* 63.

39. The Fabian Society, "Shop Life and Its Reform"; Hallsworth and Davies, *Working Life.*

40. "The Shop Assistant," 328–29.

41. Cadbury et al., *Women's Work,* 129; The Fabian Society, "Shop Life and Its Reform," 6; L. Barbara Hammond, "Equal Pay for Equal Work," *Women's Industrial News,* n.s., 28 (September 1904): 445–52.

42. Margaret G. Bondfield, "Conditions under Which Shop Assistants Work," *Economic Journal* 9 (June 1899): 277–86.

43. "The Shop Assistant," 326.

44. Bondfield, "Conditions," 282.

45. "The Shop Assistant," 336.

46. The Fabian Society, "Shop Life and Its Reform," 9; Bondfield, "Conditions," 282; "The Shop Assistant," 330.

47. Ibid.; see also E. J. M., "Truck and Fair Wages," *Women's Industrial News,* n.s., 46 (April 1909): 12–14.

48. "The Shop Assistant," 335.

49. Ibid., 332–34; Bondfield, "Conditions," 286.

50. "The Shop Assistant," 334; for more on meals and the living-in system generally, see also Mary Rankin Cranston, "London's Living-In System," *Outlook* 76 (27 February 1904).

51. "Conditions," 277; Bird, *Woman at Work,* 65–66.

52. The Fabian Society, "Shop Life and Its Reform," 10; see also Cranston, "London's Living-In System," 518, and Hallsworth and Davies, *Working Life,* 127.

53. Bird, *Woman at Work,* 2–10; Rowe, "London Shop-Girls," 398.

54. Cadbury et al., *Women's Work,* 117, 188; "The Shop Assistant," 335–36.

55. Margaret Bondfield, *A Life's Work* (London: Hutchinson, 1948), 26, 32.

56. Bird, *Woman at Work,* 14–15.

57. "The Shop Assistant" (1915), 335.

58. And not only for working-class women: middle- and upper-class women

also experienced the city as a site of both pleasure and danger. For further discussion, see Rappaport, *Shopping for Pleasure;* Nord, *Walking the Victorian Streets;* and Walkowitz, *City of Dreadful Delights.*

59. For a contemporary fictional depiction of a young woman's exposure to the pleasures of participation in the crowd, see George Gissing's *In the Year of Jubilee* (1894), in which Nancy Lord, Gissing's upwardly mobile lower-middle-class heroine, becomes assimilated with "any shop-girl let loose." The fact that Nancy later takes employment in a shop in order to support herself and her child underscores the complex assumptions about the respectability of earning one's living through shop labor and the problematics of the desire to exercise freedom of choice in work and leisure practices for women during this period.

60. Bird, *Woman at Work,* 69.

61. Feminist critics have taken up the problem of the *flâneuse* for an analysis of women's experience of the city. For the *flâneuse* as a new female spectator/consumer and urban social subject, see Giuliana Bruno, *Streetwalking on a Ruined Map: Cultural Theory and the City Films of Elvira Notari* (Princeton, NJ: Princeton University Press, 1993), and Anne Friedberg, *Window Shopping: Cinema and the Postmodern* (Berkeley: University of California Press, 1993); for the *flâneuse* as female social investigator, see Nord, *Walking the Victorian Streets.* For arguments which contradict the possibility of female *flânerie,* see Susan Buck-Morss, "The Flaneur, the Sandwichman, and the Whore: The Politics of Loitering," *New German Critique* 39 (Fall 1986): 98–140, and Janet Wolff, "The Invisible Flâneuse:* Women and the Literature of Modernity," in *The Problems of Modernity: Adorno and Benjamin,* ed. Andrew Benjamin, 141–56 (London: Routledge, 1989). As should be clear from this analysis, I believe we cannot equate the shopgirl's urban leisure practices with flânerie, since her class transitionality seems to negate, or at least complicate, this possibility. On this point see also Walkowitz, "Going Public."

62. This phrase comes from Walter Benjamin's essay on the phantasmagoric spectacles of the nineteenth-century metropolis, "Paris, Capital of the Nineteenth Century," in *Reflections,* ed. Peter Demetz, 157 (New York: Schocken Books, 1986).

63. For general surveys of British trade union history, see Hugh Armstrong Clegg, *A History of Trade Unions since 1889,* vols. 1 and 2 (Oxford: Clarendon Press, 1985); Keith Laybourn, *A History of British Trade Unionism c. 1770–1990* (Phoenix Mill, UK: Alan Sutton Publishing Ltd., 1992); and Henry Pelling, *A History of British Trade Unionism,* 2nd ed. (London: Macmillan, 1972).

64. For women's participation in trade unions and cooperative guilds, see Sarah Boston, *Women Workers and the Trade Unions* (London: Lawrence & Wishart, 1987); Katherine Graves Busbey, "The Women's Trade Union Movement in Great Britain," *Bulletin of the Bureau of Labor* (Washington: US Bureau of Labor Statistics, July 1909); Margaret Llewellyn Davies, *The Women's Co-operative Guild 1883–1904* (Kirby Lonsdale, Westmorland: Women's Co-operative Guild, 1904); Barbara Drake, *Women in Trade Unions* (London: G. Allen and Unwin, Ltd., 1920); Lucy Middleton, ed., *Women in the Labour Movement: The British Experience* (London: Croom Helm, 1977); and Mrs. Sidney Webb [Beatrice Potter Webb], "The Attitude of Men's Trade Unions toward Their Female Competitors," *Women's Industrial News* 1 (September 1897). Also useful is Deborah Thom, "'The Bundle of Sticks': Women Trade Unionists

and Collective Organisation before 1918," first published in *Unequal Opportunities: Women's Employment in England 1800–1918,* ed. Angela V. John (Oxford: Basil Blackwell, 1986), and reprinted in Thom's *Nice Girls and Rude Girls: Women Workers in World War I* (London: I. B. Tauris, 1998).

65. See Holcombe, *Victorian Ladies at Work,* 122–32. Significant attention at this time focused as well on shop assistants' lack of comfort while behind the counter; hence the union activity around the Shop Seats Bill which, although rarely enforced, signaled the public philanthropic interest in the plight of shop assistants as a class. See Margaret Hardinge Irwin, "The Shop Seats Bill Movement," *Fortnightly Review* 72 (1 July 1899): 123–31.

66. For the actual reduction in the practice of fines, see Bondfield, "Conditions."

67. See the Report of the Truck Committee, *Parliamentary Papers* (LIX), vol. 3 (1908).

68. References to the life of Margaret Bondfield are taken in large part from her 1948 memoir, *A Life's Work.* Further references will be cited parenthetically. In her preface, the author notes that over the thirty-some years since the end of the war, a dozen biographies were published in various magazines; for one example, see Mary Agnes Hamilton, *Margaret Bondfield* (New York: Thomas Seltzer, 1925).

69. For an exemplary reading of this kind, see Regenia Gagnier, *Subjectivities: A History of Self-Representation in Britain, 1832–1920* (New York and Oxford: Oxford University Press, 1991).

70. On the politics of pleasure and their relation to class, see Fredric Jameson, "Pleasure: A Political Issue," in *Formations of Pleasure,* ed. Formations Editorial Collective, 1–14 (London: Routledge & Kegan Paul, 1983).

71. "In the Days of My Youth," *T. P.'s and Cassell's Weekly* (January 1924); cited in Mary Agnes Hamilton, *Margaret Bondfield,* 35–36.

72. Ibid., 38–39.

73. Another aspect of Bondfield's life marks her story as atypical: her older brother Frank lived in London during the early years of her employment there, and was himself a member of the union at the printing house where he worked. The emphasis on familial companionship and supervision here differs significantly from the dominant story of the shopgirl, who appears almost orphaned in many of the texts which describe the work and living conditions of shopworkers. See Bondfield, *A Life's Work* (1948), 28 and *passim.*

74. Margaret Bondfield, *The Meaning of Trade,* Self and Society Booklets no. 9 (London: Ernest Benn Ltd., 1928), 15.

75. Ibid., 26.

76. For an excellent historical analysis of the Labour movement in this period, see Logie Barrow and Ian Bullock, *Democratic Ideas and the British Labour Movement, 1880–1914* (Cambridge: Cambridge University Press, 1996).

77. "'Grace Dare,' "A Tale of Tragedies," *Shop Assistant* (September 1898).

78. Hamilton considers Bondfield's close friendship with Mary Macarthur (of the National Federation of Women Workers) "the romance of her life." See Hamilton, *Margaret Bondfield,* 95.

79. "Jean," *Shop Assistant* (July 1899–June 1900); "An Imaginary Interview," *Shop Assistant* (March 1897), 148–49.

80. "The Case of Janet Deane," *Shop Assistant* (February 1898), 153; "The Manageress of the 'A' Department," *Shop Assistant* (February 1897), 128.

81. "And Gross Darkness Covered the Earth," *Shop Assistant* (December 1897), 106.

82. Bondfield, preface to *A Life's Work*, 9.

83. "'Jim'—A Memory," *Shop Assistant* (September 1896).

84. Cadbury et al., *Women's Work*, 117.

Chapter Two

1. M. Mostyn Bird, *Woman at Work: A Study of the Different Ways of Earning a Living Open to Women* (London: Chapman & Hall, 1911), 1, 63. Further references will be cited parenthetically.

2. For an analysis which describes the industrial mechanization process in terms of uneven development, see Raphael Samuel, "Mechanization and Hand Labour in Industrializing Britain," in *The Industrial Revolution and Work in Nineteenth-Century Europe,* ed. Lenard R. Berlanstein, 26–43 (London: Routledge, 1992).

3. Max Weber's work on rationalization provides a useful context for thinking through what has been called the "second industrial revolution" and its effects at the turn of the century. See Max Weber, *Economy and Society,* 3 vols., ed. and trans. Guenther Roth and Claus Wittick (New York: Bedminster Press, 1968), especially vol. 1, chaps 1–4. For a secondary source, see the introductory chapter to T. J. Jackson Lears's *No Place of Grace: Antimodernism and the Transformation of American Culture 1880–1920* (Chicago: University of Chicago Press, 1980).

4. Bird writes at length on the "Visionary Deliverer" who provides the imaginary promise of escape from the exploitative atmosphere of the shop, attempting to counter this fantasy lover's sway over the minds and hearts of young women.

5. On the relationship between consumption, gender, and pleasure in the department store, see Erika Rappaport, *Shopping for Pleasure: Women in the Making of London's West End* (Princeton, NJ: Princeton University Press, 2000), and "'A New Era of Shopping': The Promotion of Women's Pleasure in London's West End, 1909–1914," in *Cinema and the Invention of Modern Life,* ed. Leo Charney and Vanessa R. Schwartz, 130–55 (Berkeley: University of California Press, 1995). For an analysis of the parallel between the department store window and the cinema screen, see Anne Friedberg's *Window Shopping: Cinema and the Postmodern* (Berkeley: University of California Press, 1993), 66; she notes that previous film theorists and historians (among them Charles Eckert, Jane Gaines, Mary Ann Doane, and Jeanne Allen) have drawn the analogy between window shopping and cinema spectatorship (239 n. 81).

6. Of concern here is the relationship (or difference) between "work" and "labor." In Marxist criticism, labor suggests the alienating form of work, in which bodies are rendered part of a system based on industrial/capitalist progression. Work in its untainted form would look more like the fulfilling, productive experience which Bird describes as the ideal use of the energy and ability of the individual. For more on the degradation of work into labor, see Patrick Joyce, ed., *The Historical Meanings of Work* (Cambridge: Cambridge University Press, 1987),

1–30. To some extent, I use these terms interchangeably in this essay, in order to emphasize the culture of the department store which attempts through language to mask the fact that what it calls work is actually labor, disguised by the appearance of luxury and abundance in the store itself.

7. On the relationship between bodies and the "machine-culture" of turn-of-the-century America, see Mark Seltzer, *Bodies and Machines* (New York: Routledge, 1992).

8. I use this phrase in reference to Rosalind Williams's characterization of the spectacular sites for consumer pleasure in late-nineteenth-century French culture: see her *Dream Worlds: Mass Consumption in Late Nineteenth-Century France* (Berkeley: University of California Press, 1982), especially chapter 3.

9. Siegfried Kracauer, "The Mass Ornament" (1927), in *The Mass Ornament: Weimar Essays,* trans. and ed. Thomas Y. Levin (Cambridge, MA: Harvard University Press, 1995), 75–76. The Tiller Girls were named after John Tiller, a Manchester choreographer famed for his system of strict discipline which "Tillerized" his employees; the troupe was originally founded in 1890 and served as a model for future generations of chorus lines. For a brief summary of the Tiller Girls which compares them to the "girl culture" of the 1890s and early 1900s, see Peter Bailey, " 'Naughty but Nice': Musical Comedy and the Rhetoric of the Girl, 1892–1914," in *The Edwardian Theatre: Essays on Performance and the Stage,* ed. Michael R. Booth and Joel H. Kaplan, 36–60 (Cambridge: Cambridge University Press, 1996). Hollywood musicals like Warner's *Footlight Parade* (dir. Lloyd Bacon, 1933) and *Gold Diggers of 1933* (dir. Mervyn Le Roy, 1933) featured similar kaleidoscopic dance revues, choreographed by Busby Berkeley.

10. Thomas Y. Levin, introduction to *The Mass Ornament,* 18.

11. Kracauer, "The Mass Ornament," 77.

12. Other examples include: W. B. Maxwell, *Vivien* (London: 1905); Horace W. C. Newte, *Pansy Meares: The Story of a London Shop Girl* (New York: J. Lane & Co., 1912), and *Sparrows* (London: Mills and Boon, n.d. [ca. 1909]); Margaret Westrup, *Tide Marks* (London: Method & Co., 1913); and May Sinclair, *The Combined Maze* (London: Harper & Bros., 1913).

13. For the seminal argument positing a "consumer revolution" in the eighteenth century, see Neil McKendrick, John Brewer, and J. H. Plumb, *The Birth of Consumer Society: The Commercialization of Eighteenth-Century England* (London: Europa, 1982). Chandra Mukerji challenges this thesis by arguing for the earlier and more gradual development of consumer culture in a wide array of contexts; see her *From Graven Images: Patterns of Modern Materialism* (New York: Columbia University Press, 1983). For further discussion of consumer culture and commodity circulation during this period, see the essays collected in John Brewer and Roy Porter, eds., *Consumption and the World of Goods* (London: Routledge, 1993); for work focused on England, see Carole Shammas, *The Pre-Industrial Consumer in England and America* (Oxford: Clarendon Press, 1990); Joan Thirsk, "Popular Consumption and the Mass Market in the Sixteenth to Eighteenth Centuries," *Material History Bulletin* 31 (1990): 51–58; and Beverly Lemire's work on consumerism and clothing, especially *Fashion's Favourite: The Cotton Trade and the Consumer in Britain, 1660–1800* (Oxford: Oxford University Press, 1992). Lisa Tiersten provides a useful review of scholarship on consumption in her article, "Redefining Consumer Culture: Recent Literature on Consumption and the

Bourgeoisie in Western Europe," *Radical History Review* 57 (1993): 116–59. On the place of women within the development of consumer culture in the eighteenth century, see Elizabeth Kowaleski-Wallace, *Consuming Subjects: British Women and Consumer Culture in the Eighteenth Century* (New York: Columbia University Press, 1996); and on the role of privileged women as consumers in eighteenth-century England, see Amanda Vickery, *The Gentleman's Daughter: Women's Lives in Georgian England* (New Haven, CT: Yale University Press, 1998). Discussing a London linen-draper's trade card from 1720, Vickery comments, "Throughout the eighteenth century, and probably long before, genteel women were accustomed to visit fashionable London shops unaccompanied by men" (171). This argument poses a challenge to the work of Judith Walkowitz and Erika Rappaport, among others: Vickery observes, "Shopping was well entrenched as a public cultural pursuit for respectable women and men long before the advent of Selfridges and Whiteleys. . . . The urban voyager and female pleasure-seeker was no invention of the 1880s" (252).

14. Thomas Richards argues that the Great Exhibition was the first of the nineteenth-century "commodity spectacles" which contributed to the transformation of the advertising industry and the formation of a consumer culture based on commodity fetishism; see his *The Commodity Culture of Victorian England: Advertising and Spectacle, 1851–1914* (Stanford, CA: Stanford University Press, 1990), especially chapter 1, "The Great Exhibition of Things" (17–72).

15. Richards, *Commodity Culture*, 17. On the symbolic role of objects, Marx's description of commodity fetishism remains the primary source: see "The Fetishism of Commodities and the Secret Thereof," section 4 of *Capital* (vol. 1), reprinted ined., *The Marx-Engels Reader*, 2nd ed., ed. Robert C. Tucker, 319–29 (New York: W. W. Norton & Co., 1978). For criticism which reframes the relationship between culture and material objects, in addition to the sources cited above, see the essays collected in *The Social Life of Things*, ed. Arjun Appadurai (Cambridge: Cambridge University Press, 1986); Victoria de Grazia and Ellen Furlough, eds., *The Sex of Things: Gender and Consumption in Historical Perspective* (Berkeley: University of California Press, 1996); and Bill Brown, "How to Do Things with Things," unpublished manuscript presented at the American Studies/Mass Culture Workshop at the University of Chicago, January 1998.

16. This scholarship has focused largely on the rise of the department store in France (primarily Paris) and the United States, particularly New York and Chicago. Many of these critical texts center on one store: see, for example, R. M. Hower, *History of Macy's of New York 1858–1919: Chapters in the Evolution of a Department Store* (Cambridge, MA: Harvard University Press, 1943); R. W. Twyman, *History of Marshall Field and Co., 1852–1906* (Philadelphia: University of Pennsylvania Press, 1954); and Michael B. Miller, *The Bon Marché: Bourgeois Culture and the Department Store, 1869–1920* (London: George Allen and Unwin, 1981).

17. Susan Porter Benson, *Counter Cultures: Saleswomen, Managers, and Customers in American Department Stores, 1890–1940* (Urbana: University of Illinois Press, 1986), and William Leach, *Land of Desire: Merchants, Power, and the Rise of a New American Culture* (New York: Pantheon, 1993). For examples of scholarship on England which works to similar ends, see Bill Lancaster, *The Department Store: A Social History* (London: Leicester University Press, 1995), and Rappaport, *Shopping for Pleasure*.

18. On individual British stores, see the following texts (which often collapse the distinction between the history of the store and its founder or subsequent management): Richard S. Lambert, *The Universal Provider: A Study of William Whiteley and the Rise of the London Department Store* (London: George G. Harrap & Co, 1938); A. H. Williams, *No Name on the Door: A Memoir of Gordon Selfridge* (London: W. H. Allen, 1956); Reginald Pound, *Selfridge: A Biography* (London: Heinemann, 1960); [Harrods Ltd.], *1849–1949: A Story of British Achievement* (London: Harrods, n.d.); George Pottinger, *The Winning Counter: Hugh Fraser and Harrods* (London: Hutchinson & Co., 1971); Sean Callery, *Harrods Knightsbridge: The Story of Society's Favourite Store* (London: Ebury Press, 1991); and Tim Dale, *Harrods, A Palace in Knightsbridge* (London: Harrods Publishing, 1995). Several studies of individual stores do succeed in placing the store within a larger social and historical context: these include Asa Briggs, *Friends of the People: The Centenary History of Lewis's* (London: Batsford, 1956), and Michael Moss and Alison Turton, *A Legend of Retailing: House of Fraser* (London: Weidenfeld and Nicholson, 1989).

19. For a discussion of these "proto-department stores," see Lancaster, *Department Store*, 7–15. Lenore Davidoff and Catherine Hall provide a useful discussion of the growth of the middle-class household, and its emphasis on social respectability and thrift, in their *Family Fortunes: Men and Women of the English Middle Class, 1750–1850* (Chicago: University of Chicago Press, 1987).

20. On the rise of the nineteenth-century multiple grocery chains, see James B. Jefferys, *Retail Trading in Britain 1850–1950* (Cambridge: University Press, 1954), and Peter Mathias, *Retailing Revolution: A History of Multiple Retailing in the Food Trades Based upon the Allied Suppliers Group of Companies* (London: Longmans, Green & Co., Ltd., 1967).

21. For a discussion of the rise of the department store in France, see Miller, *Bon Marché*; Williams, *Dream Worlds*; Elizabeth Wilson, *Adorned in Dreams: Fashion and Modernity* (London: Virago, 1985); and Anne Friedberg, *Window Shopping*. Emile Zola's novel *Au bonheur des dames,* published serially in 1882 and translated into English in 1883, presents a fictional establishment based on contemporary department stores like the Bon Marché and the Louvre. Rachel Bowlby discusses the novel at length in *Just Looking: Consumer Culture in Dreiser, Gissing, and Zola* (New York: Methuen, 1985).

22. On Baum's influence over the transformation of the American department store, see Stuart Culver, "What Manikins Want: *The Wonderful Wizard of Oz* and *The Art of Decorating Dry Goods Windows*," *Representations* 21 (Winter 1988): 97–116. William Leach's work on American consumer culture from the 1890s to the 1930s provides useful contextualization for both Baum's and Fraser's effects on new technologies for displaying merchandise: articles include "Transformations in a Culture of Consumption: Women and Department Stores, 1890–1925," *Journal of American History* 71:2 (September 1984): 319–42, and "Strategists of Display and the Production of Desire," in *Consuming Visions: Accumulation and Display of Goods in America, 1880–1920*, ed. Simon J. Bonner, 99–132 (New York: W. W. Norton and Co., for the Henry Francis DuPont Winterthur Museum, 1989); see also *Land of Desire*. Bill Lancaster also includes a discussion of the American department store, with particular attention to Marshall Field's, in his 1995 social history.

23. Lambert, *Department Store,* provides the standard history/biography of Whiteley's, describing the founder's innovations in retailing and self-advertisement as well as the sexual innuendo and scandal which eventually culminated in his death at the hands of a young man claiming to be his son, a case described in greater detail in the conclusion to this study.

24. On the first, see Moss and Turton, *Legend of Retailing;* on the remaining three, see M. Corina, *Fine Silks and Oak Counters: Debenhams 1778–1978* (London: Hutchinson, 1978).

25. Rappaport, "'A New Era'" and *Shopping for Pleasure.*

26. Sean Callery, *Harrods Knightsbridge: The Story of Society's Favorite Store* (London: Ebury Press, 1991), 79–81.

27. Tim Dale, *Harrods: A Palace in Knightsbridge* (London: Harrods Publishing, 1995), 58.

28. Callery, *Harrods Knightsbridge,* 90.

29. *Harrodian Gazette* 35 (1950): 182. I would like to thank Nadene Hansen, archivist at Harrods, for bringing this article on Miss Waterman, one of the original "chicks," to my attention. On Miss Fowle, see the *Harrodian Gazette* 3:6 (4 June 1915): 14.

30. Unmarked ledger entries for 1891 and 1894, Harrods Archives.

31. For Richard Burbidge's synopsis of Harrods' new schemes for staff education, see his letter to the *Times,* 7 January 1914; rpt. in the *Harrodian Gazette* 2:2 (6 February 1914): 7–8.

32. On the transformation of labor politics, especially in the case of London, at the turn of the century, see Paul Thompson, *Socialists, Liberals and Labour: The Struggle for London 1885–1914* (London: Routledge & Kegan Paul, 1967); Chris Waters, *British Socialists and the Politics of Popular Culture, 1884–1914* (Manchester: Manchester University Press, 1990); and Susan D. Pennybacker, *A Vision for London 1889–1914: Labour, Everyday Life and the LCC Experiment* (London: Routledge, 1995).

33. Cited in Callery, *Harrods Knightsbridge,* 96.

34. Mrs. Norah Slade (née Irwin) described her experience as a store employee and onetime mannequin to me in a personal interview at her home in Chiswick in March of 1998. I owe her a debt of gratitude for her willingness to provide an account of one young woman's working life at Harrods from 1914 to 1916.

35. Callery, *Harrods Knightsbridge,* 91; Dale, *Palace in Knightsbridge,* 87. On Burbidge's perspective on the living-in system, see his answers to questions posed by the chairman of the Truck Committee, in the committee's Minutes of Evidence for Wednesday, 31 July 1907.

36. Harrods Stores, Ltd., "Rules and Regulations for Shopwalkers, Assistants, &c.," Harrods' Archive [n.d.].

37. "Extracts from Mr. Allen's Salesmanship Lectures," *Harrodian Gazette* 1:2 (February 1913).

38. *Harrodian Gazette* 1:2 (February 1913): 7.

39. Ibid., 13–14.

40. Ibid., 4.

41. *Harrodian Gazette* 5:8 (August 1917): 165.

42. The model of the store owner as patriarch, ruling over a family of workers with a firm hand, can be read as a descendant of mid-Victorian industrial fic-

tion: writers depicted the factory owner alternately as a good father struggling against financial constraints (as in the sentimental conclusion to Elizabeth Gaskell's *Mary Barton*) or as a bad father allowing his workers to run wild (as in Benjamin Disraeli's *Sybil*).

43. Full-page advertisement illustrated by Bernard Partridge, 15 March 1909, Selfridges Store Archives.

44. *Daily Express,* 15 March 1909.

45. Rappaport, "New Era," 130–31.

46. Pound, *Selfridges,* 11–18.

47. Lloyd Wendt and Herman Kogan, *Give the Lady What She Wants! The Story of Marshall Field & Company* (Chicago: Rand McNally, 1952), 220.

48. For a description of the case of the Bethlehem Steel shovelers, see Frederick Winslow Taylor, "Shop Management," a paper read at the meeting of the American Society of Mechanical Engineers in June 1903 and later published in *Transactions of the American Society of Mechanical Engineers* 24 (1903): 1337–80. This paper was republished in a volume which also included *The Principles of Scientific Management* (1911) and *Taylor's Testimony before the Special House Committee,* a reprint of *Hearings before Special Committee of the House of Representatives to Investigate the Taylor and Other Systems of Shop Management under Authority of H. Res. 90,* 3 (1912): 1377–1508. All citations are from this volume, entitled *Scientific Management* (New York: Harper, 1947).

49. Taylor, *Testimony,* in *Scientific Management* (1947), 30.

50. For the committee's suggestion that the worker under the system of scientific management risked becoming a mere automaton, see *Scientific Management,* 197. For analyses of the effects of Taylorization on industrial management and technology, see Alfred Chandler, *The Visible Hand: The Managerial Revolution in American Business* (Cambridge, MA: Harvard University Press, 1977), 275–81, 560 nn. 67–75; James R. Beniger, *The Control Revolution: Technological and Economic Origins of the Information Society* (Cambridge, MA: Harvard University Press, 1986), 294–98; and Daniel Nelson, ed., *A Mental Revolution: Scientific Management since Taylor* (Columbus: Ohio State University Press, 1992). For reflections on Taylor's influence on the narratives of modern life, see Martha Banta, *Taylored Lives: Narrative Productions in the Age of Taylor, Veblen, and Ford* (Chicago: University of Chicago Press, 1993).

51. See, for example, Taylor's description of the Bethlehem Steel workers' transformation into sober, steady men (*Shop Management,* 56); or Gramsci's discussion of Ford's efforts to intervene in the private lives of his employees, to shape the structure of their leisure time as well as their working hours, in *Selections from the Prison Notebooks,* ed. and trans. Quintin Hoare and Geoffrey Nowell Smith (New York: Lawrence & Wishart, 1971), 302. A useful secondary source on Ford's strategies for managing the lives of his employees is Stephen Meyer's *The Five-Dollar Day: Labor Management and Social Control in the Ford Motor Company 1908–1921* (Albany: State University of New York Press, 1981).

52. Cited in Gordon Honeycombe, *Selfridges: Seventy Five Years. The Story of the Store, 1909–1984* (London: Park Lane Press, 1984), 186.

53. "The Spirit of the House," framed testament in the Selfridges Store Archives. I would like to thank Fred Redding, the head archivist at Selfridges, for bringing this and other staff records to my attention.

54. Honeycombe, *Selfridges,* 183. For detailed accounts of the sporting and social events sponsored by Selfridges during its early years, see also the staff magazine, entitled *The Key of the House,* various issues of which are held in the Selfridges Archives.

55. Cited in Honeycombe, *Selfridges,* 175.

56. See, for example, the *Daily Express* (12 March 1909), and *Answers* (17 December 1909).

57. Honeycombe, *Selfridges,* 182, 186. For an account of the 1912 excursion, see "Business and Pleasure: Selfridges' Assistants Visit Paris," *Morning Leader,* 10 April 1912.

58. *North Eastern Gazette* (Middlesborough), 25 June 1912.

59. James de Conlay, "Personality—The Secret of Success," *London Magazine* (undated copy in Selfridges Store Archives), 688.

60. This quote is from an assistant who worked under Selfridge in the silk department at Marshall Field & Co., and who then wrote an article entitled "H. Gordon Selfridge and His Methods, by One Who Worked under Him," printed in the *Draper's Record,* 27 March 1909.

61. *Draper's Record,* 28 August 1909.

62. Percy A. Best, *The Story of Selfridges* (presentation copy in the Selfridges Store Archives), 8; originally published as a series of articles for *Women's Wear News* in 1936.

63. Recollection by Mrs. Adela Hill (store name Adela Pratt), a fifteen-year-old Selfridges employee in the Corsets department in 1909; cited in Honeycombe, *Selfridges,* 191.

64. Emile Zola, *Au bonheur des dames,* translated in England as *The Ladies' Paradise* (1883), with an introduction by Kristin Ross (Berkeley: University of California Press, 1992), 17.

65. Ibid., 16–17.

66. For details on the Williamsons' writings, see Alice Williamson's autobiography, *The Inky Way* (London: Chapman and Hall, Ltd., 1931).

67. Although the title of the novel reads *Winnie Childs,* the heroine is referred to throughout the text as Miss Child (Winnie and Win serving as nicknames), a practice I have followed here.

68. C. N. and A. M. Williamson, *Winnie Childs, The Shop Girl* (1914; New York: Grosset & Dunlap, 1916), 26.

69. Charles Dickens, *Hard Times: For These Times* (1854; Harmondsworth, Middlesex, England: Penguin Books, 1985), 102–3.

70. The centrality of the shopgirl's hands as markers of her identity and social/sexual status also emerges in early films like August Blom's 1911 film *The Shop Assistant,* in which the heroine fits a glove onto the hand of a male customer in a scene laden with erotic signification.

71. On the relation between "hands," bodies, and the capitalist production process, compare another quote from Kracauer's essay on the mass ornament: "The hands in the factory correspond to the legs of the Tiller Girls. [. . .] The mass ornament is the aesthetic reflex of the rationality to which the prevailing economic system aspires." Kracauer, "The Mass Ornament," 79.

72. For an extended discussion of the place of fantasy in the lives of shopgirl-readers, see chapter 4.

73. Arthur Applin, *Shop Girls* (London: Mills and Boon, 1914), 7–8. Further references will be cited parenthetically.

74. Compare another of Applin's passages, in which one of Lobb's spies (disguised as an employee of Bungay's) compels Martha to accept a position as shop assistant through the influence of description:

> First of all he overwhelmed her with waves of satin, silks, and brocades; muslins palpitated, silks rustled, a forest of radiantly coloured feathers beckoned them on. At her feet Martha saw a valley of velvet; the colours dazzled her. Horatio threw silks like pearls in her path, greens, azures, may-rose, and sea-blue; he whispered how fascinating it would be to live in an atmosphere of frocks and frills and sweet scents and sounds. In imagination he lured her into a ballgown, a wicked black model which he had persuaded Bungay to obtain from Vienna, and then, surrounded her with mirrors until she was frightened and blinded by her own beauty, seeing whichever way she looked, her red-black hair, white flesh, and black gown, deaf to all sounds but the rustle of silk that kissed her limbs whenever she moved. Still painting word pictures he forced her to wade through an ocean of the latest creations in fashionable French corsets, to swim through a sea of dainty lingerie until she emerged trembling, her feet sinking into the quicksands of linens and rare laces. . . . (16)

75. Kracauer, "The Mass Ornament," 76–77.

76. Ibid.

77. This event may be usefully compared with M. Mostyn Bird's description of the prospect of escape provided through marriage: "This visionary Deliverer is a powerful factor in the mental existence of the industrial worker: the possibility of his coming with all the money, pleasure, and comfort of body that she now lacks, carries her gaily through dark days that must otherwise break her spirit." Bird, *Woman at Work*, 3.

Chapter Three

1. Cicely Hamilton, *Diana of Dobson's: A Romantic Comedy in 4 Acts* (London: Samuel French Ltd., 1925). Rpt. in *New Woman Plays*, ed. Linda Fitzsimmons and Viv Gardener, 29–77 (London: Methuen Drama, 1991). For details of Hamilton's life and work, see Lis Whitelaw, *The Life and Rebellious Times of Cicely Hamilton: Actress, Writer, Suffragist* (Columbus: The Ohio State University Press, 1991); Sheila Stowell, "Drama as a Trade: Cicely Hamilton's *Diana of Dobson's*," in *The New Woman and Her Sisters: Feminism and Theatre 1850–1914*, ed. Vivien Gardner and Susan Rutherford, 177–88 (Ann Arbor: University of Michigan Press, 1992); and Sheila Stowell, *A Stage of Their Own: Feminist Playwrights of the Suffrage Era* (Ann Arbor: University of Michigan Press, 1992), chapter 3.

2. Hamilton, *Diana of Dobson's*, 38, 66–67.

3. I am indebted to Elizabeth Helsinger for a discussion of the aesthetics of boredom in this text.

4. On the disciplinary control over workers' time previous to the nineteenth century, see E. P. Thompson, "Time, Work-Discipline, and Industrial Capitalism," *Past and Present* 38 (December 1967): 55–97.

5. Hamilton, *Diana of Dobson's*, 35.

6. I take the term "proper femininity" from Lyn Pykett, *The "Improper" Feminine: The Women's Sensation Novel and the New Woman Writing* (London: Routledge, 1992), 11–18.

7. The middle-class male protagonists of these novels, Everard Barfoot (and, to some extent, Philip Carey) also must find appropriate ways to manage their experience of work and leisure and the attendant problems of boredom. However, for these men, and especially because of the gendered nature of work and industry in the nineteenth century, the experience of boredom is differently characterized. Everard Barfoot, as the symbol of a bourgeois male aspiration to the heights of aristocratic wealth and leisure, also inserts himself into a romance plot (however unconventional), but acts less from real feeling and more from a distanced intellectual perspective (especially as reflected in the struggle for dominance between himself and Miss Nunn). Philip Carey too aspires to a leisured existence, and sets about differentiating himself from Mildred Rogers, who comes to represent the impoverished, false gentility of those aspiring to middle-class status and economic security.

8. On the cultural and literary iconicity of the New Woman, see Pykett, *The "Improper" Feminine;* Ann Ardis, *New Women, New Novels: Feminism and Early Modernism* (New Brunswick, NJ: Rutgers University Press, 1990), 10–28; and Elaine Showalter, *Sexual Anarchy: Gender and Culture at the Fin-de-Siècle* (New York: Penguin, 1990), 38–58. For a useful collection of late-nineteenth-century writings on the New Woman, see Carolyn Christensen Nelson, ed., *A New Woman Reader: Fiction, Articles, and Drama of the 1890s* (Peterborough, ON: Broadview Press, 2001).

9. George Gissing, *The Odd Women* (Harmondsworth, Middlesex: Penguin, 1983), 214. Further references will be cited parenthetically.

10. In formulating this claim, I have been influenced by Lauren Berlant's work on the production of the "ordinary" in her collection of essays, *The Queen of America Goes to Washington City* (Durham, NC: Duke University Press, 1997); see especially her introduction. I have also found useful the elaboration of typicality or generality as modes of experiencing subjecthood: as Mark Seltzer suggests in his study of serial killers, "it is the intimate experience of self-generalization[,] the at once alluring and insupportable experience of a sort of hypergeneralization in typicality" that defines and assimilates the prototypical inhabitants of modern "machine" culture, "statistical person[s]." Mark Seltzer, "Serial Killers (II): The Pathological Public Sphere," *Critical Inquiry* 22 (Autumn 1995): 137. My reading of the shopgirl as a late-nineteenth-century cultural "type" suggests that she is rendered "typical" or ordinary at the same time she inhabits a position of remarkability, figured most clearly through the contemporary focus on her consuming practices.

11. For related readings of the figure of the shopgirl in this novel, see Maria Theresa Chialant, "The Feminization of the City in Gissing's Fiction: The Streetwalker, the *Flaneuse,* the Shopgirl," in *A Garland for Gissing,* ed. Bouwe Postmus, 51–65 (Amsterdam, Netherlands: Rodopi, 2001); and Sally Ledger,

"Gissing, the Shopgirl, and the New Woman," *Women: A Cultural Review* 6:3 (Winter 1995): 263–74. Also of interest is Arlene Young's chapter on Oliphant, Levy, Allen, and Gissing entitled "Bachelor Girls and Working Women," in *Culture, Class and Gender in the Victorian Novel: Gentlemen, Gents and Working Women,* 119–56 (Houndsmills, Basingstoke: Macmillan, 1999).

12. On morality and the domain of the sexual in Victorian culture, see Frank Mort, *Dangerous Sexualities: Medico-moral Politics in England since 1830* (London: Routledge & Kegan Paul, 1987).

13. See especially in this context John Ruskin's 1864 essay "Of Queen's Gardens," reprinted in *Sesame and Lilies* (1868), and Sarah Stickney Ellis's series on the wives, mothers, and daughters of England, collected as *The Women of England: Their Social Duties, and Domestic* Habits (London: Fisher, 1839).

14. Leonore Davidoff and Catherine Hall, *Family Fortunes: Men and Women of the English Middle Class, 1780–1850* (Chicago: University of Chicago Press, 1987), 404, 398 and *passim;* see also Nancy Armstrong, *Desire and Domestic Fiction: A Political History of the Novel* (New York: Oxford University Press, 1987), especially chapter 2.

15. Mrs. Humphry, *Manners for Women* (London: Ward, Lock, 1897), 18–19.

16. Ibid., 2.

17. In her analysis of the relationship between prostitution and "flanerie," that oft-discussed mode of (usually male) nineteenth-century urban experience, Susan Buck-Morss claims that "all women who loitered risked being seen as whores," a point with which I concur. Susan Buck-Morss, "The Flaneur, the Sandwichman, and the Whore: The Politics of Loitering," *New German Critique* 39 (Fall 1986): 119. Janet Wolff makes a similar argument about the impossibility of morally sanctioned female flanerie in "The Invisible *Flâneuse:* Women and the Literature of Modernity," in *The Problems of Modernity: Adorno and Benjamin,* ed. Andrew Benjamin, 141–56 (London: Routledge, 1989). For a counterargument, see Mica Nava, "Modernity's Disavowal: Women, the City, and the Department Store," in *Modern Times: Reflections on a Century of Modernity,* ed. Mica Nava and Alan O'Shea, 38–76 (London: Routledge, 1996).

18. On the relationship between artificial face color, "falseness," and the rhetoric of "fallen womanhood," see Amanda Anderson, *Tainted Souls and Painted Faces: The Rhetoric of Fallenness in Victorian Culture* (Ithaca, NY: Cornell University Press, 1993), 59–61. For more on the correlation between the stereotype of the prostitute and the physical appearance of women, see Lynda Nead, *Myths of Sexuality: Representations of Women in Victorian Britain* (London: Basil Blackwell, 1988), and Mariana Valverde, "The Love of Finery: Fashion and the Fallen Woman in Nineteenth-Century Social Discourse," *Victorian Studies* 32:2 (1989): 169–88.

19. William Tait, *Magdalenism: An Inquiry into the Extent, Causes, and Consequences of Prostitution in Edinburgh* (Edinburgh: P. Rickard, 1840), 162.

20. Gissing researched his subjects intensively before writing, as evident in diary entries that show him reading up on "woman literature" and attending lectures on the woman question. I have not found any specific references to research on shop conditions in his writings, but he clearly had a sense of the journalistic coverage of the controversy, as reflected in the level of detail in this scene. We might speculate that he drew on material from his own experience as the son of a

chemist's shopkeeper; in addition, much of the detail on shop life is reflected in writings by H. G. Wells (especially *Kipps* and *Experiment in Autobiography*, both of which trace the experiences of a draper's apprentice), whom Gissing met several years after the publication of *The Odd Women*, and who felt an instant affiliation with Gissing. For the citations from Gissing's diary, see Pierre Coustillas, *London and the Life of Literature in Late Victorian England: The Diary of George Gissing, Novelist* (Hassocks, Eng.: Harvester, 1978), 3, 427. Both authors, too, deal with a similar class of characters, in Gissing's words "a class of young men distinctive of our time—well educated, fairly bred, but without money," quoted in Pierre Coustillas and Colin Partridge, eds., *Gissing: The Critical Heritage* (London: Routledge, 1972), 244.

21. On hysteria's place within nineteenth-century British culture, see Elaine Showalter, *The Female Malady: Women, Madness, and English Culture, 1830–1980* (New York: Penguin, 1985).

22. On the relation between idleness and illness for middle-class heroines of nineteenth-century fiction—Marianne Dashwood in *Sense and Sensibility*, Emma Woodhouse in *Emma*, or Lucy Snowe as a working woman unable to experience the luxury of boredom in *Villette*—see Patricia Meyer Spacks, *Boredom: The Literary History of a State of Mind* (Chicago: University of Chicago Press, 1995), 116–25, 167–74, 183–89.

23. For further details of shop work—somewhat obliquely presented in the service of social reform: note the reiterated claim that "an account of the labour of men and women in shops must, if truthfully given, be little else than a recital of their grievances" (Amy Bulley and Margaret Whitley, *Women's Work* [London: Methuen, 1894], 49)—see "The Shop Assistant," *Women's Industrial News* (1915), 321–44, and M. Mostyn Bird, *Woman at Work* (London: Chapman, 1911).

24. Fictional versions of this ideal of female enterprise include Beatrice French's South London Fashionable Dress Supply Association in Gissing's *In the Year of Jubilee* (1894) and (rather less successfully) Lily Bart's fantasy of owning a millinery shop in Edith Wharton's *The House of Mirth* (1905).

25. Martin Waugh, "Boredom in Psychoanalytic Perspective," *Social Research* 42 (1975): 548, cited in Spacks, *Boredom*, 165. The closing quote is from Spacks, *Boredom*, 166.

26. Charles Sanders, ed., *W. Somerset Maugham: An Annotated Bibliography of Writings about Him* (De Kalb: Northern Illinois University Press, 1970), 56.

27. "Man in the Making," *Saturday Review* 120 (1915): 233.

28. Anthony Curtis, *The Pattern of Maugham: A Critical Portrait* (London: Hamish Hamilton, 1974), 85.

29. Robert Lorin Calder, *W. Somerset Maugham and the Quest for Freedom* (London: Heinemann, 1972), 89.

30. Richard A. Cordell, *Somerset Maugham: A Biographical and Critical Study* (Bloomington: Indiana University Press, 1961), 94. For a more balanced reading of the character of Mildred, see Bonnie Hoover Braendlin, "The Prostitute as Scapegoat: Mildred Rogers in Somerset Maugham's *Of Human Bondage*," in *The Image of the Prostitute in Modern Literature*, ed. Pierre L. Horn and Mary Beth Pringle, 9–18 (New York: Frederick Ungar, 1984).

31. Barbara Drake, "The Tea-Shop Girl, being a Report of an Enquiry undertaken by the Investigation Committee of the Women's Industrial Council,"

Women's Industrial News (April 1913), 115. Further references will be cited parenthetically.

32. W. Somerset Maugham, *Of Human Bondage* (1915; New York: Bantam, 1991), 272. Further references will be cited parenthetically.

33. Bird, *Woman at Work,* 65.

34. *Etiquette for the Ladies: Eighty Maxims on Dress, Manners, and Accomplishments* (London: Charles Tilt, 1837), 53.

35. *Etiquette for All, or Rules of Conduct for Every Circumstance in Life: With the Laws, Precepts, and Practices of Good Society* (Glasgow: George Watson, 1861), 47; *Girls and Their Ways: A Book for and about Girls, by One Who Knows Them* (London: John Hogg, 1881), x.

36. According to the authors of *Etiquette for Ladies and Gentlemen* (London: Frederick Warne, 1876), the term "genteel" had become a mockery of itself by the last quarter of the century, as had "polite" and other conversational "errors" which marked one's class difference from "good society" (45).

37. Sarah Stickney Ellis, *The Women of England: Their Social Duties, and Domestic Habits* (London, 1839), 17. Further references will be cited parenthetically.

38. For a primary source constructing the ideology and social practice of Victorian courtship, see *The Etiquette of Love, Courtship, and Marriage* (1847), in *Women and Victorian Values, 1837–1910: Advice Books, Manuals, and Journals for Women* (Marlborough, Wiltshire: Adam Matthew, 1996).

39. Widdowson's views, adopted from the Victorian doctrine of separate and gendered spheres, diametrically oppose those espoused by Mary Barfoot and Rhoda Nunn. Indeed, Mary's speech, entitled "Woman as Invader" (151), works as a direct counterpoint to Widdowson's argument: "I am strenuously opposed to that view of us set forth in such charming language by Mr. Ruskin. [. . . T]he fact is that we live in a world as far from ideal as can be conceived. We live in a time of warfare, of revolt" (153). [. . .] "There must be a new type of woman, active in every sphere of life: a new worker out in the world, a new ruler of the home" (154).

40. On the middle-class woman's domestic influence, see Ellis, *The Women of England.*

41. Sarah Stickney Ellis, *The Daughters of England: Their Position in Society, Character, and Responsibilities* (New York: D. Appleton and Co., 1842), 48.

42. Spacks, *Boredom,* 179.

43. For a fictional account of the effects of such literature on readers, see Oscar Wilde, *The Picture of Dorian Gray* (1891).

44. See Hamilton, *Marriage as a Trade* (1909 [London: Women's Press, 1981]), and George Bernard Shaw, *Mrs. Warren's Profession,* in *Complete Plays with Prefaces,* vol. 3 (New York: Dodd, Mead, 1963). Useful secondary sources include J. Ellen Gainor, *Shaw's Daughters: Dramatic and Narrative Constructions of Gender* (Ann Arbor: University of Michigan Press, 1991); Tracy C. Davis, *George Bernard Shaw and the Socialist Theatre* (Westport, CT: Greenwood, 1994); and the sources cited in n. 1.

45. On the figure of the barmaid, see Peter Bailey, "Parasexuality and Glamour: The Victorian Barmaid as Cultural Prototype," *Gender & History* 2:2 (1990): 148–72.

46. Judith Walkowitz, *City of Dreadful Delight: Narratives of Sexual Danger in Late-Victorian London* (Chicago: University of Chicago Press, 1992), 22. For an extended discussion of Victorian attitudes to prostitution, see Walkowitz, *Prostitution and Victorian Society: Women, Class and the State* (Cambridge: Cambridge University Press, 1980); Amanda Anderson, *Tainted Souls and Painted Faces: The Rhetoric of Fallenness in Victorian Culture* (Ithaca, NY: Cornell University Press, 1993); and Deborah Epstein Nord, *Walking the Victorian Streets: Women, Representation, and the City* (Ithaca, NY: Cornell University Press, 1995).

47. See especially W. R. Greg, "Why Are Women Redundant?" *National Review* (April 1862); rpt. in *Literary and Social Judgments* (London, 1869), 274–308.

48. See Hamilton, *Marriage as a Trade,* and Charlotte Perkins Gilman, *Women and Economics* (1898; Berkeley: University of California Press, 1998).

49. For a contemporary example of the perceived association between physical and moral decline, see Hargrave Adam's *Woman and Crime* (London: T. Werner Laurie, 1912). Adam insists upon a correlation between prostitution and the malady he terms "sexual mania," a "malign influence" driving young women to "social destruction" (41).

50. William Acton, *Prostitution Considered in Its Moral, Social, and Sanitary Aspects, in London and Other Large Cities, with Proposals for the Mitigation and Prevention of Its Attendant Evils* (London: John Churchill, 1857), 118.

51. The *Oxford English Dictionary* defines "trivial" as "Such as may be met with anywhere; common, commonplace, ordinary, everyday, familiar, trite," a now rare usage passing into "Of small account, little esteemed, paltry, poor; trifling, inconsiderable, unimportant, slight." On triviality and its connection to the "little esteemed" aspects of the ordinary, Roland Barthes writes: "I can fall in love with a slightly vulgar attitude [. . .] what is fascinating about the other's 'triviality' is just this, perhaps: that for a very brief interval I surprise in the other, detached from the rest of his person, something like a gesture of prostitution." Roland Barthes, *A Lover's Discourse: Fragments* (New York: Hill and Wang, 1978), 191.

Chapter Four

1. George Gissing, *The Odd Women* (1893; Harmondsworth, England: Penguin, 1983), 64.

2. In 1858, Wilkie Collins designated this readership the "Unknown Public," which he estimated totaled at least three million. Wilkie Collins, "The Unknown Public," *Household Words* 439 (21 August 1858): 217. There is a growing body of scholarship on Victorian reading practices. Key early texts include Amy Cruse, *The Victorians and Their Reading* (Boston: Houghton Mifflin, 1935); Richard D. Altick, *The English Common Reader: A Social History of the Mass Reading Public, 1800–1900* (Chicago: University of Chicago Press, 1957); and Louis James, *Fiction for the Working Man, 1830–1850: A Study of the Literature Produced for the Working Class in Early Victorian Urban England* (London: Oxford University Press, 1963). Relevant studies of eighteenth- and nineteenth-century readership include Jon Klancher, *The Making of English Reading Audiences,*

1790–1832 (Madison: University of Wisconsin Press, 1987); David Vincent, *Literacy and Popular Culture, England 1750–1914* (Cambridge: Cambridge University Press, 1989); and Jacqueline Pearson, *Women's Reading in Britain, 1750–1835: A Dangerous Recreation* (Cambridge: Cambridge University Press, 1999). On Victorian periodical reading, see Kelly J. Mays, "The Disease of Reading and Victorian Periodicals," in *Literature in the Marketplace: Nineteenth-Century British Publishing and Reading Practices,* ed. John O. Jordan and Robert L. Patten, 165–94 (Cambridge: Cambridge University Press, 1995); and for an excellent study of women's reading in the Victorian and Edwardian periods, see Kate Flint, *The Woman Reader, 1837–1914* (Oxford: Clarendon Press, 1993), to which this chapter is greatly indebted.

3. On sensation fiction and its consumers in the mid-Victorian period, see Ann Cvetkovich, *Mixed Feelings: Feminism, Mass Culture, and Victorian Sensationalism* (New Brunswick, NJ: Rutgers University Press, 1992).

4. Collins, "Unknown Public," 222.

5. For a comprehensive study of working-class reading in the nineteenth century, see Jonathan Rose, *The Intellectual Life of the British Working Classes* (New Haven, CT, and London: Yale University Press, 2001).

6. Friedrich Engels, *Condition of the Working Class in 1844,* 177, cited in Richard D. Altick, *The English Common Reader: A Social History of the Mass Reading Public* (Chicago: University of Chicago Press, 1957), 95.

7. Sir John Herschel, "Address to the Subscribers to the Windsor and Eton Public Library and Reading Room" (1833), in his *Essays from the Edinburgh and Quarterly Reviews* (1857), 8–10; cited in Altick, *English Common Reader,* 96.

8. Winifred Holtby, "What We Read and Why We Read It," *Left Review* 1:4 (1935); rpt. in Peter Davison, Rolf Meyerson, and Edward Shils, eds., *Bookselling, Reading, and Reviewing,* vol. 12 of *Literary Taste, Culture and Mass Communication,* 209 (Cambridge: Chadwyck Healey, 1978).

9. Agnes Reppelier, "English Railway Fiction," in *Points of View,* 209–10 (Boston: Houghton Mifflin, 1891).

10. See Sarah Stickney Ellis, *The Women of England: Their Social Duties, and Domestic Habits* (London: Fisher, 1839), and *The Daughters of England: Their Position in Society, Character, and Responsibilities* (New York: D. Appleton and Co., 1842); Athena Vrettos, "Defining Habits: Dickens and the Psychology of Repetition," *Victorian Studies* 42:3 (2000): 399–426. I thank Elaine Hadley for drawing my attention to the operation of habit in these texts.

11. Rose, *Intellectual Life,* 379–80.

12. *Christian Observer* 14 (1815): 512, cited in Altick, *English Common Reader,* 110.

13. Geo. R. Humphery, "The Reading of the Working Classes," *Nineteenth Century* 33 (April 1893): 692–93.

14. "New and Cheap Forms of Popular Literature," *Eclectic Review* 82 (1845): 76.

15. Edward G. Salmon, "What Girls Read," *Nineteenth Century* 20 (October 1886): 523.

16. On the informal and ideological censorship practiced by the circulating library system, see Terry Lovell, *Consuming Fiction* (London: Verso, 1987), 81 and *passim.*

17. Mrs. Mary Wood-Allen, *What a Young Woman Ought to Know* (Philadelphia: Vir, 1899, 1913), 123.

18. Twentieth-century texts which treat the development of the novel as a genre include John Tinnon Taylor, *Early Opposition to the English Novel: The Popular Reaction from 1760 to 1830* (New York: Kings Crown Press, 1943); Ian Watt, *The Rise of the Novel: Studies in Defoe, Richardson, and Fielding* (Berkeley: University of California Press, 1957); John J. Richetti, *Popular Fiction before Richardson: Narrative Patterns 1700–1739* (Oxford: Clarendon, 1969); Ioan Williams, introduction to *Novel and Romance 1700–1800: A Documentary Record* (New York: Barnes and Noble, 1970); Lovell, *Consuming Fiction;* and Clive T. Probyn, *English Fiction of the Eighteenth Century 1700–1789* (London: Longman Group, 1987).

19. Lovell, *Consuming Fiction,* 10.

20. For sources, see the essays in *Solitary Pleasures: The Historical, Literary, and Artistic Discourses of Autoeroticism,* ed. Paula Bennett and Vernon A. Rosario II (New York: Routledge, 1995), especially Eve Sedgwick, "Jane Austen and the Masturbating Girl" (133–53), and Thomas Laqueur, "The Social Evil, the Solitary Vice, and Pouring Tea" (155–61).

21. On the pathologized female body, see Sally Shuttleworth, "Female Circulation: Medical Discourse and Popular Advertising in the Mid-Victorian Era," in *Body/Politics: Women and the Discourses of Science,* ed. Mary Jacobus, Evelyn Fox Keller, and Sally Shuttleworth, 47–68 (New York: Routledge, 1990), and Margaret Beetham, *A Magazine of Her Own? Domesticity and Desire in the Woman's Magazine, 1800–1914* (London: Routledge, 1996), 41–42, 144–45.

22. Elizabeth Garrett Anderson was one member of an extended family of women activists in midcentury London: her sisters were the suffragist Millicent Garrett Fawcett and Agnes Garrett, who with her cousin Rhoda worked as an interior designer and campaigner for women's rights. Agnes and Elizabeth directed the Ladies Dwellings Company, promoting and building cooperative housing for single middle-class women, with rents ranging from ten to twenty-five shillings per week. For an excellent account of feminist activism in the 1850s–1870s, see Lynne Walker, "Home and Away: The Feminist Remapping of Public and Private Space in Victorian London," in *New Frontiers of Space, Bodies and Gender,* ed. Rosa Ainley, 65–75 (New York: Routledge, 1998), and "Vistas of Pleasure: Women Consumers of Urban Space in the West End of London 1850–1900," in *Women in the Victorian Art World,* ed. Clarissa Campbell Orr, 70–85 (Manchester: Manchester University Press, 1995). See also Barbara Caine, *Victorian Feminists* (Oxford: Oxford University Press, 1992).

23. Henry Maudsley, "Sex in Mind and Education," *Fortnightly Review,* n.s., 15 (April 1874): 467–83.

24. Elizabeth Garrett Anderson, "Sex in Mind and Education: A Reply," *Fortnightly Review,* n.s., 15 (May 1874): 590.

25. John Ruskin, "Of Queens' Gardens," lecture given in 1864 and reprinted in *Sesame and Lilies* (1868), ed. Deborah Epstein Nord (New Haven, CT: Yale University Press, 2002).

26. There is, however, an important body of work on romantic identification which uses reception-based historical and theoretical scholarship to discuss the ways in which women consume the mass-marketed romance. Key texts include

Janice Radway, *Reading the Romance: Women, Patriarchy, and Popular Literature* (Chapel Hill: University of North Carolina Press, 1991 [1984]), and Lynne Pearce and Jackie Stacey, eds., *Romance Revisited* (New York: New York University Press, 1995). For a provocative discussion of the ways in which female consumers might appropriate fantasy for their own uses, see Constance Penley's work on K/S fanzines (a genre produced by women narrating the development of a romantic/sexual relationship between two men, Kirk and Spock of *Star Trek*), "Feminism, Psychoanalysis, and the Study of Popular Culture," in *Cultural Studies*, ed. Lawrence Grossberg, Cary Nelson, and Paula Treichler, 479–94 (New York: Routledge, 1992).

27. For a detailed analysis of Newnes's relationship to the nineteenth-century periodical press, see Kate Jackson, "The *Tit-Bits* Phenomenon: George Newnes, New Journalism and the Periodical Texts," *Victorian Periodicals Review* 30:3 (Fall 1997): 201–26.

28. As feminist film scholars have argued, a similar trajectory can be traced in the history of film theory, in which the suturing of the spectator into the text has been complicated by alternative understandings of cinematic identification. Judith Mayne describes this trajectory in "Paradoxes of Spectatorship," an article excerpted from her *Cinema and Spectatorship* (London: Routledge, 1993) and included in *Viewing Positions: Ways of Seeing Film,* ed. Linda Williams, 155–83 (New Brunswick, NJ: Rutgers University Press, 1995).

29. Cora Kaplan, "*The Thorn Birds:* Fiction, Fantasy, Femininity," in *Formations of Fantasy,* ed. Victor Burgin, James Donald, and Cora Kaplan, 142–66 (London: Routledge, 1986).

30. Jean Laplanche and Jean-Bertrand Pontalis, "Fantasy and the Origins of Sexuality" (1968), in Burgin, Donald, and Kaplan, *Formations of Fantasy,* 22–23.

31. My argument regarding the disjunction from everyday life produced by the novelette parallels Janice Radway's argument in *Reading the Romance*. However, I want to problematize the concept of identification through an analysis of possible alternatives to the practice of imagining oneself as the heroine of these fictions, as the next section shows. Identification itself is significantly more complicated than this one-to-one relation, as feminist readers of psychoanalytic theory have taught us.

32. Thomas Wright, "Concerning the Unknown Public," *Nineteenth Century* 13 (February 1883): 282. Wright went by the moniker "the Journeyman Engineer," and wrote both fiction and nonfiction accounts of working-class life, including *Some Habits and Customs of the Working Classes* (1867), *The Great Unwashed* (1868), and *Our New Masters* (1873); for a brief discussion of Wright, see Peter Bailey, *Popular Culture and Performance in the Victorian City* (Cambridge: Cambridge University Press, 1998), 36, 122.

33. Here, Wright effects a common slippage within the category of "penny fiction," in which novelettes (short, freestanding stories) and magazine stories (often, though not always, serialized) are taken to constitute the same or similar generic models. While he is describing the magazines in this example, elsewhere he discusses novelettes in much the same language.

34. For alternative nineteenth-century claims about the readership of penny serials, see Edward G. Salmon, "What the Working Classes Read," *Nineteenth Century* 20 (1886): 108–17, and James Payn, "Penny Fiction," *Nineteenth Century*

9 (1881): 145–54; for an assessment of the "common reader" which focuses on magazines marketed to domestic servants and contradicts some of Wright's claims, see Louis James, "The Trouble with Betsy: Periodicals and the Common Reader in Mid-Nineteenth Century England," in *The Victorian Periodical Press: Samplings and Soundings,* ed. Joanne Shattock and Michael Wolff, 349–66 (Toronto: University of Toronto Press, 1982).

35. Holtby, "What We Read," 211–12.

36. Wright, "Concerning the Unknown Public," 290; see also Edward G. Salmon, "What Girls Read," which likens Aesop to the nursery and Ouida to the "full blaze of the drawing room" (523).

37. Despite her popularity as a Victorian novelist and celebrity, Ouida's writing has received little attention from twentieth-century critics. Two useful articles which seek to redress this lack of critical interest are Jane Jordan, "Ouida: The Enigma of a Literary Identity," *Princeton University Library Chronicle* 57:1 (Autumn 1995): 75–105, and Natalie Schroeder, "Feminine Sensationalism, Eroticism, and Self-Assertion: M. E. Braddon and Ouida," *Tulsa Studies in Women's Literature* 7:1 (Spring 1988): 87–101.

38. Reppelier, "English Railway Fiction," 221.

39. [Francis Hitchman,] "Penny Fiction," *Quarterly Review* 171 (July 1890): 161.

40. Kate Flint, *The Woman Reader, 1837–1914* (Oxford: Clarendon Press, 1993), 165. I am indebted to Flint for the many insights provided by this pathbreaking study.

41. Helen Bosanquet, "Cheap Literature," *Contemporary Review* 79 (May 1901): 677.

42. On women's magazines and fashion's capacity to remake the female body (particularly in the case of the tight-lacing controversy in the 1860s and 1870s, see Beetham, *A Magazine of Her Own?* especially 71–89; and Kay Boardman, "'A Material Girl in a Material World': The Fashionable Female Body in Victorian Women's Magazines," *Journal of Victorian Culture* 3:1 (Spring 1998): 93–110.

43. Quoted in Bosanquet, "Cheap Literature," 677.

44. For a discussion of Worth's influence, see Elizabeth Wilson, *Adorned in Dreams: Fashion and Modernity* (London: Virago, 1985).

45. Christopher Hosgood has noted a similar phenomenon in the social function of "the sales," which were widely advertised to lower-middle-class consumers including "young women working in offices and shops": in the penny journal *Woman's Life,* for instance, Helen Erecson-Smith "advised readers who wished to dress smartly on a limited annual budget to buy remnant material at the winter sales which could be transformed into the most fashionable summer dresses." Christopher P. Hosgood, "Mrs. Pooter's Purchase: Lower-Middle-Class Consumerism and the Sales, 1870–1914," in *Gender, Civic Culture and Consumerism: Middle-Class Identity in Britain, 1800–1940,* ed. Alan Kidd and David Nicholls, 156 (Manchester: Manchester University Press, 1999).

46. On the fashion tie-up in Hollywood cinema of the 1930s, see especially Charles Eckert, "The Carole Lombard in Macy's Window," *Quarterly Review of Film Studies* 3:1 (Winter 1978): 1–21, and Jane Gaines, "The Queen Christina Tie-Ups: Convergence of Show Window and Screen," *Quarterly Review of Film and Video* 11:1 (Winter 1989): 35–60; also useful are essays by Jeanne Thomas

Allen, Charlotte Herzog, and Elizabeth Nielsen in *Fabrications: Costume and the Female Body,* ed. Jane Gaines and Charlotte Herzog (New York: Routledge, 1990).

47. In researching examples from each of Edwin Brett's serials, I noted that he used the repetitive quality of novelette fiction to his advantage, recycling material to suit industry trends. He would publish a series of stories in successive weeks ranging in length of run from a year to eighteen months, then discontinue that serial and begin another, reprinting the previous stories years later, when readers would have forgotten the details of the plot. This happened in the case of *Something to Read Novelettes* (1881–1910) and *Gipsy Novelettes* (1900–1901), and again with *Wedding Bells Novelettes* (1880–1881) and *English Ladies' Novelettes* (1891–1892).

48. For a study of these and other early to mid-Victorian popular periodicals for women, see Sally Mitchell, *The Fallen Angel: Chastity, Class and Women's Reading, 1835–1880* (Bowling Green, OH: Bowling Green University Popular Press, 1981); and for an excellent analysis of the later period, see Mithchell's subsequent book, *The New Girl.*

49. Kracauer elaborates the concept of distraction as a mode of organizing mass experience in the twentieth century in his 1926 essay "Cult of Distraction," reprinted in *The Mass Ornament: Weimar Essays,* trans. and ed. Thomas Y. Levin (Cambridge, MA: Harvard University Press, 1995). My analysis of popular literature suggests that distraction was operative some years before Kracauer analyzed its role in the picture palace in 1920s Berlin.

50. Salmon, "What the Working Classes Read," 113–14.

51. James Haslam, *The Press and the People: An Estimate of Reading in Working-Class Districts* (Manchester: "City News" Office, 1906), 15.

52. Humphery, "The Reading of the Working Classes," 693; "'A Working Woman,' 'Do Public Libraries Foster a Love of Literature Among the Masses?'" *Chambers's Journal,* 6th ser., 3 (December 1899): 135.

53. Florence Low, "The Reading of the Modern Girl," *Nineteenth Century* 59 (1906): 278–87. Further references will be cited parenthetically.

54. Max Pemberton, *Northcliffe: A Memoir* (London, 1922), 29–30. For a concise and well-researched analysis of Harmsworth's periodicals for boys, see John Springhall, "'Healthy papers for manly boys': Imperialism and Race in the Harmsworths' Halfpenny Boys' Papers of the 1890s and 1900s," in *Imperialism and Juvenile Literature,* ed. Jeffrey Richards, 107–25 (Manchester: Manchester University Press, 1989).

55. Mitchell, *The New Girl,* 92.

56. Others have commented on the function of convent and school stories as identificatory sites for readers, whether in the case of young Roman Catholic Irish immigrants reading stories about Mary Latimer, Mother Superior at St. Agatha's convent, or Glory O'Shea, convent schoolgirl, or in the case of shop workers substituting the authority figure of the schoolteacher for a feared or disliked forewoman or employer. See Mary Cadogan and Patricia Craig, *You're a Brick, Angela! A New Look at Girls' Fiction from 1839 to 1975* (London: Victor Gollancz Ltd., 1976), 127–29, and Mitchell, *The New Girl,* 95–96.

57. For an analysis of the Pollie Green stories, see Cadogan and Craig, *You're a Brick, Angela!,* 132–35; see also Mitchell, *The New Girl,* 93–94, and Kirsten Drotner, *English Children and Their Magazines, 1751–1945* (New Haven, CT: Yale University Press, 1988), 166.

58. For scholarship on musical comedy and girl culture during this period, see Erika Rappaport, "Acts of Consumption: Musical Comedy and the Desire of Exchange," in *Shopping for Pleasure*. Also useful in this regard is Peter Bailey's article, "'Naughty but Nice': Musical Comedy and the Rhetoric of the Girl, 1892–1914," in *The Edwardian Theatre: Essays on Performance and the Stage*, ed. Michael R. Booth and Joel H. Kaplan, 36–60 (Cambridge: Cambridge University Press, 1996).

59. "London's Shop-Girls and Their Chances of Marrying Well," *Forget-Me-Not* (18 March 1899): 377.

60. "How Shop Girls Win Rich Husbands," *Forget-Me-Not* (23 August 1902): 368.

61. "Shopgirls as Wives," *Forget-Me-Not* (14 September 1901): 387.

62. Ibid.

63. "Shopgirls Make Good Wives: What Another Lady Writer Thinks," *Forget-Me-Not* (28 September 1901): 427.

64. Ibid.

65. "Confidential Chat," *Forget-Me-Not* (12 October 1901): 478; "Why I Married a Shop-Girl: The Confessions of a Happy Husband," *Forget-Me-Not* (4 October 1902): 511.

66. For some examples, see "Careers for Women: The Working Hours, Earnings, and Prospects of a Shopgirl," *Forget-Me-Not* (12 December 1903): 661; "Business Girl Chats no. 9: A Shop-Girl," *Girls' Friend* (12 August 1905): 659; "My Day's Work, by a Draper's Assistant," *Forget-Me-Not* (26 March 1904): 525.

67. *Girls' Friend* (24 October 1903): 825.

68. My commitment to the utopian element of (mass) cultural and political analysis draws from the work of Fredric Jameson and Lauren Berlant. See Fredric Jameson, "Reification and Utopia in Mass Culture," *Social Text* 1 (Winter 1979): 130–48, and Lauren Berlant, "'68, or Something," *Critical Inquiry* 21 (Autumn 1994): 124–55.

69. Tom Gunning, "An Aesthetic of Astonishment: Early Film and the (In)Credulous Spectator," in *Viewing Positions: Ways of Seeing Film*, ed. Linda Williams, 114–33 (New Brunswick, NJ: Rutgers University Press, 1995); for the earlier piece on the cinema of attractions, see "The Cinema of Attractions: Early Film, Its Spectator, and the Avant-Garde," in *Early Cinema: Space—Frame—Narrative*, ed. Thomas Elsaesser, 56–62 (London: BFI, 1990).

Chapter Five

1. Tony Davies has argued a similar point in his discussion of the popular nineteenth-century genres of the railway novel and the romance, arguing that "the pleasures of Victorian and Edwardian popular reading are associated less with the privacy of the study and the armchair than with the agitated excitements of public transport: the brittle, vivid sociability of the illuminated street, the bustle and adventure of the station platform, the transient romance of travel by bus, train, or tram." See his "Transports of Pleasure: Fiction and Its Audiences in the Later Nineteenth Century," in *Formations of Pleasure*, Formations Editorial Collective, 49 (London: Routledge & Kegan Paul, 1983).

2. However, such liaisons were not unheard of: those who married into wealth, title, or both included models employed by the fashionable West End couturière Lucile (whose second marriage to Sir Cosmo Duff Gordon in 1900 strengthened her position as society modiste). For an account of Lucile's career, see Joel H. Kaplan and Sheila Stowell, *Theatre and Fashion: Oscar Wilde to the Suffragettes* (Cambridge: Cambridge University Press, 1994), 39–44 and 115–21; for the reference to marriages of models and show girls to wealthy and titled men, see Erika Rappaport, *Shopping for Pleasure: Women in the Making of London's West End* (Princeton, NJ: Princeton University Press, 2000), 200. Actresses—women whose careers depended on self-display—had long been associated with sexual availability: on this point, see Tracy C. Davis, *Actresses as Working Women: Their Social Identity in Victorian Culture* (London: Routledge, 1991).

3. The distracted pleasures of the decade (or so) from 1894 to 1904 did not disappear entirely in the teens: the variety format extended into the 1920s, and feature filmmaking throughout the twentieth century incorporated the spectacular display of effects. Likewise, the behavior of the audience has remained to some extent based on interaction with others in the auditorium and with the narratives produced on screen: the film theatre still provides a space where couples may find intimacy in public, and where audience members can respond vocally and physically to the images presented to them. For more on these points, see Tom Gunning, "The Cinema of Attractions: Early Film, Its Spectator and the Avant-Garde," *Wide Angle* 8:3/4 (Fall 1986), rpt. in *Early Cinema: Space-Frame-Narrative*, ed. Thomas Elsaesser, 56–62 (London: BFI, 1990).

4. Bailey identifies parasexuality as "an extensive ensemble of sites, practices and occasions that mediate across the frontiers of the putative public/private divide," in a form that uses the visual signifiers of glamour: "Parasexuality then is sexuality that is deployed but contained, carefully channelled rather than fully discharged; in vulgar terms it might be represented as 'everything but.'" Peter Bailey, "Parasexuality and Glamour: The Victorian Barmaid as Cultural Prototype," *Gender & History* 2:2 (Summer 1990): 148–72; rpt. in his *Popular Culture and Performance in the Victorian City*, 151–74: 151 (Cambridge: Cambridge University Press, 1998). Bailey associates "knowingness" with the language and style of Victorian music hall and the rise of musical comedy in the 1890s: see his "Conspiracies of Meaning: Music Hall and the Knowingness of Popular Culture," *Past and Present* 144 (August 1994): 138–70; rpt. in Bailey, *Popular Culture and Performance*, 128–50; and "'Naughty but Nice': Musical Comedy and the Rhetoric of the Girl," in *The Edwardian Theatre: Essays on Performance and the Stage*, ed. Michael R. Booth and Joel H. Kaplan, 36–60 (Cambridge: Cambridge University Press, 1996); rpt. in Bailey, *Popular Culture and Performance*, 175–93.

5. Most useful on late Victorian London as a site of sexual danger is Judith R. Walkowitz's important study, *City of Dreadful Delight: Narratives of Sexual Danger in Late-Victorian London* (Chicago: University of Chicago Press, 1992). On the role of pleasure in late Victorian London, especially with regard to women's consumer practices, see Rappaport, *Shopping for Pleasure*.

6. The singular term "audience" is actually a misnomer, for music halls and cinemas targeted and were shaped by the audiences who patronized them, and contemporary accounts depict a wide range of variation in the constitution of audiences, ranging from the elite crowds who patronized the West End music halls

and theatres to the middle- and working-class populations attending local enter-
tainments in the suburbs and the East End. A useful general resource on Victorian
theatre is Michael R. Booth, *Theatre in the Victorian Age* (Cambridge: Cambridge
University Press, 1991); on the music hall, see Dagmar Kift, *The Victorian Music
Hall: Culture, Class and Conflict* (Cambridge: Cambridge University Press, 1996).
In an 1890 article in *Harper's New Monthly Magazine,* F. Anstey grouped the
London halls into four classes with a corresponding descent in the social scale:
"First, the aristocratic variety theatre of the West End, chiefly found in the imme-
diate neighborhood of Leicester Square; then the smaller and less aristocratic West
End halls; next, the large bourgeois music halls of the less fashionable parts and
the suburbs; last, the minor music halls of the poor and squalid districts." Cited
in ed., *The Last Empires: A Music Hall Companion,* ed. Benny Green, 60–61
(London: Pavilion, 1986). The same type of class segregation in purpose-built film
auditoriums was also true, reinforcing the perception of cinema as a mass entertainment patronized largely by the working classes.

   7. On the relationship between fashion and mass entertainment at the turn
of the century, see Joel Kaplan and Sheila Stowell, *Theatre and Fashion: Oscar
Wilde to the Suffragettes* (Cambridge: Cambridge University Press, 1994).

   8. Peter Bailey makes a similar argument in his "Theatres of
Entertainment/Spaces of Modernity: Rethinking the British Popular Stage
1890–1914," *Nineteenth-Century Theatre* 26 (1998): 5–22. Bailey quotes an
observer's comments on the crowds of young working women at leisure in
London's West End in 1906: "There are shopmen, clerks, and spinsters in pince-
nez; but more numerous still are the shopgirls, milliners, dressmakers, typists, ste-
nographers, cashiers of large and small houses of business, telegraph and telephone
girls, and the thousands of other girls . . . spending all their money in gadding
about, on sixpenny novels, on magazines, and above all, on the theatre." Mario
Borsa, *The English Stage of Today* (London: Bodley Head, 1908), 4–5; cited in
Bailey, *Popular Culture and Performance,* 15.

   9. On prostitution in the halls, see Bailey, *Popular Culture and Performance,*
144–47; and on the reform efforts of purity campaigners, see Lucy Bland,
Banishing the Beast: Feminism, Sex and Morality (London: I. B. Tauris, 2001 [first
published in 1995 by Penguin Books with the subtitle *English Feminism and
Sexual Morality 1885–1914*]), 95–123; and Walkowitz, *City of Dreadful Delight.*

   10. My argument has been influenced by Dave Russell's essay "Varieties of
Life: The Making of the Edwardian Music Hall," in Booth and Kaplan, *The
Edwardian Theatre,* 61–85.

   11. This migrational culture was endemic to the industrialization of the earlier nineteenth century, as Raymond Williams and others have argued. See
Raymond Williams, *The Country and the City* (Oxford: Oxford University Press,
1973); for a contemporary fictional depiction of the aspirations of the rural laborer to self-advancement in the metropolis, see Thomas Hardy's novel *Jude the
Obscure* (1895).

   12. As Tracy Davis notes, charges of indecency and obscenity in the turn-of-
the-century music hall were often based on an assumed causality between suggestive performances and the morality of the audience: "Such charges reflect comprehensively on all aspects of music hall programming—songs, ballets, sketches,
tableaux vivants and novelties—linking what occurred on stage to the 'demorali-

sation' (sexual excitement) of the audience." Tracy C. Davis, "Indecency and Vigilance in the Music Halls," in *British Theatre in the 1890s: Essays on Drama and the Stage,* ed. Richard Foulkes, 111–12 (Cambridge: Cambridge University Press, 1992).

13. The "cinema of attractions" is Tom Gunning's term for the exhibitionism or display culture of early cinema, which was concerned less with narrative and more with the presentation of "a series of views" to its audience. See his seminal articles "An Aesthetic of Astonishment: Early Film and the (In)Credulous Spectator," *Art & Text* 34 (Winter 1989): 31–45; rpt. in *Viewing Positions: Ways of Seeing Film,* ed. Linda Williams, 114–33 (New Brunswick, NJ: Rutgers University Press, 1995) and "The Cinema of Attractions."

14. Russell, "Varieties of Life," 63. The term "popular" has been taken to indicate the contested production of leisure from below or within, by the participant-consumers themselves; by contrast, "mass" has typically signified the dissemination of recreational entertainments from above, in particular by those occupying positions of power/influence within the industry. The popular/mass distinction has a long history of critical debate: primary texts include Max Horkheimer and Theodor Adorno, "The Culture Industry: Enlightenment as Mass Deception," from *Dialectic of Enlightenment* (1944), trans. John Cumming (New York: Continuum, 1994), and Dwight Macdonald, "A Theory of Mass Culture," originally published as "A Theory of Popular Culture" in *Politics Today* (1944) and expanded for *Diogenes* 3 (Summer 1953); this version is reprinted in *Mass Culture: The Popular Arts in America,* ed. Bernard Rosenberg and David Manning White, 59–73 (Glencoe, IL: Free Press, 1958). These and other indictments of mass culture often result in a revaluation of "high" or avant-garde art at the expense of "lower," mass-mediated forms of entertainment. This turn toward high cultural forms and practices has been countered by work in British and American cultural studies: analyses of the relationship between the "popular" and other forms connected to "the people," such as folk art, can be found in the work of Raymond Williams, Stuart Hall, Fredric Jameson, and Michel de Certeau, to name only a few. For an extended discussion of these concerns, see Colin MacCabe, "Defining Popular Culture," and Laura Kipnis, "Towards a Left Popular Culture," in *High Theory/Low Culture: Analyzing Popular Television and Film,* ed. Colin MacCabe, 1–10 and 11–36 (Manchester: Manchester University Press, 1986); James Naremore and Patrick Brantlinger, "Six Artistic Cultures," in *Modernity and Mass Culture,* 1–23 (Bloomington: Indiana University Press, 1991); and for the evolution of this debate within the field of cultural studies, see the collection edited by Lawrence Grossberg, Cary Nelson, and Paula A. Treichler, *Cultural Studies* (New York: Routledge, 1992).

15. For critical analyses of musical comedy, see Bailey, *Popular Culture and Performance;* Rappaport, *Shopping for Pleasure;* and Len Platt, *Musical Comedy on the West End Stage, 1890–1939* (London: Palgrave Macmillan, 2004). A useful (if more celebratory than critical) source for visual and historical detail is Raymond Mander and Joe Mitchenson, *Musical Comedy: A Story in Pictures* (London: Peter Davies, 1969).

16. See also Victor Glasstone's description of the Tivoli in *Victorian and Edwardian Theatres,* cited in Green, *The Last Empires,* 42–43.

17. F. Anstey, cited in Green, *The Last Empires,* 41.

18. Ibid., 42.

19. Kracauer's essays, "Cult of Distraction" and "The Mass Ornament," are reprinted in *The Mass Ornament: Weimar Essays,* trans. and ed. Thomas Y. Levin (Cambridge, MA: Harvard University Press, 1995). Also relevant is Walter Benjamin's discussion of distraction in his seminal 1936 essay "The Work of Art in the Age of Mechanical Reproduction," in which he observes that "Distraction and concentration form polar opposites which may be stated as follows: a man who concentrates before a work of art is absorbed by it. . . . In contrast, the distracted mass absorbs the work of art" (239). The essay is reprinted in *Illuminations,* ed. Hannah Arendt, trans. Harry Zohn, 217–51 (New York: Schocken Books, 1968).

20. Russell, "Varieties of Life," 72–75, 79.

21. W. Somerset Maugham, *Of Human Bondage* (1915; New York: Bantam, 1991); further references will be cited parenthetically. For historical commentary on the tea-shop girl, see Barbara Drake, "The Tea-Shop Girl, being a Report of an Enquiry undertaken by the Investigation Committee of the Women's Industrial Council," *Women's Industrial News,* n.s., 17:61 (April 1913).

22. This popular musical appeared at the Shaftesbury in 1898, and as Peter Bailey notes, was emblematic of the success of the musical comedy in the 1890s. Bailey, *Popular Culture and Performance,* 177. For details on the production, see Platt, *Musical Comedy.*

23. On the economic and architectural context of theatrical seating in the Victorian period, see Booth, *Theatre in the Voctorian Age,* 2, 7, 64.

24. Kift, *Victorian Music Hall,* 62.

25. See note 9 above, especially Bland, *Banishing the Beast,* chapters 1–3, and Walkowitz, *City of Dreadful Delight,* chapters 3–5; also Deborah Gorham, "The 'Maiden Tribute of Modern Babylon' Re-examined: Child Prostitution and the Idea of Childhood in Late-Victorian England," *Victorian Studies* 21 (Spring 1978): 353–69.

26. Prior to the 1890s, local licensing authority in London had been relatively diffuse and complicated by an array of parliamentary recommendations and legislation. Public entertainments were subject to the Theatres Act of 1843, which distinguished between the legitimate theatre and the "free-and-easies" attached to pubs and the song-and-supper rooms: these latter institutions, the forerunners of the purpose-built music halls which enjoyed their heyday in the later Victorian period, sacrificed the ability to stage dramatic presentations in order to maintain the license to sell tobacco and alcohol for consumption on the premises. For a summary of the chronological development of the halls, see the introduction to *Music Hall: The Business of Pleasure,* ed. Peter Bailey (Milton Keynes: Open University Press, 1986), vii–xxiii. For historical background on the transition from the Metropolitan Board of Works to the London County Council, see the series of articles from the *Times,* rpt. as *The Story of the London County Council* (1907); Sir Gwilym Gibbon and Reginald W. Bell, *History of the London County Council 1889–1939* (London: Macmillan, 1939); Sir Harry Haward, *The London County Council from Within* (London: Chapman and Hall, 1932); John Davis, *Reforming London: The London Government Problem 1855–1900* (Oxford: Clarendon Press, 1988); Ken Young and Patricia L. Garside, *Metropolitan London: Politics and Urban Change 1837–1981* (New York: Holmes & Meier, 1982); and

Chris Waters, "Progressives, Puritans and the Cultural Politics of the Council, 1889–1914," in *Politics and the People of London: The London County Council 1889–1965,* ed. Andrew Saint, 49–70 (London: Hambledon Press, 1989). For an adept analysis of the early history of the LCC and its influence on the transformation of metropolitan life during the period this study addresses, see Susan D. Pennybacker, *A Vision for London 1889–1914: Labour, Everyday Life and the LCC Experiment* (Routledge: London, 1995).

27. On censorship and the comic sketch, see Lois Rutherford, "'Harmless Nonsense': The Comic Sketch and the Development of Music Hall Entertainment," in *Music Hall: Performance and Style,* ed. J. S. Bratton, 131–51 (Milton Keynes: Open University Press, 1986).

28. Cited in Penelope Summerfield, "The Arms and the Empire: Deliberate Selection in the Evolution of Music Hall in London," in *Popular Culture and Class Conflict 1590–1914: Explorations in the History of Labor and Leisure,* ed. Eileen and Stephen Yeo, 209–40 (Sussex: Harvester Press, 1981). For a useful discussion of the role of sexual innuendo in the music hall, see Bailey, *Popular Culture and Performance,* 128–50.

29. LCC, Proceedings before the Licensing Committee, Oxford Music Hall (October 1896), 17. Susan Pennybacker argues a similar point in her article "'It was not what she said but the way in which she said it': The London County Council and the Music Halls," in Bailey, *Music Hall,* 118–40, and incorporated in chapter 3 of her book *Vision for London,* 210–40.

30. Reprinted in Green, *The Last Empires,* 60–61. For a brief discussion of the song, see Peter Davison, *The British Music Hall.*

31. In addition to its intentional use of sexual innuendo, this song incorporated a direct reference to Mrs. Ormiston Chant, one of the most well-known social purity campaigners, for comic effect:

> She met a young philanthropist, a friend of Missus Chant,
> And her golden hair was hanging down her back,
> He lived in Peckham Rye with an extremely maiden aunt,
> Who had not a hair a-hanging down her back.
> The lady looked upon him in her fascinating way,
> And what the consequences were I really cannot say,
> But when this worthy maiden aunt remarked his coat next day,
> Well, some golden hairs were hanging down the back.

32. On comic songs featuring marginally classed working girls—milliners, barmaids, waitresses—see Jane Traies, "Jones and the Working Girl: Class Marginality in Music-Hall Song 1860–1900," in Bratton, *Music Hall,* 23–48.

33. For critical discussions of the musical, see John A. Degen, "The Evolution of *The Shop Girl* and the Birth of Musical Comedy," *Theatre History Studies* 7 (1987); Erika Rappaport, "Acts of Consumption: Musical Comedy and the Desire of Exchange," in *Shopping for Pleasure;* and Peter Bailey, "'Naughty but Nice,'" 48.

34. H. J. W. Dam, "The Shop Girl: At the Gaiety," *Sketch,* 28 November 1894, 216; cited in Rappaport, *Shopping for Pleasure,* 277 n. 112. My argument in this section has been shaped by Erika Rappaport's insightful reading of this and

other musical comedies featuring shopgirls, and I would like to acknowledge her kindness in offering guidance at an early stage of my research.

35. *The Shop Girl,* written by H. J. W. Dam, music by Ivan Caryll with additional songs by Adrian Ross and Lionel Monckton, first performed 22 November 1894 at the Gaiety Theater. The manuscript is held by the British Library: Lord Chamberlain's Plays (LCP), add. mss. 53562.

36. For accounts of the Empire scandal, see Mrs. (Laura) Ormiston Chant, *Why We Attacked the Empire* (London: Horace Marshall & Son, 1895); Green, *The Last Empires, 59–75*; Pennybacker, *Vision for London,* 228–30; and Kift, *Victorian Music Hall,* 162–64. See also the sources cited in note 9.

37. *The Girl from Kay's,* written by Owen Hall, lyrics by Adrian Ross and C. Aveling, music by Ivan Caryll and others, first performed 24 November 1902 at the Apollo Theatre. LCP, add. mss. 1902/33.

38. This production was financed by Harrods' managing director Richard Burbidge as a publicity effort to counter the arrival of Selfridges on the London scene in 1909; for a detailed discussion of the competition between Harrods and Selfridges at this time, see Rappaport, *Shopping for Pleasure.*

39. *Our Miss Gibbs,* constructed by J. T. Tanner, written by "Cryptos" (Adrian Ross, Percy Greenback, Ivan Caryll, and Lionel Monckton), first performed 25 January 1909 at the Gaiety Theater. LCP, add. mss. 1909/3.

40. Rappaport, *Shopping for Pleasure,* 194–96, 201.

41. *Harrodian Gazette* 1, no. 2 (February 1913): 7.

42. I have found few exceptions to date: *A Shop Girl's Peril* was censored in 1913 but does not survive in film form or in catalog descriptions; *Shop Girls* (1915) told the familiar, if sensationalized, story of a young female shop worker suffering at the hands of exploitative store management. For a detailed description of the latter, produced by Turner Films, Ltd., see *Pictures and the Picturegoer* (6 March 1915), 48–82.

43. It is important to note that fashion films were not the only types of films to which shopgirls would have been exposed as members of the early cinema audience. Indeed, as in the case of the circus and war fictions published in the novelettes and magazines I discussed in chapter 4, early cinemas screened a wide variety of subjects and genres including westerns, war dramas, family melodramas—to name only a few. I have strategically chosen these two examples in an effort to analyze the cultural discourses producing the shopgirl as a consuming subject; further research in this area may well suggest ways in which we might read against these discourses for alternative modes of imagining the story of the shopgirl.

44. The term "penny gaff" hearkens back to the street theatricals of the mid-nineteenth century: for a description of one such entertainment, see Henry Mayhew, *London Labour and the London Poor* (London: Charles Griffin & Co., 1865), 1: 42–44; this selection can also be found in Victor Neuberg's selections from Mayhew's work, published under the same title (London: Penguin, 1985), 36–42. On traveling cinema shows, see Arthur Fay, *Bioscope Shows and Their Engines* (London: Oakwood Press, 1966). On the general exhibition context of cinema in Britain during the pre-WWI period, see Rachael Low and Roger Manvell, *The History of the British Film, 1896–1906;* Low, *The History of the British Film, 1906–1914* (London: George Allen & Unwin Ltd., 1948, 1949); John Barnes, *The Beginnings of the Cinema in England 1894–1901,* 5 vols.

(London: Bishopsgate Press Ltd., 1976–1997; rpt. ed. Exeter: University of Exeter Press, 1997); Michael Chanan, *The Dream That Kicks: The Prehistory and Early Years of Cinema in Britain* (London: Routledge, 1980); and Ian Christie, *The Last Machine: Early Cinema and the Birth of the Modern World* (London: BFI, 1994). I have found Nicholas Hiley's research on the history of exhibition and early cinema audiences especially useful in framing my understanding of early film culture in Britain: see "The British Cinema Auditorium," in *Film and the First World War,* ed. Karel Dibbets and Bert Hogenkamp, 160–70 (Amsterdam: Amsterdam University Press, 1994), and "Fifteen Questions about the Early Film Audience," in *Uncharted Territory: Essays on Early Non-Fiction Film,* ed. Daan Hertogs and Nico de Klerk, 105–18 (Amsterdam: Stichting Nederlands Filmmuseum, 1997).

45. For examples, see G. R. Baker's article in the *British Journal of Photography* 45, monthly supplement (7 October 1898): 74, cited in John Barnes, *Pioneers of the British Film,* vol. 3 of *The Beginnings of the Cinema in England 1894–1901* (London: Bishopsgate Press Ltd., 1983), 74; and George Pearson, *Flashback: Autobiography of a British Film-maker* (1957), 14, cited in Colin Harding and Simon Popple, *In the Kingdom of Shadows: A Companion to Early Cinema* (London: Cygnus Arts, 1996), 9. It is important to note that Pearson's description has been filtered through various mythologies of early cinema as a "primitive" mode of representation, and to that extent must be interpreted with some caution. On early cinema's primitivism, see Noel Burch, *Life to Those Shadows,* trans. Ben Brewster (Berkeley: University of California Press, 1990), especially 186–202, and Tom Gunning, "'Primitive' Cinema: A Frame-Up? Or, The Trick's On Us," in Elsaesser, *Early Cinema,* 95–103.

46. Hiley, "British Cinema Auditorium," 162.

47. On the estimated percentage of women in the early film audience, see Hiley, "British Cinema Auditorium," 162, and "Fifteen Questions," 112. Miriam Hansen has described a similar transformation of the American early film industry in her work on women and early cinema spectatorship: see especially her *Babel and Babylon: Spectatorship in American Silent Film* (Cambridge, MA: Harvard University Press, 1991).

48. Hiley, "British Cinema Auditorium," 162.

49. Ibid., 163; National Council of Public Morals, *The Cinema: Its Present Position and Future Possibilities* (London: Williams and Norgate, 1917), 210.

50. *Kinematograph Weekly* (14 March 1918), 87.

51. See F. M. L. Thompson, *The Rise of Respectable Society: A Social History of Victorian Britain, 1830–1900* (Cambridge, MA: Harvard University Press, 1988), 288; see also Kift, *Victorian Music Hall,* 71.

52. *Paris Fashion: Latest Creations in Gowns of the House Ernest Radnitz* (615952 A) and *Paris Fashion: Latest Creations in Hats of the House Francine Arnauld* (614842 A), both catalogued in the archive of the British Film Institute. These films have a production date of 1910, rather late in the history of the cinema of attractions but therefore an example of the enduring appeal of such nonnarrative images even as the industry progressed toward narrativization.

53. Other early fashion films include *Fifty Years of Paris Fashions 1859–1909* (1910), which according to *Bioscope* depicted "magnificent examples of the art of the dressmaker and milliner . . . a lady sitting in the picture theatre where this is being shown can imagine that she is in the showroom of a fashionable modiste with the mannequins walking around for her inspection"; the *Kinemacolor Fashion*

Gazette (1913); and early fashion serials such as *The Adventures of Dorothy Dare* (1916) and *The Strange Case of Mary Page* (1916), often with fashions designed by Lady Duff Gordon, better known as Lucile. For a discussion of these and related films, see Elizabeth Leese, *Costume Design in the Movies* (New York: Frederick Ungar Publishing, 1977), 9–14, and Kaplan and Stowell, *Theatre and Fashion*, 151.

54. Siegfried Kracauer, "The Little Shopgirls Go to the Movies," in *The Mass Ornament*, 291–304. Further references will be noted parenthetically.

55. In his writings on white-collar culture in Germany in the 1920s and early 1930s, Kracauer recognized the transitional class status of sales girls and "stenotypists," lamenting the emptiness and the physical exhaustion he viewed as characteristic of the lives of white-collar employees (one-third of whom were women). Although the national and historical context for Kracauer's work differs significantly from my own, we can trace similarities in the cultural production of the relationship between labor, everyday life, and fantasy. For a brief discussion of this transitional class, see his 1932 essay on working women, originally titled "Mädchen im Beruf," which appeared in *Der Querschnitt* 12:4 (April 1932): 238–43; an excerpt of this essay is translated in *The Weimar Republic Sourcebook*, ed. Anton Kaes, Martin Jay, and Edward Dimendberg, 216–18 (Berkeley: University of California Press, 1994). For the British context, see Geoffrey Crossick, ed., *The Lower Middle Class in Britain, 1870–1914* (New York: St. Martin's, 1997), and Jane E. Lewis, "Women Clerical Workers in the Late Nineteenth and Early Twentieth Centuries," in *The White-Blouse Revolution: Female Office Workers Since 1870*, ed. Gregory Anderson, 27–47 (Manchester: Manchester University Press, 1988).

56. Hiley, "British Cinema Auditorium," 165–68.

57. Harding and Popple, *In the Kingdom of Shadows*, 43.

58. *Times*, 25 October 1913 and 13 February 1914; for a dissenting view from the chairman of the Theatres and Music Halls Committee, H. J. Greenwood, see *The Times*, 5 November 1913. An article entitled "The Cinema Detective" in the *World's Fair* (13 April 1912) described the theft of several rings by a well-known pickpocket who apparently allowed his female accomplice to wear one of the rings; a Scotland Yard investigator discovered the thief by viewing a film which revealed the theft at the moment it was committed. These sources are reprinted in Harding and Popple, *In the Kingdom of Shadows*.

59. The 1914 report listed the following grounds for film censorship: (1) cruelty to animals; (2) indecorous dancing; (3) vulgarity and impropriety in conduct and dress; (4) indelicate sexual situations; (5) scenes suggestive of immorality; (6) situations accentuating delicate marital relations; (7) gruesome murders; (8) excessively gruesome details in crime or warfare; (9) indecently morbid death scenes; (10) scenes tending to disparage public characters and institutions; (11) medical operations; (12) executions; (13) painful scenes in connection with insanity; (14) cruelty to women; (15) confinements; (16) drunken scenes carried to excess; (17) scenes calculated to act as an incentive to crime; (18) indecorous subtitles; (19) indelicate accessories; (20) native customs in foreign lands abhorrent to British ideas; (21) irreverent treatment of sacred or solemn subjects; and (22) the materialization of Christ or the Almighty. See James C. Robertson, *The British Board of Film Censors: Film Censorship in Britain, 1896–1950* (London: Croom Helm, 1985).

60. The 1915 film *A Shop Girl's Peril* apparently violated one or more of the rules against the depiction of cruelty, immorality, or blasphemy on screen, although since I have been unable to locate an extant copy, this remains a speculative claim.

61. *Times,* 7 March 1913.

62. For further discussion of the National Council of Public Morals and its effects on cinema in the 1910s and 1920s, see Annette Kuhn, *Cinema, Censorship and Sexuality, 1909–1925* (London: Routledge, 1988).

63. I am indebted to Erika Rappaport for sharing with me her thoughts on perceptions of Piccadilly Circus in this period, and her assessment of the area as symbolizing urban danger but also new possibilities for women's leisure and urban pleasure. For more, see her *Shopping for Pleasure* (2000), 147–48.

64. On this point, see also Judith Walkowitz, "Going Public: Shopping, Street Harassment, and Streetwalking in Late Victorian London," *Representations* 62 (Spring 1998): 9–14.

65. Kuhn, *Cinema, Censorship, and Sexuality,* 51. Kuhn is among the few scholars of early cinema to write on this film and its 1914 American counterpart; others include Kevin Brownlow, *Behind the Mask of Innocence* (Berkeley: University of California Press, 1990), 58–61, and Janet Staiger, *Bad Women: Regulating Sexuality in Early American Cinema* (Minneapolis: University of Minnesota Press, 1915). Also relevant are studies of American film censorship in the teens, particularly regarding issues of sexuality: see especially Shelley Stamp, "Taking Precautions, or Regulating Early Birth Control Films," in *A Feminist Reader in Early Cinema,* ed. Jennifer M. Bean and Diane Negra, 270–97 (Durham, NC: Duke University Press, 2002), and "Moral Coercion, or the Board of Censorship Ponders the Vice Question," in *Controlling Hollywood: Censorship and Regulation in the Studio Era,* ed. Matthew Bernstein, 41–59 (New Brunswick, NJ: Rutgers University Press, 1999); and Lee Grieveson, "Policing the Cinema: *Traffic in Souls* at Ellis Island," *Screen* 38:2 (Fall 1998): 149–71.

66. Synopsis of *The End of the Road* (Public Health Films, 1918) held in the National Vigilance Association Papers archived at the Fawcett Library; cited in Kuhn, *Cinema, Censorship, and Sexuality,* 52–53. For a discussion of the production and exhibition context of *The End of the Road,* see Brownlow, *Behind the Mask,* 66–69.

67. Public Record Office, Home Office Papers, 45–10955 (6 August and 14 August 1917), cited in Kuhn, *Cinema, Censorship, and Sexuality,* 66–67.

68. Kuhn, *Cinema, Censorship, and Sexuality,* 69, 71.

Conclusion

1. "Callisthenes," "The Word 'Shop Girl' No Longer Fits," *Times,* 20 July 1926, 12. On Selfridges' advertising strategies, see Erika Rappaport, *Shopping for Pleasure: Women in the Making of London's West End* (Princeton, NJ: Princeton University Press, 2000), 156–72.

2. *Times,* 20 July 1926, 12.

3. Ibid. The article concludes, "In the interests of truth and common fairness to thousands of the happiest, most attractive, most efficient, and most dignified women in England it is time that a new name be devised to fit the new facts."

4. "Murder of Mr. William Whiteley," *Times,* 25 January 1907, 7. The murder occurred on January 24, and the *Times* provided near-daily coverage of the case throughout the following week, with subsequent occasional references in February and March. The most extensive summary of the case can be found in an article on the proceedings of the Central Criminal Court entitled "The Murder of Mr. Whiteley," *Times,* 23 March 1907, 6.

5. "Big Effort to Save Rayner," *New York Times,* 29 March 1907, 4.

6. Ibid.

7. Sigmund Freud, "Family Romances" (1909), rpt. in *The Freud Reader,* ed. Peter Gay, 297–300 (New York: W. W. Norton & Co., 1989).

8. For accounts of the Thaw-White case, see Frederick L. Collins, *Glamorous Sinners* (New York: R. Long & R. R. Smith, 1932); Phyllis Leslie Abramson, *Sob Sister Journalism* (New York: Greenwood Press, 1990); and Suzannah Lessard, *The Architect of Desire: Beauty and Danger in the Stanford White Family* (New York: Dial Press, 1996). Another useful resource is Carl Charlson's "Murder of the Century," an episode of the PBS series *American Experience* produced by WGBH-Boston in 1996; the program is reviewed by Paula S. Fass in the *Journal of American History* 83:3 (December 1996): 1124–26.

9. *Times,* 23 March 1907, 11.

10. On the continuing expansion of women's employment in the clerical and retail labor force during World War I, see Deborah Thom, *Nice Girls and Rude Girls: Women Workers in World War I* (London: I. B. Tauris, 1998), 30; for subsequent decades in the interwar years, see Miriam Glucksmann, *Women Assemble: Women Workers and the New Industries in Inter-War Britain* (London: Routledge, 1990), 46–57.

11. Memorandum from Willis Cooper, of NBC's Program Planning Board, to Sidney Strotz, head of NBC's Chicago bureau, 8 August 1934; cited in Michelle Hilmes, *Radio Voices: American Broadcasting, 1922–1952* (Minneapolis: University of Minnesota Press, 1997), 158, emphasis mine.

12. Lori Landay identifies this plot as expressing "one of the central myths of the female American dream": "the working girl marries the boss and never has to 'work' again." Lori Landay, *Madcaps, Screwballs, and Con Women: The Female Trickster in American Culture* (Philadelphia: University of Pennsylvania Press, 1998), 4.

13. "The Secret Lives of City Shopgirls," *Harper's Bazaar* (February 1998): 70, 72; "Shopgirls," *Women's Wear Daily* (9 December 1999); 6.

14. Barbara Ehrenreich, *Nickel and Dimed: On (Not) Getting By in America* (New York: Henry Holt & Co., 2001). See also Bob Ortega, *In Sam We Trust: The Untold Story of Sam Walton and How Wal-Mart Is Devouring America* (New York: Tinies Business, 1998), and Liza Featherstone, *Selling Women Short: The Landmark Battle for Workers' Rights at Wal-Mart* (New York: Basic Books, 2004).

Bibliography

Archival Sources

British Library, London
Harrods Store Archives, Harrods & Company, Ltd., London
John Lewis Partnership Company Archives, Stevenage
Metropolitan Archives, London
National Film and Television Archive, British Film Institute, London
New York Public Library, New York
Selfridges Store Archives, Selfridges, London
Special Collections, Regenstein Library, University of Chicago

Newspapers and Periodicals

Answers to Correspondents on Every Subject under the Sun. 1888–1889. Continued
  as *Answers.*
Bioscope (The).
British Journal of Photography (The).
Daily Express.
Dorothy Novelette(s) (The). T. P. Chapman. 1889–90. Continued as: *Dorothy, a
  Home Journal for Ladies,* later *Dorothy's Home Journal for Ladies.* 1890–91.
Draper's Record.
Duchess Novelette. Charles Shurey. 1898–1902. Incorporated with *Smart Novels.*
Empress Novelette. Charles Shurey. 1897–1901. Continued as: *Empress Dainty
  Novels,* later *Dainty Novels.* 1901–1924. Incorporated with *Smart Novels.*
English Ladies' Novelettes (The). Edwin J. Brett. 1891–92.
English Woman's Journal.
Era (The).
Forget-Me-Not. Amalgamated Press. 1891–1918.
Gipsy Novelettes (The). Mrs. Berkeley Fraser. 1890, 1900.
Gipsy Novelettes (The). Edwin J. Brett. 1900–1901. Incorporated with *Something
  to Read.*
Girls' Best Friend. Harmsworth/Amalgamated Press. 1898–99. Continued as:
Girls' Friend. 1899–1913.
Girls' Home. Amalgamated Press. 1910–15.
Girls' Reader. Amalgamated Press. 1908–15.
Harrodian Gazette. 1913–1930. Harrods' staff magazine.
Key of the House (The). Selfridges' staff magazine.
Kinematograph Weekly.
Music Hall [and Theatre Review].
My Lady's Novelette. 1890.

New York Times (The).

Pictures and the Picturegoer.

Play Pictorial (The).

Princess's Novelettes (The). Edwin J. Brett. 1886–1904. Continued as: *Princess Novels.* 1904–1906.

Royal Novelette. Charles Shurey. 1898–1901.

Something to Read. Edwin J. Brett. 1881–1910. Incorporated with *My Pocket Novels.*

Something to Read Novelette. 1881–1910. Included with weekly numbers of *Something to Read.*

Times (The).

Tit-Bits.

Wedding Bells. A Journal for Single and Married. Edwin J. Brett. 1870–79.

Wedding Bells Novelette. Edwin J. Brett. 1880–83.

Wide World Novelette. Shaw & Co. 1888–93.

Women's Industrial News (The).

Primary Sources

Acton, William. *Prostitution.* Ed. Peter Fryer. New York: Frederick A. Praeger, 1969.

———. *Prostitution Considered in Its Moral, Social, and Sanitary Aspects, in London and Other Large Cities, with Proposals for the Mitigation and Prevention of Its Attendant Evils.* London: John Churchill, 1857.

Adam, Hargrave. *Woman and Crime.* London: T. Werner Laurie, 1912.

Anderson, Elizabeth Garrett. "Sex in Mind and Education: A Reply." *Fortnightly Review* n. 5, 15 (May 1874): 582–94.

Applin, Arthur. *Shop Girls.* London: Mills and Boon, 1914.

"Association for Promoting the Employment of Women." *English Woman's Journal* 4 (1 September 1859): 54–60.

Baker, G. R. *British Journal of Photography* 45 (7 October 1898): 74.

"The Balance of Public Opinion in Regard to Woman's Work." *English Woman's Journal* 9 (1 July 1862): 41–44.

Barnicoat, Constance A. "The Reading of the Colonial Girl." *Nineteenth Century* 60 (December 1906): 939–50.

Best, Percy A. *The Story of Selfridges.* Presentation copy in the Selfridges Store Archives. Originally published as a series of articles for *Women's Wear News* (1936).

Bird, M. Mostyn. *Woman at Work: A Study of the Different Ways of Earning a Living Open to Women.* London: Chapman & Hall Ltd., 1911.

Bondfield, Margaret G. "Conditions under Which Shop Assistants Work." *Economic Journal* 9 (June 1899): 277–86.

———. "In the Days of My Youth." *T. P.'s and Cassell's Weekly,* January 1924.

———. *A Life's Work.* London: Hutchinson, 1948.

———. *The Meaning of Trade.* Self and Society Booklets no. 9. London: Ernest Benn Ltd., 3–32.

———. "Shop Workers and the Vote." London: People's Suffrage Federation, 1911. 3–9.

Booth, Charles. *Life and Labour of the People in London.* 2nd ser. (Industry), vol. 3 (Dress, Food, Drink, Dealers, Clerks, Locomotion and Labour). Pub. in 1896 as vol. 7 of *Life and Labour.* London: Macmillan and Co., Ltd., 1903.

Bosanquet, Helen. "Cheap Literature." *Contemporary Review* no. 79 (May 1901): 671–81.

Brabazon, Lord [Reginald Meath]. *Social Arrows.* London: Longmans, Green and Co., 1886.

Bulley, Amy, and Margaret Whitley. *Women's Work.* London: Methuen & Co., 1894.

Busbey, Katherine Graves, A.B. "The Women's Trade Union Movement in Great Britain." *Bulletin of the Bureau of Labor.* Washington: U.S. Bureau of Labor Statistics, July 1909. 1–65.

"Business and Pleasure: Selfridges' Assistants Visit Paris." *Morning Leader,* 10 April 1912.

"Business Girl Chats No. 9: A Shop-Girl." *Girls' Friend* (12 August 1905): 659.

Cadbury, Edward, M. Cécile Matheson, and George Shann, M.A. *Women's Work and Wages: A Phase of Life in an Industrial City.* London: T. Fisher Unwin, 1906.

"Careers for Women: The Working Hours, Earnings, and Prospects of a Shopgirl." *Forget-Me-Not* 12 (December 1903): 661.

Chant, Mrs. [Laura] Ormiston. *Why We Attacked the Empire.* London: Horace Marshall & Son, 1895.

Chisholm, Hugh. "How to Counteract the 'Penny Dreadful.'" *Fortnightly Review* n.s. 64 (July–December 1895): 765–75.

"The Cinema Detective." *World's Fair,* 13 April 1912.

Collins, Frederick L. *Glamorous Sinners.* New York: R. Long & R. R. Smith, 1932.

Collins, Wilkie. "The Unknown Public." *Household Words* no. 439 (21 August 1858): 217–22.

"Confidential Chat." *Forget-Me-Not* (12 October 1901): 478.

Cooper, H. St. John. "A Shop-Girl's Revenge." *Woman's World 3d. Complete Library* No. 27. London: The Fleetway House, Farringdon Street, 1914.

Cranston, Mary Rankin. "London's Living-In System." *Outlook* 76 (27 February 1904): 515–18.

Craske, May. "Girl Life in a Slum." *Economic Review* 28:2 (April 1908): 184–89.

Dam, H. J. W., and Ivan Caryll. *The Shop Girl.* With additional numbers by Adrian Ross and Lionel Monckton. First performed 22 November 1894 at the Gaiety Theatre, London. Manuscript held by the British Library: LCP, add. mss. 53562.

Dare, Grace [Margaret Bondfield]. "An Imaginary Interview." *Shop Assistant,* March 1897, 148–49.

———. "And Gross Darkness Covered the Earth." *Shop Assistant,* December 1897, 106–7.

———. "The Case of Janet Deane." *Shop Assistant,* February 1898, 153.

———. "Jean." *Shop Assistant,* July 1899–June 1900, 13, 33–34, 53–54, 72, 89, 131, 144, 163–64, 182, 232.

———. "'Jim'—A Memory." *Shop Assistant,* September 1896, 6.

———. "The Manageress of the 'A' Department." *Shop Assistant,* February 1897, 128.

———. "A Tale of Tragedies." *Shop Assistant,* September 1898.

Davies, Margaret Llewellyn, ed. *Life As We Have Known It, by Co-operative Working*

Women. 1931. With an introduction by Virginia Woolf. New York: W.W. Norton & Co., 1975.

———. *The Women's Co-operative Guild 1883–1904.* Kirby Lonsdale, Westmorland: Women's Co-operative Guild, 1904.

"The Disputed Question." *English Woman's Journal* 1 (1 August 1858): 363–67.

Dorr, Rheta Childe. "Women's Demand for Humane Treatment of Women Workers in Shop and Factory." *Hampton's Magazine,* December 1909, n. pag.

Drake, Barbara. "The Tea-Shop Girl, being a Report of an Enquiry undertaken by the Investigation Committee of the Women's Industrial Council." *Women's Industrial News* n.s. 17, no. 61 (April 1913): 115–29.

———. *Women in Trade Unions.* London: G. Allen and Unwin, Ltd., 1920.

E. J. M. "Truck and Fair Wages." *Women's Industrial News* n.s. 46 (April 1909): 12–14.

Ellis, Sarah Stickney. *The Daughters of England: Their Position in Society, Character, and Responsibilities.* New York: D. Appleton and Co., 1842.

———. *The Women of England: Their Social Duties, and Domestic Habits.* London: Fisher,1839.

Etiquette for All, or Rules of Conduct for Every Circumstance in Life: With the Laws, Precepts, and Practices of Good Society. Glasgow: George Watson, 1861.

Etiquette for Ladies and Gentlemen. London: Frederick Warne, 1876.

Etiquette for the Ladies: Eighty Maxims on Dress, Manners, and Accomplishments. London: Charles Tilt, 1837.

The Etiquette of Love, Courtship, and Marriage. 1847. *Women and Victorian Values, 1837–1910: Advice Books, Manuals, and Journals for Women.* Marlborough, Wiltshire: Adam Matthew, 1996.

"Extracts from Mr. Allen's Salesmanship Lectures." *Harrodian Gazette,* February 1913.

Fabian Society. *Shop Life and Its Reform.* Fabian Tract No. 80. London: Fabian Society, December 1897.

Fox, Stephen N., and Mrs. J. R. MacDonald. "Shop Assistants and the Truck Acts." *Women's Industrial News* n.s., no. 3 (March 1898): 17–21.

Fyfe, W. Hamilton. "The Remuneration of Women's Work." *Economic Review* 28:2 (April 1908): 135–45.

Gilman, Charlotte Perkins. *Women and Economics.* 1898. Berkeley: University of California Press, 1998.

Gissing, George. *The Collected Letters of George Gissing.* Ed. Paul F. Mattheisen, Arthur C. Young, and Pierre Coustillas. 9 vols. Athens: Ohio University Press, 1990–1997.

———. *In the Year of Jubilee.* 1894. London: Everyman, 1994.

———. *The Odd Women.* 1891. Harmondsworth, Middlesex: Penguin, 1983.

———. *London and the Life of Literature in Late Victorian England: The Diary of George Gissing, Novelist.* Ed. Pierre Coustillas. Hassocks, Eng.: Harvester Press, 1978.

Girls and Their Ways: A Book for and about Girls, by One Who Knows Them. London: John Hogg, 1881.

Greg, W. R. "Prostitution." *Westminster Review* 14 (July 1850): 238–68.

———. "Why Are Women Redundant?" *National Review* 14 (April 1862): 434–60. Rpt. in *Literary and Social Judgments.* London: 1869. 274–308.

"H. Gordon Selfridge and His Methods, by One Who Worked under Him." *Draper's Record* 27 (March 1909).

Hallsworth, Joseph, and Rhys J. Davies. *The Working Life of Shop Assistants: A Study of Conditions of Labour in the Distributive Trades.* Manchester: National Labour Press, 1910.

Hamilton, Cicely. *Diana of Dobson's.* London: Collier, 1908.

———. *Marriage as a Trade.* 1909. London: Women's Press, 1981.

Hamilton, Mary Agnes. *Margaret Bondfield.* New York: Thomas Seltzer, 1925.

Hammond, L. Barbara. "Equal Pay for Equal Work." *Women's Industrial News* n.s., no. 28 (September 1904): 445–52.

[Harrods Ltd.]. *1849–1949: A Story of British Achievement.* London: Harrods, n.d.

Harrods Stores, Ltd. "Rules and Regulations for Shopwalkers, Assistants, &c." Harrods' Archive [n.d.].

Haslam, James. *The Press and the People: An Estimate of Reading in Working-Class Districts.* Reprinted from the *Manchester City News.* Manchester: 'City News' Office, 1906.

Herschel, Sir John. "Address to the Subscribers to the Windsor and Eton Public Library and Reading Room." 1833. *Essays from the Edinburgh and Quarterly Reviews.* 1857.

Hitchman, Francis. "Penny Fiction." *Quarterly Review* 171, nos. 341–342 (July/October 1890): 150–71.

Holtby, Winifred. "What We Read and Why We Read It." *Left Review* 1:4 (1935). Rpt. in *Bookselling, Reading, and Reviewing. Literary Taste, Culture and Mass Communication* 12. Ed. Peter Davison, Rolf Meyerson, and Edward Shils. Cambridge: Chadwyck Healey, 1978.

"How Shop Girls Win Rich Husbands." *Forget-Me-Not* (23 August 1902): 368.

"How to Utilize the Powers of Women." *English Woman's Journal* 3 (1 March 1859): 34–47.

Humphery, Geo. R. "The Reading of the Working Classes." *Nineteenth Century* 33 (April 1893): 690–701.

Humphry, Mrs. *Manners for Women.* London: Ward, Lock & Co., 1897.

Irwin, Margaret Hardinge. "The Shop Seats Bill Movement." *Fortnightly Review* no. 5, 57 (1 July 1899): 123–31.

Jeune, M. (Lady Jeune). "The Ethics of Shopping." *Fortnightly Review* (January 1895): 123–32.

Kracauer, Siegfried. "Cult of Distraction." 1926. Rpt. in *The Mass Ornament: Weimar Essays.* Trans. and ed. Thomas Y. Levin. 323–28. Cambridge, MA: Harvard University Press, 1995.

———. "The Little Shopgirls Go to the Movies." Rpt. in *The Mass Ornament: Weimar Essays.* Trans. and ed. Thomas Y. Levin. 291–304. Cambridge, MA: Harvard University Press, 1995.

———. "Mädchen im Beruf." *Der Querschnitt* 12:4 (April 1932): 238–43. Rpt. in *The Weimar Republic Sourcebook.* Ed. Anton Kaes, Martin Jay, and Edward Dimendberg. 216–18. Berkeley: University of California Press, 1994.

———. "The Mass Ornament." 1927. Rpt. in *The Mass Ornament: Weimar Essays.* Trans. and ed. Thomas Y. Levin, 75–86. Cambridge, MA: Harvard University Press, 1995.

Le Bon, Gustave. *The Crowd: A Study of the Popular Mind.* 1893. 12th ed. London: T. Fisher Unwin Ltd., 1920.

London County Council. Proceedings before the Licensing Committee, Oxford Music Hall (October 1896): 17.

"London's Shop-Girls and Their Chances of Marrying Well." *Forget-Me-Not* (18 March 1899): 377.

Low, Florence. "The Reading of the Modern Girl." *Nineteenth Century* 59 (February 1906): 278–87.

Martineau, Harriet. "Female Industry." *Edinburgh Review* 109 (April 1859): 293–336.

Maudsley, Henry. "Sex in Mind and Education." *Fortnightly Review* n.s., 15 (April 1874): 467–83.

Maugham, W. Somerset. *Of Human Bondage.* 1915. New York, Bantam, 1991.

Maxwell, W. B. *Vivien.* London, 1905.

Mayhew, Henry. "The London Street Folk." Vol. 1 of *London Labour and the London Poor; A Cyclopaedia of the Condition and Earnings of Those That Will Work, Those That Cannot Work, and Those That Will Not Work.* London: Griffin, Bohn, and Co., 1861.

Mayne, Terrick. "That Pretty Shop Girl." *Inglenook Novels* no. 41. London: Aldine Publishing Co. Ltd., 1906.

"My Day's Work, by a Draper's Assistant." *Forget-Me-Not* (26 March 1904): 525.

National Council of Public Morals. *The Cinema: Its Present Position and Future Possibilities.* London: Williams and Norgate, 1917.

"New and Cheap Forms of Popular Literature." *Eclectic Review* 82 (1845): 76.

Newte, Horace W. C. *Pansy Meares: The Story of a London Shop Girl.* New York: J. Lane & Co., 1912.

———. *Sparrows.* London: Mills and Boon, n.d.

"On the Obstacles to the Employment of Women." *English Woman's Journal* 4 (1 February 1860): 361–75.

Paine, William. *Shop Slavery and Emancipation: A Revolutionary Appeal to the Educated Young Men of the Middle Class.* London: P. S. King and Son, 1912.

Payn, James. "Penny Fiction." *Nineteenth Century* 9 (January 1881): 145–54.

Pearce, Charles. "The Soul of a Shop Girl." *Mascot Novels* no. 25. London: Aldine Publishing Co. Ltd., 1915.

Pemberton, Max. *Northcliffe: A Memoir.* London, 1922.

Phillipps, Evelyn March. "The Working Lady in London." *Fortnightly Review* 52 (August 1892): 193–203.

Potter, Beatrice (Mrs. Sidney Webb). "Pages from a Work-Girl's Diary." *Nineteenth Century* 25 (September 1888): 301–14.

Report of the Truck Committee. Parliamentary Papers LIX. Vol. 3. 1908.

Reppelier, Agnes. "English Railway Fiction." *Points of View.* Boston: Houghton Mifflin, 1891. 209–39.

Rowe, O. M. E. "London Shop-Girls." *Outlook* 53 (29 February 1896): 397–98.

Ruskin, John. "Of Queen's Gardens." 1864. Rpt. in *Sesame and Lilies.* 1868. Ed. Deborah Epstein Nord. New Haven, CT: Yale University Press, 2002.

Salmon, Edward G. "What Girls Read." *Nineteenth Century* 20 (October 1886): 515–29.

———. "What the Working Classes Read." *Nineteenth Century* 20 (July 1886): 108–17.

Shaw, George Bernard. *Mrs. Warren's Profession.* 1894. Vol. 3 of *Complete Plays with Prefaces.* New York: Dodd, Mead & Co., 1963.

"The Shop Assistant." *Women's Industrial News*, n.s.,19, no. 69 (April 1915): 321–44.

"Shopgirls as Wives." *Forget-Me-Not* (14 September 1901): 387.

"Shopgirls Make Good Wives: What Another Lady Writer Thinks." *Forget-Me-Not* (28 September 1901): 427.

Sinclair, May. *The Combined Maze*. London: Harper & Bros., 1913.

The Story of the London County Council. Rpt. from the *Times*. London, 1907.

Sutherst, Thomas. *Death and Disease behind the Counter*. London: Kegan Paul and Co., 1884.

Tait, William. *Magdalenism: An Inquiry into the Extent, Causes, and Consequences of Prostitution in Edinburgh*. Edinburgh: P. Rickard, 1840.

Taylor, Frederick Winslow. *Scientific Management*. New York: Harper, 1947.

———. "Shop Management." *Transactions of the American Society of Mechanical Engineers* 24 (1903): 1337–1480.

Webb, Mrs. Sidney (Beatrice Potter). "The Attitude of Men's Trade Unions Toward Their Female Competitors." *Women's Industrial News* n.s., 1 (September 1897): 10–15.

Wells, H. B. *Experiment in Autobiography; Discoveries and Conclusions of a Very Ordinary Brain since 1866*. 2 vols. 1934. London and Boston: Faber, 1984.

Wells, H. G. *Kipps: The Story of a Simple Soul*. New York: Scribner's Sons, 1905.

Westrup, Margaret. *Tide Marks*. London: Methuen & Co., 1913.

Wharton, Edith. *The House of Mirth*. 1905. New York: Bantam, 1984.

"Why I Married a Shop-Girl: The Confessions of a Happy Husband." *Forget-Me-Not* (4 October 1902): 511.

Williamson, Alice M. (Mrs. C. N. Williamson). *The Inky Way*. London: Chapman and Hall, Ltd., 1931.

Williamson, C. N., and A. M. *Winnie Childs, The Shop Girl*. 1914. New York: Grosset & Dunlap, 1916.

Women and Victorian Values, 1837–1910: Advice Books, Manuals, and Journals for Women. 20 microfilm reels. Marlborough, Wiltshire: Adam Matthew Publications, 1996.

Wood-Allen, Mary. *What a Young Woman Ought to Know*. 1899. Philadelphia: Vir, 1913.

Woolf, Virginia. *A Room of One's Own*. San Diego: Harcourt Brace Jovanovich, 1929.

A Working Woman. "Do Public Libraries Foster a Love of Literature among the Masses?" *Chambers's Journal* 6th ser., 3 (December 1899–November 1900): 134–36.

Wright, Thomas. "Concerning the Unknown Public." *Nineteenth Century* 13 (February 1883): 279–96

Zola, Emile. *Au bonheur des dames*. Trans. as *The Ladies' Paradise*. 1883. Ed. with an introduction by Kristin Ross. Berkeley: University of California Press, 1992.

Secondary Sources

Abramson, Phyllis Leslie. *Sob Sister Journalism*. New York: Greenwood Press, 1990.

Adburgham, Alison. *Liberty's: A Biography of a Shop*. London: George Allen & Unwin, 1975.

———. *Shopping in Style: London from the Restoration to Edwardian Elegance*. London: Thames and Hudson, 1979.

———. *Shops and Shopping 1800–1914: Where, and in What Manner the Well-Dressed Englishwoman Bought Her Clothes*. London: George Allen & Unwin, 1964.

Ainley, Rosa. *New Frontiers of Space, Bodies and Gender*. New York: Routledge, 1998.

Althusser, Louis. *Lenin and Philosophy and Other Essays*. Trans. Ben Brewster. New York: Monthly Review Press, 1971.

Altick, Richard D. *The English Common Reader: A Social History of the Mass Reading Public*. Chicago: University of Chicago Press, 1957.

———. *The Shows of London*. Cambridge, MA: Belknap Press, 1978.

Anderson, Amanda. *Tainted Souls and Painted Faces: The Rhetoric of Fallenness in Victorian Culture*. Ithaca, NY: Cornell University Press, 1993.

Appadurai, Arjun, ed. *The Social Life of Things*. Cambridge: Cambridge University Press, 1986.

Ardis, Ann L. *New Women, New Novels: Feminism and Early Modernism*. New Brunswick, NJ: Rutgers University Press, 1990.

Armes, Roy. *A Critical History of the British Cinema*. New York: Oxford University Press, 1978.

Armstrong, Nancy. *Desire and Domestic Fiction: A Political History of the Novel*. New York: Oxford University Press, 1987.

Armstrong, Nancy, and Leonard Tennenhouse. "The Literature of Conduct, the Conduct of Literature, and the Politics of Desire: An Introduction." *The Ideology of Conduct: Essays on Literature and the History of Sexuality*. New York: Methuen, 1987.

Atkins, P. J. "The Spatial Configuration of Class Solidarity in London's West End, 1792–1939." *Urban History Yearbook* (1990): 36–65.

Bailey, Peter. "Conspiracies of Meaning: Music Hall Culture and the Knowingness of Popular Culture." *Past and Present* 144 (August 1994): 138–70.

———. *Leisure and Class in Victorian England: Rational Recreation and the Contest for Control, 1830–1885*. London: Routledge & Kegan Paul, 1978.

———. "'Naughty but Nice': Musical Comedy and the Rhetoric of the Girl, 1892–1914." *The Edwardian Theatre: Essays on Performance and the Stage*. Ed. Michael R. Booth and Joel H. Kaplan, 36–60. Cambridge: Cambridge University Press, 1996.

———. "Parasexuality and Glamour: The Victorian Barmaid as Cultural Prototype." *Gender & History* 2:2 (Summer 1990): 148–72.

———. *Popular Culture and Performance in the Victorian City*. Cambridge: Cambridge University Press, 1998.

———. "White Collars, Gray Lives? The Lower Middle Class Revisited." *Journal of British Studies* 38:3 (1999): 273–90.

Bailey, Peter, ed. *Music Hall: The Business of Pleasure*. Milton Keynes: Open University Press, 1986.

Banta, Martha. *Taylored Lives: Narrative Productions in the Age of Taylor, Veblen, and Ford*. Chicago: University of Chicago Press, 1993.

Barnes, John. *The Beginnings of the Cinema in England 1894–1901.* 5 vols. to date. London: Bishopsgate Press Ltd., 1976–1997. Revised edition ed. Richard Maltby. Exeter: University of Exeter Press, 1997.

Barrow, Logie, and Ian Bullock. *Democratic Ideas and the British Labour Movement, 1880–1914.* Cambridge: Cambridge University Press, 1996.

Barrows, Susanna. *Distorting Mirrors: Visions of the Crowd in Late Nineteenth-Century France.* New Haven CT: Yale University Press, 1981.

Barthes, Roland. *A Lover's Discourse: Fragments.* New York: Hill and Wang, 1978.

Baudelaire, Charles. *The Painter of Modern Life, and Other Essays.* Trans. and ed. Jonathan Mayne. London: Phaidon, 1964.

Beetham, Margaret. *A Magazine of Her Own? Domesticity and Desire in the Woman's Magazine, 1800–1914.* London: Routledge, 1996.

Beniger, James R. *The Control Revolution: Technological and Economic Origins of the Information Society.* Cambridge: Harvard University Press, 1986.

Benjamin, Thelma H. *London Shops and Shopping.* London: Herbert Joseph Ltd., 1934.

Benjamin, Walter. *Illuminations.* Trans. Harry Zohn. Ed. Hannah Arendt. New York: Schocken Books, 1968.

———. *Reflections.* Ed. Peter Demetz. New York: Schocken Books, 1986.

Bennett, Paula, and Vernon A. Rosario II, eds. *Solitary Pleasures: The Historical, Literary, and Artistic Discourses of Autoeroticism.* New York: Routledge, 1995.

Benson, John, ed. *The Working Class in Britain, 1850–1939.* London: Longman, 1989.

———, ed. *The Working Class in England 1875–1914.* London: Croom Helm, 1985.

Benson, Susan Porter. *Counter Cultures: Saleswomen, Managers, and Customers in American Department Stores, 1890–1940.* Urbana: University of Illinois Press, 1986.

Berlant, Lauren. "'68, or Something." *Critical Inquiry* 21 (Autumn 1994): 124–55.

———. *The Anatomy of National Fantasy: Hawthorne, Utopia, and Everyday Life.* Chicago: University of Chicago Press, 1991.

———. "The Compulsion to Repeat Femininity." *The City and the Politics of Propinquity.* Ed. Joan Copjec and Michael Sorkin. London: Verso, 1999.

———. "The Female Woman: Fanny Fern and the Form of Sentiment." *American Literary History* 3:3 (Fall 1991): 429–54.

———. "Pax Americana: The Case of *Show Boat.*" *Institutions of the Novel.* Ed. W. B. Warner and Deidre Lynch. Durham, NC: Duke University Press, 1997.

———. *The Queen of America Goes to Washington City.* Durham, NC: Duke University Press, 1997.

Berman, Marshall. *All That Is Solid Melts into Air: The Experience of Modernity.* 1982. Rev. ed. Harmondwsorth, Middlesex: Penguin, 1988.

Bernheimer, Charles, and Claire Kahane, eds. *In Dora's Case: Freud—Hysteria—Feminism.* 2nd ed. New York: Columbia University Press, 1990.

Boardman, Kay. "'A Material Girl in a Material World': The Fashionable Female Body in Victorian Women's Magazines." *Journal of Victorian Culture* 3:1 (Spring 1998): 93–110.

Booth, Michael R., and Joel H. Kaplan, eds. *The Edwardian Theatre: Essays on*

Performance and the Stage. Cambridge: Cambridge University Press, 1996.

Bordwell, David, Janet Staiger, and Kristin Thompson. *The Classical Hollywood Cinema: Film Style and Mode of Production to 1960.* New York: Columbia University Press, 1985.

Boston, Sarah. *Women Workers and the Trade Unions.* London: Lawrence & Wishart, 1987.

Bowlby, Rachel. *Just Looking: Consumer Culture in Dreiser, Gissing and Zola.* New York: Methuen, 1985.

Braendlin, Bonnie Hoover. "The Prostitute as Scapegoat: Mildred Rogers in Somerset Maugham's *Of Human Bondage.*" *The Image of the Prostitute in Victorian Literature.* Ed. Pierre L. Horn and Mary Beth Pringle. New York: Frederick Ungar, 1984.

Bratton, J. S. *Melodrama: Stage, Picture, Screen.* London: BFI, 1994.

———, ed. *Music Hall: Performance and Style.* Milton Keynes: Open University Press, 1986.

Breward, Christopher. *The Hidden Consumer: Masculinities, Fashion and City Life 1860–1914.* Manchester: Manchester University Press, 1999.

Brewer, John, and Roy Porter, eds. *Consumption and the World of Goods.* London: Routledge, 1993.

Briggs, Asa. *Friends of the People: The Centenary History of Lewis's.* London: Batsford, 1956.

Bristow, Edward J. *Vice and Vigilance: Purity Movements in Britain since 1700.* Dublin: Gill and Macmillan, 1977.

Brown, Bill. "How to Do Things with Things." Unpublished ms. presented at the American Studies/Mass Culture Workshop at the University of Chicago, January 1998.

Brownlow, Kevin. *Behind the Mask of Innocence.* Berkeley: University of California Press, 1990.

Bruno, Giuliana. *Streetwalking on a Ruined Map: Cultural Theory and the City Films of Elvira Notari.* Princeton, NJ: Princeton University Press, 1993.

Buck-Morss, Susan. "Aesthetics and Anaesthetics: Walter Benjamin's Artwork Essay Reconsidered." *October* 62 (1992): 3–41.

———. *The Dialectics of Seeing: Walter Benjamin and the Arcades Project.* Cambridge, MA: MIT Press, 1989.

———. "The Flaneur, the Sandwichman, and the Whore: The Politics of Loitering." *New German Critique* 39 (Fall 1986): 99–140.

Burch, Noel. *Life to Those Shadows.* Trans. Ben Brewster. Berkeley: University of California Press, 1990.

Burgin, Victor, James Donald, and Cora Kaplan, eds. *Formations of Fantasy.* London: Routledge, 1986.

Butler, Judith. *Bodies That Matter: On the Discursive Limits of "Sex."* New York: Routledge, 1993.

———. *Gender Trouble: Feminism and the Subversion of Identity.* New York: Routledge, 1990.

Butler, Judith, and Joan W. Scott, eds. *Feminists Theorize the Political.* New York: Routledge, 1992.

Cadogan, Mary, and Patricia Craig. *You're a Brick, Angela! A New Look at Girls' Fiction from 1839 to 1975.* London: Victor Gollancz Ltd., 1976.

Caine, Barbara. *Victorian Feminists*. Oxford: Oxford University Press, 1992.

Calder, Robert Lorin. *W. Somerset Maugham and the Quest for Freedom*. London: Heinemann, 1972.

Callery, Sean. *Harrods Knightsbridge: The Story of Society's Favourite Store*. London: Ebury Press, 1991.

Certeau, Michel de. *The Practice of Everyday Life*. Trans. Steven Randall. Berkeley: University of California Press, 1984.

Chambers, Iain. *Popular Culture: The Metropolitan Experience*. London: Methuen, 1986.

Chanan, Michael. *The Dream that Kicks: The Prehistory and Early Years of Cinema in Britain*. 1980. London: Routledge, 1996.

Chandler, Alfred. *The Visible Hand: The Managerial Revolution in American Business*. Cambridge: Harvard University Press, 1977.

Chandler, James, Arnold I. Davidson, and Harry Harootunian, eds. *Questions of Evidence: Proof, Practice, and Persuasion across the Disciplines*. Chicago: University of Chicago Press, 1994.

Charney, Leo, and Vanessa R. Schwartz, eds. *Cinema and the Invention of Modern Life*. Berkeley: University of California Press, 1995.

Chialant, Maria Theresa. "The Feminization of the City in Gissing's Fiction: The Streetwalker, the *Flaneuse*, the Shopgirl." *A Garland for Gissing*. Ed. Bouwe Postmus, 51–65. Amsterdam, Netherlands: Rodopi, 2001.

Christie, Ian. *The Last Machine: Early Cinema and the Birth of the Modern World*. Foreword by Terry Gilliam. London: BFI, 1994.

Clark, Anna. "Reviews in History." Ed. David Cannadine. Institute of Historical Research, University of London. http://www.history.ac.uk/reviews/paper/anna.html. September 1998. Accessed 18 November 2004.

Clegg, Hugh Armstrong. *A History of British Trade Unions since 1889*. 2 vols. Oxford: Clarendon Press, 1985.

Coffin, Judith G. *The Politics of Women's Work: The Paris Garment Trades 1750–1915*. Princeton, NJ: Princeton University Press, 1996.

Cohen, Monica. "Maximizing Oliphant: Begging the Question and the Politics of Satire." *Victorian Women Writers and the Woman Question*. Ed. Nicola Diane Thompson, 99–115. Cambridge: Cambridge University Press, 1999.

———. *Professional Domesticity in the Victorian Novel: Women, Work, and Home*. Cambridge: Cambridge University Press, 1998.

Cohn, Samuel. *The Process of Occupational Sex-Typing: The Feminization of Clerical Labor in Great Britain*. Philadelphia: Temple University Press, 1985.

Copelman, Dina M. *London's Women Teachers: Gender, Class, and Feminism, 1870–1930*. New York: Routledge, 1996.

Cordell, Richard A. *Somerset Maugham: A Biographical and Critical Study*. Bloomington: Indiana University Press, 1961.

Corina, M. *Fine Silks and Oak Counters: Debenhams 1778–1978*. London: Hutchinson, 1978.

Coustillas, Pierre, and Colin Partridge, eds. *Gissing: The Critical Heritage*. London: Routledge & Kegan Paul, 1972.

Coustillas, Pierre. Introduction. *London and the Life of Literature in Late Victorian England: The Diary of George Gissing, Novelist*. Hassocks, Eng.: Harvester Press, 1978.

Crary, Jonathan. *Suspensions of Perception: Attention, Spectacle, and Modern Culture.* Cambridge, MA: MIT Press, 1999.

Crompton, Rosemary, and Gareth Jones. *White Collar Proletariat: Deskilling and Gender in the Clerical Labour Process.* London: Macmillan, 1984.

Cross, Victoria [Vivian Cory]. "Theodora." *The Yellow Book* (1895). Rpt. in *Daughters of Decadence.* Ed. Elaine Showalter. New Brunswick, NJ: Rutgers University Press, 1993.

Crossick, Geoffrey, ed. *The Lower Middle Class in Britain, 1870–1914.* New York: St. Martin's, 1977.

———. "Shopkeepers and the State in Britain, 1870–1914." *Shopkeepers and Master Artisans in Nineteenth-Century Europe.* Ed. Geoffrey Crossick and Heinz-Gerhard Haupt, 239–69. London: Methuen, 1984.

Crossick, Geoffrey, and Serge Jaumain, eds. *Cathedrals of Consumption: The European Department Store, 1850–1939.* Aldershot: Ashgate, 1999.

Cruse, Amy. *The Victorians and Their Reading.* Boston: Houghton Mifflin, 1935.

Culver, Stuart. "What Manikins Want: *The Wonderful Wizard of Oz* and *The Art of Decorating Dry Goods Windows*." *Representations* 21 (Winter 1988): 97–116.

Cunningham, Hugh. *Leisure in the Industrial Revolution c. 1780–c. 1880.* New York: St. Martin's, 1980.

Curran, James, and Vincent Porter. *British Cinema History.* Totowa, NJ: Barnes and Noble Books, 1983.

Curtis, Anthony. *The Pattern of Maugham: A Critical Portrait.* London: Hamish Hamilton, 1974.

Cvetkovich, Ann. *Mixed Feelings: Feminism, Mass Culture, and Victorian Sensationalism.* New Brunswick, NJ: Rutgers University Press, 1992.

D'Albertis, Deirdre. *Dissembling Fictions: Elizabeth Gaskell and the Victorian Social Text.* New York: St. Martin's, 1997.

———. "The Domestic Drone: Margaret Oliphant and a Political History of the Novel." *Studies in English Literature 1500–1900* 37:4 (Autumn 1997): 805–29.

Dale, Tim. *Harrods, a Palace in Knightsbridge.* London: Harrods Publishing, 1995.

Daunton, Martin, and Matthew Hilton, eds. *The Politics of Consumption: Material Culture and Citizenship in Europe and America.* Oxford and New York: Berg, 2001.

Davidoff, Leonore. "Gender and the 'Great Divide': Public and Private in British Gender History." *Journal of Women's History* 15:1 (Spring 2003): 11–27.

———. *Worlds Between: Historical Perspectives on Gender and Class.* New York: Routledge, 1995.

Davidoff, Leonore, and Catherine Hall. *Family Fortunes: Men and Women of the English Middle Class, 1750–1850.* Chicago: University of Chicago Press, 1987.

Davies, Tony. "Transports of Pleasure: Fiction and Its Audiences in the Later Nineteenth Century." *Formations of Pleasure.* Ed. Formations Editorial Collective, 46–58. London: Routledge & Kegan Paul, 1983.

Davis, John. *Reforming London: The London Government Problem 1855–1900.* Oxford: Clarendon Press, 1988.

Davis, Tracy C. *George Bernard Shaw and the Socialist Theatre.* Westport, CT: Greenwood Press, 1994.

―――. "Indecency and Vigilance in the Music Halls." *British Theatre in the 1890s: Essays on Drama and the Stage.* Ed. Richard Foulkes, 111–31. Cambridge: Cambridge University Press, 1992.

De Grazia, Victoria, and Ellen Furlough, eds. *The Sex of Things: Gender and Consumption in Historical Perspective.* Berkeley: University of California Press, 1996.

Degen, John A. "The Evolution of *The Shop Girl* and the Birth of Musical Comedy." *Theatre History Studies* 7 (1987): 40–50.

Disher, M. Willson. *Fairs, Circuses, and Music Halls.* London: William Collins, 1942.

―――. *Music Hall Parade.* New York: C. Scribner's Sons, 1938.

Doane, Mary Ann. *The Desire to Desire: The Woman's Film of the 1940s.* Bloomington and Indianapolis: Indiana University Press, 1987.

Drotner, Kirsten. *English Children and Their Magazines, 1751–1945.* New Haven, CT: Yale University Press, 1988.

Eckert, Charles. "The Carole Lombard in Macy's Window." *Quarterly Review of Film Studies* 3:1 (Winter 1978): 1–21.

Ehrenreich, Barbara. *Nickel and Dimed: On (Not) Getting By in America.* New York: Henry Holt & Co., 2001.

Elsaesser, Thomas, ed. *Early Cinema: Space—Frame—Narrative.* London: BFI, 1990.

Engels, Friedrich. *The Condition of the Working Class in England.* Ed. David McLellan. Oxford and New York: Oxford University Press, 1993.

Enstad, Nan. *Ladies of Labor, Girls of Adventure: Working Women, Popular Culture, and Labor Politics at the Turn of the Twentieth Century.* New York: Columbia University Press, 1999.

Fay, Arthur. *Bioscope Shows and their Engines.* London: Oakwood Press, 1966.

Featherstone, Liza. *Selling Women Short: The Landmark Battle for Workers' Rights at Wal-Mart.* New York: Basic Books, 1994.

Feldman, David, and Gareth Stedman Jones. *Metropolis London: Histories and Representations since 1800.* London: Routledge, 1989.

Felski, Rita. *The Gender of Modernity.* Cambridge, MA: Harvard University Press, 1995.

Field, Audrey. *Picture Palace: A Social History of the Cinema.* London: Gentry Books, 1974.

Fielding, Raymond. "Hale's Tours: Ultrarealism in the Pre-1910 Motion Picture." *Journal of History* 3 (1957) and *Cinema Journal* 10:1 (Fall 1970): 34–47. Rpt. in *Film before Griffith.* Ed. John L. Fell, 116–30. Berkeley: University of California Press, 1983.

Fisher, Philip. *Hard Facts: Setting and Form in the American Novel.* New York: Oxford University Press, 1985.

Fitzsimmons, Linda, and Viv Gardner, eds. *New Woman Plays.* London: Methuen Drama, 1991.

Flint, Kate. *The Woman Reader 1837–1914.* Oxford: Oxford University Press, 1993.

Formations Editorial Collective, eds. *Formations of Pleasure.* London: Routledge & Kegan Paul, 1983.

Foster, Hal. "Death in America." *October* 75 (Winter 1996): 37–59.

Foucault, Michel. *The History of Sexuality, Volume 1: An Introduction.* 1978. Trans. Robert Hurley. New York: Vintage, 1990.

Foulkes, Richard, ed. *British Theatre in the 1890s: Essays on Drama and the Stage.* Cambridge: Cambridge University Press, 1992.

Freud, Sigmund. *Beyond the Pleasure Principle.* 1920. Ed. and trans. James Strachey. New York: W. W. Norton and Co., 1989.

———. "'A Child Is Being Beaten': A Contribution to the Origin of Sexual Perversions." 1919. Rpt. in *Sexuality and the Psychology of Love.* Ed. Philip Rieff, 97–122. New York: Collier Books (Macmillan), 1963.

———. "Creative Writers and Day-Dreaming." 1907. Rpt. in *The Freud Reader.* Ed. Peter Gay, 436–42. New York: W. W. Norton & Co., 1989.

Fried, Michael. *Absorption and Theatricality: Painting and Beholder in the Age of Diderot.* Chicago: University of Chicago Press, 1980.

Friedberg, Anne. *Window Shopping: Cinema and the Postmodern.* Berkeley: University of California Press, 1993.

Frisby, David. *Fragments of Modernity: Theories of Modernity in the Work of Simmel, Kracauer, and Benjamin.* Cambridge, MA: MIT Press, 1986.

Furlough, Ellen. *Consumer Cooperation in France: The Politics of Consumption, 1834–1930.* Ithaca, NY: Cornell University Press, 1991.

Fuss, Diana. *Identification Papers.* New York: Routledge, 1995.

Gagnier, Regenia. *Subjectivities: A History of Self-Representation in Britain, 1832–1920.* New York and Oxford: Oxford University Press, 1991.

Gaines, Jane, ed. *Classical Hollywood Narrative: The Paradigm Wars.* Durham, NC: Duke University Press, 1992.

———. "The Queen Christina Tie-Ups: Convergence of Show Window and Screen." *Quarterly Review of Film and Video* 11:1 (Winter 1989): 35–60.

Gaines, Jane, and Charlotte Herzog, eds. *Fabrications: Costume and the Female Body.* New York: Routledge, 1990.

Gainor, J. Ellen. *Shaw's Daughters: Dramatic and Narrative Constructions of Gender.* Ann Arbor: University of Michigan Press, 1991.

Gallagher, Catherine. *The Industrial Reformation of English Fiction: Social Discourse and Narrative Form, 1832–1867.* Chicago: University of Chicago Press, 1985.

Ganetz, Hillevi. "The Shop, the Home and Femininity as a Masquerade." *Youth Culture in Late Modernity.* Ed. Johan Fornäs and Göran Bolin. London: Sage Publications, 1995.

Gardner, Vivien, and Susan Rutherford, eds. *The New Woman and Her Sisters: Feminism and Theatre 1850–1914.* Ann Arbor: University of Michigan Press, 1992.

Garrett, John M. *Sixty Years of British Music Hall.* London: Chappell and Co., 1976.

Garvey, Ellen Gruber. *The Adman in the Parlor: Magazines and the Gendering of Consumer Culture, 1880s to 1910s.* New York: Oxford University Press, 1996.

Gay, Peter. *The Bourgeois Experience: Victoria to Freud.* 5 vols. New York: Oxford University Press, 1984–1998.

Gibbon, Sir Gwilym, and Reginald W. Bell. *History of the London County Council 1889–1939.* London: Macmillan, 1939.

Giddens, Anthony. *The Consequences of Modernity.* Stanford, CA: Stanford University Press, 1990.

Glucksmann, Miriam. *Women Assemble: Women Workers and the New Industries in Inter-War Britain.* London: Routledge, 1990.

Gorham, Deborah. "The 'Maiden Tribute of Modern Babylon' Re-examined: Child Prostitution and the Idea of Childhood in Late-Victorian England." *Victorian Studies* 21 (Spring 1978): 353–69.

Gorsky, Susan Rubinow. *Femininity to Feminism: Women and Literature in the Nineteenth Century.* New York: Twayne Publishers, 1992.

Gramsci, Antonio. *Selections from the Prison Notebooks.* Ed. and trans. Quintin Hoare and Geoffrey Nowell Smith. New York: Lawrence & Wishart, 1971.

Green, Benny, ed. *The Last Empires: A Music Hall Companion.* London: Pavilion, 1986.

Grieveson, Lee. "Policing the Cinema: *Traffic in Souls* at Ellis Island." *Screen* 38:2 (Fall 1998): 149–71.

Grossberg, Lawrence, Cary Nelson, and Paula Treichler, eds. *Cultural Studies.* New York: Routledge, 1992.

Grosz, Elizabeth. "Refiguring Lesbian Desire." *The Lesbian Postmodern.* Ed. Laura Doan, 67–84. New York: Columbia University Press, 1994.

Gunning, Thomas. "An Aesthetic of Astonishment: Early Film and the (In)Credulous Spectator." *Art & Text* 34 (Winter 1989): 31–45. Rpt. in Williams, 114–33.

———. "The Cinema of Attractions: Early Film, Its Spectator and the Avant-Garde." *Wide Angle* 8:3/4 (Fall 1986): 63–70. Rpt. in Elsaesser, 56–62.

———. "'Primitive' Cinema: A Frame-Up? Or, The Trick's On Us." Rpt. in Elsaesser, 95–103.

Gurney, Peter. *Co-Operative Culture and the Politics of Consumption in England, 1870–1939.* Manchester: Manchester University Press, 1996.

———. "The Middle-Class Embrace: Language, Representation, and the Contest over Co-operative Forms in Britain, c. 1860–1914." *Victorian Studies* 37:2 (Winter 1994): 253–86.

Hammerton, A. James. "Pooterism or Partnership? Marriage and Masculine Identity in the Lower Middle Class, 1870–1920." *Journal of British Studies* 38:3 (1999): 291–321.

Hammerton, Jenny. "For Ladies Only (Men May Glance): Eve's Film Review—The Screen Magazine for Women." Unpublished manuscript.

Hansen, Miriam. *Babel and Babylon: Spectatorship in American Silent Film.* Cambridge, MA: Harvard University Press, 1991.

———. "Benjamin, Cinema and Experience: 'The Blue Flower in the Land of Technology.'" *New German Critique* 40 (Winter 1987): 179–224.

Harding, Colin, and Simon Popple, eds. *In the Kingdom of Shadows: A Companion to Early Cinema.* London: Cygnus Arts, 1996.

Haward, Sir Harry. *The London County Council from Within.* London: Chapman and Hall, 1932.

Helsinger, Elizabeth K., Robin Lauterbach Sheets, and William Veeder, eds. *The Woman Question: Society and Literature in Britain and America, 1837–1883.* 3 vols. New York: Garland Publishing, 1983.

Herstein, Sheila R. *A Mid-Victorian Feminist: Barbara Leigh Smith Bodichon.* New Haven and London: Yale University Press, 1985.

Hiley, Nicholas. "Fifteen Questions about the Early Film Audience." *Uncharted Territory: Essays on Early Non-Fiction Film.* Ed. Daan Hertogs and Nico de Klerk, 105–18. Amsterdam: Stichting Nederlands Filmmuseum, 1997.

———. "The British Cinema Auditorium." *Film and the First World War.* Ed. Karel Dibbets and Bert Hogenkamp, 160–70. Amsterdam: Amsterdam University Press, 1994.

Hilmes, Michelle. *Radio Voices: American Broadcasting, 1922–1952.* Minneapolis: University of Minnesota Press, 1997.

Hilton, Matthew. "Class, Consumption and the Public Sphere." *Journal of Contemporary History* 35:4 (2000): 655–66.

Hirsch, Pam. *Barbara Leigh Smith Bodichon, 1827–1891: Feminist, Artist and Rebel.* London: Chatto & Windus, 1998.

Hoffman, P. C. *They Also Serve: The Story of the Shopworker.* London: Porcupine, 1947.

Hoggart, Richard. *The Uses of Literacy.* New York: Oxford University Press, 1958.

Holcombe, Lee. *Victorian Ladies at Work: Middle-Class Working Women in England and Wales.* Newton Abbot: David & Charles, 1973.

Honeycombe, Gordon. *Selfridges: Seventy Five Years. The Story of the Store, 1909–1984.* London: Park Lane, 1984.

Horkheimer, Max, and Theodor Adorno. "The Culture Industry: Enlightenment as Mass Deception." *Dialectic of Enlightenment.* 1944. Trans. John Cumming, 120–67. New York: Continuum, 1994.

Hosgood, Christopher P. "The 'Pigmies of Commerce' and the Working-Class Community: Small Shopkeepers in England, 1870–1914." *Journal of Social History* 22:3 (1989): 439–60.

———. "'A Brave and Daring Folk': Shopkeepers and Trade Associational Life in Victorian and Edwardian England." *Journal of Social History* 26 (1992): 285–308.

———. "'Mercantile Monasteries': Shops, Shop Assistants, and Shop Life in Late-Victorian and Edwardian Britain." *Journal of British Studies* 38:3 (1999): 322–52.

———. "Mrs. Pooter's Purchase: Lower-Middle-Class Consumerism and the Sales, 1870–1914." *Gender, Civic Culture and Consumerism: Middle-Class Identity in Britain, 1800–1940.* Ed. Alan Kidd and David Nicholls, 146–63. Manchester: Manchester University Press, 1999.

Hower, R. M. *History of Macy's of New York 1858–1919: Chapters in the Evolution of a Department Store.* Cambridge, MA: Harvard University Press, 1943.

Huneault, Kristina. *Difficult Subjects: Working Women and Visual Culture, Britain 1880–1914.* Aldershot, Hants, England: Ashgate, 2002.

Huyssen, Andreas. *After the Great Divide: Modernism, Mass Culture, Postmodernism.* Bloomington: Indiana University Press, 1986.

Jackson, Kate. *George Newnes and the New Journalism in Britain, 1880–1910: Culture and Profit.* Aldershot, Hants, England: Ashgate, 2001.

———. "The *Tit-Bits* Phenomenon: George Newnes, New Journalism, and the Periodical Texts." *Victorian Periodicals Review* 30:3 (Fall 1997): 201–26.

James, Louis. *Fiction for the Working Man, 1830–1850: A Study of the Literature Produced for the Working Class in Early Victorian Urban England.* London: Oxford University Press, 1963.

_____. "The Trouble With Betsy: Periodicals and the Common Reader in Mid-Nineteenth Century England." *The Victorian Periodical Press: Samplings and Soundings.* Ed. Joanne Shattock and Michael Wolff, 349–66. Toronto: University of Toronto Press, 1982.

Jameson, Fredric. "Pleasure: A Political Issue." *Formations of Pleasure.* Ed. Formations Editorial Collective, 1–14. London: Routledge & Kegan Paul, 1983.

_____. "Reification and Utopia in Mass Culture." *Social Text* 1 (Winter 1979): 130–48.

Jeffery, James B. *Retail Trading in Britain, 1850–1950: A Study of Trends in Retailing with Special Reference to the Development of Co-operative, Multiple Shop and Department Store Methods of Trading.* Cambridge: Cambridge University Press, 1954.

John, Angela V., ed. *Unequal Opportunities: Women's Employment in England 1800–1918.* Oxford: Basil Blackwell, 1986.

Jones, Colin. "The Great Chain of Buying: Medical Advertisement, the Bourgeois Public Sphere, and the Origins of the French Revolution." *American Historical Review* 101 (February 1996): 13–40.

Jones, Jennifer. "*Coquettes* and *Grisettes:* Women Buying and Selling in Ancien Régime Paris." *The Sex of Things: Gender and Consumption in Historical Perspective.* Ed. Victoria de Grazia and Ellen Furlough, 25–53. Berkeley: University of California Press, 1996.

Jones, Gareth Stedman. *Languages of Class: Studies in English Working-Class History 1832–1982.* Cambridge: Cambridge University Press, 1983.

Jordan, Ellen. *The Women's Movement and Women's Employment in Nineteenth-Century Britain.* London/New York: Routledge, 1999.

Jordan, Jane. "Ouida: The Enigma of a Literary Identity." *Princeton University Library Chronicle* 57:1 (Autumn 1995): 75–105.

Jordan, John O., and Robert L. Patten, eds. *Literature in the Marketplace: Nineteenth-Century British Publishing and Reading Practices.* Cambridge: Cambridge University Press, 1995.

Joyce, Patrick, ed. *The Historical Meanings of Work.* Cambridge: Cambridge University Press, 1987.

Kaplan, Cora. "*The Thorn Birds:* Fiction, Fantasy, Femininity." *Formations of Fantasy.* Ed. Victor Burgin, James Donald and Cora Kaplan, 142–66. London: Routledge, 1986.

Kaplan, Joel H., and Sheila Stowell. *Theatre and Fashion: Oscar Wilde to the Suffragettes.* Cambridge University Press, 1994.

Keep, Christopher. "The Cultural Work of the Type-Writer Girl." *Victorian Studies* 40:3 (Spring 1997): 401–26.

Kidd, Alan, and David Nicholls, eds. *Gender, Civic Culture and Consumerism: Middle-Class Identity in Britain, 1800–1940.* Manchester: Manchester University Press, 1999.

Kift, Dagmar. *The Victorian Music Hall: Culture, Class and Conflict.* Cambridge: Cambridge University Press, 1996.

Kipnis, Laura. "Towards a Left Popular Culture." *High Theory/Low Culture: Analyzing Popular Television and Film.* Ed. Colin MacCabe, 11–36. Manchester: Manchester University Press, 1986.

Kirby, Lynne. *Parallel Tracks: The Railroad and Silent Cinema.* Durham: Duke University Press, 1997.

Klancher, Jon. *The Making of English Reading Audiences, 1790–1832.* Madison: University of Wisconsin Press, 1987.

Knapp, Shoshanah Milgrim. "Real Passion and the Reverence for Life: Sexuality and Antivivisection in the Fiction of Victoria Cross." *Rediscovering Forgotten Radicals: British Women Writers, 1889–1939.* Ed. Angela Ingram and Daphne Patai, 156–71. Chapel Hill: University of North Carolina Press, 1993.

———. "Revolutionary Androgyny in the Fiction of 'Victoria Cross.'" *Seeing Double: Revisioning Edwardian and Modernist Literature.* Ed. Carola M. Kaplan and Anne B. Simpson, 3–19. New York: St. Martin's, 1996.

Kowaleski-Wallace, Elizabeth. *Consuming Subjects: Women, Shopping, and Business in the Eighteenth Century.* New York: Columbia University Press, 1997.

Kracauer, Siegfried. *The Mass Ornament: Weimar Essays.* Trans. and ed. Thomas Y. Levin. Cambridge, MA: Harvard University Press, 1995.

Krandis, Rita B. *Subversive Discourse: The Cultural Production of Late Victorian Feminist Novels.* New York: St. Martin's, 1995.

Krentz, Jayne Ann, ed. *Dangerous Men and Adventurous Women: Romance Writers on the Appeal of the Romance.* Philadelphia: University of Pennsylvania Press, 1992.

Kuhn, Annette. *Cinema, Censorship, and Sexuality, 1909–1925.* London: Routledge, 1988.

Lacey, Candida Ann, ed. *Barbara Leigh Smith Bodichon and the Langham Place Group.* London and New York: Routledge & Kegan Paul, 1986.

Laermans, Rudi. "Learning to Consume: Early Department Stores and the Shaping of the Modern Consumer Culture (1860–1914)." *Theory, Culture and Society* 10 (1993): 79–102.

Lambert, Richard S. *The Universal Provider: A Study of William Whiteley and the Rise of the London Department Store.* London: George G. Harrap & Co., 1938.

Landay, Lori. *Madcaps, Screwballs, and Con Women: The Female Trickster in American Culture.* Philadelphia: University of Pennsylvania Press, 1998.

Lancaster, Bill. *The Department Store: A Social History.* London: Leicester University Press, 1995.

Laplanche, Jean, and Jean-Bertrand Pontalis. "Fantasy and the Origins of Sexuality." Rpt. with a retrospect in *Formations of Fantasy.* Ed. Victor Burgin, James Donald, and Cora Kaplan, 5–34. London: Routledge, 1986.

———. *The Language of Psychoanalysis.* Trans. Donald Nicholson-Smith. New York: W. W. Norton & Co., 1973.

Laybourn, Keith. *A History of British Trade Unionism c. 1770–1990.* Phoenix Mill, UK: Alan Sutton Publishing Ltd., 1992.

Leach, William. *Land of Desire: Merchants, Power, and the Rise of a New American Culture.* New York: Pantheon, 1993.

———. "Strategists of Display and the Production of Desire." *Consuming Visions: Accumulation and Display of Goods in America, 1880–1920.* Ed. Simon J. Bronner, 99–132. New York: W. W. Norton and Co., for the Henry Francis DuPont Winterthur Museum, 1989.

———. "Transformations in a Culture of Consumption: Women and Department Stores, 1890–1925." *Journal of American History* 71:2 (September 1984): 319–42.

Lears, T. J. Jackson. *No Place of Grace: Antimodernism and the Transformation of American Culture 1880–1920.* Chicago: University of Chicago Press, 1980.

Ledger, Sally. "Gissing, the Shopgirl, and the New Woman." *Women: A Cultural Review* 6:3 (Winter 1995): 263–74.

Lefebvre, Henri. *Critique of Everyday Life*. Volume I. 1947. Trans. John Moore. London: Verso, 1991.

Lemire, Beverly. *Fashion's Favourite: The Cotton Trade and the Consumer in Britain, 1660–1800*. Oxford: Oxford University Press, 1992.

Lessard, Suzannah. *The Architect of Desire: Beauty and Danger in the Stanford White Family*. New York: Dial Press, 1996.

Levine, Donald, ed. *Individuality and Social Forms*. Chicago: University of Chicago Press, 1971.

Lewis, Jane E. "Women Clerical Workers in the Late Nineteenth and Early Twentieth Centuries." *The White-Blouse Revolution: Female Office Workers Since 1870*. Ed. Gregory Anderson, 27–47. Manchester: Manchester University Press, 1988.

Lochnan, Katharine, ed. *Seductive Surfaces: The Art of Tissot*. New Haven, CT: Yale University Press, 1999.

Logan, Peter. "Privatizing the Fad: Victorian Crowd Theory and the Popular Reader." Unpublished paper given at the Modern Language Association Conference, December 1996.

Lovell, Terry. *Consuming Fiction*. London: Verso, 1987.

Low, Rachael. *The History of the British Film*. Vols. 1–4. London: G. Allen & Unwin, 1948–1971.

MacCabe, Colin. "Defining Popular Culture." *High Theory/Low Culture: Analyzing Popular Television and Film*. Ed. Colin MacCabe, 1–10. Manchester: Manchester University Press, 1986.

Macdonald, Dwight. "A Theory of Mass Culture." Originally published as "A Theory of Popular Culture" in *Politics Today* (1944) and expanded for *Diogenes* 3 (Summer 1953). Rpt. in *Mass Culture: The Popular Arts in America*. Ed. Bernard Rosenberg and David Manning White, 59–73. Glencoe, IL: Free Press, 1958.

MacKenzie, John. *Propaganda and Empire: The Manipulation of British Public Opinion, 1880–1960*. Manchester: Manchester University Press, 1984.

Mackie, Erin. *Market à la Mode: Fashion, Commodity and Gender in* The Tatler *and* The Spectator. Baltimore: Johns Hopkins University Press, 1997.

Mander, Raymond, and Joe Mitchenson. *British Music Hall*. Fwd. John Betjeman. London: Studio Vista Ltd., 1965.

Mansfield, Katherine. *Stories*. New York: Vintage Classics, 1991.

Margetson, Stella. *Leisure and Pleasure in the Nineteenth Century*. London: Cassell & Co. Ltd., 1969.

Marshall, Nancy Rose, and Malcolm Warner. *James Tissot: Victorian Life, Modern Love*. New Haven, CT: Yale University Press, 1999.

Marx, Karl. "The Fetishism of Commodities and the Secret Thereof." Section 4 of *Capital*, Vol. I. Rpt. in Robert C. Tucker, ed. *The Marx-Engels Reader*. 2nd ed., 319–29. New York: W. W. Norton & Co., 1978.

Mathias, Peter. *The Retailing Revolution: A History of Multiple Retailing In the Food Trades based upon the Allied Suppliers Group of Companies*. London: Longmans, Green & Co., 1967.

Mayer, J. P. *British Cinemas and Their Audiences: Sociological Studies*. London: Dennis Dobson Ltd., 1948.

————. *Sociology of Film: Studies and Documents*. London: Faber and Faber Ltd., 1946.

Mayne, Judith. *Cinema and Spectatorship*. London: Routledge, 1993.

Mays, Kelly J. "The Disease of Reading and Victorian Periodicals." *Literature in the Marketplace: Nineteenth-Century British Publishing and Reading Practices*. Ed. John O. Jordan and Robert L. Patten, 165–94. Cambridge: Cambridge University Press, 1995.

McAleer, Joseph. *Passion's Fortune: The Story of Mills and Boon*. Oxford and New York: Oxford University Press, 1999.

McBride, Theresa. "A Woman's World: Department Stores and the Evolution of Women's Employment, 1870–1920." *French Historical Studies* 10:4 (Fall 1978): 664–83.

McClintock, Anne. *Imperial Leather: Race, Gender and Sexuality in the Colonial Contest*. New York: Routledge, 1995.

McKendrick, Neil, John Brewer, and J. H. Plumb. *The Birth of Consumer Society: The Commercialization of Eighteenth-Century England*. Bloomington: Indiana University Press, 1982.

Meyer, Stephen. *The Five-Dollar Day: Labor Management and Social Control in the Ford Motor Company 1908–1921*. Albany: State University of New York Press, 1981.

Miller, Michael B. *The Bon Marché: Bourgeois Culture and the Department Store, 1869–1920*. London: George Allen and Unwin, 1981.

Mitchell, Sally. *The Fallen Angel: Chastity, Class and Women's Reading, 1835–1880*. Bowling Green, OH: Bowling Green University Popular Press, 1981.

————. *The New Girl: Girls' Culture in England, 1880–1915*. New York: Columbia University Press, 1995.

Modleski, Tania. *Loving with a Vengeance: Mass Produced Fantasies for Women*. London: Methuen, 1984.

Morley, David, and Kuan-Hsing Chen. *Stuart Hall: Critical Dialogues in Cultural Studies*. New York: Routledge, 1996.

Mort, Frank. *Dangerous Sexualities: Medico-moral Politics in England since 1830*. London: Routledge & Kegan Paul, 1987.

Moscovici, Serge. *The Age of the Crowd: A Historical Treatise on Mass Psychology*. Trans. J.C. Whitehouse. Cambridge: Cambridge University Press, 1985.

Moss, Michael, and Alison Turton. *A Legend of Retailing: House of Fraser*. London: Weidenfeld and Nicholson, 1989.

Mui, Hoh-Cheung, and Lorna Mui. *Shops and Shopkeeping in Eighteenth-Century England*. Kingston: McGill-Queen's University Press and Routledge, 1989.

Mukerji, Chandra. *From Graven Images: Patterns of Modern Materialism*. New York: Columbia University Press, 1983.

Mussell, Kay. *Fantasy and Reconciliation: Contemporary Formulas of Women's Romance Fiction*. Westport, CT: Greenwood Press, 1984.

Naremore, James, and Patrick Brantlinger. "Six Artistic Cultures." *Modernity and Mass Culture*, 1–23. Bloomington: Indiana University Press, 1991.

Nava, Mica. "Modernity's Disavowal: Women, the City, and the Department Store." *Modern Times: Reflections on a Century of Modernity*. Ed. Mica Nava and Alan O'Shea, 38–76. London: Routledge, 1996.

————, and Alan O'Shea, eds. *Modern Times: Reflections on a Century of Modernity*. London: Routledge, 1996. 38–76.

Nead, Lynda. *Myths of Sexuality: Representations of Women in Victorian Britain.* London: Basil Blackwell, 1988.

———. *Victorian Babylon: People, Streets and Images in Nineteenth-Century London.* New Haven, CT: Yale University Press, 2000.

Negt, Oskar, and Alexander Kluge. *Public Sphere and Experience: Toward an Analysis of the Bourgeois and Proletarian Public Sphere.* Trans. Peter Labanyi, Jamie Owen Daniel, and Assenka Oksiloff. Fwd. Miriam Hansen. Minneapolis: University of Minnesota Press, 1993.

Nelson, Daniel, ed. *A Mental Revolution: Scientific Management since Taylor.* Columbus: Ohio State University Press, 1992.

Nord, Deborah Epstein. *Walking the Victorian Streets: Women, Representation, and the City.* Ithaca, NY: Cornell University Press, 1995.

Ortega, Bob. *In Sam We Trust: The Untold Story of Sam Walton and How Wal-Mart Is Devouring America.* New York: Times Business, 1998.

Parratt, Catriona M. *"More than Mere Amusement": Working-Class Women's Leisure in England, 1750–1914.* Boston: Northeastern University Press, 2001.

Parsons, Deborah L. *Streetwalking the Metropolis: Women, the City, and Modernity.* Oxford: Oxford University Press, 2000.

Pearce, Lynne, and Jackie Stacey, eds. *Romance Revisited.* New York: New York University Press, 1995.

Pearson, George. *Flashback: Autobiography of a British Film-maker.* 1957.

Pearson, Jacqueline. *Women's Reading in Britain, 1750–1835: A Dangerous Recreation.* Cambridge: Cambridge University Press, 1999.

Peiss, Kathy. *Cheap Amusements: Working Women and Leisure in Turn-of-the-Century New York.* Philadelphia: Temple University Press, 1986.

Pelling, Henry. *A History of British Trade Unionism.* 2nd ed. London: Macmillan, 1972.

Penley, Constance. "Feminism, Psychoanalysis, and the Study of Popular Culture." *Cultural Studies.* Ed. Lawrence Grossberg, Cary Nelson, and Paula Treichler, 479–94. New York: Routledge, 1992.

Pennybacker, Susan D. *A Vision for London 1889–1914: Labour, Everyday Life and the LCC Experiment.* London: Routledge, 1995.

———. "'It was not what she said but the way in which she said it': The London County Council and the Music Halls." Bailey, ed. *Music Hall.* 118–40.

Perry, George. *The Great British Picture Show.* London: Hart Davis/Mac Gibbon, 1974.

Poovey, Mary. *Uneven Developments: The Ideological Work of Gender in Mid-Victorian England.* Chicago: University of Chicago Press, 1988.

Pottinger, George. *The Winning Counter: Hugh Fraser and Harrods.* London: Hutchinson & Co., 1971.

Pound, Reginald. *Selfridge: A Biography.* London: Heinemann, 1960.

Probyn, Clive T. *English Fiction of the Eighteenth Century 1700–1789.* London: Longman Group, 1987.

Pykett, Lyn. *The "Improper" Feminine: The Women's Sensation Novel and the New Woman Writing.* London: Routledge, 1992.

Radford, Jean, ed. *The Progress of Romance: The Politics of Popular Romance Fiction.* London and New York: Routledge & Kegan Paul, 1986.

Radway, Janice. *Reading the Romance: Women, Patriarchy, and Popular Literature.* 1984. Chapel Hill: University of North Carolina Press, 1991.

Rappaport, Erika. "'A New Era of Shopping': The Promotion of Women's Pleasure in London's West End, 1909–1914." *Cinema and the Invention of Modern Life.* Ed. Leo Charney and Vanessa R. Schwartz, 130–55. Berkeley: University of California Press, 1995.

———. *Shopping for Pleasure: Women in the Making of London's West End.* Princeton, NJ: Princeton University Press, 2000.

———. "The West End and Women's Pleasure: Gender and Commercial Culture in London, 1860–1914." Ph.D. dissertation, Rutgers University, 1993.

Reekie, Gail. *Temptations: Sex, Selling, and the Department Store.* St. Leonards, Australia: Allen and Unwin, 1993.

Reynolds, Kimberley. *Girls Only? Gender and Popular Children's Fiction in Britain, 1880–1910.* Philadelphia: Temple University Press, 1990.

Richards, Jeffrey, and John M. MacKenzie. *The Railway Station: A Social History.* Oxford: Oxford University Press, 1986.

Richards, Thomas. *The Commodity Culture of Victorian England: Advertising and Spectacle, 1851–1914.* Stanford, CA: Stanford University Press, 1990.

Richardson, Angelique, and Chris Willis, eds. *The New Woman in Fiction and in Fact: Fin-de-Siècle Feminisms.* Houndsmills, Basingstoke, Hampshire: Palgrave Macmillan, 2002.

Richetti, John J. *Popular Fiction before Richardson: Narrative Patterns 1700–1739.* Oxford: Clarendon, 1969.

Roberts, Elizabeth. "Women's Work 1840–1940." *British Trade Union and Labour History: A Compendium.* Ed. Leslie A. Clarkson, 209–80. Atlantic Highlands, NJ: Humanities Press International, Inc., 1990.

Roberts, Mary Louise. *Civilization without Sexes: Reconstructing Gender in Postwar France, 1917–1927.* Chicago: University of Chicago Press, 1994.

———. "Gender, Consumption, and Commodity Culture." *American Historical Review* 103: 3 (June 1998): 817–44.

Robertson, James C. *The British Board of Film Censors: Film Censorship in Britain, 1896–1950.* London: Croom Helm, 1985.

Robertson, James C. *The Hidden Cinema: British Film Censorship in Action, 1913–1972.* London: Routledge, 1989.

Rose, Jonathan. *The Intellectual Life of the British Working Classes.* New Haven, CT, and London: Yale University Press, 2001.

Rosenzweig, Roy. *Eight Hours for What We Will: Workers and Leisure in an Industrial City, 1870–1920.* Cambridge: Cambridge University Press, 1983.

Ross, Ellen. *Love and Toil: Motherhood in Outcast London, 1870–1918.* Oxford: Oxford University Press, 1993.

Ross, Kristin. *Fast Cars, Clean Bodies: Decolonization and the Reordering of French Culture.* Cambridge, MA: MIT Press, 1996.

Rowbotham, Judith. *Good Girls Make Good Wives: Guidance for Girls in Victorian Fiction.* Oxford: Basil Blackwell Ltd., 1989.

Russell, Dave. "Varieties of Life: The Making of the Edwardian Music Hall." *The Edwardian Theatre: Essays on Performance and the Stage.* Ed. Michael R. Booth and Joel H. Kaplan, 61–85. Cambridge: Cambridge University Press, 1996.

Rutherford, Lois. "'Harmless Nonsense': The Comic Sketch and the Development of Music Hall Entertainment." *Music Hall: Performance and Style.* Ed. J. S. Bratton, 131–51. Milton Keynes: Open University Press, 1986.

Samuel, Raphael. "Mechanization and Hand Labour in Industrializing Britain." *The Industrial Revolution and Work in Nineteenth-Century Europe*. Ed. Lenard R. Berlanstein, 26–43. London: Routledge, 1992.

Sanders, Charles, ed. *W. Somerset Maugham: An Annotated Bibliography of Writings about Him*. De Kalb: Northern Illinois University Press, 1970.

Schroeder, Natalie. "Feminine Sensationalism, Eroticism, and Self-Assertion: M. E. Braddon and Ouida." *Tulsa Studies in Women's Literature* 7:1 (Spring 1988): 87–101.

Scott, Joan W. "The Evidence of Experience." *Critical Inquiry* 17 (Summer 1991). Rpt. in *Questions of Evidence: Proof, Practice, and Persuasion Across the Discipline*. Ed. James Chandler, Arnold I. Davidson, and Harry Harootunian, 363–87. Chicago: University of Chicago Press, 1994.

———. *Gender and the Politics of History*. New York: Columbia University Press, 1988.

Sedgwick, Eve Kosofsky. *Epistemology of the Closet*. Berkeley: University of California Press, 1990.

Seltzer, Mark. *Bodies and Machines*. New York: Routledge, 1992.

———. "Serial Killers (II): The Pathological Public Sphere." *Critical Inquiry* 22 (Autumn 1995): 122–49.

Shammas, Carole. *The Pre-Industrial Consumer in England and America*. Oxford: Clarendon Press, 1990.

Showalter, Elaine. *The Female Malady: Women, Madness, and English Culture, 1830–1980*. New York: Penguin, 1985.

———. *Sexual Anarchy: Gender and Culture at the Fin-de-Siècle*. New York: Penguin, 1990.

Shuttleworth, Sally. "Female Circulation: Medical Discourse and Popular Advertising in the Mid-Victorian Era." *Body/Politics: Women and the Discourses of Science*. Ed. Mary Jacobus, Evelyn Fox Keller, and Sally Shuttleworth, 47–68. New York: Routledge, 1990.

Simmel, Georg. "The Metropolis and Mental Life." 1903. Rpt. in *Individuality and Social Forms*. Ed. Donald Levine, 324–39. Chicago: University of Chicago Press, 1971.

Spacks, Patricia Meyer. *Boredom: The Literary History of a State of Mind*. Chicago: University of Chicago Press, 1995.

Spivak, Gayatri Chakravorty. "Can the Subaltern Speak?" *Marxism and the Interpretation of Culture*. Ed. Cary Nelson and Lawrence Grossberg, 271–313. Urbana: University of Illinois Press, 1988.

Springhall, John. "'Healthy papers for manly boys': Imperialism and Race in the Harmsworths' Halfpenny Boys' Papers of the 1890s and 1900s." *Imperialism and Juvenile Literature*. Ed. Jeffrey Richards, 107–25. Manchester: Manchester University Press, 1989.

———. "'A Life Story for the People'?: Edwin J. Brett and the London 'Low-Life' Penny Dreadfuls of the 1860s." *Victorian Studies* (Winter 1990): 223–46.

Staiger, Janet. *Interpreting Films: Studies in the Historical Reception of American Cinema*. Princeton, NJ: Princeton University Press, 1992.

Stamp, Shelley. "Moral Coercion, or the Board of Censorship Ponders the Vice Question." *Controlling Hollywood: Censorship and Regulation in the Studio Era*.

Ed. Matthew Bernstein, 41–59. New Brunswick, NJ: Rutgers University Press, 1999.

―――. "Taking Precautions, or Regulating Early Birth Control Films." *A Feminist Reader in Early Cinema*. Ed. Jennifer M. Bean and Diane Negra, 270–97. Durham, NC: Duke University Press, 2002.

Storch, Robert D. *Popular Culture and Custom in Nineteenth-Century England*. London: Croom Helm, 1982.

Stowell, Sheila. "Drama as a Trade: Cicely Hamilton's *Diana of Dobson's*." *The New Woman and Her Sisters: Feminism and Theatre 1850–1914*. Ed. Vivien Gardner and Susan Rutherford, 177–88. Ann Arbor: University of Michigan Press, 1992.

―――. *A Stage of Their Own: Feminist Playwrights of the Suffrage Era*. Ann Arbor: University of Michigan Press, 1992.

Summerfield, Penelope. "The Arms and the Empire: Deliberate Selection in the Evolution of Music Hall in London." *Popular Culture and Class Conflict 1590–1914: Explorations in the History of Labor and Leisure*. Ed. Eileen and Stephen Yeo, 209–40. Sussex: Harvester Press, 1981.

Sweet, Matthew. *Inventing the Victorians*. New York: St. Martin's Press, 2001.

Taylor, John Tinnon. *Early Opposition to the English Novel: The Popular Reaction from 1760 to 1830*. New York: Kings Crown Press, 1943.

Thirsk, Joan. "Popular Consumption and the Mass Market in the Sixteenth to Eighteenth Centuries." *Material History Bulletin* 31 (1990): 51–58.

Thom, Deborah. *Nice Girls and Rude Girls: Women Workers in World War I*. London: I. B. Tauris and Co., Ltd., 1998.

Thompson, E. P. "Time, Work-Discipline, and Industrial Capitalism." *Past and Present*, December 1967, 55–97.

―――. *The Making of the English Working Class*. New York: Vintage, 1963.

Thompson, F. M. L. *The Rise of Respectable Society: A Social History of Victorian Britain, 1830–1900*. Cambridge, MA: Harvard University Press, 1988.

Thompson, Nicola Diane. *Victorian Women Writers and the Woman Question*. Cambridge: Cambridge University Press, 1999.

Thompson, Paul. *Socialists, Liberals and Labour: The Struggle for London 1885–1914*. London: Routledge & Kegan Paul, 1967.

Thorne, Robert. "Places of Refreshment in the Nineteenth-Century City." *Buildings and Society: Essays on the Social Development of the Built Environment*. Ed. Anthony D. King, 228–53. London: Routledge & Kegan Paul, 1980.

Thurston, Carol. *The Romance Revolution: Erotic Novels and the Quest for a New Sexual Identity*. Urbana: University of Illinois Press, 1987.

Tiersten, Lisa. *Marianne in the Market: Envisioning Consumer Society in Fin-de-Siècle France*. Berkeley: University of California Press, 2001.

―――. "Redefining Consumer Culture: Recent Literature on Consumption and the Bourgeoisie in Western Europe." *Radical History Review* 57 (1993): 116–59.

Traies, Jane. "Jones and the Working Girl: Class Marginality in Music-Hall Song 1860–1900." *Music Hall: Performance and Style*. Ed. J. S. Bratton, 23–48. Milton Keynes: Open University Press, 1986.

Twyman, R. W. *History of Marshall Field and Co., 1852–1906*. Philadelphia: University of Pennsylvania Press, 1954.

Valverde, Mariana. "The Love of Finery: Fashion and the Fallen Woman in Nineteenth-Century Social Discourse." *Victorian Studies* 32:2 (Winter 1989): 169–88.

Vicinus, Martha. *Independent Women: Work and Community for Single Women, 1850–1920.* Chicago: University of Chicago Press, 1985.

Vickery, Amanda. *The Gentleman's Daughter: Women's Lives in Georgian England.* New Haven, CT: Yale University Press, 1998.

———. "Golden Age to Separate Spheres: A Review of the Categories and Chronology of English Women's History." *Historical Journal* 36:2 (1993): 383–414.

———. *Women, Privilege, and Power: British Politics, 1750 to the Present.* Stanford, CA: Stanford University Press, 2001.

Vincent, David. *Literacy and Popular Culture, England 1750–1914.* Cambridge: Cambridge University Press, 1989.

Vrettos, Athena. *Somatic Fictions: Imagining Illness in Victorian Culture.* Stanford, CA: Stanford University Press, 1995.

———. "Defining Habits: Dickens and the Psychology of Repetition." *Victorian Studies* 42:3 (2000): 399–426.

Walker, Lynne. "Home and Away: The Feminist Remapping of Public and Private Space in Victorian London." *New Frontiers of Space, Bodies and Gender.* Ed. Rosa Ainley, 65–75. New York: Routledge, 1998.

———. "Vistas of Pleasure: Women Consumers of Urban Space in the West End of London 1850–1900." *Women in the Victorian Art World.* Ed. Clarissa Campbell Orr, 70–85. Manchester: Manchester University Press, 1995.

Walkowitz, Judith R. *City of Dreadful Delight: Narratives of Sexual Danger in Late-Victorian London.* Chicago: University of Chicago Press, 1992.

———. "Going Public: Shopping, Street Harassment, and Streetwalking in Late Victorian London." *Representations* 62 (Spring 1998): 1–30.

———. "Male Vice and Feminist Virtue: Feminism and the Politics of Prostitution in Nineteenth-Century Britain." *History Workshop Journal* 13 (Spring 1982): 79–93.

———. *Prostitution and Victorian Society: Women, Class and the State.* Cambridge: Cambridge University Press, 1980.

Walsh, Claire. "Shop Design and the Display of Goods in Eighteenth-Century London." *Journal of Design History* 8:3 (1995): 157–76.

———. "The Newness of the Department Store: A View from the Eighteenth Century." *Cathedrals of Consumption: The European Department Store, 1850–1939.* Ed. Geoffrey Crossick and Serge Jaumain, 46–71. Aldershot: Ashgate, 1999.

Walton, John K., and James Walvin, eds. *Leisure in Britain, 1780–1939.* Manchester: Manchester University Press, 1983.

Walvin, James. *Leisure and Society 1830–1950.* London: Longman, 1978.

Waters, Chris. *British Socialists and the Politics of Popular Culture, 1884–1914.* Manchester: Manchester University Press, 1990.

———. "Progressives, Puritans and the Cultural Politics of the Council, 1889–1914." *Politics and the People of London: The London County Council 1889–1965.* Ed. Andrew Saint, 49–70. London: Hambledon Press, 1989.

Watt, Ian. *The Rise of the Novel: Studies in Defoe, Richardson, and Fielding.* Berkeley: University of California Press, 1957.

Waugh, Martin. "Boredom in Psycho-analytic Perspective." *Social Research* 42 (1975): 538–50.

Wendt, Lloyd, and Herman Kogan. *Give the Lady What She Wants! The Story of Marshall Field & Company.* Chicago: Rand McNally, 1952.

Whitaker, Wilfred B. *Victorian and Edwardian Shopworkers: The Struggle to Obtain Better Conditions and a Half-Holiday.* Newton Abbot: David & Charles, 1973.

Whitelaw, Lis. *The Life and Rebellious Times of Cicely Hamilton: Actress, Writer, Suffragist.* Columbus: The Ohio State University Press, 1991.

Williams, A. H. *No Name on the Door: A Memoir of Gordon Selfridge.* London: W. H. Allen, 1956.

Williams, Ioan, ed. *Novel and Romance 1700–1800: A Documentary Record.* New York: Barnes and Noble, 1970.

Williams, Linda, ed. *Viewing Positions: Ways of Seeing Film.* New Brunswick, NJ: Rutgers University Press, 1995.

Williams, Raymond. *The Country and the City.* Oxford: Oxford University Press, 1973.

———. *Culture and Society 1780–1950.* London: Chatto and Windus, 1958.

———. *The Long Revolution.* London: Penguin, 1961.

Williams, Rosalind H. *Dream Worlds: Mass Consumption in Late Nineteenth-Century France.* Berkeley: University of California Press, 1982.

Wilson, Elizabeth. *Adorned in Dreams: Fashion and Modernity.* London: Virago Press, 1985.

———. *The Sphinx in the City: Urban Life, the Control of Disorder, and Women.* Berkeley: University of California Press, 1991.

Winstanley, Michael J. *The Shopkeeper's World 1830–1914.* Manchester: Manchester University Press, 1983.

Wolff, Janet. "The Invisible *Flâneuse:* Women and the Literature of Modernity." *The Problems of Modernity: Adorno and Benjamin.* Ed. Andrew Benjamin, 141–56. London: Routledge, 1989.

Wright, Thomas. *Some Habits and Customs of the Working Classes, by a Journeyman Engineer.* London: Tinsley Brothers, 1867.

Yeo, Eileen and Stephen, eds. *Popular Culture and Class Conflict 1590–1914: Explorations in the History of Labour and Leisure.* Sussex: Harvester Press, 1981.

Young, Arlene. *Culture, Class and Gender in the Victorian Novel: Gentlemen, Gents and Working Women.* Houndsmills, Basingstoke, Hampshire and London: Macmillan Press Ltd., 1999.

Young, Ken, and Patricia L. Garside, *Metropolitan London: Politics and Urban Change 1837–1981.* New York: Holmes & Meier, 1982.

Zimmeck, Meta. "Jobs for the Girls: The Expansion of Clerical Work for Women, 1850–1914." *Unequal Opportunities: Women's Employment in England 1800–1918.* Ed. Angela V. John, 153–77. Oxford: Basil Blackwell, 1986.

Zlotnick, Susan. *Women, Writing and the Industrial Revolution.* Baltimore: Johns Hopkins University Press, 2001.

Index